# RECONSIDERING TRENTON

# RECONSIDERING TRENTON

## The Small City in the Post-Industrial Age

Steven M. Richman

McFarland & Company, Inc., Publishers
*Jefferson, North Carolina, and London*

LIBRARY OF CONGRESS CATALOGUING-IN-PUBLICATION DATA

Richman, Steven M., 1955–
    Reconsidering Trenton : the small city in the post-industrial age / Steven M. Richman.
        p.   cm.
    Includes bibliographical references and index.

    ISBN 978-0-7864-4822-7
    softcover : 50# alkaline paper ∞

    1. Trenton (N.J.)— History.  2. Trenton (N.J.)— Description and travel.  3. Industries— New Jersey— Trenton— History.  I. Title.
    F144.T757R53    2011
    974.9'66 — dc22                                             2010041684

British Library cataloguing data are available

© 2011 Steven M. Richman. All rights reserved

*No part of this book may be reproduced or transmitted in any form or by any means, electronic or mechanical, including photocopying or recording, or by any information storage and retrieval system, without permission in writing from the publisher.*

Front Cover: Sunlight glints off the golden dome of the Statehouse in Trenton as seen from Pennsylvania across the Delaware River. One of the city's skyscrapers, State Street Square at 50 West State Street, was added to the skyline in 1989 and houses private and government tenants (photograph by the author)

Manufactured in the United States of America

*McFarland & Company, Inc., Publishers*
   *Box 611, Jefferson, North Carolina 28640*
      *www.mcfarlandpub.com*

When asked to whom I should dedicate
this book, she said, "Me." So here it is:
To Hannah Nicole Richman,
born in Trenton on October 18, 1992.

*Table of Contents*

*Preface* 1
*Introduction* 7

PART ONE: ESTABLISHING A CONTEXT

1. The City of the *Flâneur*   13
2. The City Defined and Considered   33
3. The City and the Persistence of Memory   58

PART TWO: THE ELEMENTS OF CITY LIFE

4. The City of History   78
5. The City and Its Architecture   95
6. The City of Lost Factories   116
7. The Urbanist City   136
8. The Engineered City   153
9. The Landscaped City   173

PART THREE: PEOPLE REACTING TO THE CITY

10. The City of Thought   185
11. The Territorial City   200
12. The City and Its Footprint   215
13. The City and the Photographer   238

*Epilogue* 254
*Chapter Notes* 255
*Bibliography* 273
*Index* 281

# *Preface*

This is a book about a particular city and, at the same time, about the city in general. It is about Trenton, New Jersey, a one-time major industrial city along the East Coast, and about the generic post-industrial small city fallen on hard times. It is a photographic essay that seeks to capture the present-day essence of Trenton, as well as the patterns discernible in Trenton that transfer and resonate in other cities. It is a search for identity, not only what makes a city a city, but what attracts the affection and loyalty in those who stay, and variously, the opposite emotions in those who leave. In short, this is a meditation on *place*, and more particularly, urban place. By focusing on selected readings and classical works on aspects of the city, I have sought to place Trenton in a larger context without losing sight of its own uniqueness. In Trenton is every city, and in every city, Trenton.

It is useful to state up front what this book is not. It is not a definitive book on the history, politics or economics of Trenton, nor is it an extended sociological tract using Trenton as a case study. It does not attempt to make abstract arguments or fit Trenton into a particular school of thought. It is, however, a series of topical discussions using Trenton as a prism through which to extrapolate thinking about the place of the small city in contemporary America. It is an examination of the facets of a city, whether small, large or medium (however defined). To the extent there is an argument, or theme, that runs through the book, it is that most cities—as we think of *cities*—have certain common denominators. And while certainly Trenton is not New York, and Newark is not Shanghai, the interested observer may use his or her small, familiar, local city to increase understanding and awareness of the essence of urban existence, and find connections to cities around the country and the world. This is not to say every city is alike, or even contains every component on an element-by-element basis. Rather, it is to provide an introduction to the city, both as concept and reality.

In short, it is an effort to take one city as a prism for understanding why people stay in or leave a place, and what makes a city a city. What are the bonds of attachment of a city? The history of the world has been one in which people kill and die in defense of place, of particular pieces of ground. What makes a city a city and worth dying for?

The subject is an important one. Cities are often the subject of stereotype, and the conversation often seems to fall into familiar routine. The photographer's eye — indeed, the eye of the *flâneur*, the urban wanderer — can provide a fresh look and consideration. If nothing else, anything that increases awareness and the need for continued and meaningful dialogue is important. Notwithstanding loss of industrial and population bases, the nation's cities remain and persist; dismissal is simply not a viable option or a desired mindset. They remain an essential part of societal restructuring as the world faces, together, environmental and economic challenges. We cannot and should not ignore the tangible and intangible assets of the city — its history, infrastructure, culture and society. A place like Trenton must not be dusted under the rug.

It is important to renew interest, beyond narrow artistic or scholarly endeavors, in the city as a city. Words like "scholar" or "amateur" or "journalist" or "professional" do not always suffice. One need only think of Jane Jacobs, an inspirational example of the enlightened and educated "amateur," and photographers or journalists such as Jacob Riis or Lewis Hine, to be able to argue effectively for points of view not necessarily the result of "expert" opinion or based on academic foundation. Like the boy in Hans Christian Andersen's *The Emperor's New Clothes*, sometimes it takes the "uninformed" to expose a reality for what it is. As the United States seeks to come to grips with whether "American exceptionalism" can last through the 21st century, and whether its "superpower" status will be eclipsed by China, India and the European Union, it may well find that part of the solution to its economic and cultural survival is within the lost cities like Trenton, the post-industrial urban enclaves that retain certain tangible and intangible characteristics that warrant attention.

A city should be accessible. The curious and intelligent amateur should be able to sample the scholarship as a prelude to deeper readings and meditations. It is my hope that this book serves as appetizer.

Over a generation ago, in 1978, Temple University Press published *Gritty Cities*, subtitled as a "second look" at a dozen small to medium-sized cities in Connecticut, New Jersey, Pennsylvania, New York and Delaware — more or less, the mid–Atlantic region. Trenton is one of the three New Jersey cities featured (the others were Hoboken and Paterson). What is striking is how much Trenton's visual nature has changed in those 30 years. A photograph of the Old and New Masonic Temples shows the sign for the Hotel Hildebrecht over the roof of the "new" temple; that hotel was demolished in 1984. A picture of North Broad Street shows large signage dominating the street, with the Battle Monument in the background; nothing like that is present today. Of the city itself, they write, "In a very real sense, Trenton today is an example of the post-industrial society. The major challenge the city faces is making those who work in

Trenton want to live in Trenton."[1] When they wrote their book in 1978, the population was falling dramatically — 104,638 people reflected in the 1970 census, and a 12 percent drop to 92,124 as per the 1980 census — the most dramatic drop in population, percentage-wise, since the first census capturing Trenton itself in 1810. The city is even less populated in 2010.

My photographs were made over an extended period, with regular visits to Trenton across seasons and times of day, in an effort to paint both broadly and deeply. Not every neighborhood is pictured; some will contain several images. Nor is every historic landmark or house the subject of its own photograph. An effort was made to make representative and aesthetic images, without manipulation of fact or judgment. This is the city as I have seen it.

In order to photograph, one must know the subject. Given my themes of connection and pattern, my readings sought out the common denominators of cities across a variety of thematic and topical subjects. I of course reviewed the classic works on Trenton's history, with particular attention (and gratitude) to the extensive websites maintained by the Trenton Historical Society and others with an interest in the city's past and present. To gain a deeper appreciation of critical thinking about cities in general, American cities in particular and their post-industrial fates, I explored the city through readings in sociology, urban studies and political science. I wanted my focus to be more a set of meditations and reflections, as if I were a tourist off the beaten path. To accomplish this, I sought a background sufficient to understand what I was seeing and experiencing, and provide resources for those interested in pursuing such areas in depth.

Primarily, though, I wanted to see if I could peel back the layers of Trenton and find its essence, and to see if it could still be considered a "city," and what that might mean. I sought to place Trenton within the broader theoretical, sociological and historical discussions, to provide a basis for induction, to move from the particular to the general, to make people see a place they deem familiar, like Trenton, in an unfamiliar way, to see it not as a "Jersey city" but as a place of importance that is not only real, but also symbolic and emblematic of deeper currents in the 21st-century dialogue. As photographer Dorothea Lange wrote in "Photographing the Familiar," discussing the need to accept the familiar without manipulation, we nonetheless need to be attuned to its nuances, so that "through familiarity the photographer will find not only the familiar but the strange, not only the ordinary but the rare; not only the mutual but, the singular."[2]

Such inquiries into the nature of the city in general have been the source of significant and voluminous commentary and study at least over the past century; I did not want to wade too deeply in those waters. Rather, I wanted to sample the discussion, dipping in and out, and provide a context for understanding what has happened to industrial America from ground level.

It is time for an honest conversation about our cities and, in particular,

***Cadwalader Heights.*** Designed by Frederick Law Olmsted (creator of Cadwalader Park) and Trentonian Edmund C. Hill (1855–1936), this hundred-year-old neighborhood remains a diverse mix of professionals. Trenton's residential areas expanded westward; beyond Cadwalader Heights and in the vicinity of the park are Parkside, Hillcrest, Hiltonia and Glen Afton.

our smaller and medium-sized cities. To have that discussion, it is essential to walk the streets and understand them. One can have such a conversation and still believe in the possible. What does no good is to refuse to call things what they are. Trenton's commercial success, its ability to draw people in to a revitalized downtown or central business district, will be a function of dealing effectively with its crime (most notably, its gangs), its deteriorating housing stock, and its infrastructure. Whether money or political will exists, or can be found, is a question. But what is not a question is the importance and relevance of the attempt.

In the post-industrial world, in which service industries dominate and we live in the world of the intangible, of intellectual property, what happens to places like Trenton that bore the physical needs of 19th-century industrial America? What happens when their factories shut down or leave, when their populace flees, their houses deteriorate and their streets become unsafe? Do we enter the post-apocalyptic landscape of *Bladerunner*? Are we in the realm of Langston Hughes's deferred dreams? Do cities like Trenton just dry up like so many raisins in the sun? Or do they, as in his poem, explode?[3]

I would like to acknowledge the staff of the New Jersey State Museum, on whose board I have the honor to sit and serve as vice president, for their enthusiasm and input for things New Jersey. I also acknowledge the College of New Jersey, where I taught as an adjunct professor for several years, for access to library resources. A few kind words are offered to Small World Coffee, a highly individualistic coffee shop in Princeton, that doesn't seem to mind how much time one sits at the laptop as long as one drinks coffee. And finally, I acknowledge the city of Trenton — the city in which all four of my children were born, and in which I was first sworn in as a lawyer to commence my career.

Finally, every attempt has been made to ensure accuracy and correct citation, but mistakes happen. Errors are my own. If appropriate acknowledgment has not been made, please write to me in care of the publisher.

# *Introduction*

What does it mean to love a city? To identify with a place? To feel loyalty to one's city? To live an urban existence? Do cities fit together? Does the citizen of Trenton have more in common with the citizen of San Francisco, some 3,000 miles away, than she does with the resident of the Borough of Princeton, in the same county and state? Can she found common ground with the urban inhabitant of ancient cities in Mesopotamia? Can the inhabitant of Trenton today identify with the Trentonian of one hundred years ago?

In a conference paper discussing peoples' affinities and loyalties, if not affection, for their city, Jeffry M. Diefendorf tried to get at the question of why people would love Cologne or any other city, and asked:

> What are the objects of this love? The buildings? The streets? The shops? Customs or food? Certain cultural institutions, such as theaters, museums, orchestras, or, yes, sports teams? Who loves which of these? Moreover, to make matters more complex, both the people who love the city and the objects of love change over time. Generations change, people move in and out, the ethnic composition of a city changes. And institutions and structures change too ... even in the normal course of events, buildings burn or are torn down.... Theaters close. Teams go into decline or move away. So what *is* the relationship between changes in the city — everyday changes and catastrophic changes — and the ways and degrees to which people love and identify with the city?[1]

He then compared three cities to reflect upon these questions: Cologne, Basel, and Boston. Although he evaluates these cities in terms of various factors, of interest to me are his comments on identity formation through public festivals. He notes that this is not an abstraction, and that significant monies were spent in the three cities under consideration "to create or reinforce the ways in which citizens understood their cities as well as to project images of the cities to outsiders."[2]

It would seem important, then, in seeking to define a city to consider not merely the physical elements of it, but the psychological, or intangible, elements of what is considered a city, and a particular city, by not only its inhabitants but also outsiders.

What about Trenton? Say the name, and all kinds of stereotypical images are conjured up. For many people, Trenton, Newark and Camden embody not only negative images of New Jersey, but also the worst of urban decay. And yet Trenton remains a city in fact as well as name, a member of the national and world community of urban places, that continues to have reason to celebrate its metropolitan existence.

It is useful to provide some context for Trenton's place in New Jersey. A municipality in New Jersey may be called a city as a legal matter based on certain historic issues, or based on certain population and other legal criteria, but that is not necessarily (and often is not at all) what we think of when we think of cities. Indeed, the 2000 census lists over 50 municipalities as "cities."[3] These include, for example, Somers Point, with 11,614 people, and Gloucester City, with 11,484 people, as well as Newark and Jersey City, with 273,546 and 240,055 people, respectively. Apart from the census, in New Jersey some municipalities are statutorily defined as a city; Trenton is one of them. On the other hand, various townships are listed in the 2000 census with populations that rival cities proper such as Trenton and Camden; in Mercer County, Hamilton Township with 87,109 people was more populous than Trenton, at 85,403. In Middlesex County, Woodbridge Township far outdistances New Brunswick in population by approximately double.

Trenton, like New Jersey, is perhaps much maligned these days, but there was a time when Trenton was the 50th largest city in the United States and boasted worldwide leaders in the iron and steel, rubber and pottery industries. Like many, if not most, cities of its comparative size and prowess that came of age in the Industrial Revolution, it diminished in the aftermath of World War II and was further buffeted by the social unrest that marked the 1960s and 1970s. It has become, for many, one of the lost cities, a place of reduced population, abandoned houses and factories—in short, just another aggregation of concrete and clay in the vast "Bos-Wash" network.

But if you rub away the dust and grime from the window, so to speak, might you see a different place? In 1860, New Jersey—the "Garden State"—fielded eight cities in the 100 largest in the United States; in the 1890 census, Trenton peaked at position 50, at the time having a greater population than Los Angeles, California, or Portland, Oregon. In the 1990 census, Los Angeles was second, and Portland 30th, in population in the country. So where did Trenton go?

Once upon a time Trenton was among the most important cities in the Western world. Not in the sense of Paris or London, and not in the sense of having been a "world-class" city (whatever that really means), but in the sense of having been one of the relative handful of cities in America and Europe that lifted up, shouldered, and carried the Industrial Revolution to the end, ultimately enabling post-industrial society. It was the site of the pivotal battle that inspired the Continental army and injected new life into the American War of

Introduction 9

***Passaic Street.*** This is the beginning of Passaic Street, just past North Willow (which separates this street from its continuation, called Bank Street, which itself leads into Perry Street), and is in the heart of the Central West neighborhood. Across from these homes is 48-50-52 Passaic Street, one of the city's historic landmarks, and originally a barn, reflecting the rural nature of this part of the city at the time of the Revolution. Now the street is marked by rowhouses of both wood and brick. The Trenton Historical Society speculates that the street was named for either the county or city of Passaic in New Jersey. Barely visible at the extreme right are a group of people sitting on the stoop of one of the homes; Jane Jacobs, in ***Death and Life of Great American Cities,*** notes the importance of stoops as a means of knitting neighborhoods together and establishing a sense of watchfulness over the city.

Independence. It was a significant point along the Eastern seaboard in the early years of the country, the site of great industrial breakthroughs, and the home of the men who built the Brooklyn Bridge. For a few moments, it was the capital of the United States, and almost the permanent capital of the country. Having done its duty, judgment was passed. Trenton, like its other New Jersey Industrial Revolution compatriots Camden and Paterson, became lost.

Driving into the city of Trenton southbound on Route 1 seemingly is to pass into a jungle reclaiming the vestiges of civilization. Inconsistent and incoherent trees and brush hide and surround the erstwhile factories of this erstwhile city. We feel, possibly, as if we are somewhere in the Yucatan Peninsula, glimpsing the remains of an ancient Mayan stronghold. Soon we see the city's modest skyline — the federal courthouse, the Department of Environmental Protection, the Labor Building, the Kingsbury Towers. The latter — twin apartment buildings — at 21 stories are Trenton's tallest buildings. They are also examples of Brutalist architecture, which in itself makes a profound statement about this lost city. We see the rusting, graffiti-strewn water towers rising above the weeds and scraggly trees.

A leading urban scholar in New Jersey over a decade ago pronounced judgment that none of New Jersey's "Big Six" cities—Newark, Elizabeth, Paterson, Jersey City, Trenton and Camden—were built to last. They were essentially ephemeral, "company towns" built around the need of the factories. Once those factories vanished, the purpose of the city vanished.[4] Is that really so? Must we accept that?

As late as the 1950s, as with other such industrial cities, Trenton maintained a particular civic identity. If one flips through historical photographs, particularly those in the 1890 to 1920 range, one imagines this place as the kind of city with the kind of urban lifestyle indicative of a city. This is not a town or village. This is a concrete jungle, within the context of its size. Paved roads filled with traffic, a downtown shopping and office area with new skyscrapers and multitudinous offerings, factories in and outside the city center, civic buildings, elegant hotels, and a social stratification of the well-to-do and famous at one end, and immigrant factory workers at the other. A place where presidential candidates such as Wendell Willkie and John Kennedy passed through. A place that looked like a city, thought itself a city, and was a city.

Two "out of the box" sources have influenced this book. These are Italo Calvino's *Imaginary Cities* and Marco Polo's account of travels to China. The manner in which Marco Polo sought to relate, compare and contrast each new city to his experiences in Venice is helpful in creating the appropriate mindset. Similarly, Calvino's imagined Marco Polo, in describing different cities to the equally fictionalized Kublai Khan, pressed home the notion that there were connections and commonalities to all cities, despite their particularized differences and character. The overriding word is "connection." And sometimes we see best viscerally, rather than directly, and learn by metaphor and analogy.

This book, then, is at the same time neither paean nor condemnation. It is a series of observations and meditations, an attempt to get at the essence of a place through word and image. In some places we tread lightly, and in others, in more detail. A city is a place of infinite variety and depth. It is a place of human endeavor and commitment. In each city there is something of beauty and value, no matter how tarnished, rusty or worn.

The advantage of the camera is it makes you see in a certain way. Armed with a certain objectivity and empathy, I thought I could find the city beneath the city, or at least my interpretation of it. I thought I might do so in the form of meditating on the city, considering things such as *place*. Approaching the subject with a fair degree of humility and realism, I set out to see what connections I might make between Trenton, as a prototypical American city, and the post-industrial 21st-century. Perhaps I could approach it in the vein of a *flâneur*, a wanderer in the city, as the French poet Charles Baudelaire wandered around Paris, observing and absorbing. Maybe I could provide, as Walter Benjamin said of Baudelaire, for whom everything was allegory, "the gaze of the allegorist, as it falls on the city," the "gaze of the alienated man. It is the gaze of the flâneur, whose way of life still conceals beyond a mitigating nimbus the coming desolation of the big-city dweller. The flâneur still stands on the threshold — of the metropolis as of the middle class."[5]

Such an exercise elicits questions. What is it about a city such as Trenton that holds meaning for its citizens? How does a city look on a physical level? How does it feel to live in it, or visit, on an emotional level? What does it stand for, or contribute, on an intellectual and cultural level? If we can ask if androids dream, can we also ask about the personality, the living essence, of the city? And if so, are the questions any less legitimate if the city is small? More to the point, perhaps, can we even hope to define a city? Why is that relevant?

Such questions will be explored in this book in the format of a series of thematic chapters, making use of primary and secondary sources, exploring and synthesizing what others have had to say about "The City," as I filter it through a journey through Trenton. Part One sets the stage and seeks to establish context. The first chapter begins with a series of casual observations, much in the matter of someone wandering through a city, attempting to form initial impressions and place Trenton in context. I take the opportunity to touch briefly on two other of the state's cities, Newark and Camden, north and south, with Trenton in the middle. The mind flits from details to broader pictures and back again. It wanders and makes connections. We begin to tug gently at the fabric of the city. But we know we are not the first to engage in such an exercise. We pause in this chapter to consider three significant sociological frameworks that have underlain much of the discussion of how to view a city and its functions. In the second chapter, we move beyond initial impressions and look at how the city has been defined. This is done so that we can return to Trenton and see if it still functions as a city — if we can find the patterns of city existence in Trenton, and find elements of Trenton in other cities we may care to examine. Finally, in chapter 3, we contemplate the soul of a city, its persistent memories and ruins, and their impact on the city in its present.

In the second part I look for different elements of contemporary urban life in Trenton. Chapter 4 provides an overview of Trenton's history, and how that has shaped its ethos. In chapter 5, we find Trenton to encompass various of the architectural trends that prevailed across the country during the relevant time periods; Trenton becomes a kind of open-air museum for these styles. A former industrial city with world-class industry, Trenton is now, as we see in chapter 6, a city of lost factories. The abandoned or readapted buildings are physical reminders of the essence of what this city was; their persistence as part of the landscape helps define Trenton. Another component of city life, in addition to its history, architecture and industry, is the nature of its urban existence, as discussed in chapter 7. We move from that perhaps more intangible factor to the concrete engineering achievements of Trenton, focusing on its infrastructure that in some instances achieves aesthetic and iconic status. Finally, in this part we look at the city's parks and cemeteries, in chapter 9, as we explore the landscaped city.

Whereas Part One lays out what it means to be a city as a matter of fact and theory, and Part Two focuses on more identifiable facets of the city's existence, in Part Three the discussion is oriented toward the way in which people react to the city in general and Trenton in particular. The place of the city in American life as an intellectual center has been the subject of controversy; chapter 10 looks at this and also notes Trenton's particular contributions to intellectual life, and the importance of the museum to the city and its surrounding region. Chapter 11 goes in the other direction and looks at the city in terms of territoriality, juxtaposing criminal and gang activity on the one hand, and the attempt of urban planners to find the city's legible points on the other. This provides a segue into how the city's territorial aspects can be made to work better; I discuss in some detail in chapter 12 the current master plan for Trenton, and its context in terms of the "new urbanism." Finally, in chapter 13, I discuss an aesthetic reaction to the city by the photographer, coming full circle to the original impetus for this work.

There is no conclusion as such, no final argument to be made. I have not focused on the city's contemporary politics, or other aspects, such as the religious life of the city. Trenton is reconsidered as we should be reconsidering other former manufacturing cities in the post-industrial age. They require our attention. Failure to understand them and pay attention to them is not a viable policy. If this book serves to cause attention to be paid, it will have done its job.

# PART ONE
# ESTABLISHING A CONTEXT

## 1. The City of the Flâneur

I saw in my dream the great lost cities...—John Berryman, *His Toy, His Dream, His Rest* (Poem 197)

Consider a photograph of Trenton from 1915 showing the corner of State and Broad streets, the city's core. In those pre-mall, pre-shopping center days, the caption tells us that "residents who lived in the Mercer-Hunterdon region came to the city for everything from farm equipment to the finest clothing to a restaurant for a special occasion."[1] The image shows a four-story building, with United Cigar Stores Company on the ground floor, and three layers of signs: Coca Cola, The Baby Carriage Factory Store on South Broad, Keeler's Shoes on East State, Correct Millinery on South Broad, Howards on North Broad, Hutchinson's Storage Battery on South Warren, Sam's Shoe Shop on South Broad, and Combs & Reed Furniture on West Hanover. A large hand with an extended index finger points to Heroy on North Broad.

Almost 30 years later, in the mid–1940s, another picture of the corner of Broad and State streets shows another urban scene.[2] A bus, several automobiles, pedestrians on a crossed sidewalk (a well-dressed couple studying a map or flyer), and in a row on State Street: Woolworth, Grant's and Kresge's. A movie theater marquee shows current listings; a sign on the street pole points to the Soldier's Club. It could be the corner of 14th Street in New York, or any other central business and shopping district in any other major city.

And some 30 to 40 years after that, in the first decade of the 21st-century, the corner of Broad and State Street is a desultory affair. On a Saturday morning, perhaps a few people are waiting for a bus, or leaning against the side of a building. State Street has some pedestrian traffic, but there are not the jostling crowds of the faded images. Just small groups. During the week, the city usually is filled primarily with state employees, with no significant industry or shopping or private office usage downtown. Even South Warren Street, undergoing a bit of a renaissance, is dormant. On a typical Sunday morning, downtown is not particularly busy. Not for Trenton are the touristic *flâneurs*, looking for endless possibilities around every corner.³ In the past, this was a significant urban center. Today, it is one of the lost cities of the United States, yet it provides a place where connections may be made to all cities throughout time. Lost is not a permanent state. There are those who seek to reset the course. But there is no denying that the city is not what it was. That is not necessarily bad; the operative question is what it can, and will, become.

Trenton is not just part of the heritage of America. On one level, it can be considered the midwife of the country, with the First Battle of Trenton that birthing. And its vision as an industrial center, a world leader—and a cultural hub with an urbanist existence during its "Golden Age"—warrants capture, before those vestiges disappear into the post-industrial decades of the 21st-century.

Let us put Trenton in context more locally before proceeding more globally. It is situated in a compact state, in the central part, as distinct from the northern and southern parts. For those in New Jersey, this geography is meaningful. And so are the state's cities different. Newark is a north Jersey place, and Camden a south Jersey place. But there are similarities to these three cities that grew to prominence in the Industrial Revolution and came to symbolize New Jersey's industrial prowess.

New Jersey's cities are no longer among the nation's largest. They are small cities now or, at best, perhaps considered medium-sized. They have their own identities and character. And they have the same parabolic journey through rise, fall and (in Newark's case, at least) perhaps another rise.

Trenton, like the state's largest city, Newark, was established during the Colonial era, and helped not only to launch the nation, but also to carry it into industrial importance. In his study of the rise, fall and resurrection of Newark, Brad Tuttle notes the importance of understanding cities such as Newark to understand not only the rise of America as a superpower, but also how its cities were brought down in the latter half of the 20th century by political corruption, loss of manufacturing, and racial issues, among other things, calling it "Everycity, U.S.A."[4]

The same patterns and comments could be made, and were in fact so noted, regarding both Trenton and Camden. The fate of these cities may have had factual differences, but the essential social, political and economic causes and ramifications were the same. Howard Gillette, discussing comparable issues vis-à-vis Camden, writes in tandem with Tuttle and notes the nostalgia for Camden as its suburbs drained the city's population as its own manufacturing base evanesced.[5]

Trenton's fate was summarily similar. In his study of the city's steady fall from its so-called Golden Age, John Cumbler noted the decrease in workers in Trenton's stagnant industries, and the concomitant rise of its suburban working population. Unlike Camden and Newark, though, as a result of the location of state government, Trenton was shedding its industrial character and "was fast

*1. The City of the* Flâneur

**Brunswick Avenue.** Brunswick Avenue is part of the original King's Highway, the colonial route enabling travelers to go from New York to Philadelphia by way of the Trenton ferry. The rowhouses of Brunswick Avenue are varied; the detached twin rowhouses here feature bracketed cornices and continuous stone bands, comparable, according to the Trenton Historical Society's North Ward Survey, to other such rowhouses built in the late 19th century along Brunswick Avenue.

becoming a city of reports and forms and of clerks, nurses and waitresses. The new Trenton workers were white and held white-collar jobs, but the city was increasingly becoming populated with black migrants who lacked the skills and skin color to find employment in the new jobs."[6]

The comparisons and the same story played out in the state's northern, central and southern cities, whether in the New York or Philadelphia vicinity, or in between, as with Trenton. To use Tuttle's word, they are "Everycity."

In their now somewhat-dated book on New Jersey's urbanization, Bebout and Grele note the phenomenon of the extended city, and comment that "Newark, Jersey City, Elizabeth, and Paterson have become satellites of New York, just as Camden may be called a satellite of Philadelphia."[7] What is interesting about that remark is that it excludes Trenton. In the 21st century, the trains to Newark and New York run from Trenton as an express during the early morning rush hour, with Trenton and neighboring Hamilton contributing sizeable numbers. The trains stop at Princeton Junction, where they virtually fill, and proceed to Newark and New York. Perhaps at present they might conclude that Trenton is a satellite of both Philadelphia and New York. Or, perhaps, Trenton has sufficient geographic and political distance from both of those cities to do what neither Newark nor Camden can do—establish itself as the only viable, "real" city in a particular region.

What Tuttle writes about Newark may well have been said about Trenton: "The manner in which Newark had grown — in piecemeal, haphazard fashion, with a factory here, tenements thrown up there, various trolley lines strewn about almost randomly — was traditionally blamed for many of the city's mid–twentieth century problems."[8]

Interestingly enough, Trenton began as a more populous place; it took Newark at least two decades to catch up and surpass Trenton. In 1810, the United States Census reflected Trenton as 42nd of the 46 largest urban places in the United States.[9] Newark was not on the list. Elizabeth was, at 43rd place. No other New Jersey city made the 1810 list. Trenton had 3,002 people; New York, in first place, had 96,373. Newark was still not there in 1820, when Trenton was 46 out of 61; Elizabeth had dropped to 52nd. By 1830, though, Newark sprang to 21st place with 10,953 people, and Trenton was in 71st place out of 90, with 3,925 people. In 1840 Newark, in 23rd place out of 100, had 17,290 people, and Trenton fell off the list. Newark continued to climb, and in 1850, with Trenton still off the list, Newark placed at 19 with 38,894 people. However, by 1860 Trenton had experienced a significant decade of growth, returning to the list at 53rd place, with 17,228 people, compared with 11th place Newark and its 71,941 people.

In 1860, just before the Civil War and its need for industrial product to fight the war, Trenton's place as a leading American city would not have been questioned. It ranked just ahead, populationwise, of Nashville, Tennessee, and well ahead of 99th place Atlanta, Georgia. Newark remained in front of Trenton. In 1890 Trenton peaked at 50th place with 57,548 people. In 1950, the last census report in which Trenton remained in the 100 largest American cities, it placed at 80 with 128,009 people; Newark was in 21st place with 438,776 people. The Census Bureau's estimate of Newark's population for 2008 was 278,980; Trenton's was 82,883.

Trenton's history also has been one of acquisition. To an extent, it grew by acquiring neighboring independent towns. What if neighboring Ewing and Hamilton Townships, with populations of about 37,000 in 15.6 square miles, and 87,000 people in 40.4 square miles, were part of the city? Trenton today would be about 64 square miles, with a population of about 207,000 people. At present, Vineland, a small "city" in South Jersey with 58,164, is the largest geographic area in the state, at 49 square miles. In other words, if Trenton's area had expanded in the way of some other cities that acquired not only land but also population, what would, or could, it be?

By way of comparison, Port St. Lucie, Florida, with a comparable population to Trenton of 88,769 (2000 Census) has 75.5 square miles. Jonesboro, Arkansas, with 55,515 people (2000), has 79.6 square miles. Knoxville, Tennessee, has 92.7 square miles. California, with a massively larger geographic area than New Jersey and many times the population, has 480 municipalities, ranging from Vernon (population 95) to Los Angeles (population 4,045,873). Issues of consolidation of municipalities remains a controversial topic in New Jersey, and is usually considered regarding a smaller municipality surrounded completely by another. New Jersey's cities are relatively compact, geographically.

The abiding uniqueness of Trenton among New Jersey's cities stems in part from its position as the state's capital. Notwithstanding one writer's comment about certain state capitals being sent to "cow towns" so that the largest city in a state could remain an uninhibited economic engine,[10] Newark does not appear to have been in serious contention for the state capital of New Jersey. Perth Amboy had been the capital of East Jersey, and Burlington of West Jersey; Trenton did not become the state capital until after the Revolutionary War, in 1790. After its failed effort to become the national capital, the city's leaders pushed for state capital status; a significant factor appears to have been its geographic location.

While New Jersey may have begun as East and West Jersey, it is known today more in terms of North and South Jersey. There is no definitive line between the two. Some might consider a line from Trenton to Asbury Park as a suitable dividing line. Others refer to a third area, Central Jersey, that includes an amorphous area from Trenton to Lambertville to Woodbridge to Asbury Park and back across. So if Newark is representative of "north" Jersey, we might think of Trenton not of "central" but even of "south" Jersey, more like Camden than Newark.

These "regional" differences do not seem to have affected the demographics; Trenton remains comparable to the state's northern and southern cities. Together with Newark and Camden, Trenton has most of the principal accoutrements of a city as we think of it, though of the New Jersey cities, Newark probably comes closest to the contemporary city image. Newark has skyscrapers that are actually tall buildings, and not just historical curiosities. It has a subway system, a monumental train station in the classical tradition and a city hall to match, and a nationally renowned art museum. Like Trenton, Newark has an Olmsted-designed park. Unlike both Trenton and Camden, Newark features an international airport, as well as hotels, business centers, and professional hockey and basketball teams. In 2000, it placed 63 out of the 75 largest cities, in the company of Buffalo (58), St. Paul (59) and Louisville (66).

Per the U.S. Census Bureau's 2008 population estimates, Newark has about 24 square miles and a population of 278,980; Trenton has an area of about 8 square miles and a population of 82,883.[11] If Trenton were three times as large and had three times its population, would it be the virtual equivalent, population-wise, of Newark?

Demographically, the 2000 Census reports Trenton as having a white population of 32.6 percent and a black population of 52.1 percent. Newark's numbers were 26.5 percent and 53.5 percent, respectively. Camden's white population was 16.8 percent; its black population 53.3 percent. The New Jersey statewide percentages were 72.6 percent and 13.6 percent, respectively. Trenton's Hispanic population was 21.5 percent; Newark's, 29.5 percent and Camden's, 38.8 percent. Newark's population grew by 3.3 percent from 2000 to 2006; Trenton's declined in the same period by 1.7 percent, and Camden's declined by 0.7 percent. In 1999, Trenton had 21.9 percent — over a fifth — of its population below the poverty line. Newark was 28.4 percent — over a quarter. Camden, one of the poorest cities in the country, had over a third — 35.5 percent. Trenton's median household income (1999) was $31,074; Newark's was $26,913 and Camden's $23,421. The home ownership rate in Trenton in 2000 was 45.5 percent; in Newark, 23.8 percent, and in Camden, surprisingly, 46.1 percent. New Jersey's was 65.6 percent.

So we have Trenton, with a higher median household income, losing population; Newark, with a significantly lower median household income, gained population. And Camden, leading (barely) only in home ownership.

Numbers never tell the entire story. There are analogous histories to the state's northern, central and southern cities, and that analogy is based in manufacturing. New Jersey's cities, exemplifying the vision of Alexander Hamilton observing the Paterson Falls, were about industry. Physical things you could touch. Whereas Trenton's post–Revolutionary industry was steel, Newark's began with shoes. If Trenton had John Roebling, Newark had Seth Boyden and a burgeoning leather industry. Boyden then moved into iron, and established a malleable iron foundry in the 1820s. Through the decades leading up to the Civil War, Newark grew, aided in part as was Trenton, by a canal. In Newark's case it was the Morris Canal; in Trenton, the Delaware and Raritan Canal. Both cities were part of the great Canal Age of America, transportation and industrial centers that were part of the Anthracite Trail from Pennsylvania to New York — America's answer to the great Silk Road of Marco Polo.

By the closing decades of the 19th century, Newark was as diversified as Trenton in factory and industry production. In 1872, the year of the Newark Industrial Exhibition, it ranked third in industrial output and was the 13th largest city in the country. Trenton, per the 1870 census, ranked 58th in population among the country's 100 largest cities, and was about one fifth the population of Newark. Camden placed at 69th. During this time Newark also diversified beyond manufacturing, and its banking, insurance, retail, utility, entertainment and education sectors expanded. The city further proved attractive to Thomas Edison, who established himself there prior to relocating to nearby Menlo Park.

In the antebellum era, regardless of its political classification, Newark had typical and contemporary "city" problems: "crime, poverty, housing shortages, general filth."[12] It shared these with larger cities, such as Boston and New York. Interestingly, in this period, Newark lost territory, areas that became some of the wealthier towns in the area. This may be contrasted with Trenton and its growth by acquisition of abutting towns.

Camden also saw its position deteriorate in the 1950s. Unlike Newark and Trenton, Camden did not have a particularly separate Colonial identity. It was an adjunct to Philadelphia, known originally as Cooper's Ferry for its transportation role. Like Newark and Trenton, early European settlers were Quakers. Between 1800 and 1840, the three settlements around three principal ferry sites consolidated into the city of Camden. Like Trenton and Newark, its industrial growth was facilitated by its proximity to rivers. In Camden's case, two rivers — the Delaware and the Cooper — together with stage coach service, were foundations upon which Camden's businesses could be built.

Trenton, along with New Jersey's other principal cities, experienced three major population shifts at the turn of the 19th to the 20th century: between 1890 and 1910 (1) the beginnings of post-industrial society were established by the emerging class of technicians, managers and white-collar workers, (2) commuters coming in by rail from outside the city, and (3) the shift from mainly northern European immigrants to southern and eastern Europeans, as well as African Americans.[13]

So Trenton, like New Jersey's other cities, is compressed and dense, ethnically diverse, a 19th-century magnet for immigrants and with a history of manufacturing. Until World War II, Trenton went hand in glove with other of the country's East Coat powerhouses that built things. On the other hand, its distance from New York and Philadelphia has helped shape its unique historical identity.

The perception after World War II, was that Trenton had lost its luster. In 1957 Trenton was an object of national ridicule. *House and Home* magazine described a University of Pennsylvania study that "described Trenton as old, decaying, and suffering from multiple ills: obsolescence, overcrowded housing, antiquated schools, lack of planning, and inadequate transportation."[14] Efforts at urban renewal in the 1960s and 1970s might be considered a response to this. However, the problems of Trenton as a post-industrial city are deeper than simply its politics. Much broader forces were at work. In the case of Trenton, it was not simply a question of short-sightedness, or individual greed; the best efforts of its civic leaders were not sufficient to stem the tide of the nationalization of corporate life as a much more universal phenomenon.[15] As companies nationalized, and local industries were acquired, the influence of the venue waned. Decisions were made by people who no longer lived in Trenton. However, to blame the city's political leaders is, on a certain level, like blaming Canute for not being able to hold back the ocean. There were forces at work that affected many of the nation's small- and medium-sized industrial cities as the post-industrial, automobile-driven, service-oriented economy took hold.

We have looked at Trenton in a particular context — that of a New Jersey city — and briefly compared it with two of its companion cities in both the northern and southern parts of New Jersey. This overview has been brief and contextual. I now want to act more like the *flâneur* and explore the concept of the city in a purely visual manner. We will do this through reference to a particular artist. To help provide a way of looking at Trenton in a pictorial context to examine the notion of the visual city, we turn to one artist's attempt to capture his own city, "between the wars," in the course of a single day. It is a way of placing Trenton, of connecting it and other cities like it, in a common frame of reference. As such, we move toward the meditative exercise on the nature of a city and what we may make of Trenton. The parallels, or connections, are often not hard to find. More to the point, we can start to see Trenton as a prism for the urban scene.

Frans Masereel (1889–1972) was a Belgian woodcut artist who created *The City*, a collection of 100 woodcuts published in Germany in 1925. Without his own words, it nonetheless tells the story of this anonymous European city through macro and micro scenes, ranging from the estrangement and loneliness of the prostitute in her room to the massed crowd getting on or off a train. The only text is the quote from Walt Whitman: "This is the city and I am one of the citizens, Whatever interests the rest interests me." It is a quote from *Song of Myself*; the full sentence reads: "This is the city and I am one of the citizens, Whatever interests the rest interests me, politics, wars, markets, newspapers, schools, The mayor and councils, banks, tariffs, steamships, factories, stocks, stores, real estate and personal estate."[16]

An industrial city, in which people's individual lives are drawn against the background of skyscrapers and smokestacks. The book opens with an image of a well-dressed man, back to us, standing on a hill and overlooking the smoke-stacked buildings of the city. In the foreground and background are trains billowing smoke. Factory stacks belch black and white smoke. The city is a compact, dense, defined set of buildings, with the empty distance beyond the skyline. Next image is a railroad station, trains coming and going, with more smoke. We move after another image of trains to the streets of the city, with mostly men, all hated, in black, moving through the crowded streets. And then — a woodcut of mostly men, with a woman peeking between them, staring at a supine man in the street. Dead? Dying? Attacked? The skyscrapers form a border of over half the space behind them. A man peers through the rear window of an automobile.

> [Interlude]
> *A city man has been indicted for the brutal stabbing death of his girlfriend in March. Brian Carlos Oliver, 40, is charged with murder, theft and a weapons offense in the death of 38-year-old Lisa Glennon, the mother of his daughter. Prosecutors say Oliver brutally beat and stabbed Glenn 23 times before stashing her body under the basement steps of a Melrose Avenue home.*[17]

Masereel's City is a mass of buildings, automobiles, businessmen, elegantly dressed women, crowds, desperation. A city of one's imagination, of another time and place — an observed reality, or an unobserved unreality? Scenes of workers wielding shovels, the builders of the city, cranes and pickaxes. The music hall, jammed, culture spewing forth and spilling out. A city overflowing with culture, with intellect. A city where a man, his face a grotesque, contorted mask, stands over a secretary at her typewriter, her head bowed: the 20th-century city of industry, of business, of money and power and — in these woodcuts — dominated by men. Monocled and spectacled men in their clubs, beneath triangular lights. Women looking from shuttered windows, between hanging laundry; children surrounding the legless beggar on his cart in the street. A bowler-hatted man leaning back on his cane, studying the pane glass window filled with corsets. It is a city of advertising billboards, of financial dealings, of public squares and displays of military prowess, of the elegance of the grand ball and the squalor and sordidness of lonely people in small rooms, of churches and weddings, of suicides and deathbed scenes. A city of hope and despair, of a shared daily experience but a mass of people strangely disconnected.

> Interlude, Trenton: "A lovers' quarrel led Arthur Laster to fatally stab a woman he claimed to care for after she called out another man's name while they were having sexual relations."[18]

Lives of the city. Trenton, Berlin. Across time and oceans, there are patterns and connections. Size is not necessarily relevant. We can find in contemporary Trenton the same raw emotions and humanity that Masereel captured in Berlin. Every city has its stories, as they say.

Back to Masereel.

Of vast paintings in the grand hall of a museum, and of the haggard woman alone in her bed, a crooked picture of a man (husband? father?) above her bed. A city of laws (there is a courtroom woodcut) and of lust, of birth and death, of oratory and murder, of food and hunger. A scene with a young mother holding a forlorn child, outside the window of a posh restaurant, confronted by the Lurch-like doorman. Of factories and workers in crowded streets and bars. Of black smoke seeping into the black night from the incessantly operating factories. The lone woman at night, head in hands, running down steps against a background of Precisionist-cut buildings. And the drunks carousing in the street.

Reportedly, Masereel was inspired by Georg Heym's poem "Die Stadt" ("The City"), with one translation:

> Very much this night. Clouds and light
> Rend before the moon fall.
> And thousand windows along the night stand
> And blink with their eyelids, red and small.
>
> How Aderwerk go through the city streets,
> Countless people wash in and out.
> And ever a dull dull sound of his
> Monotone matt comes out in silence.

> Give birth, death, knitted monotony,
> Babbling of labor, long Sterbeschrei,
> Change is in the blind by muffled.
>
> And sham and fire torches and red fire
> To threaten in the distance with a drawn hand
> And seem to be high with dark clouds.[19]

The city is imagistic. The city is the composite of its lives. The city overwhelms our senses.

Another way to approach the city is through the sounds it makes. Not just the sounds of the traffic and voices, but the creative sounds by those who imagine the city in music. Music also provides an introduction to the essence of the city, its neighborhoods and pulsing life. To note but a fraction of what is out there — listen to Dmitry Shostakovich's *The Golden Age*, Opus 22. A ballet in three acts, with six scenes, it takes as its subject a Soviet soccer team's visit to a Western city ("U-town") at the same time that the Western city features an industrial exhibition, sometime around 1930. Captions of the various movements reflect, as Masereel's images do, different facets of the prototypical city. Another composer, Ralph Vaughan Williams, seeks to capture London in his eponymous Symphony No. 2. The first movement begins slowly, quietly, as day breaks over the city; the sound of Big Ben leads to a frenzy of activity in the streets off the Strand as the city comes to life, and so on. And of course, George Gershwin's *Rhapsody in Blue*, to my ear, is the essence of urbanism, and the night life of a city. Listen to *Rhapsody in Blue*, then look at Edward Hopper's *Nighthawks*, and contemplate the city. As you wander Trenton, or other seemingly familiar cities, listen to them.

Contemplate Trenton. And cities of its ilk. The movie *The Full Monty* opens with a promotional film clip of the English city of Sheffield, and then moves to its present scene of abandoned factories and desolation. The popular English series *The Office* was set in Slough, and its American counterpart was set in Scranton, Pennsylvania. The post-industrial city remains a piece of contemporary Western culture. Trenton is an industrial city. Therefore....

There is something about a city: the sound of footsteps echoing on old streets, the connection of walking over a place that hundreds, thousands, tens of thousands of people have walked across the centuries, observing a detail in a building previously unnoticed. These tactile sensations are not discernible from the ether. They are not found in the telephone line–riddled roads of the suburbs. Cities are valuable places, the ballast of civilized society. They are open-air museums and testaments to what we can be. We let them decay and vanish to our considerable loss.

The city is a singular human creation that marks our aspirations as communal beings. It provides connection, and grows out of a human need for connection. In the virtual age, companionship still matters. We remain descendents of the extended tribe. There are those who argue definitionally

*101 to 107 South Warren Street.* This building on South Warren stands where the Golden Swan Tavern stood. A plaque on the side of the building reads, "Built about 1815. An inn 1826–1857. 'The Daily True American' published by the Naar family 1857–1872. Subsequently housed various industrial and commercial activities." The signing of the ratification of the United States Constitution occurred about 100 yards from the site. Such markers identify the physical ground that has historic connection and helps anchor us with the city.

that the city is a place of strangers, but my point is different. As in a movie theater, the strangers share a common experience, and there remains a connection. You may never have seen someone from your city, but when you encounter that same person in a foreign city and learn of the connection, that connection proves powerful. Suddenly the person is a friend. You have a connection.

Society provides the political parameters of a physical infrastructure in which a group of people live and work. The city itself has stayed with us through the centuries as the epitome of social organization. Constantly changing in its demographics and population, as well as physical shape, it is also a function of its intangibles—its history, culture and personality. Whether we think in terms of primitive bonds driven by a need for safety in numbers, or more sophisticated economic relationships to drive efficiency and survival, or even a transcendent, psychological need for tactile human contact, the city is a collective identity within a finite space. The vaster the space, the more attenuated that connection and possibly identity; too large an area, and the city breaks down into its component regions. Similarly, the fewer the people, the less there are to be connected. Nations have come and gone, borders have shifted, but the city seems to have remained, and survived, in one form or another.

The city is palpable, sensory. Despite the present digital age of the avatar, where people live "second lives" in the photonic ether, people remain drawn to the physical city. There is something about knowing a city, becoming familiar with it. Embracing the familiar, knowing which streets lead where. Understanding a city. It provides a comfort; it is *home*. We need a sense of place, of belonging. In an era of isolation, of communion over computers instead of in person, of an ethic that sacrifices friendship for work, a familiar city provides a kind of comfort. We may take particular pleasure in visiting a foreign city for a third or fourth time, when we've gotten to know it a bit, and no longer need a map, when we recognize what I remember. A city is a living thing, a thing made by people for people.

Can a city, like a person, be clinically depressed? Is it also capable of moments of sheer happiness? Can we find pieces of Trenton in every city in the industrialized United States? Can we find pieces of America in the broken streets of Trenton?

If a city sleeps, does it dream? Does Trenton dream?

We have, by way of introduction, now glanced at Trenton in the context of New Jersey, and briefly compared it with Newark and Camden. We have moved farther afield to explore a city, as one artist has done, through visual images that purport to capture a "day in the life." The broader question remains: how does Trenton "measure up" in terms of defining the city as a city?

The poet Wallace Stevens once suggested "Thirteen Ways of Looking at a Blackbird." Are there 13 ways of looking at a city? How do we define "the city?" How does it shape us? Sociologists attempt to define a city and get at a theory of a city. Wander through the streets of Trenton, and try to understand the place. Ultimately, the task of definition may be impossible, as historian Blake McKelvey noted; the inability of scholars to agree "reflects the fact that [cities] are human aggregates and historic experiences, not abstractions."[20]

Architect Spiro Kostof, in *The City Shaped*, asks what a city is, and offers nine (as opposed to Wallace Stevens' thirteen) ways of looking. More particularly, he suggests nine glosses on the premise of the city as a place of a large and concentrated population. He calls the city a place (1) "where a certain energized crowding of people takes place"; (2) that is clustered near other cities; (3) that itself is physically circumscribed; (4) with specified differentiation of work; (5) "favored by a source of income"; (6) that relies on written records; (7) "intimately engaged with" the surrounding countryside that provides food; (8) "distinguished by some kind of monumental definition" encompassing public buildings and landmarks; and (9) "made up of buildings and people."[21]

Today, perhaps, "countryside" might be replaced with "suburbia" or "sprawl," although food would still come from outside the city, even if shipped in from across the country, but otherwise this presents a working set of concepts or parameters with which to think about Trenton.

Essentially, though, whatever anyone says, the city begins and ends with its people, and generally the focus is on the interaction or result of the concentration of people within a finite space.

We are, for the moment, on a casual stroll. One way to begin is to look at different sets of viewpoints, or three theoretical prisms reflecting certain "schools" of thought as to approaching the city. They provide something to think about as you wander your way through the post-industrial streets of Trenton or cities like it. That is, more ways of looking at the blackbird, and meditating more broadly upon the urban existence as a reaction to the impressions of Trenton. Put another way, can we take a mini-course in urban studies, with the broadest of brush strokes, to allow us to think about a place we may have taken for granted, with a fresh mindset?

The three broad ways of looking at the city, three hypotheses attempting to define the City, have been denoted as determinism, compositionalism, and subcultural theory. We need not go into all the intricacies of such theories or variations; the purpose here is to note three principal viewpoints, and some of the main works articulating them, as a starting point for reconsidering Trenton in the 21st century.

Regarding determinism, or the view that the city fosters estrangement and isolation, we turn first to socialist Louis Wirth. In his 1938 essay "Urbanism as a Way of Life," Wirth argues that "for sociological purposes a city may be defined as a relatively large, dense, and permanent settlement of socially heterogeneous individuals."[22] Size alone is important but not determinative, and is also relative. The features of urbanism may be reflected in those areas surrounding the city. The city itself encompasses other factors apart from simply size; communication, transportation, cultural and government functions are present within the city. One feature of Wirth's analysis has particular applicability to determining Trenton's continuing place as a city—that is, to the extent that the city exerts influence over the surrounding "rural" areas based on its aggregation of economic and cultural institutions. In the case of Trenton, it could be just as easily stated that the surrounding suburban areas have become dominant in terms of all but government—certainly economic, cultural and transportation centers have migrated outward.

Wirth's writings borrowed from another "Chicago school" sociologist in the opening decades of the 20th century, Georg Simmel.

In 1903 Simmel published an essay titled "The Metropolis and Mental Life." He opens that essay by saying, "The deepest problems of modern life derive from the claim of the individual to preserve the autonomy and individuality of his existence in the face of overwhelming social forces, of historical heritage, of external culture, and of the technique of life."[23] He argues that the city fosters an intellectualization of the person, as opposed to the emotional behavior of those living in rural areas. The relationship between urban existence and the "money economy" leads to an impersonal, objective approach by anonymous urban citizens toward one another that is steeped in matter-of-factness that links justice with hardness; it is the result of purely economic calculations and ego that have no fear because personal relationships are not deep or, as Simmel puts it, they are "imponderable."[24]

Ultimately, the effect of urban existence, the hardness and anonymity of relationships, leads to a "blasé attitude" that ultimately has a destructive effect:

> In the blasé attitude the concentration of men and things stimulate the nervous system of the individual to its highest achievement so that it attains its peak. Through the mere quantitative intensification of the same conditioning factors this achievement is transformed into its opposite and appears in the peculiar adjustment of the blasé attitude. In this phenomenon the nerves find in the refusal to react to their stimulation the last possibility of accommodating to the contents and forms of metropolitan life. The self-preservation of certain personalities is brought at the price of devaluating the whole objective world, a devaluation which in the end unavoidably drags one's own personality down into a feeling of the same worthlessness.[25]

This causes a reserve among the various groups that act in self-preservation. In other words, one seeks to distance one's self in the city for survival rather than seeking the assistance of others to achieve survival.

These works, among others, denominated "determinist" suggest the destructive effects of the city. The concentration of people causes a particular psychological result on urban inhabitants. Stated differently, the city itself is the causal factor, with an across-the-board application. The conclusions were challenged by Herbert Gans (among others), in what is referred to as compositionalism, that is the city itself and its concomitant population is *not* in and of itself the determining factor. Rather, the city is not homogeneous, and we need to recognize the city's disparate parts and their reflection of these factors.

Gans criticized Wirth's view as not taking into account the entirety of the metropolitan area. In "Urbanism and Suburbanism as Ways of Life: A Reevaluation of Definitions," Gans broadly criticizes Wirth's theory in part on the grounds that it is based on society as being completely urban, and does not distinguish between lifestyles as reflected in different kinds of communities in contemporary society.[26] More specifically, he challenges Wirth's analysis on three bases. First, one cannot apply general conclusions based on the inner city to the broader urban region. Second, he specifically disputes the conclusion that number, density and heterogeneity are sufficient to generate the consequences described by Wirth, based on the variable evidence (or lack thereof). Third, he contends Wirth did not take into account other "social structures and cultural patterns" that affected the city's inhabitants.[27] Gans divides the urban population of the city into five types: cosmopolites (students, artists, writers, musicians, entertainers, professionals, intellectuals), unmarried or childless (temporary and permanent), ethnic villagers (isolated nationalities), the deprived (emotionally disturbed, handicapped, poor white), and the trapped (those who can't leave their neighborhoods due to economics, including the old).[28] Consequently, the inner city is different from the outer city, and both are distinct from the suburbs; there are different types of people in and out of the urban environment, as well as physical differences.[29] These conclusions render a sociological definition of the city impossible; "the sociologist cannot, therefore, speak of an urban or suburban way of life."[30] Thus, in contrast to Wirth's urbanism definition of the city, Gans offers the non-definition in a compositionalism format. The city is a diverse place, with specific groups that have their own rules and codes, and who are not necessarily isolated or estranged.

Let us pause a moment to think about this in the context of Trenton. Has it become the "hard" place of Wirth and Simmel? Does it retain, on the other hand, a more empathetic, "small town" atmosphere despite its city-sized population and density? Considering it in terms of what Gans has to say, we can note that Trenton retains considerable diversity, despite migration to the suburbs by a sizeable portion of its population. It has neighborhoods with varying

***Taxis.*** Although taxis frequent suburban venues, the image of the taxi goes hand in hand with urban identity, as in this image of West State Street. Long before the automobile, rented transportation included ferries and animal-drawn coaches. With the advent of the automobile in the 1890s, electric-powered cabs made their appearance in certain American cities. In 1900, the New York Taxi Cab Company brought over 600 French-made, gasoline powered, red and green cars. In England, the first gasoline cabs appeared in 1903. The name "taxi" is derived from the taximeter, invented by Wilhelm Bruhn in 1893, From the French "taxe" (price) and Greek "metron" (measure); the device measured both distance and time. The word "cab" derives from cabriolet, a horse-powered carriage.

economic and nationality components. As noted above, the Census Bureau reports in the 2000 census a city population that is 32.5 percent white and 52.1 percent black; 21.5 percent of the city's residents reported themselves as Hispanic or Latino, which could include either race.[31] So arguably Trenton retains diversity reflective of its immigrant history as well. For example, the Italian-American community accounts for just over 7 percent of the city's white population.[32]

It is not my intention here to engage in a full-blown case study of Trenton in terms of these schools of thought, or to seek to apply them in detail to Trenton. As *flâneurs,* we are strolling and wandering not simply through the physical space of Trenton, but through the intangible. And simply providing some things to think about by reconsidering Trenton in view of what some urban sociologists have had to say about cities in the abstract.

But these are not the only theories of the city for our consideration. A third perspective, offered by subcultural theory, is mainly attached to Claude Fischer, and offers perhaps a "middle ground" between Wirth and Gans. I agree with Fischer that the city itself has a significant influence in shaping social life; he does not, however, view it as destructive or isolationist, but rather as producing particular subcultures. Fischer questions Wirth's conclusions that disorganization and alienation were the inevitable result of urban living, and sets out to determine the effects of population concentration.[33] He posits that Wirth's "higher rates of 'deviance and disorganization' in cities are not accounted for by such factors as alienation, anonymity, and impersonality, but instead by the congregation of numbers of persons, 'critical masses,' sufficient to maintain viable unconventional subcultures. It is the behavioral expressions of those subcultures which come to be called 'deviant.'"[34] He rejects the notion that concentrated population in and of itself produces an urban phenomenon or that that is the definition of "urban."

If Wirth viewed all who live in a city as affected in the same manner, and Gans challenged that by pointing to groups that nonetheless thrived without such estrangement in the urban environment much as others in non-urban environments, Fischer notes that at a minimum, "urban residents do differ significantly from residents of nonurban places, and they differ to a degree insufficiently accounted for by the individual traits each group brings to its locale. They are more likely than rural residents to behave in ways that diverge from the central and/or traditional norms of their common society."[35] In short, cities produce *unconventionality,* which Fischer defines to include "unusual, divergent, idiosyncratic, nonglobally normative."[36] Unlike Gans, though, Fischer views the unconventionality of urban existences as more than incidental to urban life.

Setting out his premises, he defines urban "solely in terms of population concentration—the greater the number of persons aggregated at a place of settlement the more urban the place," and a "subculture" as "a set of modal beliefs, values, norms, and customs associated with a relatively distinct social subsystem."[37] He posits several propositions; I am omitting the quotations for ease of reading. Essentially, the more urban a place, then (1) the greater its subcultural variety, (2) the more intense its subcultures, (3) the more numerous the sources of diffusion and the greater the diffusion into a subculture and (4) the higher the rates of unconventionality. Ultimately, Fischer provides his own self-critical analysis and concludes that work remains to be done to test his propositions.[38]

So consider Trenton as the laboratory for a class in urban sociology.[39] As students — or as *flâneurs* — we may ask ourselves: which of these views of the effects of urban existence better explains or applies to Trenton? These are attempts to understand urbanism and social organization within the city. Whether or not any of these views provides a meaningful prism for viewing Trenton as such is less important than thinking about Trenton on a broader theoretical plane in order to place it with other cities. It is to facilitate looking at the familiar through a different set of analytical eyes, and attempt to understand the larger importance of a place like Trenton. The way people live in Trenton, view Trenton, and view other Trentonians has relevance. Can it be explained? Accounted for? One can conduct interviews and surveys: will that help us *understand* the place better? Trenton is a place of good and bad, light and dark, like any city. The thing about theory is that it is abstract. Trenton is real. However, when we think about Trenton, and walk its streets, we may bear in mind these approaches to the city and consider how Trenton fits in — or not.

If we move beyond the stereotypes and the stale jokes, can we reexamine Trenton and its value as a living place within the broader theoretical discussion?

But Trenton is not theory. It is a real place. A pragmatic place. And so, on a more pragmatic level, we can join urban historians who look to more tangible factors. Urban sociologist and historian Lewis Mumford, in noting the cooperative nature of the city, the evolution of order from chaos and allowing human contact in a physical space to facilitate cultural growth and expand upon civilization's heritage, nonetheless looks to the city's concentrated power, and the negative result was aggrandizement, slavery and other evils that have persisted even into the 20th century. At its core, though, the city began with human beings and needs to return to classical conceptions of the city. As Mumford writes: "We must now conceive the city, accordingly, not primarily as a place of business or government, but as an essential organ for expressing and actualizing the new human personality — that of 'One World Man.'"[40] Beyond theoretical abstractions, the city is a place where there are real consequences to real people.

The city may be considered the achievement of humanity, replete with shattered dreams. Trenton is the city of industrial prowess and significance, and is also the industrial city in the post-industrial world abandoned factories and rowhouses.

[Interlude]
*NEW JERSEY DAILY BRIEFING; Condom Plant to Close*
By Susan Jo Keller (New York Times, May 19, 1995)
    Carter-Wallace, one of Trenton's largest private employers, confirmed yesterday that it will close its plant here, which makes Trojan brand condoms. That means 500 fewer manufacturing jobs in a city that once boasted "Trenton makes, the world takes." Carter-Wallace's other New Jersey operation, a research and manufacturing plant in Cranbury, is not affected.[41]

A city has a soul. This is another way to think about Trenton and what makes a city a city. Let us draw another completely different connection in this opening chapter, this *flâneur*-like meandering in and about Trenton. This one takes us to the cutting edge of what is, or is not, acceptable.

In his controversial and far-reaching writings on the *Gaia Hypothesis*, scientist James Lovelock writes of the interconnected system that comprises both animate and inanimate objects to form a complex life unit. Like Lovelock's vision of "our planet as something possibly unique in the universe, something alive,"[42] each city is unique and, in its way, alive. It is more than metaphor to Lovelock; the Gaia theory is that "the Earth behaves like a living system."[43] It is not a reach to apply Gaia in a more microcosmic way. In short, the same kinds of interrelationships that led Lovelock to view the planets as a living system are applicable to the city.

Lovelock speaks of *Gaia*, and the "living" nature of the planet, the admixture into a living system of animate and inanimate components. Philosopher Mark Kingwell acknowledges that while cities "are not biological entities ... they exhibit certain organic features, such as growth, disease and decline."[44] However imaginative or fantastic we become in our thinking, we need to look at the city — the post-industrial American city — as something more than a physical thing. To do so, in many cases, is to see only wreckage. We need to look beyond the detritus and find the beating heart. We need to look at its history, its physical components, its parks, its dead, its neighborhoods and downtown, its pulse, its good and its bad.

I mentioned in the Introduction that two "out of the box" sources inspired the approach to this book. In Italo Calvino's speculative *Invisible Cities*, the emperor Kublai Khan felt it imperative to send a fictionalized Marco Polo to describe the cities of the empire. Khan needed to know and understand these cities. Ironically, despite the series of individual descriptions of individual cities, Marco Polo observed that "traveling, you realize that differences are lost: each city takes to resembling all cities, places exchange their form, order, distances, a shapeless dust cloud invades the continents."[45] Marco Polo has a series of conversations with Kublai Khan in which the explorer seeks to identify the few core characteristics of each, in inductive fashion, moving from the particular to the general. It is suggested that all are really facets of one city, which was

Venice. (As an intriguing historical aside, Trenton was actually compared to Venice in an article in the *New York Times*, noting, "It is remarkable that an island town should have so many waterways running parallel with the streets and avenues. Trenton has one-fourth as many bridges as Venice, and it has just one-third the population...."[46])

Is Trenton Venice? Is Venice Trenton? Posing the question seems ridiculous in 21st century eyes. But that is part of our purpose here — to pose the questions no one would even think to ask. And to transcend current time and space, and reshape our paradigms.

Are all cities Venice?

The city is a home.

In photographing Trenton for this book, I came upon two different people, in two different neighborhoods, on two different days, doing something I hadn't seen people do for decades: they were sweeping the street and sidewalk in front of their homes. One, in the Ewing-Carroll area near the federal courthouse, and the other, in South Trenton on Center Street. I was struck by these very urban moments. Both lived in rowhouses. There was a sense of pride in their actions. They were determined to keep their particular pieces of the city — of the universe — tidy.

The city is its secrets.

Trenton is a city with architectural and historical jewels. Like an old man or woman who hears a few bars of a song or catches a whiff of something in the wind, and is immediately transported to another place by a recovered lost memory, a long-forgotten image of something thought irretrievably gone, so Trenton continuously sees bits of its past in its present. The mansions of West State Street still continue to impress, if now in converted offices rather than residences. The eyebrows on rowhouse windows on Grant Avenue or the cupola on the decayed New Berkeley Hotel on Brunswick Avenue or a weed-covered statuette of a drunk man clinging to a pole in the Berkeley neighborhood — all compel a smile of recognition of some deeper layers of aesthetic concern and sense of place. Details form part of the mosaic and concomitant personality of place. Historical markers on the sides of buildings, ignored and unread, nonetheless state unequivocally, desperately: *Look at me. This was here, on this spot. You are connected. I still exist. I live.*

As on the corner of West State Street and North Warren Street, the former site of the Abraham Hunt House: "Colonel Rall was entertained on Christmas night 1776 in the house owned by Abraham Hunt which stood on this spot." Rall was killed during the First Battle of Trenton, and was buried in Trenton. Here he was, on this spot, over two hundred years ago. Someone considered this important enough to go to the trouble and expense of preparing this marker. Look at it.

We have introduced the city in general and the city of Trenton but barely scratched the surface. Wandered a bit here and there, not delving too deeply, suggesting. Letting our minds flit about — just as we do when we walk in a city. Connections, meditations and reflections, photographic images — all are part of the inquiry into the cognizable character remaining in this lost city, like others of its kind, and all the more unique for that.

Trenton matters. The small lost cities of the Atlantic seaboard, tracing their roots back to the formation of the country deserve, if not demand, our attention.

# 2. The City Defined and Considered

I have written of connections, the taking off from one point and proceeding to another, even if the reason is not immediately transparent — like a Rorschach response to the images of the city. We considered, preliminarily, different ways of viewing a city generally, and of viewing Trenton particularly. In this chapter, we look more broadly, thinking about Trenton in the broader context of how people think about cities in general, and seek to define them to get at their essential characteristics. We move beyond the abstract theories to the more particular and concrete aspects of defining and considering a city. We will seek to place Trenton in this context, or at least provide a set of "reading glasses" for looking at Trenton — or any other such city, for that matter — through those lenses. We move beyond the three theoretical frameworks discussed in Chapter One, and beyond the census data, and demographics. We consider different ways that people have defined a city and what it means to be in and of a city.

The first cities were in Mesopotamia.[1] They developed from a combination of commercial, security and religious reasons. Early Mesopotamian cities were often dominated by the ziggurat, the large stepped towers of the ancient communities that served as temples. One can also note this combination of functions not only in ancient world cities, but also in the formation of American cities in particular, which began with a core admixture of religion and social concern.[2] Various New Jersey cities — Newark and Trenton among them — began with Quaker roots and a search for religious freedom, coupled with a desire to take advantage of the commercial advantages of the particular locale. The Industrial Revolution was such that at mid–19th century, the development of the city — of urbanized America — was seen as a "phenomenon," and one for which political leadership was not prepared. Indeed, the chaos generated by the unmet social needs of the burgeoning populations was viewed as a threat to American democracy itself.[3] However, led by such as William Ellery Channing, founder of the Unitarian Church, and American transcendentalists like Ralph Waldo Emerson and Walt Whitman, the city was seen as a noble human pursuit, something that could, and should, be properly planned to give voice and vision to that which was most ideal in the human condition.[4]

Cities need a sense of place that is greater than the sum of its parts, and to that end they provide physical elements of place. A city comprised primarily of office and residential space, and limited public spaces and monuments, will be deficient: "People tend to select something prominent, something that has played a role in the life of their city, for a landmark: a town hall, a market cross, fountains, monuments, theaters, church porches, and the like."[5] They provide a sense of cultural identity, but equally important to these civic symbols is the sense of "place," the "territory within which important personal memories are inscribed and which also provides windows of opportunity to sustain hope for the future."[6] Every city has at least one fundamental icon that proclaims to the world, like a brand logo, its identity and its essence. It may be a skyline, a plaza, an iconic building—but there is something that becomes the face of the city.

For the city of Trenton, that symbol is a bridge. Crossing the Delaware River at virtually the same location as the earliest bridge crossings of that river, the Lower Trenton Bridge is more affectionately and locally known as the "Trenton Makes" bridge, derived from the slogan "Trenton Makes, the World Takes" emblazoned across it. The first bridge on the site opened in 1806, and was a

**Trenton Makes Bridge.** The iconic bridge, reflecting Trenton's motto, "Trenton Makes, the World Takes," stands on the site of its 18th-century predecessor bridge that was an engineering wonder of the time across the Delaware River.

wooden covered bridge that was internationally known for its engineering. The current bridge dates to 1928; the slogan's letters, testifying to Trenton's industrial heritage, were placed on the bridge in 1935. It is, perhaps, difficult for those outside of the city itself and the surrounding area to understand the emotional resonance of the sign and the bridge.[7]

To be sure, there are other iconic symbols in the city — the War Memorial Building, the golden-domed Statehouse, the mansions of West State Street, the Roebling steel factory, the Battle Monument, the Old Barracks, even Cadwalader Park, designed personally by Frederick Law Olmsted — but it is this bridge, with its bold statement that defies and denies current economic and commercial reality of the city, that remains the symbol of the city.

If the "Trenton Makes" bridge is the most visible physical structure to capture the spirit of the city, there is other physical evidence of Trenton's "cityness" that establishes Trenton's sense of urban place. When one looks at the pictures of Trenton from half a century ago, or even a full hundred years ago, there is no question of its *urbanness*. It *looks* like a city. Today, even with its decreased population and commercial activity, its *footprint* is still that of a city. While other cities have grown, both physically, architecturally and economically, Trenton has not, but the definition need not be a comparative one. Trenton remains a city, and it is important to retain that definition in considering its present and its future.

Cities matter, and not just economically. They matter because of what has

*War Memorial Building.* One of the great monumental buildings of the city, the War Memorial Building was constructed in 1931-1932, another example of American Renaissance architecture and neo-classicism. Dedicated to the fallen of World War I, it was refurbished in 1999 and serves as Trenton's premier performing arts venue.

***Roebling Factory.*** Among the most famous Trenton factories was the steel wire factory of the Roeblings. Shown here is Building 104. John A. Roebling opted for Trenton in part on the recommendation of his friend, Peter Cooper, whose Iron and Steel Works was already in the city (and is now a restaurant/bar). He bought land in 1848 on South Broad Street and by 1849 began production. Advantages of the city included its location on the Eastern seaboard, accessible water and rail transport, and nearby related industries.

gone into them and what is lost if they are gone. A place like Trenton would be missed. We think *city* and, at least in the United States, we think concrete and skyscrapers. We think population. We think things. But a city is more than that. A city may need a physical composition to be a city, and all that it connotes, but a city is something more.

In the initial instance it might seem that to ask what is a city is in part a fool's errand; definitions abound, objective and subjective, real and surreal. Still, we are a naming people, and we need to name this thing we are observing, and are part of. We attempt a definition. But do we focus on the physical? The emotional? The intellectual? The city is all of these things. Perhaps like Justice Potter Stewart's definition of obscenity, we simply know it when we see it. Mark Girouard, in *Cities and People*, expressed a similar thought: "There is a certain stage of cosmopolitanism and complexity at which a town becomes a city; everyone is aware of it, although the border between the two is inevitably imprecise."[8]

Trenton provides a basis to consider three interrelated things: first, the definition of a city, and how we think of cities; second, what it means to have a sense of place; and third, what the industrial city looks like through the lens

***Battle Monument in Snow.*** The blizzards of February 2010 blanketed the city. The Battle Monument seems a more vivid reminder of the actual battle in this setting.

of Trenton. The scholars send us to the abstract and the theoretical, and the streets and life return us to the reality of Trenton. We make connections. To understand them, it is helpful to have some background and framework. In the first chapter we discussed broad themes and schools of thought as to the impact of the city. We can now look a bit more closely at particular ways in which some have sought to define a city.

## *Defining the City*

At present it is estimated that nearly half of the world's people live in cities, and by 2030, the figure will be two-thirds; this should be compared with about 10 percent living in cities in 1800.[9]

In the context of metropolitan world, what remains of the city identity itself? The world is becoming urbanized, with more people living in urban environments. What may seem a self-evident statement should not be taken for granted or dismissed too quickly. This is a relatively recent phenomenon. Throughout the eighteenth century, the population was primarily rural, and towns were the norm as opposed to large cities. With the 19th century and the movement of rural populations towards burgeoning industrial centers, this began to change, and European cities' boundaries expanded beyond medieval walls. In the Western Hemisphere, the "New World," there were no such walls to break, so in the alternative, cities often expanded by aggregating outlying towns. So it is worth reflecting on the impact that this has on the way we look at ourselves in the twenty-first century, and what it means culturally, intellectually and otherwise to be an urban society as opposed to a rural society. And since, at the heart of urban existence are the cities, in one form or another, it warrants attention.

The cities of the world continue to grow significantly, at the expense of rural areas.[10] A standard metropolitan statistical area is not the same as a city.[11] The city itself is less easily defined, or perhaps even intuitively known. It has tangible and intangible assets. However we define it, primarily the city is a physical place, not simply a census measuring device. Forget the "virtual" city or the temptation to look for the characteristics of a city in the digital byways of the Internet. Put aside notions of suburban "cities," or "sprawl," or complex sociological theories as to what the city of the twenty-first century is, has been or will become. Leave Joel Garreau's "edge cities" aside for the moment—that notion of a vast geographical blob that may have replaced the core functions of the city in the new extended sprawl. The physical American city remains, even if it has shrunk and withered, as Trenton. Its footprint remains.

America's urbanization has been continuous and accelerated. Paradoxically, in the post–World War II era, the urbanization of the country increased while simultaneously many of its smaller and medium-sized cities—including those that once were among the nation's hundred largest—diminished. The standard metropolitan statistical area skews our concept of city.[12] We are interested in the city *proper*, the thing we seem to know without having to necessarily define it. Once we understand its physical contours, we can get at its intangible being, its essence, its soul, its *urbanity*.

Municipalities, particularly in New Jersey, where there are 566 of them, may often run together, bleeding borders. Most are not, have never been, and frankly, will not become, cities. The city proper is a particular thing. New Jersey still has a few of them — the East Coast cities, the Colonial towns that grew up and, like Carl Sandburg's Chicago, had broad shoulders.

We tend to think today of cities with skylines, filled with skyscrapers, drawn by the image of New York. This is an Americanism; many of the larger cities of Europe lack these tall buildings in their city centers, though one finds them sprouting on the peripheries. Even Paris, sprawling and medieval Paris, sprouts one essential central skyscraper (apart from the Eiffel Tower and the domino-like fringe of Defense), the gray finger pointing up from Montparnasse. The American cities, visible from the great Eisenhower-spawned interstates, seem like cut-outs stood on end. A few, many — it doesn't matter. To the American, tall buildings define the city. Even Trenton, with its handful of skyscrapers generally between fifteen and twenty stories, sports a discernable skyline from across the Delaware River. It can be a city by appearance, still.

But looks are not enough. It is time to shift our focus, to think about one of the questions of this book: What makes a city?

It cannot be just a matter of population, though population itself must be the starting point for determining a city. It is counterintuitive to refer to a city of, say, 1,000 people, in the contemporary world, no matter how concentrated they are. However, there are suburban areas with more people than many other "traditional" cities, and yet we do not think of them, either anecdotally or in scholarly fashion, as cities. Let us consider this more in the context of Trenton.

Trenton is hemorrhaging people. The city now has a population of less than 90,000 individuals. Surrounded by suburban communities, those New Jersey townships with housing developments built over farmland, it no longer dominates merely by its number of people. We might note in passing that the "downsized" city may not necessarily be a bad thing, and that a constructive view of that may lead to a more positive use of resources, as suggested elsewhere.[13] There are other places, of much smaller populations, such as Venice, Italy, with even less people than Trenton within its city limits,[14] that we nonetheless still consider to be cities. As we look at the geopolitical structure of the United States and Europe, we may well wonder what it means to be a city in the 21st century. More particularly, at what point does a city cease to exist and turn into something else — part of suburban sprawl, an "edge city," or just a large town? Conversely, at what point do we think of a place as a city instead of a town or village, or something else? The words themselves are not determinative, but they have impact, as words carry connotations. When we hear "city," we, at least in the United States, tend to think of something different than when we hear "town" or "village." Beyond nomenclature and definitions, though, we have a sense of what makes a city a city.

As made evident by the prior discussion that population is the starting point, ultimately population in and of itself does not the city make. Aristotle refused to identify a particular number, but rather qualified it as the number sufficient to establish the "good life;" Plato quantified the number at 5,040.[15] Put another way, Aristotle felt the size of a society was a function of citizens to recognize each other, and Plato looked for 5,000 citizens.[16] We do not think of a city without sufficient numbers of people, whatever that is, but population is only an initial factor, if that, and by no means the end. Numbers are numbers. They are not *place*.

In considering Trenton, now a small city, and discussing whether it may even still be deemed a city, we can turn to some of the classical analyses on the subject. It provides a starting point. Dictionary definitions are tautological. For example, the *American Heritage Dictionary*'s first definition is "a center of population, commerce, and culture; a town of significant size and importance."[17] Clearly, we cannot leave it at this. There are a wealth of definitions and attempts to define the city, ranging from the physical to the more abstract. Consider the following non-exhaustive survey.

German sociologist Max Weber (1864–1920), in his posthumously published *The City*, rejected size as the defining factor; such would rule out smaller, successful cities. He started with an economic definition: "The city is a settlement the inhabitants of which live primarily off trade and commerce rather than agriculture," though he acknowledges that this, too, is insufficient, since economic versatility can come through both a market and a permanence to exchange.[18] Put more specifically, Weber wrote, "We wish to speak of a 'city' only in cases where the local inhabitants satisfy an economically substantial part of their daily wants in the local market, and to an essential extent by products which the local population and that of the immediate hinterland produced for sale in the market or acquired in other ways."[19] Cities may be divided into producer, trade and consumer cities.[20] The notion of "city" is complex; in part, it inhabits a place between the rural and household economy on the one hand, and the national economy on the other.

Weber rejected the thought that understanding the conceptual city cannot end with identification of its "merchants and tradesmen" living and working in a crowded place to meet the daily needs of the citizens.[21] Other non-economic factors are relevant to defining and understanding the composition of the city, such as governance—the "politico-administrative concept"—and security— "fortress and garrison."[22] The city fuses the "political fortress and the civil economic population," and this combination has critical importance for the institutionalization of the city.[23] Weber distinguished the Western city as having another relevant factor: community. An essential feature of an urban community is the "relative predominance" of trade and commerce, "displaying the following features: 1. a fortification; 2. a market; 3. a court of its own and at least partially autonomous law; 4. a related form of association; and 5. at least partial autonomy and autocephaly, thus also an administration by authorities in the election of whom the burghers participated."[24] So while Weber's city has clear economic underpinnings, the analysis moves far beyond simply population concentration, and looks to factors that, while also common to other types of communities, nonetheless in combination with the other factors move the community into the realm of "city."

Gideon Sjoberg calls a city "a community of substantial size and population density that shelters a variety of nonagricultural specialists, including a literate elite."[25] The city is further defined "as a residence of specialists, has been a continuing source of innovation."[26] This definition notes population and density, but also the need for diversity. Implicitly, this recognizes that unlike the small town, the city will embody a degree of anonymity.

This point picks up on another way of defining the city in terms of its citizenry and their relationship to each other. Once we accept a certain population base — whatever it is — do we then define a city less in terms of the other components identified by Weber, or look to a more psychological approach? For example, sociologist Lyn Lofland in *The Public Realm* accepts a definition of the city as "a permanently populous place or settlement."[27] However, earlier, in her 1973 *A World of Strangers*, she noted that a city is "many things"—a physical space, a political entity, a simultaneous magnet for "ambition and hope" and repellent filled with "inconvenience and fear," a place of work and recreation, and *apart from size*, those characteristics might be found as well in what we consider small towns.[28] Size, though, remains a critical definitional component of the city not so much for its quantitative number, but because it mandates that the citizens of the city are essentially strangers to one another, and therefore, "the city then, among all the other things that it may be, is also a world of strangers, a world populated by persons who are personally unknown to one another."[29] Numbers breed anonymity. To some extent, the notion that the city must by definition be a place of strangers—and therefore be large enough to accommodate that — has resonance in a variety of formulations.

For Lofland, the city as a unique social-psychological environment is a place of strangers, of people who do not know each other, and this is of importance.[30] The "urban settlement," that is, the *public realm*, is the city — and regardless of where that city is, the experience of the city dweller is unique from that of the village dweller. In other words, the city dweller in Chicago has more in common with the city dweller in Buenos Aires, she argues, than the Chicagoan does with someone from a small town in Illinois. The public realm is urban public space.[31]

Public space has meaning, and its misuse, or denigration, has consequences. The city is a place of public as well as private space, and the use, or non-use, of that space in the city has consequences that form a part of urban, or city, existence. Eamonn Canniffe observes that "whereas Modernism had inverted the urban fabric of the traditional city into a landscape of isolated objects, the void between them, the 'dead public space' ... might now be deemed to have meaning by virtue of its potential privatization.... Space is treated as a commodity from which it is necessary to deter the undesirable, and the surest way to effect this deterrence is to introduce an economic barrier. We therefore have the phenomenon that the most common form in which to enjoy public space in the city is to be engaged in commercial activity."[32]

In thinking about how we define a city, therefore, we need to think of those places that are common and public, the backdrop for a multitude of use by persons connected solely by the physical space they share.

The city and its composition of strangers reflect a change in human existence; tribal existence and villages developed around a knowing of one's compatriots. Lofland in particular notes that being strangers, as opposed to being familiars, "has been the exception, not the rule."[33] What are the consequences of this for defining a city? If tribes, and then early settlements, were composed of those who knew each other, were familiar with each other, and the city is no longer defined as the exception, but rather the rule — that is, where *estrangement* and anonymity are defining characteristics — then what does that say about where we are as a species in our development?

Archeologist V. Gordon Childe uses ten criteria to determine whether a place is a city: size, composition and function, taxation, public buildings, a ruling class, systems of record keeping, writing, artistic expression, trade, and craftsmen.[34] Once again, while we may start with size, there are other components — some if not all of which may be found in communities we do not necessarily consider a city. One could apply all these factors — except size — to a small college community in the United States, but we would probably not consider such to be a city.

The American urban sociologist Robert Park understood that size alone was not the defining factor, but also even all of the composite factors, in and of themselves or even in combination, were not enough to capture the essence of a city. The city is not just its physical space; it is its ethereal space as well. He calls the city

> something more than a congeries of individual men and of social conveniences — streets, buildings, electric lights, tramways, and telephones, etc.; something, more also, than a mere constellation of institutions and administrative devices — courts, hospitals, schools, police and civil functionaries of various sorts. The city is, rather, a state of mind, a body of customs and traditions, and of the organized attitudes and sentiments that inhere in these customs and are transmitted with this tradition. The city is not, in other words, merely a physical mechanism and an artificial construction. It is involved in the vital processes of the people who compose it; it is a product of nature, and particularly of human nature.[35]

In the twilight of the twentieth century, Edward L. Glaeser discussed whether cities were dying, and provided a definition rooted in economics: "Conceptually, a city is just a dense agglomeration of people and firms. All of the benefits of cities come ultimately from reduced transport costs for goods, people and ideas. The positive impact of agglomeration that comes from reducing the costs of moving goods lost most of its importance over the 20th century as transportation costs fell and large-scale manufacturing declined."[36] Again we have a city's definition stated in terms of population and density, with economic functions that could be found in smaller places, but are of sufficient scale to be something else, something more akin to what we consider a "city."

Douglas Rae is a writer who focused on the city of New Haven, Connecticut to get at the nature of the city in general. In his book on that city, he remarks that during the time frame covering the latter decades of the 19 century through the 1920s, the urbanist city consisted of five essential elements: concentrated industrial activity that drew people into the city, a diverse and concentrated economic base, centralized housing, multiple and concentrated civic organizations, and political integration.[37] A city is not just a physical place, but an emotional place as well. Certain elements were necessary to come together, but in the end, what defines a city was the conflation of these elements into a particularized self-vision of the city's inhabitants.

Notwithstanding a sociological analysis of population, density and heterogeneity as Wirth posited in terms of defining a city, does Trenton remain as an idea? Can the question of a city be as much a state of mind as a physical state? Can the idea of a place come to it over time, if it was not built in accordance with it? Do Trentonians have an urban self-vision?

Architect and writer Witold Rybczynski also has developed this theme, and considers the semantic difference between "town" and "city" to be of little significance, particularly when one crosses language barriers, and concludes that what distinguishes a "city" is as much a matter of perception and connotation as any physical criteria:

> Today, to call a place a town implies that it has close economic and emotional ties with the surrounding countryside. A city, on the other hand, while it may appropriate natural areas for weekend recreation, is considered self-sufficient.... Thus, to say one place is a large town and that another is a small city is to insinuate that while their population sizes may be similar, their character is not."[38]

In short, *character* becomes a defining element of what makes a city a city.

Another writer from academic circles, Daniel Monti, in *The American City*, makes a comparable point; the American city is defined as much by its motion and sense of *business* as by anything else:

> City dwellers occupy a world filled with spontaneity and, yes, sometimes a lot of scurrying around.... There really is something different about the way city folk live and make sense of their world. It is seen in their willingness to embrace some new ideas or neighbors even as they run away from strangers. It is apparent in the obedient way they follow some rules while willfully violating others. And it is found in their insistence to be whomever they like and still go to church, declare their fidelity to an ancestral people, buy the same items their neighbors do, and pay their taxes.... Not everyone who lives in cities has to act this way for cultural practices to work their special magic on us."[39]

The notion of a city is also the notion that there are certain common denominators and patterns to the definition of the city, or at least the Western city, regardless of size. Writing in 1935, Walter J. Matherly of the University of Florida stated that "externally, every city, especially in America, resembles every other city. Urban development has tended to follow a single pattern. Little distinction of any kind has been achieved.... They differ from each other only in that some are constructed more of reinforced concrete than of brick and others more of brick than of reinforced concrete.... In outward form the American city is standardized. When a traveler sees one he has seen all."[40] His is a view that might resonate with Italo Calvino's Marco Polo. Mark Kingwell identifies a city with its airport and observes an "increasingly spectral" relationship to cities entered as such.[41] Others seek to redefine the city as an area, based on functionality and other concerns.[42]

If we start looking for patterns in the least common denominators, we can find a consensus that while population, and population density, are generally accepted as essential to defining the city, it is also apparent that other elements are critical components of discernible patterns in the development and institutionalization of the city, and which distinguish it, if even on a visceral level, from communities or towns or settlements that are *not* cities. And the importance of the discussion seems to be that understanding what makes a city helps understand how its citizens view themselves. Ultimately, self-vision would seem relevant to efforts to transform a city, or otherwise adapt it to the current needs of the 21st century and post-industrial life.

Or maybe not. Maybe the core functions remain the same, but the technology and desires that are met by those functions have changed. Joseph Rykwert, in *The Seduction of Place*, notes that little seems to have been transformed in the functions of the city for the past hundred years or so: "That the nineteenth-century city was confusing, congested, and unhealthy, as well as dangerous, is a truism. Action to remedy the defects was constantly stymied by an underlying belief in the liberal concept of the free-floating value of money and the ultimately benevolent, 'natural' working of industrial development. *Nor has this changed.*"[43]

This is but a sampling of various writers who have sought to define the city; such efforts are as varied as the number of writers attempting it. Perhaps we need to change our notion of "the city." Perhaps we need a new paradigm for the concept of city that recognizes its function in the post-industrial world. Perhaps we simply need to pause and reflect, and let our minds wander, as we sift through what may be relevant and important to understanding a place like Trenton.

## A Sense of Place

We have been looking at a variety of efforts to define a city in terms of its tangible (or at least measurable) and intangible components. I want to return to the subject of sense of place, one of the more intangible ways of defining a city. A sense of place is not confined solely to a city, but we may look to the city to see if it can be defined in terms of place. Whether objectively others might not view a place as a city, it does seem that a city can be a city to its inhabitants because they believe it to be so, and because for them, it functions as a city. At the very least, it functions in a conventional sense of how a city ought to function, and ought to be perceived. In *Cities*, journalist John Reader comments that "the integral role of the city in human affairs runs deep — well beyond the streets and buildings and into the realms of conscious and sub-conscious awareness that makes us who we are."[44] Cities provide a sense of cultural identity, but equally important to these civic symbols is the sense of "place." Urban scholar and historian Lewis Mumford has referred to "a more general truth about cities: their marked individuality, so strong, so full of 'character' from the beginning that they have many of the attributes of human personalities."[45] Joel Kotkin in *The City: A Global History* speaks of the commonality of cities, whether ancient or modern, Eastern or Western, and notes, "There is the visceral 'feel' of the city almost everywhere — the same quickening of pace on a busy street, an informal marketplace, or a freeway exchange, the need, to create notable places, the sharing of a unique civil identity."[46] The urban writer Lewis Mumford refers in *The City in History* to "a more general truth about cities: their marked individuality, so strong, so full of 'character' from the beginning that they have many of the attributes of human personalities."[47]

A city provides identity, a sense of community, of belonging, of place. We return to this. We need something physical to anchor us. The city streets provide a sense of place. In virtually every city there is one street, or one intersection, synonymous with the particular city. Hollywood and Vine define Los Angeles, Fifth Avenue for New York, Piccadilly Circus in London. Kotkin adds: "In the end, a great city relies on those things that engender for its citizens a peculiar and strong attachment, sentiments that separate one specific place from others."[48] Say its name, and we have an identity that fits within a more global identity.

Cities are the stuff of songs, of movies, of books and poems. Edward Hopper's painting *Nighthawks* conjures up the quintessential city at night. We are strangers on the street, peering in through the plate glass window, looking at strangers. And yet we share a moment in the city, and are connected.

Cities matter in part because *place* matters. We know that intuitively. We feel safe in a known place, a familiar place. At home, comfortable. But what exactly is place? More particularly, a sense of place? Place is important. It grounds us. We speak of home, not simply housing. The sum is greater than the parts. It encompasses memory, experience, sensory perception. A place fills us. We meet someone, a stranger, from our home in a faraway place, and we feel an immediate kinship. There is a pleasure in the identification. If we can't define it, we certainly miss it when it is gone, and envelop ourselves when within it.

So what exactly is *place*? Can we even use such a word as exactly to discern meaning in something so gossamer-like?

Mark Kingwell wrote in *Concrete Reveries* that cities are places, and readily admits "that may sound obvious ... but the ostensible obviousness of the concept belies a depth of challenge." For him, place "is an area of significance, a physical staging ground. But it is more than that. It is somewhere that matters, where we find or lose ourselves, where understanding good and bad is forced upon us. Places are environments, sites of action, horizons of concern. They are infused with our aspirations and beliefs, reflecting and shaping them both."[49]

One writer has devoted an entire book to discussion of place. In *The Experience of Place*, Tony Hiss has argued for the intimacy of this bond with place in terms of both environment and personal experience, and the need to be sensitive to this as we make changes to our places. He writes, "Paying careful attention to our experience of places, we can use our own responses, thoughts, and feelings to help us replenish the places we love."[50] It is an extra sense, a "simultaneous perception," that he suggests generates a profound, often unconscious, association with place. Like a painting whose colors have darkened unrecognizably through centuries of neglect and are then realized with an appropriate restorative cleaning, so "the fading and discoloration of places has been going on around us for generations."[51] The environment provides experience, but Hiss's concern is that as we expand our urbanization, if we are not attentive, we will lose the experiential relevance of place.

In recounting sensory perception, he uses Grand Central Station as an example, and describes that experience in terms of sight, touch, sound, and his overall reaction to the simple act of walking across the concourse. With appropriate concentration, simultaneous perception can "pick up what we could call cross-sensory, or multisensory, patterns of information — things or events we can recognize only when information from two or more senses is taken all together."[52] It allows us to aggregate an experience that, like the sum, is greater than the individual parts. It helps provide an interconnectedness and awareness that gives us more information about our surroundings that we absorb, even if on a subconscious level. And, when some of that information is cut off, we eventually reach our limits of tolerance — in short, there is a certain amount of experience we must have, regardless of our overt awareness. To that extent, "people are often drawn to places that offer rich experiences.... But changes made over the years to such places which fail to consider the experiential impact produced by physical alterations can turn pearls into past and convert the real into a mirage."[53]

Another writer has taken a somewhat different approach to getting at the importance of place. Lucy Lippard, in *The Lure of the Local: Senses of Place in a Multicentered Society*, says simply and evocatively that "place for me is the locus of desire."[54] Instead of "sensory perception," she writes of multicenteredness: "Every time we enter a new place, we become one of the ingredients of an existing hybridity, which is really what all 'local places' consist of."[55] And unlike Hiss, who (at least to my reading) intimates that we are all aware of place on a variety of levels, Lippard proclaims that "few of us in contemporary North American society know our place."[56] However, like Hiss, she recognizes the importance of sensory perception; it is that perception, together with physical space, that constitutes *place*.[57] Regarding the city, she notes that "where the city dweller may revel in her daily anonymity and freedom from self within crowded spaces, she also struggles to find an emotional community that will offer the intimacy for which Americans pine, even after we have made the choices that make it less and less likely."[58]

The city is backdrop and foreground. The city permeates. Place envelopes is. We are more connected — rooted — to place than we may think. But, like Dorothy in Oz, the knowledge is useless unless we want it. We need to want to be home.

We have considered defining a city in terms of quantitative measurements and immeasurable *gestalt* qualities. The city becomes part of our individual character as well, and our experiences in the urban environment shape our moods and being. This was explored intensely in an atmospheric novel by Georges Rodenbach. In 1892, Rodenbach's novel *Bruges-la-Morte* ("Bruges the Dead") was published in France. Its plotline consists of a widower who sees a woman who resembles his deceased wife, and follows her around the city of Bruges, ultimately establishing a relationship with her and then, in a fit of passion and rage, killing her. Throughout, the deadness of *fin de siecle* Bruges becomes a metaphor for his life and, apparently, many of the inhabitants. As that author wrote in his essay *The Death Throes of Towns*, "how many who not so long ago were handsome and wealthy towns, suffer an abandonment at their life's end; poor ancestors who grow stiff with an air of fallen grace, preserving at the most a few monuments; coasts of arms in stone, armorial bearings which alone attest to their ancient and authentic nobility."[59]

Over a century later, a popular film is made, *In Bruges*, also threaded with murder and estrangement, and yet oddly celebratory of place. In that film, a criminal sends two of his hitmen to Bruges, with the intention that one of them kill the other for the latter's bungled prior job. Being a man of some "compassion," the criminal wanted the intended victim to share the experience of Bruges and experience that place as a final treat.

Yes. Place matters. Urban space matters.

A place has familiarity and comfort. When I lived in Hoboken in 1980, I walked most nights to the overlook by Stevens Institute of Technology that faced Manhattan. When I lived in London, it was Trafalgar Square that always drew me, and whenever I return to London, no other part of that city so establishes place for me as that square. It has pieces of my personal history, as well as the city's, and it is a point of connectedness for me. In New York, it is the area around the United Nations, where I had spent a lot of time as a student. In Washington, D.C., it is the Jefferson Memorial. Each of these spots is intertwined with my personal experiences, and no matter how long it has been since I visit any of these cities, when I go to the particular spot, I feel a sense of belonging. This is my city, still. I am a cell in this great life force that is the city.

In Trenton, I am always drawn to West State Street, and in particular, the section between Stockton Street and Calhoun Street, covering the heart of the Revolutionary-era city, with its reminders of the city's industrial greatness in the mansions lining the street. Nearby is the War Memorial Building, where I was sworn in as a lawyer. I participated in the state spelling bee championship in the State Museum auditorium. Within the city are the hospitals in which my four children were born. The Statehouse building—among the oldest in continuous use in the United States—personal and historic ghosts travel with me. There is no other place in New Jersey, or the world for that matter, that looks just like this or carries the catalysts of resonance for me. Trenton has a sense of *place* for me.

But place is not unique to the city, though a city carries its own sense of place. The city carries with it, though, a separate kind of sense—that of being an urban place. Urban identity should not be confused with living in an *urbanist* way, that is, in the sense of being part of the culture, work and leisure,

*North Montgomery Street.* Originally known as Quaker Lane for the Friends Meeting House at the corner of Montgomery Street and Hanover Street, the street was renamed for Richard Montgomery, a Colonial naval officer who died in 1775 at Quebec as part of the American invasion of Canada.

of a city. (Indeed, if suburban sprawl is irrevocable, it may be that urbanist principles need to become part of such an "extended" city.[60]) In the United States, small and medium-sized cities could still boast, into the 1950s, urbanist lifestyles, in which people of a city lived, worked and played in that city. There was still a sense of identity of place, of culture, of a civic sense, if not pride, before the era of sprawl, "Edge City,"[61] and so forth. To be urbanist is to have a sense of place, an identification with one's city, and be part of its personality. It is different to live and work in a city than it is to live and work in a small town. We understand that on an intuitive level.

Trenton is a *place* and has a sense of place. It seeps history. It is a haunted place, a place where over two hundred years ago English and Hessian soldiers bled into its ground. It is a place where virtually every significant figure of the American Revolution stayed or passed through. It is a place that, like ancient European cities, still bears the footprint of its original settlement.

## *The Post-Industrial City*

In our explorations of defining the city, we have noted the importance of population in a concentrated area, with the physical accoutrements of a city, and the anecdotal references to city. Timing is a factor; the city of the 19th century may well be a very different, if not unrecognizable place, in the present. Much of Trenton's identity, though, was tied to Trenton's manufacturing stature. As that vanished after World War II, what of Trenton's contemporary urban identity? Consider Trenton now as a post-industrial city. In other words, do we need new definitions and parameters in the post-industrial world to define the "traditional" city? Arguments have been made as to what may or may not be a city based on function. What of the traditional city, the urban footprint, and its contemporary relevance? Indeed, the title of this book compels us to reconsider Trenton, the industrial large city of its time, as the post-industrial small city in the 21st century.

The post-industrial city has been categorized as the third of three historic stages of city development, following the traditional or historical, and the industrial.[62] What has been missing from the discussion has been the ethical component, which has been under-represented, as argued by Eammon Canniffe: "Commercial values prevail which ultimately serve the need of only a minority of citizens. The motivations of the democratic representative system remain disconnected from the populations they are intended to serve. The views of citizens have to be actively sought, and their individual aspirations addressed for them to be able to endorse any shared shaping of the city."[63]

Daniel Bell, in his prophetic *The Coming of Post-Industrial Society*, decades ago identified the primary characteristics of the new paradigm of nations that had gone through pre-industrial and industrial societies and become "post-industrial." The economic sector moved beyond the primary (extractive) and secondary (goods producing) stages to include tertiary (transportation and recreation) and quaternary (trade, finance, insurance, real estate). A professional class is predominant over a semi-skilled worker class. Information replaced energy as the primary technology. Abstraction replaces empiricism, and what he calls the "time perspective" shifts toward the future as opposed to ad hoc adoptions. Centralization and codification of theoretical knowledge becomes the axial principle as opposed to economic growth.[64]

Put another way, the evolution of American cities in the 21st century has led to "a new form of American urbanism: the festival city has replaced the service city, which itself replaced the industrial city nearly a century ago."[65] One definition proposed for the "prototypical" post-industrial city defines it as "a city in which traditional industry maintains a significant but decreasing share of economic activity, replaced as an engine of economic growth by the production of various types of services, from producer services, to medical, educational and governmental services, to consumer services."[66] The loss of manufacturing has led to the departure of a strong middle class; "thus the broad middle of urban societies may be shrinking, while the income gap between the well paid and the working poor widens. The post-industrial city, then, is also likely to be a dual city, in which rich and poor draw further away from each other spatially within the urban region, as well as in terms of differential access to economic resources."[67]

The post-industrial city reflects population loss and increased class disparity. While central business districts still provide the commercial core of most American cities, they are generally surrounded by poor, inner city areas.[68] Spatially, the post-industrial city can be envisioned as a series of concentric circles: at the center is the central business district core, surrounded by its frame, and that itself is within the low income inner city. Next come the inner, middle and outer suburban fringes, with rising income levels from lower-middle to middle. The outer suburban ring comes next, with the rural-urban fringe and ultimately, the exurban area.[69] The city is marked by older housing stock, often pre–World War II. There is often an identifiable, even if small, skyline and coterie of tall buildings.[70]

Post-industrial cities embody these characteristics and may be marked by "edge city" characteristics, with office parks on the outskirts, and within the city, dramatic class differences. They reflect the loss of an industrial manufacturing base, and with it, sizeable portions of a middle class.

Trenton is situated in an almost prototypically defined post-industrial area dominated by Princeton University. Nearby are the Princeton Plasma Physics Lab, various pharmaceutical companies, and other research and development companies. It remains a transportation hub on the Northeast Corridor train route between Philadelphia and New York or, more broadly, Washington and Boston. It is in the neighborhood of some of the wealthiest communities in the country. Trenton, in the post-industrial age, is an island in Einstein Alley, the high-tech rubric applied to Princeton and its swollen and figurative boundaries.

## *The Failure of Cities*

We read occasionally of a once-great city unearthed in an archeological find. Beyond the dust, dirt and foundations of buildings, we try to imagine the life-force and look of the place. While Trenton and other such post-industrial, "gritty" cities have not been reduced to rubble in an apocalyptic vision, one wonders whether, in a few centuries, such places will also have vanished. What is unthinkable or unimaginable is often the prelude to reality.

In this last section of this chapter, I want to comment on another defining characteristic of the city — its soul. Soul is obviously an intangible and amorphous concept, particularly when applied to the city, but as we will see, it has figured in some of the discussion as to what makes, or does not make, a city. It may even mean the difference between success and reinvention on the one hand, and failure on the other.

Cities have lifespans, some exceptionally long, others less so. But cities, like people, can and do reinvent themselves. Sometimes the entire civilization fails and the city with it. Peoples like the Aztecs and Mayans built and sustained great cities; such are cases in point. On the other hand, there are a handful of cities some 2,500 to 3,000 years old — Rome, Damascus, Jericho, Jerusalem, Benares — that continue to thrive.[71]

I previously referred to one contemporary writer on cities, journalist John Reader. He has identified three principal factors by which to gauge the failure of cities — "economics, politics and religion — have been the primary motivating forces of urban history.... Most cities contain elements of all three categories, and their relative significance is blurred.... But in the modern world, even where the determinant factors of a large city's origin and rise are quite obvious, their relevance has long since been rendered subservient to the practical expediencies of everyday life."[72] He does not address natural disasters, which of course eradicated Pompeii. What he explains is that the city thrives to the extent it serves diverse interests; when it ceases to provide such means to an end, the particular city ceases to be relevant.

Reader cites Edward Gibbons' *The History of the Decline and Fall of the Roman Empire,* and its factors including a decline in morals and values, public health, political corruption, unemployment, inflation, urban decay, inferior technology, and military spending. Gibbons comments on the decline of Sumerian cities — among the world's oldest — as a result of the inability of their agricultural systems to sustain cities that ran out of space and resources.[73]

The city as physical community is engrained in the ethos of those who live in it, whether by birth or later choice. The city, like a living organism, depends upon its varied parts to achieve something greater, something that in turn is given back in the form of identity, of satisfying a human need for community. In his *The City in History,* Mumford is more abstract: "The chief function of the city is to convert power into form, energy into culture, dead matter into the living symbols of art, biological reproduction into social creativity."[74] In other words, the intangible qualities of what makes a city are no less real than the tangible characteristics we see, smell, hear and touch.

The institutions of the post-industrial city have changed. Mumford identified the factory, railroad and sum as the principal elements of the city of the Industrial Revolution, though complained that while this may have been a "city," it was not sociologically mature and even lacked the elevating factors of a stone-age city.[75] As these industrial-era cities emerge, shaken and battered, into the post-industrial world, do they have the capacity for institutions to enable the sociological maturity in this new world? It is important to understand where they have been in order to understand where they can go.

If cities began with agricultural roots, it was industry that formed the backbone of the new city of the 18th century. New Jersey cities were no different, and although some may have had religious roots, such as Elizabeth, they became commercial centers at the height of the Industrial Revolution. Critical to the success of the rise of the American city at the height of the Industrial Revolution of the 19th century was, as exemplified by New York, not merely industrialization but the ability for upward social mobility. Culture could take root in such an economic environment, and the physical shape of the city interacted with the citizens' images of their city. The skyscraper rose not merely literally but figuratively, and relevant to New Jersey's cities, even smaller cities like those in New Jersey sought to define their skylines. Down in the streets, though, the 19th century was as grim for many as it was inspirational for some.

If the practical expediencies of everyday life in Trenton are measured by numbers, the story is grim. According to the 2000 census, its family median income was $36,681, compared to the overall (and surrounding) Mercer County median income of $68,494. In 1990, the figure for Trenton was $48,490. If Trenton has lived as a city, and once having had the potential for greatness, has it now been rendered — to use Read's word — subservient? Has it become irrelevant? Does it no longer serve the ambitions of its citizens?

Rae refers to the "accidents of urban creation" that began in the mid–19th century that were the result of a confluence of six major factors: the rise of stream-driven manufacturing, an agricultural revolution, an integrated railroad system and automotive and truck transportation — both facilitating national markets— sustained immigration and its concomitant increase in labor, and technological developments (such as electricity) that shrank distances.[76] With the increased urban density and the development of outlying agricultural areas to feed the city, the ability of the American city to grow increased. The country moved from a relatively limited number of "large" cities to what Rae calls a "middle tier of industrial cities" between 1880 and 1910 — which included New Jersey's Newark and Jersey City.[77] The "rail-before-trucks-and-cars period" facilitated growth in cities such as New Haven (Rae's focus) but also, for example, Trenton.

Trenton, like Camden, Reading and other East Coast industrial cities identified with the 19th-century manufacturing prowess of the United States, was a victim of and participant in the 20th century's economic mugging of its factories, and the social upheavals as the country came to grips with its post-war social upheavals. Some of the smaller cities, like corks in the ocean, road the waves. Others went under.

The fate of Trenton can be viewed through, if not completely explained by, the common experience of other post-industrial medium and smaller cities. New Jersey's cities experienced at the end of the 19th and beginning of the 20th centuries as a result of significant population changes, brought about as a result of an emerging technician middle class, the advent of the automobile, and the development of commuter lines and commuting as a lifestyle choice, the proliferation of layers of government over overlapping geographic areas, and the changing demographics as earlier European groups left the cities in the latter 20th century that their forebears had entered in the 19th, and African Americans and Latinos accounted for larger percentages of the city's population.[78]

Where did Trenton go? The *flâneur* wandering Trenton is the *flâneur* of the lost city. It is Trenton and Everycity. It is the city lost to the suburbs and amid the suburbs and yet it persists as a *place*.

In the 20th century the "suburban model" took root, exemplified by Los Angeles. Not only in the United States but worldwide, the downside of industrialization, the increase of crime in the city and the "universal aspiration" for an idealized better life outside the city streets facilitated the demise, and ghettoization, of the 20th-century city. Of course, the emergence of the automobile as an indispensible factor in American life in the post–World War II era made the suburbs an option, even for those still working in cities.[79] The expansion of the interstate highway system under President Dwight Eisenhower is another contemporary recognition of the primacy of the automobile in the 1950s, with the concomitant development of office parks to accommodate the "road" mindset. In New Jersey, housing developments sprang up on the state's farms to feed the growing demand of relocated New Yorkers. Beginning in the 1970s, parking passes at train stations such as nearby Princeton Junction became valuable commodities as potato farms were ground up and developed into housing. New York was "the city" for these transplants; Trenton, something else.

To define the nature of the contemporary post-industrial city is also to understand the relationship of violence to the nature and character of a city, or at least certain aspects of the city. We find that such characteristics are not new; particular issues and stakeholders may change, but the relationship of violence to defined urban conditions remains the same. The violence that engulfed various cities after World War II in the United States had complex causes, some of which were the product of socio-economic changes after World War II and others may well be endemic to American life. But we can look back to Alexis de Tocqueville, who viewed the American cities of the 19th century with concern: "In towns men can hardly be prevented from assembling, getting overexcited together, and adopting sudden passionate resolutions. Towns virtually constitute great assemblies with all the inhabitants as members. In them, people wield astonishing influence over their magistrates and often carry their desires into execution without the latter's intervention."[80] "Cities may be looked upon as large assemblies, of which all the inhabitants are members; their populace exercise a prodigious influence upon the magistrates, and frequently execute their own wishes without the intervention of public officers."[81]

De Tocqueville also wrote, "I look upon the size of certain American cities and above all the nature of their inhabitants as a genuine danger threatening the future of the democratic republics of the New World and I do not hesitate to predict that that will be the source of their downfall unless their government succeeds in creating an armed force which will remain under the control of the majority of the nation, but which will be independent of the town population and thus able to repress its excesses."[82] Architect and author Witold Rybczynski similarly notes de Tocqueville's predictions of the need for armed bodies to suppress mob excesses in commenting on the more individualistic nature of American city life, compared with more communalistic European cities.[83]

Trenton in particular, and New Jersey's cities in general, may be viewed against this background. They are, after all, representative urban centers. Newark and Jersey City, in the past, have been among the nation's largest cities, and the state's other cities certainly fall within the scope of small and medium-sized cities. And like others of the nation's urban centers, New Jersey's cities exploded in the 1960s. It is apparent that simply the creation of an armed force under control of the majority of the nation is not sufficient to prevent the downfall of a city. As the National Advisory Commission on Civil Disorders (the "Kerner Commission") concluded,

> A study of the aftermath of disorder leads to disturbing conclusions. We find that, despite the institution of some post-riot programs: Little basic change in the conditions underlying the outbreak of disorder has taken place. Actions to ameliorate Negro grievances have been limited and sporadic; with but few exceptions, they have not significantly reduced tensions.
> In several cities, the principal official response has been to train and equip the police with more sophisticated weapons. In several cities, increasing polarization is evident, with continuing breakdown of inter-racial communication, and growth of white segregationist or black separatist groups.[84]

Certain New Jersey cities were of course among those that were reviewed by the Kerner Commission. What de Tocqueville identified more than 150 years before the riots came to pass.

After New Jersey's cities exploded in the 1960s, the prophetic nature of Freidrich Engel's comments also became apparent. The definition of the city in terms of its characteristics were a cauldron for violence a century before the events of the 1960s. For class and social causes, we only need read Engel's "The Great Towns" in his *The Condition of the Working Class in England in 1844*. He wrote of "the turmoil of the streets," of "hundreds of thousands of all classes and ranks crowding past each other," and "of all great towns," that "everywhere barbarous indifference, hard egotism on one hand, and nameless misery on the other, everywhere social warfare, every man's house in a state of siege, everywhere reciprocal plundering under the protection of the law, and all so shameless, so openly avowed that one shrinks before the consequences of our social state as they manifest themselves here undisguised, and one can only wonder that the whole crazy fabric still hangs together."[85]

We may still find particular relevance in these words today as we consider the status of post-industrial Trenton.

The fate of Trenton, like other lost post-industrial cities, was the result of specific and general causes. Specific to New Jersey is the unique governmental structure, the position of the state between two great cities (New York and Philadelphia), and the particular demographics. General factors would include the post–World War II change in the American economy, the nationalization and globalization of industry and the transformation of a goods-based to service-based economy in the 1970s, and the near-institutionalization of gangs. It would not be fair to attribute the decline of New Jersey's cities to the racial disturbances of the 1960s alone. Underlying causes, not least of which economic and a seismic shift in societal priorities, factored. With the growth in the 1950s of the interstate highway system and the movement out of the city for residential purposes while maintaining a working relationship in the city, as well as the sprouting of the "office park," fostered exurban movement.

Wander the more desolate streets of East Trenton and think about Friedrich Engels. And think about Uruk, the "mother of cities," located in Mesopotamia (now Iraq) that had not only the architecture and public spaces of the contemporary physical city, but also a functioning centralized bureaucracy, relocated rural population, law and order issues, but also a venue in which changing attitudes toward sexuality (if not urban liberalism) developed.[86] Three thousand years later, Uruk — a major urban center of its times — is no more than an archeological dig.

Three thousand years from now, what will archeologists make of Trenton?

Cities have come and gone, and the ancient cities of Mesopotamia and Egypt are not the cities of the contemporary world. But the cities that were born in the United States all still survive, in some form or another. There have not been enough centuries for them to vanish. And they are the product of America, and Americans. They are not hyphenated or ethnic. They are composites, living systems whose whole is by definition greater than their parts. The city, even in deterioration or the apparent downward arc, is a place worth saving. In its way, each city is a living museum to its citizens. It is a collective memory and a mentor to its future self.

Indeed, Patsy Healey posited the city as a "shared collective resource," with a focus that "could encompass an everyday-life perspective on urban conditions and experiences, along with an economic and environmental one."[87] She argues that the current challenge "is to mould multidimensional conceptions of 'city' which both reflect and interrelate the rich diversity and complexity of contemporary urban life, while generating a discursive public realm within which people can argue about what their city is and should be."[88] She faces the same questions as the rest in trying to define the city. The city to the geographer and planner was a "physical artifact,"[89] but "the economic and social relations of the city keep escaping these definitions."[90] She notes that "the social space of what we take to be the city is thus a complex layering of the time-space rhythms of multiple time-space relations, some of which are narrowly confined to a particular part of the city, others of which spread across many places near and far from the city.... It is the density and mixity of these relational layers and multiple identities which, for some commentators, create the key qualities of a 'city-type' ambience, of 'citiness.'"[91] Cities are also, of course, economic entities; "in this conception of the city as a container of economically exploitable assets, the ambition of some policy-makers is to position 'their city' in a wider landscape of competing cities."[92]

She writes:

> I have so far argued that cities are not just material artifacts, although we experience the materiality of urban life. Still less is a city a material subject which can 'act.' Cities are neither people nor technologies with the power to act locked in them. What is 'city' lies beyond these specific existences and materialities, although as conceived, cities are full of people, technologies and power relations. But yet cities do exist and have material effects. Their existence and their power to act lie in the way they are imagined and brought to life, and in how these imaginings then become mobilized to shape politics, public policy and projects.[93]

And so this is the point, and what we have been exploring in this and the first chapter. We are trying to move beyond the physical, the tangible, into what makes a city a city — because, as Healey argues, it matters — not in some esoteric sense, but to conceive and implement sensible policy. We still maintain free will. A place like Trenton must understand itself, engage in self-reflection as to the kind of city it has been, is, and will be. Without vision there is simply rote action. Soul matters.

Mumford traces the history of the city as a progression of the loss of soul.

As cities became exploitive and class-oriented, the poor compressed inward, while the more wealthy spread out to the country. He writes of the acceptance of, if not complacency toward, the permanent existence of poverty and an underclass. What he calls "Coketown," the industrial city of the 19th century, became an accepted utilitarian and ugly creation.[94] To a large extent, he seems to argue, we have never recovered.

The concept of the city with a soul finds resonance among other writers on the city. I have mentioned Monti's comments in terms of seeking to define the city. He writes in *The American City:*

> The heart and soul of our decline, and possible resurrection, remains in cities, just as many persons have said over the years. That is where social critics and reformers have been telling us to look for signs of our discontent with public life. It also is where the impulse to reconstitute a community of believers around religious beliefs and morally upright practices has been expressed most fully. The city has been the place where our civic culture will be reclaimed, if it can be salvaged at all.[95]

If it can be salvaged at all. But the point is that, like the Tin Man in *The Wizard of Oz*, you need heart. Vision without faith and money produces an unattainable desire. Faith provides the staying power, but without vision and money, will be unchanneled. Money without faith and vision will be sidetracked and ineffective. It is important to understand what a city is, and what Trenton is, and how it fits in within the urban framework, to be able to take the city to the next century. This is not to ignore the reality of street crime and the need to put food and health care into the hands of the city's families that need it, or to address urgent educational needs. But without the triad of factors, the future becomes sacrificed to the present.

Soul is what keeps a city from becoming a failed city. As long as Trenton retains its soul, it will survive, and remain a city. Beset with poverty and violence, the city nonetheless remains intact and viable.

In this chapter I have noted a sampling of writers who have attempted to define the city, and we have seen that population and density, while perhaps predicate, are not enough. I have suggested that the inquiry is important not only to those in the city, but to those in the region, since the city provides a sense of place that is important to us. It is not simply of academic interest, because we need to have an analytical framework, or at least analytical awareness, of what we are talking about if we are to understand the potential of the small city — of a place like Trenton — in the post-industrial era. We have seen that various writers on the city have recognized the intangible aspect of what makes a city a city in general, and a particular city a particular city. I have also suggested that it is possible to place Trenton as part of the overall pattern present in consideration of the city. What we can do is view Trenton as a prism that reflects the elements of the city in history and the city in theory.

# 3. The City and the Persistence of Memory

Trenton persists.

It is a city of memory, and those memories form an essential part of its psyche. Let us explore this city in a more personal vein.

From across the Delaware River, a clearly delineated skyline: this place looks like a city. Not towering skyscrapers, but nonetheless enough tall buildings to take it beyond the appearance of a large town, and enough to at least resemble what we consider a 21st century American city to look like. A varied skyline reflects the beginning and end of 20th-century architecture. Historic bridges frame the city. Approaching from land down one of the main Northeast Corridor arteries, U.S. 1 (locally known as Route 1), shells of factories attest to its former industrial glory: *Trenton Makes, the World Takes.*

Trenton Makes, the World Takes. A city once ranked 50th among America's hundred largest cities, a world leader in pottery and steel production, home of one of the world's preeminent engineers. A city chronically ill like an old arthritic man, rubbing his hands in an attempt to make them useful again. A code word for urban decay: say Camden today and that is what the world thinks. It was not so in 1950.

Yet despite its political infighting, its drumbeat of assaults, shootings and robberies, the infestation of gangs and the boarded-over buildings, the barbed wire and pot-holed streets, Trenton follows Dylan Thomas's advice and perversely refuses to "go gentle into that good night." A bookstore returns to downtown, on Warren Street, and at least as of this writing, survives. A park built on top of a bypass "tunnel" along the Delaware River hosts an annual festival celebrating the state's diverse cultures. A World War II memorial is dedicated on West State Street across from the Statehouse. Cadwalader Park, an urban park designed by Frederick Law Olmsted himself, features a well-attended and popular Easter egg hunt. The State Museum has reopened after years of renovation, with a state-of-the-art planetarium. Charter schools form a self-

***World War II Memorial.*** Set in a small plaza across from the Statehouse Building, the New Jersey World War II Memorial was dedicated in November 2008 and opened to the public in 2009. The 12-foot bronze central sculpture of Lady Victory was done by Thomas Jay Warren, who was also one of the sculptors for the Korean War Memorial in Atlantic City, and the Vietnam Veterans Memorial in Holmdel, New Jersey. This image also shows the Lone Soldier, an "everyman" for all branches of service, and behind him, a helmet resting on a rifle, symbolizing the fallen soldier.

determinative backbone of the city's education system. A state capital that went years without a major hotel within its borders now again has one. A light rail system now runs between Trenton and Camden. The city has a "Double A" minor league ballfield and a significant concert and arena.

It is not just a highly populated suburban sprawl of housing developments and office parks and shopping malls and schools. It is relatively compact, with the ecto-skeleton of its urban infrastructure. If it no longer has the working factories, cultural centers and shopping downtown it once did, that does not necessarily change its essence, its nature. People do still commute into Trenton to work, even if they are mainly state employees. It is not a village or town. If we believe it to be a city, it remains a city.

In its day, Trenton was a quintessential American city, itself a metaphor for the American persona, and maybe today, it is the quintessential post-industrial-age "brick-and-mortar" city. From modest beginnings of grist mills, it propelled itself through hard work into an industrial power. *Trenton Makes, the World Takes.* Number 50 in the 1890 census listing of the 100 largest cities in the United States. Trenton, New Jersey, right in the middle. A mainstream, working place.

***Government Buildings.*** The geometry of New Jersey's government buildings is revealed in part in this image made from the top of a parking garage. The square building in the right foreground is the Labor and Workforce Development Building. The Departments of Agriculture and Health and Senior Services are in the square and round buildings in the left foreground. Behind and between these two building is the Richard J. Hughes Justice Complex, which houses the state's Supreme Court, Appellate Division and the Attorney General's office.

### 3. The City and the Persistence of Memory

Consider Trenton from the perspective of its ruins. What bits and pieces remain to anchor us? Put another way, let us talk to Trenton's ghosts.

Among Salvador Dalí's iconic works is *The Persistence of Memory*, the instantly recognizable small painting of limp watches and an ant-covered gold pocketwatch in a desolate landscape by cliffs and river. Ants for Dalí represent decay; here, they clamber over a symbol of opulence, a gold watch. What is the thing lying on the ground, draped by a melting watch? Often interpreted as Dalí's profile, or with sexual overtones, the object seems dead, or at least sleeping, a lost, bizarre creature that has been overtaken by time. Time itself seems to have stopped. A fly — another symbol of decay — sits on top of one of the watches. In addition to the timepieces, though, are two other seemingly man-made items, suggesting ruins or at least abandoned structures. The title suggests that what was, must still be there, if not physically then at least in memory, despite the barrenness and decay.

Memory persists in Trenton, a paradoxical place of contemporaneous decay and vitality.

In May 1907, construction was completed on the "Coney Island of New Jersey," the White City Amusement Park just outside Trenton, in what is now the Trenton-Hamilton Marsh area. Anchored by Spring Lake in present-day John A. Roebling Park, this amazing place, also known as Capital City Park, boasted seemingly state-of-the-art amusement features, like those found in Chicago and New Orleans at other "White City" parks. Each of the houses reportedly was painted white. Postcards from the time seem like scenes from a period movie of the opening years of the 20th century, a *Masterpiece Theatre* set piece of images, of women in long flowing dresses and wide, colorful hats, with men in thick wool suits, strolling arm in arm. Part of the White City amusement chain centered in Chicago; the Trenton site was feted as a massive success during the course of its brief life. Nonetheless, by April 12, 1910, it was in receivership and on the block. The owner, Trenton White City Company, included among its directors F.W. Roebling, Jr., of Trenton's illustrious and renowned family. The 120-acre property included "carrousel [sic], shute the shutes, concert hall, dancing pavilion, down and out, crystal maze, moving pictures, theatres, boating and numerous other amusement devices...."[1]

[Interlude]
(Advertisement from 1893, in the Trenton Battle Monument Association Souvenir and Programme) *United States Hotel, Warren Street, near State St., Trenton, N.J., Rates from $1.50 to $2.50 per Day, Special Rates by the Week: The above Commercial Hotel has been refurnished throughout, and under its new management will be conducted as a first class house. The sanitary arrangements of the house are perfect, and the cuisine of the establishment is unexcelled. This is a hotel with home comforts. Electric cars pass the door from both Railroad Stations. Good Stabling. John J. McCarthy, Prop.*

During the same time frame of White City, the New York resort, Coney Island, was at its peak. Like White City, Coney Island was, in the words of Rem

Koolhaas, "the technology of the fantastic."[2] The three parks on Coney Island, outside the thrusting, industrial, slum-filled Manhattan, were places of unreality and escape. Magical, unbelievable things were built in the parks in this seaward area of Brooklyn. Luna Park was "the first City of Towers: functionless, except to overstimulate the imagination and keep any recognizable earthly realities at a distance."[3] It burned down in 1914. Dreamland, home of the steel pier, Canals of Venice, and the Leap Frog Railway, was, like White City, painted white; it burned down in 1911. Steeplechase survived but with "its attractions more debased with every new season."[4] What these places did, in addition to providing the turn-of-century Twilight Zone for New Yorkers, was also to provide a laboratory for architecture that found its way back into Manhattan. Life imitated art, or vice versa.

## *Remnants of the Industrial City*

We cannot view White City as the same kind of testing ground for the building of Trenton, but we can note the hysteria for entertainment that Koolhaas attributes to the parks built on Coney Island. As urban personas go, White City and Trenton find some connection to the larger phenomenon occurring in New York.

Today the only thing remaining is the staircase, overgrown with vegetation and the intruding surrounding woods. It is at the entrance to the Trenton-Hamilton Marsh natural area. A few anglers ply the lake, and hikers wander the trails. You look again at the postcards, and then at the dilapidated stairs and the struggling Spring Lake, and battle a sense of bewilderment. It is like looking at Dalí's painting? Is Trenton that indistinguishable object buried by time? There before you is an unreal staircase, "painted" realistically, yet so incongruous in its setting as to suggest a vision. Surrounded by the grid of residences between this place and South Broad Street, it is not easy to imagine the trolleys bringing thousands of Trentonians here to stroll on a summer night. What was this place of magic? One almost wonders if it ever really existed or if it was really just some kind of dream. A dream by a city in the early decades of the 20th century, the Age of America, that shouldered industry and was the master of its fate.

So its civic leaders must have thought.

Memory persists. Perhaps the staircase ruins, like the flaccid watches, are symbolic of the city of Trenton as a whole, or perhaps even the entire country in meltdown. But then, did the Romans foresee the ruins to be while the gladiators killed each other to cheers in the Coliseum?

Or the remains of the great factories, the ones that gave rise to Trenton's homegrown motto: *Trenton Makes, the World Takes*.

Only the world is no longer taking.

## 3. The City and the Persistence of Memory 63

***White City Stairs.*** These elegant stairs leading to nowhere, amid a tangle of vegetation, provide a surrealistic tombstone to the dead amusement park that once stood here. Now part of the Trenton-Hamilton Marsh, a natural area, it was once the hopeful and renowned entertainment enterprise of Trenton's business community.

These factories were vibrant and real before they became husks. The past swirls around this lost city, caught up like bits of paper in a draft. A city once among the top hundred cities in the United States, now mugged and left for dead in the post–World War II years. Over 30 years ago places like Trenton were called "gritty cities."[5] We might well still consider it gritty, but that word is insufficient. Today at times it appears to be a city that can't seem to get sufficient oxygen to breathe. It is a city that paradoxically has brought in a film festival (notwithstanding its complete absence of movie theaters, as of this writing), a minor league ballpark and a major concert and arena venue, all set against a crescendo of gang murders and often daily acts of violence against person and property. Like all such cities, it has financial challenges; hope and good intentions are not enough.

Boosters may tout it for having been voted among the top ten (out of 500) walking cities in the country in 2008,[6] but it is also among the more violent.[7] In this new millennium of the 21st century, its homicide statistics for the opening years were staggering relative to its population. The city was (and remains) plagued by brutal gang warfare, although recent efforts to dent the situation may be yielding progress.[8] It is not uncommon to read reports in *The Times* (also known today as *The Times of Trenton*, but to old-timers, the *Trenton*

*Times*) of innocent bystanders being shot or assaulted. And yet, it remains a city of diverse and important architecture, with a fiercely loyal cadre of defenders, a place that can still inspire affection, a city not merely steeped in history, but whose history was essential to the formation of the United States of America, a city with a vibrant and important past, a place that was urbane. A city that still insists in bold letters on its signature bridge across the Delaware: *Trenton Makes, the World Takes*.

Kenneth Gibson, the first African American mayor of New Jersey's largest city, Newark, has had attributed to him the statement that "where American cities are going, Newark will get there first."[9] By the time of Gibson's ascendancy, Newark's rank among the hundred most populous American cities had fallen. It had been torn apart by rioting. Its political leaders were part of a corruption in New Jersey municipal government that included the state's second largest city, Jersey City. Was this truly where America's cities were going? Had Newark gotten there first? Was Newark, and other of the state's cities like Trenton, truly canaries in the mine, predicting the future of urban life in the United States in general?

The mayor of New Haven, Connecticut, said something eerily comparable of his city: "If New Haven is a model city, God help America's cities."[10] Trenton as well is a kind of advance guard to where the United States is going.

So if Newark got there first, perhaps Trenton got there second. Newark may be said to be resurgent. Most would agree that Trenton cannot yet claim to be there, despite steps like its arena and minor league ballfield, and certain adaptive reuse for downtown housing. Newark retained certain significant financial and legal firms; the private sector never completely fled, as it largely did in Trenton. A Master Plan for Trenton was proposed in May 2008[11] that envisions implementation by 2020 and a restoration of accessibility to such cut-off areas as Stacy Park and integrating residential and office development within the city's downtown areas. Is this realistic? The staircase ruins of the bankrupt and ghostlike White City Amusement Park compel our attention. This is a city of high hopes. But have we been here before?

Two of my children were born at then-called Mercer Medical Center, now Capital Health System-Mercer, on Bellevue Avenue in Trenton. Nearby and parallel is Stuyvesant Avenue, one of the more violent and gang-infested streets.[12] Barely a few blocks from where the first two were delivered, on Bellevue Avenue between Calhoun and Fowler streets, a man was gunned down in a drive-by shooting; as reported by *The Times*, one bystander said "This is crazy. It don't make no sense. They're killing each other for nothing."[13] Blocks away, babies are born and doctors tend to the sick. Blocks away, a 23-year-old man became the 18th homicide in Trenton for 2008 in October—more than one a month that year.

In November 2008, notwithstanding the length of the presidential cam-

## 3. The City and the Persistence of Memory 65

***Stuyvesant Avenue.*** In the Stuyvesant/Prospect neighborhood, Stuyvesant Avenue has been an area of reported gang activity, as noted by the graffiti on the abandoned house at the left of this image. The use of graffiti by gangs has multiple purposes, including the marking of territory and delivering of threats. The street appears to have been named for Peter Stuyvesant, according the Trenton Historical Society.

paign, I was struck by the near absence of discussion of the fate of cities such as Trenton. Surprisingly, and contrary to a generation ago, there remains virtually no dialogue on the cities. The economy in general, yes, but not the cities. I remember Ronald Reagan and Jimmy Carter standing in the South Bronx to call attention to the plight of the American city. In 2008, there seemed to be virtually no public discussion by the presidential candidates apart from some website commentary.[14]

It was not always this way. In 1960, candidate John F. Kennedy addressed a crowd standing before the War Memorial in Trenton, and Dwight Eisenhower and Harry Truman also spoke from its steps.[15] No presidential candidate stood in on the steps of the War Memorial in Trenton in 2008 to address crowds on the plight of the city in this millennium, although Barack Obama did speak in that building in May 2007 to the AFL-CIO New Jersey chapter on other issues.[16] Meanwhile, on Bellevue Avenue, in this ruinous city, lives still begin and end. If a tree falls in the forest and there is no one there to hear it, does it make a sound?

Recall Trenton in its prime as the prototypical American city, the product of the Industrial Revolution, an internationally recognized *place*, a pocket of urbanism along the Atlantic seaboard of the United States. A city that knew it was a city. A city that was among the largest, population-wise, in the country.

*Waterfront Park.* Two modern office structures frame the entrance to Trenton's Waterfront Park, a pastoral setting along the Delaware. Nearby is the minor league stadium that hosts the Trenton Thunder, and also the KatManDu bar and restaurant, housed in the former New Jersey Iron and Steel Company factory. Also nearby is the plaque dedicated to John Fitch, oft-forgotten inventor of the steamboat who was overshadowed by rival Robert Fulton. On game days, the area is lively and filled with people.

## 3. The City and the Persistence of Memory    67

A city whose factories had world-renown. Now, as we contemplate the physical and emotional remnants of what this city was, consider it as a potential harbinger of where America is headed in the 21st century, now that the so-called American Century — the 20th — may be over. And if we are to understand ourselves, and what the country will look like in the post-industrial, post-racial world, we need to understand places like Trenton. The history of the United States is replete with fallen and resurrected cities, cities that have reinvented themselves and cities that have simply eroded away. What do we remember of them?

We discussed earlier the soul of a city, and the manner in which a city's residents can believe a place to be a city. We can think of Trenton as state of mind, a place that persists despite and because of its physical, tangible history. There are those who still call themselves *Trentonians*; indeed, that is the name of one of the city's two daily newspapers. An urbanist way of life can exist in suburbs, but it is arguable that it is facilitated by the components of the city: a relatively compact area of workplace, cultural and political center, and residence. A place of strangers that nonetheless share a common sense of place, an understanding of where they are, and a loyalty to it. Were the Trentonians visiting White City in the years before World War I conscious of their urbanist lifestyle? Presumably not, as such, for they were living it. But we can see it in the retrospective mists of hindsight, looking at the old photographs, or listening to the removed stories and anecdotes, passed down within families. Memory persists or, more accurately, much-revisited and embellished memories persist. And memory crashes against the jagged rocks on the shores of contemporary reality.

It is this notion of urbanism that is interesting to contemplate as we think of White City. When we look at the old photographs, we are aware of an entire way of life that has vanished.

In his book on New Haven, Connecticut, Rae writes, "In the era of urbanism, one could very nearly describe the city as a vast network of implicit conspiracies between business and heir customers. City life was sustained by a layered fabric of business relationships."[17] He defines "urbanism" as a function of five factors characterizing American city life between the 1870s and 1920s: (1) industrial convergence (products outflow and capital inflow); (2) dense fabric of enterprise (neighborhood retailing); (3) centralized housing clusters (multi-class populations within central city); (4) dense civic fauna (charitable and other societies); and (5) pattern of political integration (civil and business leaders within the city).[18]

He refers to an "urbanist city" whose citizens deliberately and affirmatively chose to either move to their city, or who remain there by choice after being born there, or who by virtue of economic need must stay, citizens who live and work and seek entertainment within the parameters and confines of the city. They shop, eat, work, drink and play in the city, which is their point of reference.[19]

Let us consider Trenton as such a place — a self-contained yet cosmopolitan city of the world, a city of manners and culture. The urbanist Trenton of the Roeblings, of the Stacy-Trent Hotel and the Hotel Hildebrecht, of the West State Street mansions and opera house, of concerts in the park, of a city whose industrialists lived, worked and played. The city is gone, in many cases physically but also metaphorically and imaginatively. Lawyer-historian Francis Beazley Lee, in 1895, described the city's culture: "Trenton as a commercial center is known the country over. The traveling men of the potteries and iron companies usually make their headquarters in the city, and start from the city on "trips" which reach to Mexico, Vancouver, Quebec or Havana. This leads directly to fact concerning Trenton; it is that no other city in the State is so well equipped in the matter of hotels. This is owing not so much to the daily travel as to the fact that Trenton is the capital of the State."[20]

But gone, too, is the darker side of those years— but what has replaced it may not necessarily be a coherent personality of the city. Whatever it meant to be a Trentonian in the 1920s, it means something different today, and it is questionable whether a new persona has replaced it. It is hard to maintain the mindset in the presence of the numbing violence, the poverty and the desolation that marks much of this place. To admit it is not disloyalty; to deny it is naïve.

Trenton's past was industrial. If it is indeed post-industrial, we need to remember what is what to understand not just how Trenton got to where it is, but to make sense of the physical reminders, the souvenirs, all around. Tangible evidence of its past permeate the city.

We do well not to glamorize the past. Sepia-toned pictures of well-dressed men and women strolling through the festive atmosphere of White City do not change the reality of the city of the Industrial Revolution or even of the first quarter of the 20th century. One need only read Engels' description of the Victorian city, or Lincoln Steffens's descriptions of American cities, or look at Jacob Riis' pictures in his groundbreaking book *How the Other Half Lives*, to know that the late 19th century had its share of urban issues. If not the contemporary gang warfare, there certainly were criminal elements. Not to mention child labor, racism and other elements of the urban existence of the times.

And yet, an extended quote from a Victorian-era chronicler of Trenton insists on a view through rose-tinted glasses. As described by Francis Bazley Lee:

> Trenton has been too remote from either Philadelphia or New York to become the storehouse for the surplus of metropolitan life. The characteristics of the present East and West Jersey towns lying contiguous to the great cities are wanting in Trenton. The vast die of humanity which ebbs and flows across the Hudson and the Delaware, making near-by towns miniature reproductions of the metropolis, scarce touches this city. Trenton is highly individualized. It is a city

where the home is in constant touch with the financial and social powers which treat that home. Trenton's history, in short, is unique, and whatever she is today is very largely the result of her own actions and of the energies of the men and women who dwell within her borders. This, however, is not provincialism. It is not a lack of sympathy with humanity which dwells in the greater cities. Upon the other hand, Trenton's name has reached the most remote districts of every European country. The foreign population of Trenton is very large and constantly increasing. But it is not a "drifting" class; its permanency is proverbial. Were the city "provincial," would this be true? Did other cities offer greater inducements, would the foreign-born residents, who have no associations with our older hearthstones, remain within our limits?[21]

In a later chapter I discuss Trenton's factories, but for our purposes here, these buildings, like the White City staircase, like Dalí's watches, adorn the current landscape of the city and offer their own persistent reminders of the character and core of this city. They also remind us of Trenton's place in the American industrial story and legend.

The growth of the American factory city from the Civil War era through the pre–World War I years of the 20th century challenged New York's status, particularly as the Civil War caused disruption in previous trade routes.[22] In addition to the competition with New York, cities (such as Trenton) competed for control in regional areas.[23] Trenton is some 30 miles from New Brunswick, and some 40 miles from Camden; it was also sandwiched, geographically speaking, between Philadelphia and New York. Benjamin Franklin's attributed quote compares New Jersey to a barrel tapped at both ends. It was also a central point along the Delaware and Raritan Canal, built in the 1830s. It is easy to sense the self-importance and urgency its business leaders must have felt, with the proof that Trenton, by 1890, was the 50th largest city in the United States, outranking at the time Dallas and Los Angeles. (Newark, also arguably within Trenton's "province," was the 17th largest city in the country then. In fact, New Jersey had seven of the top 100 cities, and five of those were in the top 50.) Of New Jersey's six largest cities (Newark, Jersey City, Paterson, Camden, Trenton and Elizabeth), Trenton's percentage population increase from 1880 to 1890 was by far the largest, jumping *92.1 percent*, some three times the rate of growth in that decade of Newark, Jersey City or Elizabeth).[24]

New York was "the" city. Nonetheless, other cities refused to concede absolute control. Trenton was no different. Pride was reflected in the civic leaders' efforts to market and establish Trenton, like other smaller cities around the country, as entities in their own right, and not mere satellites of larger urban centers.

In addition to the challenge to New York and quest for regional superiority, Blake McKelvey identified a theme of the growth of the American city in this period the "gradual evolution of a community out of the welter of conflicting individuals and groups that surged into each growing town."[25] Finally, this thrust for growth in an increasingly competitive environment was underway at a time of limited legal regulation, "injecting the city more positively into state and national politics."[26]

McKelvey's historical approach to the development of the American city during this period notes "the economic vitality [cities] drew in large part from the private enterprise of their residents. Not only did the cities build the railroads and the railroads the cities, but the latter also encouraged, almost compelled, their trade arteries to develop the far-reaching monopoly systems; they then fought for preferred service and, failing that, for some form of government control. Again, not only did the cities develop the industries and the industries the cities, but the latter also supplied the market for agriculture expansion and battled fiercely for domination over regional hinterlands."[27] But Mumford paints a somewhat more poetic picture of the ramifications of this industrialization: "If capitalism tended to expand the province of the marketplace and turn every part of the city into a negotiable commodity, the change from organized urban handicraft to large scale factory production transformed the industrial towns into dark hives, busily puffing, clanking, screeching, smoking for twelve and fourteen hours a day, sometimes going around the clock."[28] This was Coketown to Mumford. America's cities, until the mid-19th century, were centers of support for an agrarian society; after the Civil War they facilitated the country's industrialization.[29]

Rae identifies "four events and two nonevents" that, around 1840, propelled the growth of American cities: (1) steam-driven manufacturing, (2) improved agricultural methods, (3) integrated railroads, (4) the gap between rail and automobile dominance in transportation that facilitation centralization, and later decentralization, of cities, (5) immigration policies that fueled the labor supply, (6) delayed development of "distance-compressing technologies," such as the electrical AC grid, that further allowed centralization of cities.[30] American cities, therefore, "enjoyed" a kind of incubus that facilitated their growth.

Those factors are gone. Post-industrial cities face a new reality.

## *The Idea of the City*

Memory is linked to idea.

In the introduction to his modern epic work *Paterson*, the New Jersey physician and poet William Carlos Williams made an argument for individuality and distinctiveness of the city-dweller. He wrote "that a man in himself is a city, beginning, seeking, achieving and concluding his life in ways which the various aspects of a city may embody-if imaginatively conceived-any city, all the details of which may be made to voice his most intimate convictions."[31]

If we move beyond population and focus on structure, and on to the *look* of the city, we come to another common aspect of a city, a place of concentrated architecture. Architect David Mayernik has written of the idea of the city, and how certain Renaissance Italian cities were constructed (or reconstructed) with a particular state of mind, and how now that has been lost: "Something had changed since the eighteenth century in the sense of what cities were all about, and it is our misfortune that the great growth of American cities happened well after the Idea of the City had lost its allure to the Western mind."[32] He discusses five Italian cities from the standpoint of how they were conceived based on certain ideas, during the Middle Ages, and reinvented from ancient beginnings. Those five cities "drew on the specifics of their location to infuse the broad principles of classical form with local meaning."[33] As cities developed and changed in the 19th century to focus on utilitarian issues, with their purpose of organizing people and systems, Mayernik believes something was lost. That something was the equivalent of removing religious artwork from their context and exhibiting them elsewhere.

Consider Trenton in those terms, or the broader range of Eastern seaboard cities in the United States. Few of Trenton's colonial buildings survive intact. Most notable among these is the Trent House, which itself has seen addition and renovation. It dates back to 1719 and is named for one of the city's earliest

*Trent House.* The Philadelphia merchant William Trent moved to Trenton and built this house in 1721. The house served as executive mansion for New Jersey's governors at various times, the last being Governor Rodman Price (1854–1857). New Jersey's governor's mansion is not in the capital city; it is now at Drumthwacket, in Princeton. It is an example of Georgian style that predominated in the colonies until the American Revolution and was notable for its symmetry and hipped roofs.

residents, William Trent. Trenton's idea, if it had one, was commercial — it began as a mill town along the Delaware River. Our memory of Colonial Trenton has relevance to our idea of post–Industrial Trenton, just as the memory of a middle-aged person can shed light on that person's self-image at present.

American architecture in the Colonial period was a kind of stepchild; for example, in his time, Thomas Jefferson decried the then-state of American architecture. Survival took priority over expression, and utility over form. Part of this was attributable to a Puritan disdain for that which was not purely useful.[34] It is ironic, or perhaps commendable, that at present, city planners are starting to think like those Renaissance architects and contemplating what the buildings of the city should *say*, and how the city should physically look. There seems to be at last a recognition that an unattractive city has a direct impact on its citizenry. Ugliness breeds ugliness. Trenton's physical appearance did not begin as an aesthetic idea. It was born of necessity. We are reminded of that in its ruins.

Cities are their people and their architecture, their location and their geography, their weather and their natural environment, their streets and their past, their buildings and their art, their parks and waterways, their aspirations and their sense of themselves. They are greater than the sum of their details. The same building looks different in the infinite variation of sun and cloud. They are places of work and leisure, of stress and quietude, of beauty and ugliness. They are places of peace and violence. They reveal themselves to us in colors and patterns. They are, to an extent, vibrant, living things. Their buildings, too, are individuals and "speak."[35] Even without people in the frame, their work is the embodiment of the city as well, in bicycles left standing by a lamppost, lighted buildings at night, sounds of footsteps on cobblestone, and a myriad of other details. The city is communal life, individual and aggregate. It is an Escher print, forming and reforming with each look. The spirits walk among us in Dickensian fashion.

American cities are the product of American mindsets. And so Trenton, this most prototypical of American cities, founded by religious and industrious Western Europeans, put its mind to it, believed in itself, didn't give up, and until the 1950s, accomplished what it set out to do. And, like most Americans, has now found that the platitudes don't hold true. Bubbles burst, again and again, and economies crash. What is fortunate, though, is that America is also the land of the second chance, the land of no past and of reinvention. The land where, as Scarlett O'Hara noted, there is always tomorrow.

It is important that we know them, for our cities are our creation. Our *ideas*. They are a kind of living thing, changing with time and circumstance to reflect current inhabitants. They yield accents, ways of thinking, perspectives on their people and the outside world. They represent the civilization of the planet.[36] How can we ignore what they are, what they were, and what they might be? A place like Trenton has been a city on the North American continent for over three centuries.

## Details of the City

Peace Street is a narrow way connecting Front Street and Lafayette Street in the downtown area. The land here was owned by Joseph Peace upon purchase in 1732 from James Trent, whose father, William Trent, was the city's namesake. It was officially named Peace Street by city ordinance in 1842. Its rowhouses, with their bricks and shutters and symmetry, could find a place, I would think, in Philadelphia's Society Hill or Boston's Back Bay. The connection between America's East Coast cities may be imagined. This street was a surprise to me. I had driven down Lafayette Street hundreds of times to park at the state capital complex, and never noticed this remarkable oasis. That is the pleasure of a city.

Or the detail on the Kelsey Building on West State Street, of a girl with a laurel crown on her head, surrounded by symbols of agriculture and learning. A building dedicated to the industrial arts of the Industrial Age, at a time when all things suddenly seemed possible.

***Lafayette Street.*** Originally known as Washington Street, in 1889 the name was officially changed to honor the French general. Federal and Italianate row houses on Lafayette and Peace streets in this neighborhood lend a Colonial, early Republic feel to the city.

To see these things you have to be on foot. To know a city you have to walk it; to understand what it means for a place to be a city, you have to see it and touch it from within. You have to feel the distance pass beneath your feet. The city is mastered space. You cannot understand a city from 30,000 feet up, looking down through small oval windows, nor can you really understand a city from inside the passing train or through the taxi window. You have to be out and about, in the restaurants and stores, in the movie theaters and parks, on the sidewalks. You have to walk past the houses and apartments and offices. You have to look at the people and interact with them. Maybe you have to sit on a bench for a while. If you want to understand a city, you have to experience it on its various levels—physical, intellectual, commercial, cultural, and emotional. As Jane Jacobs observed, "The way to get at what goes on in the seemingly mysterious and perverse behavior of cities is, I think, to look closely, and with as little previous expectation as is possible, at the most ordinary scenes and events, and attempt to see what they mean and whether any threads of principle emerge among them."[37]

A city looks a certain way. A political unit may have more people than another, but if the former is spread out, with single-family homes, wide streets and strip malls, we do not readily think of it as a city. On the other hand, a smaller number of people living in a compact area with a few moderately tall buildings, and a mix of retail and residential, and we are more accepting of that as a city. In the 19th century, American cities were traditionally places of industry, built around factories. Ports and railroads and airports, with landscaped parks. Today, the post-industrial city may see those factories converted to residences and office buildings, or colorful shopping districts. The post-industrial city has grown vertically, if not horizontally. We see them appear on the horizon from the interstate highways.

A city feels a certain way, and thereby conjures up certain sensations in us. A city provides identity, a sense of community, of belonging, of place. Say its name, and we have an identity that fits within a more global identity. Cities are the stuff of songs, of movies, of books and poems. They are political, with a political culture and a history. And a city is a place of thought. Museums and universities form and shape the city's intellectual life. Cities become centers for art and creativity, which in turn shape the city's image. The café, bar, hotel, bookstore, concert hall, stage, all comprise the mosaics and the individual stories that are the city. We know when we are a stranger in a city and when we know a city, when we feel like a tourist or when we feel like we belong. In *Moment of Grace*, discussing the apogee of American cities in the 1950s, Michael Johns refers to the "culture of urban song, dress, and manners, achieved by its consummate expression."[38] In the first half of the 20th century, Trenton certainly boasted such expression.

Walk again these streets, downtown, the original streets where James Monroe was wounded in the First Battle of Trenton. Look beyond the graffiti and boarded windows. Ghosts lurk. Memories.

One of the more intriguing plaques is the one situated on the Calhoun Street Bridge, connecting Trenton to Pennsylvania, across the Delaware River. The bridge, carrying Calhoun Street traffic westward, was part of the famed Lincoln Highway, that purely American dream of the road, of a national highway uniting the coasts. Pursued aggressively by Indiana industrialist and automobile enthusiast Carl G. Fisher from 1913 through the 1920s, this road was actually an aggregation of other roads, hammered into a named route in honor of the president. Until shifted southward to Route 1 across the Delaware River, the Calhoun Street Bridge was an important link. The road took travelers from Times Square, New York, to Lincoln Park in San Francisco. The plaque on the bridge points to both those cities. It is fascinating to stand on the bridge and look at that. Trenton was a key city along the road that states fought to include in their jurisdictions.

The Calhoun Street Bridge may be second to the "Trenton Makes" bridge in the hearts of Trentonians, but in some ways it is of more historic value. Once known as the Trenton City Bridge or simply City Bridge, it was featured in a 1995 catalog of its maker, the Phoenix Bridge Company, as one of the most advanced bridges in the country. Part of the Lincoln Highway before it moved south. Like the ruins of the staircase in White City Amusement Park, it is another remnant of lost dreams and what was. *This way to San Francisco*, says Trenton. *I will take you there.*

So where is here, today? The past competes with the present. The *Times* reported on November 3, 2008, "a pregnant woman huddling terrified in bed with her three young children and a woman who tried to save her boyfriend from a beating were among the victims of violent crime in the city early yesterday, police reported," and in a separate unrelated incident on the same day, "20 minutes earlier, a couple was beaten and an innocent bystander stabbed outside a bar on the 900 block of Anderson Street, police said."[39]

What is this place? Like the melting watches in a desolate landscape, Trenton is impenetrable, indiscernible.

## *Living with the Might Have Been*

The near-miss of Trenton's candidacy for capital of the new United States had helped catapult the city into a political and economic center. It edged out Perth Amboy (a predecessor state capital of the colony) as capital of the new state, and its position on the New York–Philadelphia route, together with the area's natural resources, made it into an important rail, canal and industrial hub. Trenton's population propelled it into one of the hundred largest cities in the country from 1810 (when it surfaced at position 42) through 1950, when it occupied 80th place; only from 1840–1850 had it dropped below the top hundred. In 1860 it appeared at 53rd place, and in 1890, as noted earlier, it held position

50. In that census year, and the last decade in which Trenton achieved its highest post–Civil War ranking, 57,458 people lived in Trenton. New York, holding the number-one position, had a population of 1,515,301. Only Chicago and Philadelphia broke a million in that census, and Brooklyn, still its own city, was in fourth place. Twenty-eight of the top hundred cities broke the 100,000 mark.

Out of sight, out of mind.

That contrarian urbanist, Jane Jacobs, admonishes us to not equate the "great" cities with towns, suburbs or even "little cities," since these "are totally different organisms from great cities."[40] She does not elaborate, but one assumes that she knew a great city when she saw one. The American cities mentioned in her book are Baltimore, Boston, Chicago, Cincinnati, Houston, Los Angeles, Louisville, Miami Beach, New Haven, New York, Oakland, Philadelphia, Pittsburgh, St. Louis, San Francisco, Spokane and Washington, D.C. New Haven is noted as a "little-scale city," and places like Miami, San Diego, and Atlanta are not mentioned. She does refer to "great" cities that are great not because of size, and contends that they are not merely large suburbs; "they differ from towns and suburbs in basic ways, and one of these is that cities are, by definition, full of strangers."[41] It is this diversity that gives a city its greatness.

By those terms, Trenton was once a great city. It was ethnically and racially diverse, with over a hundred thousand people, a commercial center with hotels, theaters, cultural halls, civic and business chambers and organizations that propelled the city. On its 250th anniversary, literally on the eve of the stock market crash in October 1929, Trenton celebrated with parades and other activities. And following that crash, and the Great Depression, New Jersey's cities and suburbs were hit hard: "The larger cities began to lose population as jobless men went back to the farm or hit the road. Suburban growth was smothered by a wave or mortgage foreclosures."[42]

In the current millennium, the opening of a Marriott hotel in and of itself was such a newsworthy event that it made the *New York Times*.[43] This is even more remarkable when put in the context of one of the significant histories of Trenton, published in 1895, when that author declared: "Trenton as a commercial center is known the country over. The traveling men of the potteries and iron companies usually make their headquarters in the city, and start from the city on 'trips' which reach to Mexico, Vancouver, Quebec or Havana. This leads directly to fact concerning Trenton; it is that no other city in the State is so well equipped in the matter of hotels. This is owing not so much to the daily travel as to the fact that Trenton is the capital of the State."[44]

Trenton might now be considered a "little scale" city, perhaps, or more technically, a "small" city, that is, having had a population between 100,000 and 200,000 over the 30-year period from 1970 through 2000, even where the population at present might be somewhat above or below this.[45] Once larger than Los Angeles, and once in the top 50. Was Trenton merely a company town, now ready to close that the factories have gone? Was it something more? Bits of revival are underway. Many have not yet given up. Some other once-"lost" industrial cities, like Greenville, South Carolina, now boast active cultural centers and vibrant downtowns. Can Trenton follow? Will it be rendered redundant or irrelevant in the face of "sprawl" and the "Edge City?"

Some, and perhaps many, believe the American Century is over. Debates rage over "American exceptionalism." In the first decade of the 21st century, the United States has begun to come to grips with the hitherto unaccepted, if not unacceptable, notion that its first-place position is not forever. We look to the lost post-industrial cities that have also had to come to terms with not being number one, with a realization of their limitations and the need to adapt, to rechannel civil pride from arrogance to acceptance. Trenton rises or falls in the American tide, and becomes a window into the future of the American psyche.

One day in my wanderings in Trenton I saw a man in-line skating on East State Street. In its way, it was a shocking image, out of place. If someone can in-line skate in Trenton, what does that say about subservience to practical expediencies? Another day I saw two kids sledding down a hill formed by the elevation of the railroad track leading to the train station on the fringe of the Mill Hill district. One of Calvino's chapters in *Invisible Cities,* "Cities and Memories 1"[46] references details and the moment of one woman on a terrace saying "ooh," and that is the moment that stands out and that one remembers, that identifies a particular city, even if other details may be replicated in others. In Trenton, a moment of a skater on East State Street, or sledders off Market Street, at a glance, and Trenton is fixed in memory, in detail.

Marco Polo would tell Kublai Khan that he visited a city of great desolation, of faded promise and ruins, but when he saw a man in-line skating on its main thoroughfare, or children sledding, in that instant, he understood the city.

In this chapter we circled back to Trenton itself, to its memories and its ruins, to draw connections to the bigger picture. We now turn to its more specific history as we peel back another layer of the city to find its past in order to appreciate its present.

# Part Two
# The Elements of City Life

## 4. The City of History

A city is its history. Among Trenton's intrinsic values and identity is its unique position as a pivotal place in American history as well. Washington fought here twice and passed through on his way to being inaugurated as the first president. The city was prominent in early national politics. But for the famed Christmas Day crossing of the Delaware River and ensuing First Battle of Trenton, there might not have been a United States of America, or at least not in the time it took to achieve it. Return to Trenton of the 1770s, bits of which still remain in the city today, and which provide the city's uniqueness. After all, this was the site of the battle between Washington's Continental army and the Hessians on the day after Christmas, 1776, following the heroic, historic and iconic crossing of the Delaware River, a victory that was among the most psychologically important in history. In this chapter we wander about that history and feel it around us.

Trenton of course was inhabited prior to the advent of Europeans by the Sanhican tribe of the larger group of Native Americans known as Leni Lenape. Trenton's colonization by Europeans built on well-established footprints: "The Indian village became a convenient, central stopover place for the travelers of the north and the south. Many Indian trails led directly to it. Today, Brunswick Avenue, Broad Street, and Ferry Street, Trenton's oldest streets, are built on the early Indian trail."[1] Kildorpy was the principal Native American village near to where Trenton is. To the south were Swedes; the Dutch had also colonized the area. The English King Charles conveyed the lands of "New Caesaria," that is, New Jersey, to his brother James, who in turn conveyed the provinces of East and West Jersey to Lords Berkeley and Carteret, respectively. Quaintly, title to the physical lands was claimed under the laws (English, of course) of discovery and conquest. The aboriginal peoples already on the physical land were deemed to have only possessory interests. European settlers were obligated to clear title with the Native Americans, and the questionable nature of the acquisitions for trinkets and baubles from a people who had no clue what English law was all about, or the fictional nature of such property ownership, is well known today. The legal claim was to give Native Americans certain defined rights in accordance with European-based jurisprudence. The new lands belonged to the foreign sovereign, and the Native Americans were deemed only to have rights of possession. And so the colonies (and Trenton) sashayed into European hands.[2]

On a Saturday morning one November, I stood in the graveyard of the First Presbyterian Church of Trenton on East State Street. The Hessian commander in charge of Trenton during Washington's fateful attack in December 1776, Colonel Johann Rall, purportedly was buried here, but a marker lists his name among those "names of persons interred in the west yard of the church whose markers have been destroyed by time." Some miles toward Princeton, on the grounds of the Princeton Battlefield, lie unknown British soldiers from the Battle of Princeton a few days later. To the north, near Bowman's Hill and along the Delaware, is another burial spot for American soldiers from the Revolution.

The First Presbyterian Church building now on the site was built in 1839–1840, but the church traces its origins and original stone building on the site to 1726.[3] Among its early and famous congregants was the "other" inventor of the steamboat, John Fitch. Following the razing of that building in 1804, a replacement church, of brick, was finished in 1806; that was replaced in 1839 by the present structure. It is the largest Greek Revival church in New Jersey, reportedly designed by Nelson Hotchkiss, the Connecticut architect.[4]

Hallowed ground, this. And a sad end for Colonel Rall, unmarked, unregarded in body if not spirit in the instant century, nearly 250 years after his fateful stand. In his meticulously researched book *Washington's Crossing*, David Hackett Fischer cites ample authority to dispute what he calls the "legend" of Rall's drunkenness in particular and Hessian drunkenness in general that led to their defeat. Other recent authors seem less inclined to accept the conventional wisdom. In actuality, Rall attempted to rally a defense and, despite a court martial that ultimately found him guilty of failing to adequately defend Trenton, the evidence Fischer cites shows that his men defended him, and that significant blame lay elsewhere.[5]

Such details aside, there is a a near-physical connection with the past amid the seeming indifference of those passing by on State Street. We take for granted what is familiar and in front of us, standing in this churchyard on a street that was part of the original city, and that was extant during the battle, knowing that Rall was laid to rest here. Unlike Washington, who was here and gone, Rall remains, quite literally. And when you stand on Warren or Broad street and look toward the Battle Monument, you see the hill where Lt. Alexander Hamilton's artillery was positioned. You look in the direction of the approaching Continentals and see what Rall must have seen. Future president James Monroe, then a lieutenant, led the attack on the Hessian artillery and was wounded in Trenton.

***First Presbyterian Church.*** The spires of this historic church are one of the most recognizable features of the Trenton cityscape. Dating to 1839, this building was the third on the site; the Revolutionary era building, the "Old Stone Church," was built in 1726 and replaced by the second building in 1804. Its adjacent graveyard features Revolutionary-era interments.

4. *The City of History*

***Hessians on Warren Street.*** Contrary to popular belief, the Hessians did not stumble around drunkenly during the First Battle of Trenton, per David Hackett Fischer in *Washington's Crossing*: "The German responses to the American attack were not those of intoxicated revelers. When the alarm sounded, the three Hessian regiments in the center of town formed rapidly near their garrisons" (Fischer 240). Colonel Rall led the Hessians in a counterattack up King Street, now Warren Street, where this modern re-enactment image is set.

Or consider the Old Barracks, another of Trenton's most iconic structures. Dating to the end of the French and Indian War, it was authorized in 1758 and finished in 1759. Both British and American troops occupied it at various times during the Revolution. The Barracks was one of five erected in New Jersey during the French and Indian Wars; the others were in Burlington, Perth Amboy, New Brunswick and Elizabeth.[6] Its rationale and construction reflected a serious concern about Indian attacks. Trentonians had received notice of so-called murders by Indians in Sussex County, in the northwest corner of the colony.[7] During the Revolution, in addition to housing British troops, the Barracks also housed Tory refugees from Burlington and Monmouth Counties.[8]

One December I attended the recreation of the First Battle of Trenton. The troops, both Hessian and American, assembled at the Barracks. I wandered around, taking in the color, watching the drills. For a moment, you can imagine the same calls from officers centuries distant. This was the building, and this was the ground. It is a tangible, tactile connection. It is not just a connection to Trenton, but a connection to the founding of this country. It is a place of contemplation, a physical space to think of where we have been.

The Five Points, located where the Battle Monument stands, and where the contemporary Broad and Warren streets converge, still stands and reflects a historic crossroads dating back to Colonial times. It was the entranceway to the city from various routes. The "five points" were (1) Brunswick Avenue (then old Kings Highway [now generally parts of Route 206] from Lawrenceville to Trenton, also known as Old Maidenhead Road), (2) Princeton Avenue (then known as the Post Road to Princeton), (3) Pennington Road (between Pennington, Hopewell and Trenton), and King Street (now Warren) and Queen Street (now Broad).[9] From Indian trails to Dutch trading paths to stagecoach routes and, ultimately, with the Lincoln Highway in 1913, a point on the cross-country automobile route, the Five Points remains a place to reflect on history. Benjamin Franklin is reported to have passed through this spot.[10] Today, the Monument Park, on my visits, is usually empty. The intersection is not busy. It is like an ancient gateway in Rome, noted and marked, but no longer the prime means of entry to the city.

An isosceles triangle forms from the Battle Monument as the apex, Warren and Broad streets as the sides, and Front Street as the base. We now have the locus of the First Battle of Trenton. Standing at the corner of Front Street and South Warren Street (known, in 1775, as King Street), the Battle Monument is visible, looking up Warren. Move over to the corner of Broad (then Queen) Street and State Street, where Hessian commander Johann Rall had been celebrating Christmas festivities, and look down North Warren Street to the Monument. Standing on the corner of North Warren and West State Street, we can read the plaque that states "Colonel Rall was entertained on Christmas night 1776 in the house owned by Abraham Hunt which stood on this spot."

You are looking to where George Washington's forces set up artillery to pound the Hessians, and from which point Washington's troops charged toward the center of the city. Rall unsuccessfully tried to rally his troops up Warren (King) Street; they then tried Broad (Queen) Street and again failed, and were routed. The Presbyterian Church yard, on State Street, was where Rall was buried after dying from his wounds. The entire battle took about two hours. More than eight hundred Hessian troops were captured; others escaped over the Assunpink.

There are many detailed accounts of this First Battle of Trenton, with a surprising amount of first-hand quotes that seem to have survived. It is not my intention to rewrite the history of the battle. It is enough for our purposes here to recognize that places like this are sacred ground. The Old Barracks, at Front Street, still survives. The lay of the land, with the rise of ground where the Battle Monument stands, is as it was. The Assunpink Creek still marks where many Hessians escaped over the bridge built in 1774 (long since replaced), which itself was the focal point of the Second Battle of Trenton. After the First

## 4. The City of History

***Dayton Grave.*** Riverview Cemetery traces its origins to a Quaker burial ground. Located in South Trenton with magnificent views of the Delaware River, it features several prominent Americans. William L. Dayton (1807–1864) was the newly formed Republican Party's vice-presidential nominee in 1856, beating out Abraham Lincoln for the position. When Lincoln won in 1860, he appointed Dayton as Minister to France and was instrumental in keeping France from supporting the Confederacy. Also buried in Riverview Cemetery is George B. McClellan, the original commander of the Union forces in the Civil War and later Governor of New Jersey.

Battle of Trenton, Washington moved his troops with their prisoners back across the Delaware, and then returned to Trenton, where they established a line south of the bridge across the Assunpink Creek. Lord Cornwallis, having moved superior forces quickly down from New York to Princeton and on to Trenton, opted for a strategy that we might today call "shock and awe"—superior, concentrated forces in a direct assault. As it happened, the Second Battle of Trenton on January 2, 1777, was more a series of probing attacks by the British, one attempted across the creek and the rest across the bridge, all of which were repulsed. On the evening of January 2, Washington and his officers met in the Douglass house on Queen Street (now South Broad Street), at which time it was decided to march to Princeton and assault the British from the rear.

The Douglass House was originally owned by Alexander Douglass since its construction around 1766, and it was used for a strategy conference by Washington following the Second Battle of Trenton on January 2, 1777. It has been restored, and relocated several times to its present location at the corner of Front Street and Montgomery Street. If not in its original place, it is still intriguing to look at the physical building and reflect the conference that helped determine the course of not only the Revolution, but the future of the United States as well. In the words of General Arthur St. Clair, whose quarters it was, "The General summoned a council of the general officers ... and after stating the difficulties in his way, the probability of defeat, and the consequences that would necessarily result if it happened, desired advice."[11]

The "Corner Historic," at the intersection of South Warren and West State Street, is, as its name proclaims, steeped in history. It, too, is a kind of hallowed ground. Originally the site of a stone residence in the 1730s, by the 1740s it was home to the first Royal Governor of the colony of New Jersey, Lewis Morris.[12] By 1780 it became a tavern, in which the Continental Congress met, and by 1782 was known as the French Arms Tavern. Lafayette took leave of Congress in the tavern.[13] The New Jersey Assembly purportedly met here.[14] Other names included the Thirteen Stars, the Blazing Star and the City Tavern.[15] In the opening decades of the 19th century, purchased in 1836 by the Mechanics and Manufacturers Bank.[16] It has remained a bank to this day; the present building was built by the First Mechanics National Bank in 1930.[17] This is another place in which one can touch history. It is part of the sense of place.

We don't use the word "tavern" much anymore. We talk of "bars." Yet the

*Corner Historic Building.* Seen from the Roebling Building across from it, through the George Segal sculpture of men working, the Corner Historic Building occupies the site of important historic events in the history of Trenton and the country.

tavern was a core element of the city's social life and its urban existence; Trenton was replete with taverns in Colonial and post–Revolutionary times. It was a key point on the stagecoach route from New York to Philadelphia, and an important ferry site. Almost the nation's permanent capital, the scene of the meeting of Colonial representatives from up and down the eastern seaboard, it was a *place*. And the tavern was an important part of the community. Among the other sites is a block away at the corner of South Warren and Front streets, where the Golden Swan Tavern held sway. Built around 1815, it was the largest tavern in the city.[18] It later became the site of the *True American* newspaper in the 1850s.

These taverns are no longer visible. Other buildings stand where they were, and their physical presence ceased to be used as taverns. There is one remnant, though, dating to the Revolutionary era, if not the actual war itself, as a tavern. We can, however, find one that survives, another ruin, another figurative melting watch in the surreal landscape. The Eagle Tavern, on South Broad Street. A plaque on it states: "A Bicentennial commemorative site recognizing America's 200th year of liberty **Old Eagle Tavern.** During the 19th century this tavern served travelers, soldiers, and Trentonians as a social and political center." Added to the National Register of Historic Places in 1972, it is now vacant,

*The Eagle Tavern.* Forlorn and abandoned on South Broad Street, near the city's sports arena on the edge of the Ferry Historic District, the Eagle Tavern dates to the second half of the 18th century, and by most accounts, post-dates the Revolutionary War. Nonetheless, it was a stopping point for those on the New York to Philadelphia route.

boarded up. Its architect unknown, and its periods of significance vague, ambiguous: 1750–1799, 1825–1849, 1850–1874.

The original portion of the building was built in the late 1760s by Robert Waln, a Philadelphia merchant and member of Congress who, like William Trent, came to Trenton for financial gain; the original building is presumed to have been his residence.[19] The building appears to have been depicted on several Revolutionary War maps. It is unlikely that Waln lived there during the Revolution, and it is also believed to have functioned as a schoolhouse briefly in this time frame. In 1811 it passed from Waln family ownership and underwent subsequent sales, with the first documented application for a "liquor license" being filed in 1817.[20] The popularity of horse racing and the nearby Eagle Race Course in the 1820s and 1830s helped business at the tavern. Also beneficial was its location on the New York–Philadelphia route; the establishment in the 1840s of the Cooper wire mills helped as well. The tavern also served as a gambling house.[21] It served as a hotel and, in 1864, site of a campaign rally for Democratic presidential nominee George B. McClellan (himself buried in Riverview Cemetery in Trenton). It seems to have ceased functioning as a tavern by the turn of the 19th century, and early in the 20th, it was in disrepair. Acquired in 1946 with plans to develop it into apartments, it was later purchased by Trenton in 1965, leased to the Trenton Historical Society in 1973, served for about ten years from 1980 onwards as a restaurant, and closed.[22]

Backes reports in his article on "Landmarks, Taverns, Markets and Fairs" in the 1929 History of Trenton[23] that this was the oldest hotel south of Assunpink, though as of 1929 it was no longer used as a hotel, though purportedly was active as such at the time of the Revolution. An article in *American Heritage Magazine* in 1987 urged readers visiting Princeton and Trenton to "have a drink or a meal there," and noted it was originally a private residence during the Revolution and then became a tavern,[24] though Backes notes it was a tavern before the Revolution. He adds it was reportedly a popular stop on the route between the ferry and the center of the city, and in the 19th century, was a hangout for politicians and racing aficionados, the latter due to the proximity of the Eagle Race Course. It was shut as a tavern in 1896 and remains shut and vacant as of this writing.

When in London or Rome, you stumble over ruins a thousand, two thousand years old. In the New World, you make do with ruins a hundred, two hundred years old. You imagine life in the tavern, the drinking, the talk, the sense of being in a place that at one time was, quite literally, understood to be on the edge of the world. The Old Eagle Tavern now stands in proximity to the sports and entertainment arena that seeks a resuscitation of the cultural and sports life of the city. South Broad Street, also known as Route 206, still can carry travelers from the fair north to the relatively deep south of the state. No one will stop at the Old Eagle Tavern, and no one will be taking the ferry across toward Philadelphia on a journey from New York. This is not merely a ruin. It is a ghost, a ghost that bore witness to the Revolution and sits silent, boarded up, a relic on an unremarkable section of street in a somewhat rundown area of the city.

Among the group of Quaker settlers of what was known as the Falls of the Delaware, was Mahlon Stacy, in 1679. One of the Council of Proprietors of West Jersey, he established a grist mill in 1680, and in 1714 his son sold lands to William Trent. Trent was a Philadelphia lawyer, who laid out the rudimentary plan of the city, in the form of the isosceles triangle mentioned above. By the time of the Battles of Trenton in the winter of 1776–1777, Trenton had been described as a town or village of about 100 homes, an attractive if not particularly important city in the colony.[25] The actual city was by then encompassed more in a rhomboid, marked by Calhoun Street to the north west, up to the "Five Points" where Warren and Broad met Brunswick Pike (part of the King's Highway that led on to Princeton and Elizabeth), and southeast to Ferry Street and near where Trent built his mansion, which still stands. In 1784, Trenton served as the national capital for two months under the Articles of Confederation.[26] By 1792 and the time of the city's first petition for charter, it had expanded up along the river and inward, to form a kind of reverse "L." The streets, according to the early maps, were straight, but with no particular attention paid to grid or other organizing principle. This was a place along the route of the "flying machine," that is, the early high-speed stage coach on the route from New York to Philadelphia.

Certain buildings within Trenton anchor it to its past and in their persistence and survival, establish indelible links of the present to that past. Trenton's Quaker roots, for instance, are exemplified in the Friends Meeting House in Trenton, which was built originally in 1739; the Quakers in the Delaware region had met in people's homes.[27] The Quakers first settled Trenton in 1679,[28] and religious activity by them formally began in 1684.[29] A meeting house was first proposed for Trenton in 1691, and one was built in 1693 in Crosswicks. Later deemed inadequate, it was replaced by the current building. With the Revolution also came the beginning of the decline in membership of the Friends. Mahlon Stacy, the principal settler of early Trenton, was a Quaker. The most famous of the regional Quakers was William Penn; it is a reminder of the prevalence of Quakers and their importance in the early days of the country to look at the now largely incongruous Colonial meeting house at the intersection of Hanover and Montgomery streets.

Another prominent feature of the city's skyline, the First Presbyterian Church, as Harry J. Podmore writes in *Trenton Old and New*, presents an important image of the city: "Few landmarks in the city are more expressive of early Trenton than the First Presbyterian Church and its graveyard."[30] The current physical building itself dates to 1839; the predecessor church on this site and Congregation predate the Revolution. Perhaps the presence in its graveyard of

*Friends Meeting House.* Trenton was settled as a city by Quakers around 1679, but they did not construct their local meeting house until 1739. It was occupied by the British Light Dragoons in December 1776. The building as shown in this image reflects an 1873 addition. In the adjacent burial ground is the grave of George Clymer, a signer of the Declaration of Independence (although as a Pennsylvania delegate), who spent much of his career in Philadelphia but who died in Morrisville, Pennsylvania.

Revolutionary notables, including the Hessian commander Rall, adds to its mystique. Trenton was important enough to be part of Anglican minister George Whitefield's visit to New Jersey in 1739–40, speaking to more than 3,000 people in Trenton as part of the Great Awakening.[31] In John Hall's *History of the Presbyterian Church in Trenton, NJ*, this period was described as "one of the most exciting and tumultuous epochs" in the church's history.[32] Whitefield records preaching at Trent-town on November 12, 1739, and later than month, on November 21, 1739, on the occasion of a hanging. Hall notes several visits by Whitefield, including another in 1740 and further ones through 1770.

Another significant home from Revolutionary War days, though fairly well modified, is the Hermitage. The Hermitage on Colonial Avenue was built prior to the Revolution, but was most known as the home of Major General Philemon Dickinson, who purchased it from the original owners in July 1776. Dickinson's friend, President John Adams stayed here at various times. The Hermitage and the Dickinsons exemplified Trenton's "high society" at the time. It is remarkable to read a description of it from 1903 by Weymer Jay Mills in *Historic Homes of New Jersey*:

## 4. The City of History

October days of 1798 were bright ones for Trenton, and the rooms of the Hermitage were always taxed with large gatherings of the first company of the republic....

English carriages became quite the rage in the city about this time, and the Hermitage stable possessed a beautiful and expensive example used by the second Mrs. Dickinson, pretty Rebecca Cadwalader, a sister of the general's first wife.... The whisper-room of the Hermitage is one of the most famous rooms in the social history of New Jersey. There Madame Moreau, "the beautiful Parisian," displayed her wonderful pearls and played on the harp for select audiences. In its dim recesses Louis Philippe, a future king, paid graceful compliments to the ladies of the Dickinson household."[33]

Today, the Hermitage is nestled among attached homes on a relatively narrow street, and while conspicuous in its design, otherwise does not attract much attention. With imagination, perhaps, one can block out the highway and the other houses that block the view of the Delaware River, and try to conjure up such a party seen at the end of the 18th century.

A short survey of the city's historic buildings would not be complete without mention of one of the most significant state capital buildings in the country. The Statehouse building deserves its own mention, and while not a "Trenton city" building, nonetheless is an integral part of the city's culture. Trenton was chosen as the state capital in 1790, and construction on the Statehouse began

*The Hermitage.* One of the more famous and elegant Colonial-era mansions in the city, this was Major General Philemon Dickinson's home and has been significantly renovated and changed to its present form. President John Adams stayed here in 1777 and again while president in 1798 during the cholera epidemic.

in 1791. It has undergone substantial additions and renovations, and was severely damaged by fire in 1885. Among those who have spoken in the building are Lafayette, Daniel Webster, Abraham Lincoln and William Henry Harrison.[34] It is commonly referred to as the second oldest statehouse in continuous use in the country.[35]

In the course of his monumental *The City in History*, Mumford refers to "a more general truth about cities: their marked individuality, so strong, so full of 'character' from the beginning that they have many of the attributes of human personalities."[36] In the case of Trenton, the city celebrates the First and Second Battles of Trenton, and Washington's crossing of the Delaware some miles north of the city, by way of reenactment. In one of the most recent comprehensive accounts of the battles, David Hackett Fischer quotes two Colonial soldiers and notes that, facing a force that clearly outnumbered them, "the American troops long remembered that moment, when the enemy appeared before them in their full strength.... Most shared a deep sense of foreboding, deeper than any recalled at any other battle."[37] It remains part of the city's psyche that it was the turning point in the American Revolution, and the knife-edge balance that tilted in favor of independence over continued colonial rule happened in Trenton. We can today walk the streets and see the parameters of the battle. When we stand on the ground where history was made, we are doing more than making a physical connection. We are allowing our thoughts to move towards the *being* of that period, and relate it to the present.

Even when the physical house has moved, we can draw the connection. We can still see the Douglass House, moved from its original location and now at the corner of Front and Montgomery streets, where Washington held council with his officers as to his next course of action. Like looking at the displaced Elgin Marbles at the British Museum or any number of altarpieces in an art museum, and not in their original churches, we nonetheless are in a kind of time machine. We see the house where Washington sat, whose walls absorbed the voices of the men those centuries ago. It remains a direct connection to the past.

So—we can see the unmarked graves of the Hessians in the cemetery of the First Presbyterian Church on East State Street. We look up Warren and Broad streets to the Battle Monument, and see the same rise in land that the Hessians saw as the artillery from that height pounded them. We see the same stone bridge over the Assunpink that Washington held. We see the Friends Meeting House. We see the Old Barracks. These are now sacred places in American history. They were physically touched by those who fought and lived in Trenton in 1776, and we can touch them today. They are integral to the city, and part of its psyche.

They are fundamental, if now unsung, places in American history. And yet we take them for granted and become complacent. These buildings, streets and plaques are virtually ignored by most people going about their day-to-day business. Once a year, the devout history buffs get together, and for a little while, Trenton is a kind of tourist attraction. *The persistence of memory.* But if we look at the familiar through the eyes of a stranger, we come to see them in a new light. As familiar as Trenton was to me from growing up in and around the area, as I looked through the camera's lens I saw them afresh.

I once took an English colleague to Washington's Crossing; it was in fall, and a chilly, foggy day. The atmosphere was conducive to imagining history, and there was a real connection to the place. Similarly, in the right moments, simply standing by the plaque on the building at the corner of State and Broad streets where Colonel Rall was dining, and looking up Broad (then Queen) Street as he would have done, provides a bit of a window on Trenton's soul. It is its history. Yet familiarity, perhaps, does breed contempt. As I photograph the plaque, I am unregarded and alone. This is not New York, or even Baltimore or smaller cities, where tourists with cameras are expected. The photographer in Trenton, in pursuit of history, is a whimsical sight.

A rusty pole holds up a plaque that states: "On this site, late in the afternoon of January 2, 1777, General Washington's 'Little Band' of determined men and boys won the Second Battle of Trenton. Having amassed a great concentration of artillery and small-arms power, the Americans withstood three powerful charges by the enemy and exacted a heavy toll in killed and wounded. This stand enabled the Americans to outflank the enemy during the night and march on to another victory at Princeton, thus completing the ten days that kept a dying revolution alive."

This is important. Joel Kotkin has identified three core purposes of the city in its historical genesis: provision of a sacred place, security and commerce.[38] Cities originally were built around and to sustain designated holy places, and run by the religious hierarchies. In the more contemporary city, such religiosity has been replaced by more civic institutions or functions. The sacred place was a cornerstone of the particular city's persona, and was essential to the establishment of the urban center. If we think in those terms, it is possible to image the triangle formed by Warren, Broad and Front Street as Trenton's sacred place. Not in the religious sense, but in the sense of its importance to the fabric of this place. In Paris, there are bricks in the road to mark where the Bastille stood. In Boston, the site of the Boston Massacre is marked along its red line Freedom Trail by a circle in a median in the street. These are defining places. It is not too much to call them sacred places in the context of the particular city and its history, to the extent they provide an American identity.

One of the missing elements of historical Trenton is physical recognition of its Colonial significance as a port along the Delaware River. Near the baseball stadium — indeed, the parking lot abuts both the stadium and a stairway to the elevated park on top of the Route 29 tunnel — was the Colonial town and port of Lamberton, later annexed by Trenton. In 1789 Lamberton was recognized as an official port of entry in the new country.³⁹ A casual walk along the park's pathway leads to various markers and plaques. Here the *flâneur* can look out over a wide expanse of the Delaware River and begin to escape from the now to the then. Here, the northernmost point on the Delaware River that was still navigable, about a mile and a half south of the "falls" the precluded more northern shipping, except for the rafting of lumber, was Lamberton, home to the shallop and the sloop, and the warehouses that facilitated trade up and down the river, between New York and Philadelphia. It was one of the Colonial ports in New Jersey; even as late as the early 20th century, steamships docked in the area.

Lamberton and pre-industrial Trenton pass for the American equivalent of the Middle Ages. Also known as Trenton Landing, the area was not only a port, but also a fishery. A first effort, by the Englishman Edward Broadfield, to supply sturgeon and shad to New York and Philadelphia merchants failed due to weak demand. A decade later, the politician and businessman Charles Read succeeded by developing a significant commercial entity. The facility included "a boiling house for converting fish into oil, glue, or isinglasss, a cellar for curing sturgeon and herring, a cooper's shop, and a dwelling."⁴⁰ Read sold the business to William Richards, another ambitious local entrepreneur, who ran retail shops in Philadelphia and Lamberton, and who expanded the business to include pickled sturgeon and shad. His was one of several thriving fisheries at the time. By the 1780s he had built a series of warehouses along the waterfront.⁴¹ During the Revolution, Lamberton's significance held military importance; Washington designated Trenton and Lamberton as a "provision magazine" where rations were stored.⁴² With the loss of Trenton to Washington for the national capital, the frenzy of post–Revolutionary War activity and investment faded, though the area held on throughout the 19th century, and was host to various industry, including several breweries.⁴³ A sad reminder remains the Champale Office on Lamberton Street as one of the city's historic landmarks.

The opening of the Trenton Marine Terminal downriver, near Duck Island, in the 1930s ended the reign of Lamberton. Looking at old photographs from the time and seeing the large ships conjures up a different image of Trenton.

Let us also pause also to reflect on Lieutenant John Fitch, who ran a gun shop on King Street (now Warren) during the Revolution. Fitch was also, arguably, the inventor of the steamboat, conceiving the idea in 1785, though he gained little recognition for it, and most people today think of Robert Fulton when they think of the steamboat. John Fitch's steamboat was test run in 1788 and the source of Trenton-Philadelphia runs by 1790.⁴⁴ His steamboat dock was near the site of the New Jersey Iron and Steel Company, now the KatManDu Restaurant. A plaque set in stone states: "This commemorates the genius, patience and perseverance of Lieutenant John Fitch, inventor of the first steamboat. It made successful trips between Philadelphia and Trenton in 1790 and docked near this site." Fitch was granted a patent by Congress in 1791, and in France by Louis XVI, but the French Revolution destroyed his ambitions. Reportedly, he had left his plans in France, where Robert Fulton got hold of them. Fitch left New Jersey for Kentucky and died in 1798.[45]

These places are not only part of the physical nature of Trenton; they are part of its psyche. There is a deep and abiding respect and affection among significant portions of the city's residents for Trenton's place in American history. This appreciation was documented over a century ago. In 1904 an anonymous booklet, *Souvenir of Trenton*, was published. It described Trenton like this:

> The historic city of Trenton traces its existence back to the year 1680 at which time a mill was built at the mouth of the Assanpink [sic] Creek. The place was then known as "The Falls" and held that title until 1714 when the interests of the original founder, Mahlon Stacy, were transferred to Colonel William Trent, and thus was derived the name Trent-town, later shortened to the present Trenton. Trenton has been a city since 1792, when it was granted a charter by the State legislature. It became capital of the Stare in 1790. The population in 1810 was approximately 3,000, which has increased steadily until now her inhabitants number 80,000 persons. It covers an area of nine square miles of which one hundred and fifty acres are devoted to parks. The assessed valuation of the city

*Trenton Poster Advertising Company.* This neo–Classical building housed the Trenton Poster Advertising Company and, after its merger into the R.C. Maxwell Company in 1923, that entity, until 2000, when R.C. Maxwell was sold to Interstate Outdoor. Maxwell was one of the more prominent outdoor advertising companies, and is reflective of the broad diversity of Trenton's industrial and commercial interests.

is forty millions and the public debt two million dollars. There are forty miles of electric railroad; one hundred miles of streets, thirty miles of which are paved.

Trenton is a strictly American city, modern and up-to-date in every respect, and her streets which in Washington's time resounded to the tramp of the contending armies now tell with unmistakable voice the story of the armies of industry. Trenton is splendidly equipped for the education of her young. Thirty public schools cater to the needs of over nine thousand pupils.

On account of her adjacency to the great cities of the Atlantic Seaboard, Trenton offers unusual advantages for the shipment of manufactured goods. Her means of communication by rail and water are unsurpassed. Her citizens cordially extend the hand of welcome to all comers.[46]

Eighty thousand people in 1904 was just about the population the city has now, a century later. The photographs by J.S. Neary in that booklet of downtown might well be those of a Western town in an old black-and-white movie. The images of the pottery factories and the Roebling steel plant might be something out of turn-of-the-century England. Whatever the definition of "city," in 1900 it was clear that Trenton had all the accoutrements of a vibrant urban center.

Note the language of a century ago proclaiming Trenton "a strictly American city." So it was said then, and so it remains true today. Where Newark and Trenton go, so goes America. If we look to define the country, we do well to consider Trenton.

Our memories are vital. They anchor us. We know where we have been. A shared collective memory establishes connection among us and, more particularly, among the city's people. Trenton's history is both tangible and intangible, and real. The places noted in this chapter are tiles in the mosaic of the city in particular and a way of thinking about cities in general. In Boston, the "freedom trail" causes one to follow a series of bricks inlaid in the pavement that traverses the city, connecting its various historic sites. If such existed in Trenton, one would walk in the footsteps, quite literally, of Washington, Monroe and Hamilton in the Battle of Trenton, and of John Adams, and be able to touch the building where Washington held his war council, or the house where William Trent lived and laid out this city. One can stand on the spot where Fitch's steamboat was launched. One can stand on other comparable spots. They are a tactile connection, a means of contemplated these physical presences as reminders of the history and spirit of the city.

# 5. The City and Its Architecture

Trenton has the advantage of being one of the original Colonial cities in the United States. Like other such East Coast cities, it reflects the birth and growth of American architecture. As the new country struggled for its political identity, it also sought to establish its own aesthetic identity. As the country matured and developed industrially, it also developed uniquely American forms of architecture, borrowing and combining ideas from abroad. Trenton, of course, developed along with and as a fundamental part of the United States as it turned from an aggregation of colonies to a world superpower in the 20th century. A large part of the intrinsic importance of Trenton, therefore, is found in its architecture and contributions to the American story.

Architecture matters. We individually decorate our residences because we respond to our environment. The most utilitarian cubicle in the most homogenized workplaces still will often contain the small framed picture of a loved one, or a bent postcard from a colleague on vacation, or even a coffee mug urging some clichéd advice. There is a human need for aesthetics, if that is the word, or at least, some making of the environment pleasant for our particularized perspective. In their forward to *The Rise of an American Architecture,* Thomas Hoving, then-director of New York's Metropolitan Museum of Art and James Biddle of the National Trust for Historic Preservation observed that historic buildings in America's cities "are not employed as museums but, through imaginative adaptation, serve as homes, offices, business establishments, restaurants and community centers. Their preservation and use can counteract — and prevent — the rootlessness and spiritual alienation that result from living in degrading circumstances and among amorphous structures to which one cannot possibly relate."[1] For a post-industrial city such as Trenton, bleeding population and business, rootlessness and spiritual alienation need counteraction. We need to pay attention.

We need to understand that buildings communicate, and have symbolic meaning as well as functional utility. Not only the buildings, but the public spaces of the city are also significant. I have touched on the city's architecture briefly in prior chapters, in the context of its historical significance. In this chapter, we consider the importance of architecture by taking a look at what Trenton has to offer.

## Public Space

Any discussion of architecture, particularly in a city, must take into account the concept of public space. We can think of this as accessible, visible space open to all.[2] We live in the city; we walk its streets. What messages, both explicit and subliminal, are being sent? How has that message changed with the decline of the industrial city and the advent of the post-industrial city? Just as we cannot fully appreciate music by listening only to the notes and ignoring the rests between them, so we must appreciate the pauses and rests in the urban symphony.

Public places are available to all. Nonetheless, there are limits — public spaces involve the tension between freedom of action and the right to stay inactive.[3] They involve the opportunity for chance encounter and the planned event, the latter including the rituals or celebratory rites of the city.[4] Architect Spiro Kostof, who noted these points, further stated that "the fundamental aim of the public place is to encourage community and to arbitrate social community."[5]

I have briefly referred to Lyn H. Lofland's work in the earlier discussion of how a city may be considered or defined. Her comments are relevant in another context, namely, the analysis of public space and its relationship to the city. Public space can be considered a facet of the architectural make-up of the city.

Lofland argues that public space should serve four essential purposes for the cosmopolitan city: (1) compactness of the city, to facilitate a natural and essential flow through the public space; (2) small areas of spatial segregation of person and function, to facilitate diverse encounters; (3) unsanitized areas of difference that force diverse peoples to see and experience meaningfully different viewpoints; and (4) the public space must have an "edge," that is, it "must — at least occasionally — generate mild fear ... [but] not be viewed by its citizenry as 'too' dangerous."[6] Another important contemporary urban commentator, William H. Whyte, offers a corollary observation regarding the social life of the street: "What attracts people most is other people. Many urban spaces are being designed as thought the opposite were true and what people like best are places they stay away from."[7]

I am talking now about public spaces like plazas, as opposed to parks, playgrounds or the physical street itself. What causes them to be popular or not? Used or not? Are they of value? Whyte weighs in, having conducted a three-year study of the use of plazas in New York that are adjacent to buildings—contrasting, for example, the success of the plaza in front of the Seagram Building but the failure of others. His study emphasizes "an elemental point" that a "good" public space supports the proposition that supply creates demand, and if a city facilitates public spaces, they will be used. Such uses can range from dining outdoors to meeting places to segments of the daily routes of city travelers, all of which leads to interaction and social concourse.[8] I would agree. Such are valuable components of urban existence and also distinguish the city from towns and "suburban" sprawl where the only non-parkland open space is the strip mall parking lot.

Trenton experimented with open space in the middle of downtown, called the Trenton Commons, by closing off a portion of East State Street to vehicular traffic and rendering it a pedestrian zone. The experiment was deemed a failure; it not only failed to attract anchor businesses downtown, but also wreaked havoc with traffic patterns.[9] Enhancing open space in downtown Trenton, and eliminating the current eyesores of flat parking lots as unappealing open space, and transforming the city into more of a "green" place, is among the visions and themes of the Downtown Capital District Master Plan.[10] Another area of the city, the site of the former Roebling factory that includes readaptive use as the Roebling Market, also contains plaza-like areas. Even without sculpture, more interpretive signs to explain the history of the place and more seating might move this space toward the realization of a utilized and popular place for people to congregate. The new World War II memorial across from the Statehouse also has potential, as does the plaza-like areas around the capitol building and its annex, overlooking the Delaware River. The area in front of the Statehouse is commonly used for demonstration or protest; in the post–9/11 world, there are unattractive cement barriers to prevent vehicles from jumping the curb. Still, there is plenty of nearby open space to be more efficiently utilized, surrounded by the State Museum and State Library, for example. Trenton, as a walkable and compact city, would benefit from these areas being used in this fashion. Supply creates demand, but there also needs to be pedestrian traffic.

If more extensive private office usage can be drawn back to the city in its State Street high-rise buildings, a more diverse mix beyond state workers would also benefit the city, in terms of the mix of strangers. In the past, Trenton's working population was diverse in terms of jobs. Opportunities and vision come from such cross-fertilization. It enriches the city. The public space facilitates that. In the post-industrial city, in the face of abandoned streets and neighborhoods, of lost factories and declining population, public space — safe, accessible, utilized — becomes essential, lest the city decay into factionalized mini-cities.

Public art goes hand in hand with public space. There is a value to public art in a city's downtown area. Trenton's is minimal (a sculpture of an artist painting in Waterfront Park; another sculpture of a lawyer speaking to his client on the steps of the Hughes Justice Complex; one of construction workers in front of building on State Street; some outdoor sculpture by the parking garage near the train station). Still, a city with public art, combined with relevant public space, can increase the value and interaction of that public space.[11] Just outside the city's borders in adjacent Hamilton, the Grounds for Sculpture serves as an anchor for scattered and intriguing sculpture appearing on industrial properties. The more valuable and utilized the public space, the more contact diverse sections of the city can have, and the more of a cosmopolitan identity the city achieves. At present, there is a depressed level of street activity in Trenton not only on weekends, but during the week as well, and a nearly nonexistent recreational night life downtown. (KatManDu, the restaurant, bar and nightclub near the Trenton Thunder stadium, may be an exception; on game nights, that part of Trenton is vibrant and populated). There are not crowds of people on State and Warren Street at night. There are no movie theaters. There are occasional functions at the War Memorial Building and the Mill Hill Playhouse. One need only read the blogs and listen to the anecdotal evidence as to safety issues, but this also suggests that it is a chicken and egg situation: if the open space is appropriately designed and utilized, will the numbers deter criminal activity? Wishful thinking? Space matters to the small city just as it does to the large.

Beyond questions of the use of the ground, the city's buildings are important as well for the city's self-image and relate to its use of public space. Another commentator, Jack Burgers, writing on public space in the post-industrial city, has stated that "first and foremost, the architecture of the post-industrial city is focused on status and prestige. In an increasingly globalized economy, local activities have to be staged internationally. By exhibiting architectonic objects that are as prestigious as possible, local authorities are demonstrating that they are to be taken seriously as sites where commerce can flourish. The more impressive the skyline is, the more impressive the urban economic potency seems to be."[12] In other words, architecture matters. It communicates. People want to live, visit and work in aesthetically pleasing, comfortable and rewarding places.

He distinguishes between six different forms of non-exclusive public space. There are (1) erected "service sector" space, that is, space connected with finance and economic power, as the space outside a large office building; (2) displaced space, such as advertising and communications space; (3) exalted space, involving areas generating excitement, including sexual; (4) exhibited space, relating to things like museums and culture; (5) colored space, reflecting ethnic differences; and (6) marginalized space, which is the space of poverty and deprivation.[13] His point as I read him is that by categorizing or thinking about public space more deeply, we can understand what public space exists, and how it might be used, or whether and what kind of intervention is required.

So in order to feature the local activity, public space is needed, and dedicated for the particular purpose. I have noted that just as music is dependent upon the pauses between the notes, so a city's vibrancy is as dependent upon the silences—the public space—as it is upon the notes—that is, its buildings and other features. It is interesting to reflect upon Trenton as a symphony in this regard and wonder how it might sound with the right combination of public space and private space.

Philosopher Michel Foucalt, in his influential essay *Of Other Spaces* (1967), discussed *heterotopias*, or other spaces. These other spaces interrupt the normality of public space. When we think of public space, we might think of the large plazas of a European city, or we may think of the Americanization of that space, with private shopping malls serving as "public" space with concomitant legal issues. In the post–9/11 world, public space now needs to balance security with the essentialities of city life. But that does not mean it becomes, or is left, abandoned. Trenton needs to reconsider its public spaces, its *heterotopias*, and how they might be utilized. They are a part of its essential architectural heritage. Why not a "freedom route" with bricks, as is done in Boston, to direct the pedestrian up and down Broad Street and to other sites linked to the Revolution, and a circle of bricks, as reflecting the Boston Massacre, on the spot where Colonel Rall was mortally wounded? The use of public space is as varied as the imagination allows. Anything that causes a person in a city to pause and reflect, or make a connection, and be linked to *place*, has value in deterring the kind of estrangement that seems even more prevalent in the migratory, if not nomadic, post-industrial economic world of America today.

Might not the Battle Monument serve as a kind of plaza? It stands at the apex of a park, adjacent to a large grassy area, and at the center of the "Five Points" convergence of roads that do not carry significant traffic. It is a few minutes' walk from the center of the city. As a public space, it would seem appropriate. The current Trenton Master Plan does not consider this, although it does suggest a plaza adjacent to the courthouse and the restored Assunpink Creek area.[14] Consideration of the Battle Monument area as place of congregation and concourse could provide a central point reminiscent of the area's original place as entryway to Trenton.

## *The City and the Courthouse*

Having considered the pauses of public space, let us now turn to the notes of the architectural symphony, and look at certain types of public buildings that have particular importance to city identity. Two of Trenton's principal public buildings—its city hall and its old county courthouse—were reflective of national trends at the time, and continue to serve the purpose of using Trenton as a microcosmic prism through which to consider broader patterns and practices in the country.

To a greater or lesser extent, we identify with our public buildings, and

*Mercer County Courthouse.* Built in 1903 in Beaux Arts style, this building replaced the prior courthouse on this site. In that courthouse in 1853, Daniel Webster (while serving as U.S. Secretary of State) argued a patent case here on behalf of Goodyear Rubber that enjoined infringement of its patents and helped the nascent rubber industry in Trenton.

*City Hall.* Built between 1908 and 1910, the "new" city hall was an expression of Trenton's civic pride and stature at the height of the city's Golden Age, replacing the old city hall at the corner of Broad and State streets. The Neo-Classical design and columns, evoking Greek architecture, contrast with the previous, more Colonial-looking red-brick city hall.

our public buildings and monuments identify our cities. Big Ben and the Parliament Building (the Palace of Westminster, to be more precise) define London. The Grand Square in Brussels, with its grand buildings, is another source of civic pride. In my observation, much more frequently than in the United States, public sculpture is also more prevalent in European cities. If American cities lacked the cultural soul that preceded economic utility in the construct of cities, then they have sought to achieve some of that through favored public buildings.

Public buildings generally serve more than simply utilitarian purpose. Frank Hague, mayor and political boss of Jersey City, built the Hudson County Courthouse (now the Brennan Courthouse) as a showcase, with no expense spared. It is a beautiful example of Neo-Classical architecture; with its massive white pillars it resembles a Greek temple. The Essex County Courthouse in Newark was built as well to send a message and not simply to house courts. As James O'Gorman notes in *ABC of Architecture*, "architecture is a form of communication. It speaks. It can convey through its design its place in society, its content."[15] We can consider the courthouses in Trenton and expand upon our understanding of their architecture in general.

In New Jersey the state courts are located in the county seats of the states 21 counties, many of which would be considered towns as opposed to cities. Its courthouses run the gamut from classical to modern. There are three federal vicinages, one each in Newark, Trenton and Camden, and each has its own distinctive federal courthouse. In addition to the old Mercer County Courthouse, Mercer County's "new" civil courts building is also in Trenton.

Legal proceedings did not begin in specialized courthouses, or law courts. Taverns and other buildings served equally well. Nikolaus Pevsner, in *A History of Building Types*, writes, "Separate monumental buildings for law courts began in the English provinces with York, where in 1705 a Debtors' Prison had been built in a Vanbrughian style close to the castle keep."[16] He identifies separate buildings for law courts in France to date from the late 18th century.[17]

The courthouse in particular has a message to communicate. Rykwert speaks in terms of "ought," that is, a city ought to ensure justice. In this regard, it is not simply the presence and use of the courthouse, but the appearance of it as well. Embodying both public and private space, the courthouse should not only do justice, but also "be seen" to do justice. Appearances matter and should be consistent with the message.[18]

We as Americans pride ourselves on attentiveness to, and respect for, the rule of law. Architectural design is more than physical: it is meant to capture something of the spirit of the building, express its personality. As the American legal community became more professionalized in the 19th century, rituals as well as the message they were sending to the community through their courthouses became important and a focus.[19] Indeed, it has been argued that a legal system must be understood not in isolation, but in the broader relationship of it to its social and cultural context.[20]

An interesting study was made in Padua, Italy, in 2000, which asked whether courthouse architecture could affect a perceived likelihood of conviction. The authors concluded architectural design could affect the way in which participants in the justice system perceived their chances. The authors compared this perception of two courthouses in Padua. The first, and older one, was originally located in a 14th-century convent and turned into a courthouse in the 19th century, and was rebuilt in the 1930s after the original was destroyed by fire. The second was built in 1991. The former had a residential look, with warm colors and a large wooden door, and the latter was a massive, steel-gray, semicircular structure. The authors showed the participants photographs and questioned them as to their imagined feelings on entering the buildings and the likelihood that a hypothetical friend of theirs would be convicted. The study participants could not identify any particular feature or reason, but had less faith in a favorable outcome in reacting to the new building. Despite a variety of caveats, and non-definitive results, the study nonetheless felt there was something there, and suggested the subject was worth further investigation, providing a perhaps intriguing scholarly investigation into what many lawyers and architects may intuitively believe.[21]

As an instance of public space, the courtroom is a tangible and intangible place. It has a look, feel and appearance; its architecture is a message. And within its space, good and bad, horrible and wonderful, things happen. It is a place of realization of theory and ideal into practical and real. Politically, and fundamentally, though, the courtroom (as well as the parliament) are "the presumptive province of each and every citizen."[22]

Ultimately, though, as a practical matter, it is not a question as to whether courthouses intimidate. No matter how many "warm" touches, to the average citizen facing legal process for the first time, the building is more than likely intimidating. They are public buildings, and just as the "third branch," the Judiciary, of the United States considers its courthouses representative of itself, so the state's courthouses speak for the state. More particularly, the county's seat of justice speaks for the county, and even more specifically, the city's courthouse represents the face of the city to its citizens in the most important and fundamental philosophical component of the American psyche: the sense of justice, and the need to do justice. Law is not enough: there must be a notion that justice goes hand in glove with law. These buildings purport to speak to that, or so their designers intend. Put another way, "a building *condenses culture* in one place. Like the body itself, which is always cultural and social as well as physical, it pleats presuppositions and ideas in and relationships into a material fold, a container of meanings."[23] It is this recognition that appearance, as much as function, matters that seems to drive the design of many courthouses to a certain conformity of monumentalism.

Mumford discusses the importance of the citadel in the development of cities, in which military and religious powers were consolidated. The citadel became the central point of the city and its most protected place. In New Jersey, as in many states, it is arguable that the courthouse has replaced that function, or at least fulfills a component of it in the modern state. The rule of law has replaced the rule of the military, although force is implicit in judicial enforcement, if occasionally explicit. The secular authority has replaced the religious authority in the enforcement of law and the keeping of order. To some extent, state courthouses such as the old Mercer County Courthouse in Trenton in their classical design, are based on the Greek and Roman temples, which themselves connote more ancient citadels. Like those in Jersey City and Newark, they have this in common: they are meant to convey more than merely utility. They are meant to instill respect, if not fear. They are meant to compel compliance and establish authority. The newest federal courthouse in Newark is a modern building, with an intriguing sculpture of "blind justice" that has a figure of a kind of androgynous person with closed eyes, beyond a somewhat transparent blindfold. It is an interesting juxtaposition between the stark message of justice with the more humanistic, and ambiguous, contemporary notion of justice.

More prosaically, some facts. Trenton was originally part of Hunterdon County; Mercer County was formed in 1838 and named for General Hugh Mercer, who died at the Battle of Princeton. Prior to that time, New Jersey courts were established pursuant to the Act of 1676, with Hunterdon County Court held in varying places until ordered to be in Trenton by the Colonial governor in 1719.[24] John O. Raum,[25] in his detailed and voluminous 1871 *History of the City of Trenton*, reports the court in Trenton was held originally in a private home, but a courthouse was built "probably ... about a year after, or it might have been in erection at that time."[26] It would have been apparent that the kind of respect and awe deemed a necessary component to law would not have been realizable in someone's kitchen.

The first courthouse for the newly formed Mercer County, built in the Mill Hill area at the corner of South Broad and Market streets (as now known), was a brick structure built in 1839, Greek style with Corinthian columns, topped by a cupola with a bell that rang to notify of court sessions.[27] Many courthouses have Corinthian columns, since the Corinthian was the highest order of columns, the most elegant and associated with beauty. This courthouse was demolished in 1901. Prior to that, in 1852, Daniel Webster took time out from his tenure as Secretary of State in President Fillmore's administration to argue the case in Trenton. Although a federal case (and federal court was held in a room in the state Errors and Appeals Court that sat in the Statehouse),[28] the trial was moved to the county courthouse to accommodate the number of spectators. Webster represented Goodyear in a defense of its patent on rubber against Day's claims of invalidity; Webster's victory helped propel Trenton's significance in the rubber industry. The site in Mill Hill, at the corner of Market and Broad streets, is marked today with a plaque to this effect.

***Mill Hill.*** **Mill Hill is split by Market Street and surrounded by Broad Street and the complex of highway ramps for Route 1, as well as the railroad. Pictured here are Federalist-style rowhouses on Jackson Street. Mill Hill is one of the city's most historic districts; Mill Hill Park, on the other side of Market Street, was the site of aspects of both battles of Trenton.**

The "old" Mercer County Courthouse in Trenton on that site must count among the state's more impressive constructions, and is particularly reflective of its time and the renewed interest in American architecture in the influence of the Renaissance. The Beaux Arts sandstone building was built in 1903. The cornerstone was laid on May 14, 1902, with New Jersey's Mahlon Pitney, justice of the United States Supreme Court, in attendance to say a few words.[29] It has become one of the county's iconic buildings. In 2007, the Mercer County Executive recognized its importance:

> "The Courthouse has served the Capital County and its residents well beyond what could have been predicted when it was built," Hughes said. "Even as we phase our court facilities and other important functions into the new courthouse, we cannot neglect this historic building."
> "We will work with the State Historic Preservation Office to ensure this building will last another hundred years," he added.[30]

As that historic building deteriorated, a new courthouse was built nearby, and civil cases primarily moved there, with criminal cases remaining in the old building.

This courthouse was built at a time of retrospection in American architecture, a revival of interest in classical form.[31] As such the courthouse contains the columns, pediment and symmetry of ancient Greek temples. Courthouse architects recognize that functionality is only one purpose of the courthouse; the building must also convey a sense of fairness, impartiality and justice. The monumental look of this building supports that. I tried cases and argued motions in that courthouse very early in my career. There is an intangible aura about practicing law and being in a courtroom that carries with it the imagery and iconography of law.

On the other hand, the more recently constructed civil courts building with its more contemporary look, nonetheless in postmodern fashion, seeks to incorporate classical elements with distinctive and unusual design. Designed by the Trenton architectural firm of Clarke Caton Hintz, it accommodates civil, chancery and family law courts. The firm describes the project on their website: "The entry door is marked with free standing classical columns and a pediment. The façade design recalls 19th-century civil buildings while at the same time being an expression of more recent contemporary design ideas."[32]

The New Jersey Supreme Court is housed in the Richard J. Hughes Justice Complex, named after the former governor and Chief Justice. Built in 1978, it is actually "three" buildings in one, consisting of two wings for administrative and offices, such as the Attorney General, and a component for the courtrooms. Appellate arguments are also heard there. There is sculpture by J. Seward Johnson depicting lawyer and client conferring. This building is modern in design, vaguely reminiscent of the triangle construction at the Louvre in Paris. It more resembles, though, an office building than the traditional courthouse.

Another example of Classical design is the federal courthouse, built in 1931–1932 under the auspices of the Works Project Administration, which resembles other such buildings of that ear. As described by Daniel Brook, such buildings were meant to establish a common look, a representative "federal presence"; in other words, "for the first half of the 20th century, the federal government had insisted on an official style.... The federal courthouses built at this time were solemn, neo–Classical style structures that looked like, well, courthouses."[33] The federal district court in New Jersey is among the oldest of the federal districts.

This building, known as the Clarkson S. Fisher United States Courthouse, together with its more recent addition, houses the district court judges, bankruptcy judges and magistrate judges in the Trenton vicintage. It was designed by James Wetmore, who was responsible for numerous other federal buildings. Like its counterparts in Camden and Newark, it was a Works Project Administration (WPA) project that combined courthouse and post office. Wetmore was acting supervising architect of the Treasury Department in 1913 and from 1915 to 1934. Interestingly, he was also a lawyer. Wetmore also designed numerous other federal buildings and courthouses around the country, including the federal courthouse and post office building in Camden, New Jersey, constructed in 1932. They promoted uniformity of appearance during the Depression, with perhaps the subtle message of unifying the country and establishing a sense of stability in these solid structures, a sense of federalism at a time of increased governmental involvement in everyday affairs.

The current U.S. Courts Design Guide emphasizes the consideration of the impact on the citizenry:

> Courthouses must be planned and designed to frame, facilitate, and mediate the encounter between the citizen and the justice system. All architectural elements must be proportional and arranged hierarchically to signify orderliness. The materials employed must be consistently applied, be natural and regional in origin, be durable, and invoke a sense of permanence. Colors should be subdued to complement the natural materials used in the design.[34]

Consider the issue of intimidating buildings from another standpoint. Perhaps the question is less whether these buildings intimidate; anyone entering a massive, pillored lobby and facing security officers with uniforms and guns is intimidated. The question is whether the message remains effective. They are public buildings, and just as the "third branch," the Judiciary, of the United States considers its courthouses representative of itself, so the state's courthouses speak for the state. More particularly, the county's seat of justice speaks for the county, and even more specifically, the city's courthouse represents the face of the city to its citizens in the most important and fundamental philosophical component of the American psyche: the sense of justice, and the need to do justice. Law is not enough: there must be a notion that justice goes hand in glove with law. These buildings speak to that.

The website of the United States courts contains an article that compares four federal courthouses in Scranton, Montgomery, Phoenix and San Francisco. The anonymous article appeared in June 1996 and starts with the assertion that "a courthouse and its architecture play a central role in a community, both as a structure open to the public and as a representative of the nation's justice system."[35] We see the example of this in Trenton, and relate it to the broader world.

For example, there is an interesting organization titled "Justice Environment" which combines architects, psychologists, engineers, lawyers and other law enforcement officials in Australia and New Zealand, in an effort to improve the environment in which justice is administered.[36] Among the papers on that site is one by a group of Princeton-based architects that notes the transition from Classic-based architecture for courthouses to the more modern glass and steel structures.[37] The Classic influence, adopted from Greek architecture and the symbolism of the ancient Greek temple by the Romans and transformed to represent principles of justice, was reflected in American courthouse architecture through the early 20th century. In the 18th and 19th century, an American "Federalist" variation on English Georgian classicism was the result of Jeffersonian influence. This particularized style served to emphasize the distinction of the role of the courthouse. Classicism was reinforced by the 1893 World's

Columbian Exposition in Chicago. Lagging behind the gradual abandonment of classical design were courthouses; "in general, the middle decades of the twentieth century brought a shift away from the idea of the courthouse on the town square, away from the grandiose and the exuberantly decorated, and away from a building that sought, in each detail, to instruct and uplift. The courthouse became a place of function and a place of business, in response to a growing volume of caseloads and a concurrent increase in the county and federal workloads."[38] Thus, glass and steel become representative of the new vision of democracy — transparency and typicality, a workplace building, rather than the reminder of the isolated Greek temple. Even the new Mercer County civil courthouse reflects a symbolic pediment on the front of its otherwise very modern construction.

Compare the steel and glass of the Hughes Justice Complex with the stone of the federal and old county courthouse, and think about the messages.

One historian, Mary P. Ryan, has studied several iconic public buildings — courthouse and city hall — in terms of their symbolism, based both on interior and exterior architectural features. Evaluating the Cabildo house of government for Louisiana, the New York city hall and the "Tweed" courthouse, and the San Francisco city hall, she concludes:

*Carroll Street.* The Ewing/Carroll historic district is within the Coalport/North Clinton area, near the federal courthouse. Its architecture dates from the latter half of the 19th century, and in the words of the Trenton Historical Society, "is a classic example of a 'railroad age' community developed when middle class workers and industry's successful executives lived side-by-side in order to be near the place of their livelihoods." The Universal Hagar's Spiritual Church began in 1923 in Detroit.

> The architectural record ... denote[s] a halting, erratic development from imperial absolutism to republican polities to a tenuous and imperfect democracy. In their materiality and three-dimensionality, these public buildings served as both the schoolhouses and the theaters of political change. They opened up, and sometimes closed down, access to municipal government and on a prosaic, everyday basis-in legislative chambers, administrative offices, and in the stairways, parks, and promenades outside.[39]

So in this set of comments on the "courthouse," consider what we have seen. Trenton, of the oldest of American cities and a prototypical post-industrial city, allows us to see and speculate upon, and draw connections to, much more profound philosophical issues relating to the justice system as a whole. We look at its judicial buildings, and we can identify with such other buildings around the country, if not the world.

## The City and the City Hall

If the courthouse symbolizes law and justice, the city hall symbolizes the executive and legislative branches of municipal government. Here, too, the search for meaning has deep roots in American architecture. There were few native American architects, and these were primarily educated amateurs at the time of the Revolution. With the exception of Thomas Jefferson and a handful of others, most had never been to Europe, and knew European architectural styles second-hand, through often outdated publications that made their way to the new United States. Following the Revolution and in the early 19th century, American architects looked to Greek and Roman inspiration, seeking to create an American architecture that reflected the influence of at least a perception of democracy as practiced in Greece.[40] Architecture in the United States took some time to catch up to what was occurring in Europe in the 17th and 18th centuries. Resources were limited, and Colonial America was dominated by the educated amateur. New Jersey was dependent upon, and heavily influenced by, leading architects of Philadelphia and New York more so than by European influences. Nonetheless, New Jersey architecture, called conservative by some, appears to have provided examples of the major architectural schools and styles of the past three centuries.

The city hall is the focal point of the city's political life. William L. Lebovich, in *America's City Halls*, writes that the American city hall "can be seen as an oration of a local government's will to power, symbolizing triumph over the natural and human obstacles to its growth and prosperity. Taken collectively, America's city halls, therefore, symbolize the will to power of cities and towns as the United States became an ever increasingly urban country."[41]

The oldest surviving city hall or government building is the Palazzo del Brotto, constructed in 1215, in Como, Italy.[42] The Medieval city hall reflected the transition from religious and aristocratic power to the economic classes. Early European city halls were generally two-story structures, with the upstairs the meeting place and records center, and the first floor the marketplace.[43] Put another way, "The plan becomes standard: an open ground floor with arcades and one large room above."[44] Between 1250 and 1300, Pevsner notes, a variation developed in Tuscany that saw the separation of the market function from the governmental function; the building now comprised basically two halls, one on top of the other. To a large extent these were multipurpose government buildings, including judicial functions. This was the case through the 17th century.[45] From the 18th century onward, however, functions split off, and development of the city hall became more one of style than utilitarian development.[46]

The old city hall in Trenton was on the corner of Broad and State streets, and though no longer used as a city hall, the building stands there still. Retail establishments occupy the first floor. Built in 1837, it was used for the first time on January 1, 1838, as a dance hall.[47] It also contained a jail and police headquarters; in addition, "at one time [it] embodied most of the public activities of the city, succeeding the City Tavern."[48] Prior to the construction of the Taylor Opera House (named for its founder and the creator of Taylor Ham, also known as pork roll, John Taylor (1836–1909), the old city hall featured such celebrities of the day as General Tom Thumb and Horace Greeley.[49] This mixed use recalls ancient municipal buildings that also combined private enterprise in the same space as governmental regulation; in Greco-Roman cities, "symbolic of this partnership between the public and the private interest, government and business shared the same open space, the same civic container — even the same building."[50] With the relocation of the city's governing house down East State Street, the building was converted for purely commercial use. It served as the seat of municipal government in Trenton until 1910.

The current Trenton City Hall building, built between 1908 and 1910, reflects the preference for classical architecture at the beginning of the 20th century. Made of marble, brick and bronze, in the Renaissance style, Lebovich writes of this building that its "marble, symmetrical facades, with two-story columns, bronze gates, banding and elaborate lintels, were designed to impress the viewer with the importance of the institution housed within."[51] The interior is no less ornate. The building was designed by Spencer Roberts, who also designed Trenton's library building. The annex, behind the original building, was built in the 1970s and has a much more contemporary look.

The city hall building was reflective, internally and externally, of the vision Trenton had of itself at the time, at the peak of the so-called Golden Age. Everett Shinn, a member of the Ash Can School, was responsible for the murals, which featured workers in Trenton's dominant industries of pottery and steel.[52] He remarked that this mural pictured the "grand and glorious work that makes the city and city hall possible. Keep that before the men that sit in the Council

Chamber and you keep the interests of the city ever before them."⁵³ Trenton's use of murals was not unique; popular in that latter half of the 19th century through the Depression, "they were larger-than-life depictions of early settlers and history," later becoming "less realistic in style, dealing with less serious themes."⁵⁴ The mural, made in 1911, was "done at the height of the American Renaissance," and is "an example of that era's emphasis on civil price and urban beautification."⁵⁵ The mural was innovated in its presentation of "sweaty, muscular workers, many stripped to the waist, involved in strenuous activity."⁵⁶ When looking at this, consider that thought, as well as other murals across the country that depict this kind of American realism of the time.

The "new" City Hall was built during what Lebovich calls the Age of Discipline and Imperialism (1893–1919).⁵⁷ The 1893 World's Columbian Exposition in Chicago increased interest in, and awareness of, classical and Beaux Arts design.⁵⁸ It was also the period of the "American Renaissance," generally the five decades from the 1870s to the 1920s.⁵⁹

The statue of the fireman, another Trenton landmark and example of its memorial public sculpture, is on the lawn in front of the City Hall and commemorates the city's fire department, founded in 1747; the sculpture itself was made in 1892. *The New York Times* reported on July 28, 1892, that "many of the prominent citizens of Trenton assembled this morning in the Council Chamber to witness the official transfer of the new Firemen's Memorial Monument, which is now in position in front of the City Hall.... The monument is of bronze and represents a life-size fireman, with a child in his arms, standing on a pedestal, the basis of which is a drinking fountain."⁶⁰ It is somewhat difficult today to image such an event being notable enough to figure on page 5 of one of the leading newspapers of the world, but perhaps it is a testament to the relative importance that was attached to the city of Trenton at the time.

Trenton's paid fire department began shortly thereafter, in 1896; 18 firefighters have died since then. The most recent, Manny Rivera, died March 31, 2009, from injuries in a fire on February 9, 2009, and his name was added to the monument.⁶¹ Such things matter. Monuments are not just stone. They are symbols. Today, in the no-man's land that characterizes much of East State Street, sliced by the metal river of Route 1 that separates the City Hall from the federal courthouse, it is good to pause a moment to think of the importance of this monument over a hundred years ago, and its symbolic resonance of today.

## *The Prison*

Another public building that has an interesting architectural significance is the prison. It is tempting to dismiss the prison *qua* building as purely functional, but that is not the case. Like the courthouse, city hall and other public buildings, there is an architectural philosophy to the prison. Trenton's principal prison enables us to reflect on that.

New Jersey State Prison, previously known as Trenton State Prison, remarkably dates back to 1836–1837 when the north and south wings were completed. The underlying philosophy of prisons in the first opening decades of the 19th century was a choice between the Pennsylvania approach, supported by Quaker principles, of Bible readings and solitary confinement to isolate the prisoner from temptation, and the Auburn approach, which involved communal workshops and enforced silence.[62] With the New Jersey legislature opting for the former, it also engaged the architect behind Philadelphia's Eastern State Penitentiary, John Haviland. It was a premier example of Egyptian Revival in New Jersey architecture, which "seemed a better symbol of eternity or security than Green Doric for cemetery gates or prisons."[63]

It was also the subject of a classic study of maximum security prisons in the 1950s by Gresham M. Sykes, *The Society of Captives: A Study of a Maximum Security Prison*. He describes conditions inside: "Hot in the summer and cold in the winter, cramped and barren, the stone and steel cellblock would seem to express the full nature of imprisonment as seen in the popular fancy. Indeed, if men in prison were locked forever in their cells, shut off from all intercourse with each other, the dimensions of the cell would be the alpha and omega of

*Trenton State Prison.* Now known as New Jersey State Prison, this maximum-security facility in South Trenton has been on this site since the 1830s. The mural showing scenes of the city makes for a strange contrast. The prison sits square in a residential area, a block or so from the South Broad Street thoroughfare.

life in prison."⁶⁴ Of this particular prison, he added: "Yet the New Jersey State Prison does not represent acute physical discomfort, nor is there evidence of shockingly bad living conditions. Rather, it gives the impression of a grinding dullness, an existence lacking the amenities of life we take for granted, but an existence which is still tolerable."⁶⁵

It is interesting that this prison remains where it has been for just about 175 years, and retains the Egyptian architectural style of its original construction. It is in the middle of a residential neighborhood. On one of its walls, modernistic murals depict contemporary Trenton. Some of the most hardened, dangerous and despised criminals have been sentenced here. There have been riots and escapes, and near escapes. I was once a visitor to the prison, interviewing a prisoner in connection with a case I had, and still recall the sense of otherworldliness inside. And yet, here it is.

## *The Monument*

A significant public structure that marks and defines a city is the war memorial. New Jersey's cities generally have limited public sculpture. The most dramatic one of which I am aware is the Katyn Memorial in Jersey City, in remembrance of the 1939 massacre of 15,400 Poles by the Soviets. The sculpture shows a bayoneted rifle through the torso of a soldier arching his back. The combination of public art and memorial is striking. Also dramatic in more understated and muted ways are the memorials to the victims of the 9/11 attack on the United States that appear in various towns in New Jersey, as well as the various and updated war memorials that list the engagements of the United States and attest to each town's own contributions.

In Trenton, the War Memorial building is a testament to the armed forces in World War I, and in Cadwalader Park, there is a Civil War memorial. However, it is the Battle Monument, the central and towering monument to the Revolutionary War's First Battle of Trenton, that takes pride of place. The Battle Monument, dedicated in 1893, stands where one column of Washington's forces began their assault into the city. It is 155 feet tall and capped by a statue of Washington. The *New York Times* report on the dedication ceremony in 1893 notes some 20,000 people attended, with "at least 100,000 people crowd[ing] the principal streets of the old capital."⁶⁶ Eight governors attended, from Maryland to Vermont; President Grover Cleveland, identified on the program, did not appear but sent a letter of regret. Some 5,000 people were estimated to be in the parade. As one stands in Monument Park today, looking out over a bedraggled field, a renaissance of sorts of new homes and the general desolateness of the area, it is quite a contrast to the event of a century and a quarter ago, as reported by the *New York Times*: "The scenes around the grand stand were impressive. There was a solid wall of humanity that blocked all view of the thoroughfares that centered on the historical site. At one time the crush was so great that a dozen women fainted. Children had narrow escapes from being trampled to death."[67]

The souvenir booklet contains many ads of the city's businesses. Perhaps none capture the character of Trenton better than the one by Wilson & Stokes, who claimed "Next to dedicating the Monument comes our COAL YARD.... With three cheers for Washington as the savior of his Country, and Jumbo, as the boss Coal."[68]

The Battle Monument was designed by John H. Duncan, who also designed Grant's Tomb in New York. It is an example of Beaux Arts architecture, and was modeled after the 1671 memorial to the Great Fire of London in 1666. It stands on the site where Alexander Hamilton's artillery—the New York State Company of Artillery—fired into the city. The monument is topped by a statue of Washington pointing down Warren Street to direct Hamilton's aim of fire. The two soldiers at the base, on either side of the entrance, are Private John Russell of the 14th Regiment from Massachusetts and Private Blair McClenachan of the Philadelphia Troop of Light Horse.

The bronze relief of Washington crossing the Delaware River was done by Philadelphia artist Thomas Eakins; the original now is exhibited in the State Museum with a copy on the Battle Monument. The largest monumental column in the world[69] commemorating a battle is in San Jacinto, Texas. One is also reminded of the tradition of such memorials, such as the Place Vendôme Column in Paris.[70] Setting aside the Statehouse, the Battle Monument is Trenton's most significant, iconic and visible landmark in the city itself. While the Trenton Makes Bridge has a certain affectionate appeal, it is the Battle Monument as one of the tallest structures in the city that is visible, to the extent anything is, from a wide variety of places. From the observation platform, the whole of Trenton spreads before you. It is a perspective-shifting experience.

## *The Theater*

Trenton once boasted an opera house, but that no longer exists. Presently, its principal auditorium is the War Memorial Building, built in 1930–1932, on the site of a sawmill. According to *The Trentonian*'s Capital Century website, "The idea of a community performing arts center took hold in the early '20s. Arts lovers thought it was a shame that Trenton should have a dozen movie theaters and vaudeville houses, but no hall for opera, ballet and music recitals."[71] Built in Italian Renaissance style, it was conceived as a memorial to the fallen of World War I. Its official name is the Soldiers' and Sailors' Memorial Building. The State Museum auditorium, on West State Street, is housed in a building of Modernist construction.

What about "monumental" architecture? What are we trying to say? Kingwell observes that "the question then becomes: Are the monumental-conceptual works living up to the responsibility of public money and public attention, or are they large-scale con games feeding the self-indulgence of a new breed of installation artists, the architect as seer?"[72] Ultimately, architecture and politics collide. Architecture persists; it is visible, and transcends generations. Kingwell observes that architecture cannot be isolated as "autonomous art," but rather must live "in a larger and more complex context where its boundaries with the street, the cityscape, the world of social meaning are permeable and fluid."[73] In other words, it seems to me that while the architect as artist must answer to his or her own aesthetic, a building or monument that ignores its broader context becomes less inspiring than it does arrogant and selfish.

These memorials form part of the public art and history of a city. They are reminders of these cities' roots and their roles in the Revolution and every significant war in which the country has been involved.

## The City and the Rail

The railway station is another unique architectural form that remains represented in its grand sense in New Jersey in Newark and Hoboken. A train station should announce arrival. New Jersey's cities were built on the development of the railroad. Rybczynski links the attention to railroad station architecture to the same impetus that propelled the City Beautiful Movement and the attention to civic art and parks at the end of the turn of the 19th century into the 20th.[74] Newark's Penn Station and the Hoboken Terminal are two that are still in use and truly reflect the great age of railway construction. Trenton's new railroad station, still undergoing renovation as of this writing and known as the Trenton Transit Center, lacks the grand sense of arrival that greets one in a place such as Philadelphia or Washington. It is a functional place. There is something to be said for arriving in a city in grand style, as when one enters New York through Grand Central Station as opposed to the deadening maze of Penn Station. The current Trenton railroad station does not rise to such lofty levels, but nonetheless its size and step up from its predecessor does send a message of the continued importance of Trenton as a transportation hub.

The public building and the public space are part of the architecture of the city. They speak to us. These old, massive buildings convey a sense of seriousness and majesty, consistent with law. They are courthouses that fit comfortably within the paradigm of the city as a place of order. These are not the buildings of small towns. They are imposing structures that one generally associates with the great cities. The spaces punctuate the notes. Can we hear the city sing? What does the voice of Trenton sound like?

At this point in this meditative journey through Trenton, we are surrounded by monuments and buildings that are symbolic not only of the events they purport to memorialize, but also of a kinship stretching across time and space to other nations, other histories, and other cultures. We find traces of Greek and Roman culture on East State Street in the City Hall. We find a link to Napoleon and French battles in the Battle Monument. We find affinity with the development of the rule of law across centuries in the architecture of the city's courthouses. If we listen, we can hear what the architecture is saying. Buildings, streets, memorials, plazas, all have something to say to those who can hear.

# 6. The City of Lost Factories

There is something about a factory—like looking at a confident athlete, there is a sense of power and strength. The poet Carl Sandburg's "broad shoulders" description of Chicago, for example, could apply to Trenton as well. The factory is a place of substance, where tangible things are made. In a world of services and intangibles, it is comforting to remember when the economy was based on the actual physical production of things. Craft and style were often as important as the usefulness of the item. Today, wandering among the abandoned husks and frames of these places is like walking through a graveyard.

As noted earlier, Trenton was a city that was almost the national capital, that established one of the first steel mills in the country (Isaac Harrow's on Petty's Run), that was widely recognized at the end of the 19th century as one of two of the nation's pottery centers (East Liverpool, Ohio, claiming joint status), and whose historic heritage included two of the fundamental and pivotal battles of the American Revolution. It was still in the hundred most populated cities in the country as it entered the 1950s, virtually dropped out of the national commercial consciousness a decade later, only to enter it as a symbol of the lost post-industrial American city. Plagued by violence and in need of funding, these cities no longer have the private industrial base to support much of what government is now called on to do.

The breadth and depth of the city's industries was extraordinary. Shortly after the formation of the Republic, Trenton's industries were quintessentially American—as Eleanore Shuman tells us, "they included grist, fulling, paper, and iron and steel mills."[1]

Before there were factories there were mills. A plaque stands in Mill Hill Park off South Broad Street that states:

> **Mahlon Stacy's Grist Mill**
> Trenton's first industry. Built near here in 1679. Heirs sold mill and 800 acres to William Trent after 1704. He replaced it with a larger mill which continued under successive owners until 1828. Later converted to a cotton, and then to a paper mill. The structure was carried away by a flood in 1843.

## 6. The City of Lost Factories

Joseph Raum, in his *History of the City of Trenton*, published in 1871, puts the date of Stacy's mill as established in 1680, and notes the mill was originally a flouring mill.[2] William Trent bought it in 1690, razed it and rebuilt it in stone, which lasted until it was destroyed in the flood of 1843. John Sines, in his chapter on industries and trades in Trenton in *A History of Trenton: 1679–1929*, notes the next manufacturing facility as the 1723 iron works of Samuel Green and Trenton, and the 1734 plating and blade mill near the Old Barracks, established by Isaac Harrow.[3] In 1756, a stone paper mill was built by Daniel W. Coxe, later used to make linseed oil and grind paints. Trenton's early mills also included the 1814 cotton mill built by Gideon Wells, destroyed by fire in 1845. A steel works was built on Front Street in 1776 by Stacy Potts. A "Factory Street" still exists today, surrounded by government buildings.[4] Regardless, we understand that Trenton began as a mill town.

Architecturally, Pevsner suggests that "the earliest factories were the workshops of some printers."[5] He notes early writers who stress that factories (derived from the word *manufactory*) should be built in utilitarian fashion, "simple and solid" or "simple but proud."[6] The first American factory is reputed to be the Old Slater Mill in Pawtucket, Rhode Island, built in 1793.[7] Following the War of 1812, mills began to transform into real factories, distinguished by their materials used and construction methods, using, for example, masonry walls instead of clapboard.[8] Between the 1820s and 1830s, decorative elements were used, which were deemed to help promote the image of individualism: "The extraneous nature of these embellishments was crucial because it demonstrated to public view that money was not the measure of all things—that, in effect, the corporation was not heartless."[9] As the 19th century progressed, the architecture of the factory also became part of its advertising image.[10] There began a recognition of the importance of marketing—and therefore the communicative message—of the building itself.

Trenton was a diverse manufacturing center, but its principal industries were pottery and porcelain, iron and steel, and rubber; others included furniture, boat, paper, cigar, watch and doll factories. The rich geological deposits in the area, and proximity to the Delaware River, facilitated the early industrial development of the city, as well as its proximity to significant markets and a skilled immigrant labor force, and the engineering of the Delaware and Raritan Canal. Ultimately, as with many of the country's small and medium cities, the years following World War II saw labor unrest, racial turmoil, the loss of local control of industry, the collapse of the city's downtown and the flight to the suburbs of its population, as well as the impact of global competition. Trenton's great factories and industrial prominence—in short, the city that proclaimed in the 1930s that "Trenton Makes, the World Takes"—were abandoned, sold, destroyed or converted to other uses.

We might compare Trenton to Lowell, Massachusetts, which also grew up in the early days of American manufacturing (with a focus on textiles) and has had a comparable population. As long as we are thinking about Trenton in its industrial stage, the comparison to Lowell is legitimate as far as it goes. That Massachusetts city was the subject of a detailed study of the relationship of architecture and industrial growth. The author of the study, John Coolidge, observed that in addition to the migration of people from rural to urban areas, the concentration of power, of those in charge, the "ruling elite," moved from the country to the city as well. This led to centralization of control over not only economic but also social activity. If prior economic power was found in seaports, the ruling elites there were merely "influential rather than dominant"; but the Victorian cities of the 19th century were "the ganglia from which the whole country was run." Consequently, it was "small wonder that the meaning of nineteenth-century architecture can only be grasped if that art is understood as an expression of urban life, for the buildings of the cities are the record of the way the masses lived; they are the monuments of the intelligentsia; taken as a whole, they are the mirror of communal ideals."[11]

These reflections lead us back to another time and place, with remarks about the industrial city. Trenton, as window and mirror, again reminds us of Friedrich Engels, mentioned earlier for his description of the 19th-century English industrial city. Engels, more popularly known for his collaboration with Karl Marx on *The Communist Manifesto*, devoted a chapter titled "The Great Towns" in his book *The Condition of the Working Class in England*. As we saw, he painted a desolate picture of the city of the industrial revolution as the product of capitalism. With regard to the Victorian cities studied and commented on by Engels, Asa Briggs, in his *Victorian Cities,* suggests another way to look at these factory-driven cities. In calling them "a characteristic Victorian achievement" in the railway age, he commented that "perhaps their outstanding feature was hidden from public view — their hidden network of pipes and drains and sewers, one of the biggest technical and social achievements of the age, a sanitary 'system' more comprehensive than the transport system."[12]

Was Trenton a place of "hard egotism" and "barbarous indifference," to use Engels's words that I quoted earlier? I have also quoted elsewhere the more glowing words of others at the turn of the 19th to the 20th century to depict Trenton. As with Coolidge's observations about Lowell, we can look at the remaining mansions on West State Street — including particularly the Roebling Mansion — and fully understand the message of power and wealth being conveyed. We might contrast that, without going into the details, with Trenton's particular history of industrial strife, attesting to less-than-ideal working conditions and pay scales.[13]

The remains of the factories let us stand on the streets of Trenton and think about this vital struggle in not only American, but also world history. We see the symbols of the battle that took place, both here and abroad. The chimneys no longer belch smoke, but the red bricks, pierced here and there by weeds, remind us of what has been.

Tremendous growth occurred between the end of the American Revolution and 1840, the initial phase of the American Industrial Revolution. One of the core events that facilitated that growth was the War of 1812 and the concomitant English embargo and blockade, as well as domestic needs for weaponry and transportation.[14] By 1840, Trenton and most of the state's other major cities were "linked by rail, canal, steamboat, or turnpike to New York or Philadelphia."[15] One of the darker sides of these developments, with which the state unsuccessfully grapples today, was the "balkanization of local government" and emphasis on "home rule," where the growing urban areas flexed their muscles and sought greater independence.[16] "Home rule" is a New Jersey idiom for the assertion of power by municipalities and counties, and their political representatives, over anything happening within their territorial borders.

More broadly, this transition from political to business clout was not simply a localized phenomenon. Seismic changes happened to the country and consequently its cities during the course of the Industrial Revolution. While the factories were an impetus to growth of that revolution, they also sowed the seeds of the post-industrial city. In other words, as factories and companies expanded, local control was lost, ultimately, as capitalism was nationalized and the national, and then multinational, corporation became the way of life.

In *The Incorporation of America*,, Alan Trachtenberg addresses the rise of the corporate culture in the United States following the American Civil War through the turn of the century. Trachtenberg notes "the shift from one form of capitalism to another, from predominantly self-employed proprietors to large corporations run by salaried managers."[17] Within a relatively short period of time, towns and smaller cities evolved to industrial metropolises, replete with educational and cultural institutions, and an overriding philosophy of professionalism.[18] He argues that this economic development transformed American culture with it, and in particular, its importance to development of cities, transportation, education, politics, the arts. He further states that this "economic incorporation wrenched American society from the moorings of familiar values, that the process proceeded by contradiction and conflict."[19] A core component of this transformation was the machine, which created a fissure between traditional American notions of free will and individual effort on the one hand, and automatic and efficient operation on the other.[20] This had a profound effect not only on labor in general, but also on local hegemony: "The mighty river of industrial expansion threatened to take dominion everywhere, converting all labor to mechanical labor, to the production of commodities for distant markets. The spread of the machine meant the spread of the market.... Along with regional and local autonomy, age-old notions of space and time felt the impact of mechanization as a violent wrenching of the familiar."[21] Other industries followed suit.[22] Power was shifting from the more egalitarian structure of rural society to rule by "self-conscious classes of mechanics, professional men, businessmen, and capitalists...."[23]

For Trachtenberg, the city "came to embody the reciprocal relations between production and consumption in their most acute form. Consumption emerged as the hidden purpose of cities: consumption crystallized in advertising as a perpetuation of the corporate form of private ownership of production."[24] And yet, others note, the period from 1830 through 1860 was one of the greatest freedom that urban dwellers had known.[25] The city had been a paradoxical construct in American life; on the one hand, the shining city on the hill embodied Puritan ideals and utopian visions, and on the other hand, it also exemplified sin and corruption. Trachtenberg observes that the rise of the middle class during the post–Civil War period under study, in the age of reform, penetrated some of the mystery of city life.[26] With the consolidation of businesses, there was less opportunity for advancement; this, coupled with the growth of tenements and slum living, poor sanitation, and political corruption at the end of the 19th century, the state's urban centers went into crisis.[27]

Ultimately, "a middle class version of the city emerged and became widespread in these years; it took on tangible shapes in new neighborhoods, public buildings, redesigned downtown regions, and parks."[28]

We look at the sepia prints of Trenton, and particularly Cadwalader Park, and see images showing members of Trenton's nascent and developing middle class.

In the years following World War I and leading up to the Great Depression, the localized civil capitalism of the Roeblings and their set transformed into national capitalism, a phenomenon addressed by John Cumbler in *A Social History of Economic Decline*, specifically with regard to Trenton. Another example in one of Trenton's principal industries involved the leading pottery manufacturers, Maddock and Sons, which sold out to American Radiator and Standard Sanitary; a company that had been in the family for 50 years lost management control to a New York–centered headquarters and became a part of an international company.[29] Trenton was just another piece in the American puzzle. It is reflective of the economic shifts in America to a dominant national business class, transplanting political primacy and also local control.

Cumbler describes this transformation of American cities from civic to national capitalism, that is, from a locally governed place in which indigenous business leaders made decisions, to a system in which national corporations, with distant home offices, imposed decisions on the local branches and divisions. The prelude to this was New Jersey's sympathetic environment for homegrown corporations that became large for a variety of reasons. Bebout and Grele concur, and observe that "concentration of industrial control and management was a prime objective of the new corporate leaders. Smaller firms became parts of larger ones through failure, lease, or sale. The easy incorporation laws of New Jersey allowed interlocking directorates, stock-watering, and trust-building. That the big corporations wanted was large-scale production, so that the resulting economies would yield higher profits."[30] New Jersey, like Delaware, raced to the bottom, so to speak, in liberalization of corporate laws, seeking the least common denominator to attract business. Trenton is a prism for understanding this.

Cumbler devotes his concluding remarks to an entire chapter titled "Trenton as America," and notes that "the story of Trenton's transformation from civic to national capitalism is not unique to Trenton."[31] He places Trenton in the context of other capital and industrial cities, like Harrisburg, Pennsylvania, and St. Paul, Minnesota, or even Scottish cities, which fell by the wayside after the Industrial Revolution in the United Kingdom. As to the question of why Trenton is important, he writes: "But what do Trenton's changes mean to the United States? They are part of a national pattern. The restructuring of the political economy is a long and complicated phenomenon that affects communities, neighborhoods, families, and individuals."[32] This pattern, or set of connections, is why we need to reconsider Trenton. If it was emblematic of cities during the rise of the Industrial Revolution, it remains emblematic of the post-industrial city in the current millennium. Its lessons are not isolated.

The size of the new corporate entities and the rise of the national, and birth of the multinational, company changed not only economic but also cultural attitudes; the capitalist owner was being replaced by the "managerial group."[33] Culturally, other institutions—in entertainment, the press and publishing—yielded to popular taste and profit considerations at the expense of more traditional influences.[34] Put another way by one of the leading muckrakers of his time, Lincoln Steffens, in his introduction to *The Shame of the Cities* in 1904, railed: "The commercial spirit is the spirit of profit, not patriotism; of credit, not honor; of individual gain, not national prosperity; of trade and dickering, not principle."[35]

If cities began with agricultural roots, it was industry that formed the backbone of the new city of the 18th century.[36] New Jersey cities were no different. Critical to the success of the rise of the American city in the height of the Industrial Revolution of the 19th century was, as exemplified by New York, not merely industrialization but the ability for upward social mobility. Culture could take root in such an economic environment, and the physical shape of the city interacted with the citizens' images of their city: New York's "glass towers and darkened streetscapes seemed to reflect a new, bold expression of the modern metropolis."[37] The skyscraper rose not merely literally but figuratively, and relevant to New Jersey's cities, as even smaller cities "raced to make their statement."[38] Down in the streets, though, the 19th century was as grim for many as it was inspirational for some. Rykwert notes, "The chaotic and often wretched nineteenth-century city was a constant challenge to the passion and energy of the utopians."[39]

This challenge was replaced by the advent of quasi, or "light" industrial activity, outside the city. Whyte refers to the "semi-city" that competes with, if not drains, the smaller industrial city, growing up in "corridors" outside the

122   Part Two: The Elements of City Life

city. Trenton and the Princeton corridor are a particular focus, with the Route 1 corridor; however, he cites a study that refuses to attribute this corridor as the cause of urban decline in Trenton and New Brunswick says it was but rather, simply accommodating the increase in white-collar jobs. The blue collar jobs, it seems, would have been lost in any event.[40]

We know all this from personal observation. We have lived through it. We may not know all the details, or the precise academic pinpointing of cause and effect, but we get the big picture. Perhaps we can reflect a bit more specifically on what we see. The "Golden Age" of industry, of which we see the physical remains, had its tarnished side as well. Ultimately, the most meaningful stories are the ones lived by each of the citizens of the city. We can hear their whispers in the air, and take off from our walk to explore the ether and see what we can find.

In the course of my perambulations in the "clouds" of the internet and the hard pages of the libraries, and my own pedestrian wanderings along the streets of Trenton, I found this poignant commentary on Trenton's industrial past in a blog on the internet, by someone self-identified as "Decaying Angel." I quote at length, without correcting any of the typos or incorrect names or spellings, to give voice to one person's nostalgia about Trenton:

> Hey, don't forget Taylor's Pork Roll or Loefflers Bologna and hot dogs. I don't even want to know what was in those things but no other ones tasted like them and talk about those dogs plumping when you cooked them!
> The Champale factory — and I admit I am old enough to remember the smell of ketchup being made at Stokely-Van Camp every fall. The scent became synonymous with school starting up again as most of the ketchup was produced from the summer's crop of tomatoes from all over.
> And the cigar factory (can't remember its name) and E.L.Kerns Beverages on Smith Street. We used to watch the assembly line as the bottles went by and the machine put the caps on them. The lable [sic] had an elk on it for obvious reasons.
> Don't forget Artic Ice cream ... and the Chambersburg Dairy, a kid's dream. Those streets were very narrow with parking both sides and they were all one way EXCEPT for the one which led to the Dairy. The city made it so people could get there easily rather then having to go around the block even though two cars could barely pass each other on that street, esp. when it was full of parked cars.
> Hoffman doll factory, where one of my grandmothers worked. Once in a while the workers would throw dolls to us out of the windows. They were the "seconds" but we girls didn't care![41]

Not the Hoffman Doll factory, but in actuality, the Horsman Doll Factory.[42] Now abandoned, occupying a block in South Trenton at Grand Street, the Horsman Doll Factory was built in the 1930s of typical brick construction. Preservation New Jersey includes it on Mercer County, New Jersey's, ten most endangered buildings list for 2003 (and still threatened), and notes that it was considered in its day to be the largest doll factory in the United States.[43] It

*Horsman Doll Factory.* There is melancholia to an abandoned factory, particularly one that was nationally preeminent. Prior to World War I, dolls in the United States were generally imported; thereafter, companies like Horsman made its own dolls. When Shuman published her history of Trenton in 1958, she called it "the largest manufacturer of dolls in the United States" (Shuman 204).

ended production in the 1960s and at one point, had in excess of 800 employees. The large factory actually consisted of two connected three-story buildings, and several brick one-story additions.

The original Horsman dolls were created by Edward Imeson Horsman (1843–1927), who began his toy store in New York City in 1865. Horsman was born in Brooklyn, the son of an English immigrant father and Massachusetts mother. His original dolls were the cloth "Babyland Rag Dolls." Sometime in the 1920s the company ceased to be family controlled as a result of the premature death of Horsman's son and then, in 1927, of Horsman himself; thereafter, it acquired a competitor, Louis Amberg & Son, in 1930. The financially distressed company was acquired by the Trenton and New York–based doll company Regal Doll Manufacturing Company, originally known as the German Doll Company, but it changed its name in 1937 for obvious reasons. Regal already owned the underutilized Trenton factory at the Grand Avenue location. It acquired Horsman in 1933, but by 1940, only the Horsman name was being used.

Politically, the Horsman factory was an important player in the 1936 strike, when 600 workers walked out to organize, bucking both the owner as well as union leaders. By 1953 the company was in financial distress, and the factory was purchased by Botany Mills, Inc. In the 1980s the name was sold to Gata

Box, Ltd., in Hong Kong, where the dolls are now made. Horsman dolls remain collectors' items.

Reportedly, in the 1940s and 1950s the company's Trenton factory produced 12,000 dolls *per day* in the peak months of August and September.[44] The factory was also notable for making all components of the doll in the one place, including the body, outfit and boxes. Women operated the sewing machines and men the heavier blades to cut the fabric. As a result of cutbacks in material during World War II, Horsman developed an expertise in using vinyl, and while it was not the first to make plastic dolls, it become known for its extensive use of vinyl.

Horsman made German toys and items until the beginning of the 20th century, when the company began making composition dolls. Unlike European dolls made from porcelain or bisque, composition dolls were made of wood pulp and glue, and then painted. As such, they were more durable and less expensive than the porcelain and bisque dolls. Doll sizes ranged from 12 to 26 inches. The company also developed dolls that walked, used a kind of vinyl that dramatically improved the "skin" quality and look of the faces, and further introduced Saran fibers for hair on the dolls' heads.

As of this writing, the factory remains vacant, and though there has been some interest expressed in residential development, that has not borne fruit. All that action, and history, and now this abandoned, lost building. When you look at it, with its broken glass, it is like a sarcophagus.

Contrast this with an example of the successful re-use in the J.L. Mott Iron Works, which now constitutes a nursing and rehabilitation facility in South Trenton.[45] Jordan Lawrence Mott joined his father in the iron works business, and grew the company into a significant porcelain manufacturer. J.L. Mott Iron Works was incorporated in 1853. In 1866, the younger Mott took over, and in 1876, he moved its factory from New Haven, Connecticut, to Trenton. The Trenton factory was known for developing the built-in bathtub and also manufacturing plumbing supplies. A print from 1911 shows at least 15 buildings in the complex. The 1918 Industrial Directory of New Jersey described this factory as "probably the largest of its kind in the country."[46]

J.L. Mott Company, in 1873 has been reported to be "the first company to make bathtubs out of cast iron with a baked enamel finish," which superseded all other bathtubs.[47] J.L. Mott's patent survived challenge in federal court in New Jersey in 1907. The company acquired the Trenton Fire Clay and Porcelain Company in 1902, forming the Mott Company of New Jersey. This was the company that made the famous, and large, bathtub for heavy-set President William Howard Taft. By 1928, it was heavily in debt and despite selling to Lail Pottery Corporation in 1928, did not survive the 1930s.[48] J.L. Mott was also the subject of a verdict, among other porcelain manufacturers, for violating the antitrust laws in a suit brought by the United States.

And it is now a nursing home. But more to the point, there is a story behind each building, each physical representation and connection to the past. Those stories and personalities and histories become part of the tapestry of the city, and inform its present.

Perhaps less well known today was Trenton's place in the world of cigars. The Henry Clay and Bock Company cigar factory, located at 507 Grand Street in the Chambersburg area, was one of several cigar factories in Trenton that, according to one source, was one of the city's most significant industries.[49] Now utilized as residential units, this factory was one of several contributing to the prominence of Trenton as a manufacturer of cigars. The building is on the National Register of Historic Places. The factory is located within a larger residential area in South Trenton. The building, in Spanish Mission Revival style and modeled after a Cuban cigar factory, produced La Corona and other cigars from Cuban tobacco, and counted Winston Churchill as one of its customers. The Henry Clay factory was originally in Cuba; after a strike there in 1933, the company relocated its plant to Trenton. The factory's life ended in the 1960s with the mechanization of cigar making, the Cuban embargo and the company's relocation to Pennsylvania. Writing in 1899 about the cigar industry in Cuba, Robert Percival Porter noted in *Industrial Cuba* that the Henry Clay and Bock Company was one of the great Havana companies.[50] Interestingly, the cigar industry in New Jersey in general, and Trenton in particular, was a significant employer of women.[51]

Another example of urban readaptive use is the H.D. Lee Factory on East State Street, acquired in 1920, having first located to Trenton in 1917. The company began in Kansas City in 1912. Beginning in 1916, "it became the first clothing maker to start carrying a union label and consequently identified its popular coverall as "unionalls."[52] The factory was built the year the property was acquired, and it ceased operations in 1967. The New Jersey Historical Bridge Survey, addressing background to the small 1930 stringer bridge providing access to the plant, notes the factory "survives in a remarkably complete state of preservation and ranks as one of the finest examples of the Moderne style in the area. Lee, employing as many as 600 workers at its peak, was an important Trenton industry. The well-preserved facility, which symbolizes both Lee's corporate history and the industrial development and prosperity of Trenton, appears to be an eligible resource."[53] Lee Jeans continues to thrive today, though not in Trenton.

What is interesting about this building is that it is visible from downtown Trenton. Standing at the State Street overpass over Route 1, near the City Hall and federal courthouse, the Lee factory is seen down East State Street. It is a reminder of how close the factory was to the rest of Trenton, whether in residential areas or near the downtown.

Classic automobile aficionados will know the "Mercer Raceabout."[54] The Mercer Automobile Company was founded in 1909 by the Roebling and Kuser

*Lee Union Alls Factory.* Henry D. Lee began business in Kansas as H.D. Lee Mercantile Company in 1889. By 1899 he had expanded into other areas, including clothing. He designed his "union alls" for mechanics and farmers in 1915 and opened a factory that year in Kansas City. The company, ultimately dropping "Mercantile" from the name, established this factory in Trenton, New Jersey, on East State Street, which is now being converted to residential use.

families to replace the defunct Walter Automobile Company they had funded. The incorporators were Ferdinand W. Roebling, Sr., Anthony R. Kuser, John L. Kuser and Charles Roebling.[55] The Mercer Raceabout, selling for $1,950, was the outcome of this endeavor. Ferdinand Roebling, son of the Brooklyn Bridge builder, John A. Roebling, was president; industrialist and financier John L.

Kuser was secretary/treasurer. The factory was located at 400 Whitehead Road, just outside the Trenton city limits in Hamilton Township, the site of a Kuser abandoned brewery. The company experienced a riot during the industrial strike of 1914, with the plant closing until safety and order could be restored. In 1916 the company came out with the 22–73 models, a new series that held to the traditional Mercer but made refinements based on "simplicity." The company passed out of Roebling and Kuser hands in 1919 through merger, and went downhill until ceasing production in 1925.It had showrooms in Trenton, New York, Los Angeles and Chicago. According to an article in the May 19, 1909, *State Gazette*, the company was not yet even incorporated when it produced its prototypical model, and had orders for taxicabs.[56] Though its production lasted only fifteen years, "the Mercer Raceabout is considered the model sportscar of the era, the perfect blend of speed and finesse."[57]

I mention this factory and industry because it was a revelation to me. I had known, of course, of the three major industries, and some of the more peripheral ones. But it is worth noting, as a point of civic pride, that Trenton participated in a splashy way as a city in the history of the automobile in the United States. The intriguing thing about a city is that its past retains the ability to surprise in the present.

Another famous factory and another example of recycled building use in Trenton is the Exton Cracker Factory. In 1847 John and Adam Exton established a bakery on Centre Street, in what was then Lambert Town (now obviously part of Trenton). They shipped their product out through the Reading Freight Station on Willow Street, near the Battle Monument.[58] Over the next half century, the factory grew, in stages, with the Exton family continuing to own part of the site through the 1950s. In the new millennium, the success of the conversion was hailed in some quarters as evidence of success of the stimulus funding during the 2008–2010 recession.[59] The Oyster cracker is attributed to Adam Exton.[60]

And then there is ice. Originally built as a stable for the Roeblings, the Saxony Ice Company's building at 20 Swan Street in Chambersburg has been turned into readaptive use.[61] The breadth and diversity of Trenton's industrial output at the height of its prowess was staggering.[62]

But it was the big three — iron and steel, rubber, and ceramics— that dominated Trenton's brawn. One writer on the city has divided the steel industrial history of Trenton into three eras.[63] The first, from 1734 through 1800, saw the city's iron and steel works grow, supplying arms and weaponry for the Continental Army. With the discovery and development of anthracite coal in the Lake Superior region, Trenton's iron and steel industry faltered, the state's limited mines unable to compete. The second era, from 1840 through 1890, was led by the Trenton Iron Company, founded by industrialists Peter Cooper, James Hall, Edward Cooper and Abram S. Hewitt.[64] Peter Cooper was one of the 19th century's leaders of the Industrial Revolution, with the "Tom Thumb" engine

***Griffith Electric Supply Building.*** Across from the Sun National Bank Center Arena, on the fringe of South Trenton and part of the Ferry Historic District, this building is part of the Griffith Electric Supply company, founded in 1938. The main entrance is across the street. The sign proclaims it as the Dobbins Building, which was built in the 1880s and owned by John P. Dobbins. The company's website describes the building: "The historic Flat Iron Building still stands as a symbol of Griffith Electric Supply Co. Inc., at the intersection of Broad Street and Second Street in the heart of what was Trenton's industrial center."

to his credit. This plant was reported to the British Parliament to be "the leading establishment of the United States, not only in regard to production but also in regard to working arrangements. They produce rails, chains, and wire."[65] It was also the originator of the wrought iron beam that facilitated skyscraper construction. The company became the New Jersey Steel & Iron Company after the Civil War, was acquired by the American Bridge Company in 1900 and ceased production in 1976.[66] Trenton also made weaponry during the Civil War. The Trenton Iron Company, also known as Trenton Iron Works, produced the Trenton Springfield Rife, as well as mortar carriages for naval vessels.[67]

The importance of Trenton as a steel production center based on Cooper's plant was enhanced by the arrival of his friend,[68] engineer and industrialist John Augustus Roebling, to establish his wire rope factory. Perhaps the most famous of the factories in Trenton was the Roebling Steel and Wire Company, founded by Roebling. As described by David McCullough in his classic book on the Brooklyn Bridge:

> He was called a man of iron. Poised ... confident ... unyielding ... imperious ... severe ... proud ... are other words that would be used in Trenton to describe

him. There had always been something distant about him; he kept apart and had no real friends in Trenton, but he had always been accepted on those terms long since and he in turn was always extremely courteous to everyone. "He was always the first to say good morning," a man from the mill would tell a reporter after Roebling's death. When he spoke they listened.[69]

Born in the small German town of Mühlausen in 1806, he came to America in 1831 to found a Utopian colony with his brother. He held an engineering degree from the Royal Polytechnic Institute in Berlin, where he had studied bridge-building, hydraulics and architecture, among other related subjects, including studying under the philosopher Georg Hegel. He and his brother Karl bought land near Pittsburgh, and built their farming town, Saxonburg. By 1837, McCullough reports Roebling was "bored,"[70] and resumed his engineering work.

As he worked with dams, locks and railroads, he conceived the idea of replacing rope hawsers with iron rope, based on writings in Germany but not yet introduced into the United States. He made prototypical products in 1841 in Saxonburg with primitive equipment. In 1844 he used his product to fulfill a commission to build an aqueduct for the Pennsylvania Canal across the Allegheny River.

By 1847, though, it was apparent that Roebling needed a more propitious location to expand his business. He picked Trenton, after consultation with friend and fellow industrialist Peter Cooper (founder of Cooper Union in New York). Cooper was one of the co-founders in 1847 of the Trenton Iron Works, and now the site of KatManDu restaurant on the Delaware River, at the end of South Warren Street. As discussed in Chapter 9, thanks to the work of William Borrow, this facility produced the key iron beam that enabled skyscraper construction. Cooper's advice was not altogether altruistic; Hamilton Schuyler, in his book on the Roeblings, notes that Cooper "obviously had a shrewd eye open to the possibility of securing profitable relations with the new venture for the sale of his own products."[71] As it turned out, Roebling's plant became more of a competitor than purchaser of Cooper's products. Roebling envisioned an industrial center in Trenton, then a relatively small city of 6,000 people, but well-located between Philadelphia and New York, with excellent river, canal and rail transportation facilities, as well as readily available raw materials such as pig-iron and coal.[72] The location of the wire rope factory, purchased in 1848, was farmland in what was then Hamilton Township. Construction was completed in 1849.

The site encompasses some 45 acres. The machine shop, built originally in 1890, houses the science center. The administration building of the factory now houses Mercer County Administrative offices, and features a small suspension bridge connecting the building to another — one of two suspension bridges in Trenton, the other being a small "model" of the Brooklyn Bridge in Stacy Park.

Roebling's sons, Ferdinand W. Roebling, Charles G. Roebling and Washington Augustus Roebling, became instrumental in the business, John A. Roebling's Sons Company. Ferdinand and Charles acted more on the financial and sales side and Washington on the engineering side, the latter including the conclusion of the Brooklyn Bridge construction following John Roebling's death.[73] By the 1870s business had expanded beyond bridge construction and comparable uses to the communications area, and others.

As a result of the need to expand, though, the sons decided to move the business to a new town south of Trenton, creating Roebling, New Jersey, as the site for the other mills, including a "steel mill, blooming mill, rod mills, wire mills, cleaning houses, annealing and tempering shops and a woven wire fabrics factory."[74] John Roebling's grandsons, Karl W. Roebling and Ferdinand William Roebling, Jr., took over the company and remained in control until 1936, at which time control passed to a cousin, William A. Anderson. In 1974, the Roebling plants shut down.

An article in *The Times* in May 2009 indicated potential interest in developers in the site.[75] The site remains a curiosity in Trenton, a kind of open-air museum that, with appropriate signage, and both financial and political commitment, should be developed into usable office buildings and educational facilities.

The third steel era began after World War II in 1948 with United State Steel's acquisition of the Fairless Works across the Delaware River from Trenton.[76] This was seen as beneficial to Trenton, even if not within the city's borders, to the extent it would act as a magnet for the region. Shuman's book was published in 1958; its optimistic tone has been belied by the facts of history. Robert P. Rogers notes in his more recent *An Economic History of the American Steel Industry* that "it is hard to draw any definite conclusion about the performance of the steel industry during the 1950s and 1960s.... Numerous causes of the later decline [in the 1970s and 1980s] could be traced to the postwar period, including unhealthy labor relations, technological conservatism, and disorderly add-on expansion."[77] From 1970 through 1989, production fell, and layoffs resulted due to a variety of factors, such as changes in the production process and how the technologies were implemented, much of which was impeded by lack of capital resulting from the 1982 recession.[78] In addition, in this period, consumption and shipments fell, due to declines in such sectors as "automobile, containers, oil and gas, railroads, and industrial and electrical machinery."[79]

Steel attracts us. Maybe it is the ultimate connotation of power, of consummate strength. Pottery breaks, and rubber bends, but we refer to steel nerves and steel personalities to connote unyielding commitment. We speak of iron will. As we walk about this city, and consider the details of what we see, we reflect on the histories and lives who are now figments of imagination but who were once the "broad shoulders" of this place.

The second industry of the triumvirate was pottery. Trenton is particularly proud of J.L. Mott Company's massive 600 pound 50 gallon bathtub produced in 1909 for President Taft.[80] Fostered by the clay deposits in central New Jersey, Trenton's pottery industry dates to 1723 and John de Wilde's establishment.[81] However, the first "permanent" pottery has been identified as established around the 1730s in the vicinity of North Warren Street and St. Mary's Cathedral.[82] It was not until the 1850s and the Civil War era, though, that the city's pottery industry came into its own, fueled by the need for sanitation pottery. Among the reasons for its development was the development of hotels, improved housing, and a general improvement in the "American standard of living."[83]

Trenton's pottery industry established itself as a force in the 1850s with two companies—Taylor and Speeler, and William Young & Co.[84] Trenton held sway for a century as one of the country's major pottery centers.[85]

Two names stand out in the pantheon of Trenton pottery: Maddock and Lenox. Walter Scott Lenox was born in Trenton in 1859 was according to Shuman's almost Dickensian account was one of "[m]any Trenton boys in the late 19th century ... ambitious to become ceramists."[86] With several others he formed the Ceramic Art Company in 1889, which he wholly owned by 1894. His vision was to create ceramics "that had all the beauty of Belleek [an Irish-made ceramic with egg-shell texture] but greater translucency and strength.[87] Lenox himself suffered paralysis and blindness, yet prevailed in establishing his company as a worldwide leader: "From London to Istanbul, from Caracus [sic] to Teheran, in more than 30 United States embassies, legations and consulates, Lenox has been used as the official china. Presidents of Ecuador, Cuba, Venezuela and Mexico, many state governors and other dignitaries use china made at the famous Trenton plant."[88]

The other major figure, Thomas Maddock, headed the largest sanitary-ware company in the country, and among the largest in the world, commencing in 1872.[89] Beginning with an interest in a pottery in the Ewing/Carroll area, he developed appropriate formulas that accommodated new firing methods to better the glazing. Apparently his efforts concerned his partners from a cost perspective, and ultimately, buying them out, he formed Thomas Maddock and Sons. Successful, the business expanded and, according to Shuman, "in 1895, 100 per cent of all sanitary-ware of the United States was made here [in Trenton]."[90]

And then there was rubber, the third of the trio of Trenton's great industries. I mentioned in the last chapter the famous Goodyear rubber case argued and won by Daniel Webster. The city's rubber industry commenced in the 1850s when a small rubber plant was established and then ultimately acquired by Hiram P. Dunbar and Garret Schenck; it concentrated on small items, such as rubber dolls.[91] In 1856, Goodyear Rubber Company considered Trenton. Its agent, Charles Meade, made a site visit, charged Dunbar with patent infringement, and the resultant victory for Goodyear solidified its position in the city in particular and in the rubber industry in general.[92] Goodyear was also successful in its famous victory in 1852 through its counsel, Daniel Webster, against the infringer, Horace H. Day, of New Brunswick over vulcanization.[93] Although once known as the "tire capital" of the country (due to its eastern location, Detroit-manufactured automobiles could be fitted with additional tires to save shipping costs), it fell victim to the costs of infrastructure to accommodate changing production methods after World War I.[94]

The Roebling and Maddock families were among the more important families in Trenton civil society during its "Golden Age." With the end of the 19th century and the beginning of the 20th, though, social as well as economic forces began to gnaw at the industrial roots of the city and ultimately contribute to the loss of Trenton's factory civilization. By the 1920s, national capitalism "eclipsed" the local civil capitalism.[95] One example was the purchase by U.S. Steel of the Trenton Iron Works and the New Jersey Steel Company.[96] But apart from national capitalism and a spreading of the city's industries into national markets and national concerns, labor and capital on the municipal level fissured. In 1914, the International Association of Machinists sought standardization of wages based on skill, and a system for arbitration. Though many factory owners agreed, the largest — including Roebling — did not. On June 1, 1914, the strike began. It lasted for three months, ending in August as a result of economic depression, scabs, and the threat of intervention of the state militia.[97]

Trenton's Golden Age staggered on past World War I and into the 1920s. Two strikes erupted in 1925 and 1926. Following the Great Depression and World War II, Trenton, like other cities of its kind, entered the 1950s with "decline of manufacturing and the increased bureaucratization of jobs in the manufacturing sector [which] combined with an increased growth of service and government jobs."[98] Other factors contributing to the decline of the factory society was the fact that the city's "work force became increasingly divided between older male industrial workers and younger female service workers."[99] The city's loss of manufacturing caused its citizens to look afield for employment; that movement coincided with the change in ethnic and racial composition within the city, creating a different social dynamic that ultimately exploded in the riots in the 1960s.[100] The major forces of the era of the automobile and the electric grid shrank distances and diminished the need for physical centralized cities like Trenton.[101]

I have a personal and singular footnote in the history of the Roebling factory. I represented Trenton Studios, Inc., in a lawsuit brought by the Mercer County Improvement Authority to recover a portion of the old Roebling plant that had been sold to this company, affiliated with Manex Entertainment, the company that did the special effects for the first *Matrix* movie. Trenton Studios had missed payments on its mortgage, and the creditor, the MCIA, sued both in foreclosure and for forfeiture and money damages. I became involved somewhat late in the proceedings, and took the matter through an unsuccessful appeal. The unreported decision is captioned *Mercer County Improvement Authority v. Trenton Studios, Inc.*, DOCKET NO. A-2475–06T32475–06T3, decided October 11, 2007.[102]

But more to the point, if anything symbolizes the industrial revolution and the might of Trenton and the 19th century promise of America, it is the Roebling facility. And if anything speaks to us from the grave, it is this factory site.

A full history of industrial Trenton, both specifically to its factories and how it fits in, is beyond my endeavors here. Look at the images of factories in this book. They are the briefest of examples of the richness and power of this city. They enable us to reflect not just on 19th-century capitalism, but on the lives of those who were part of this place. They are bookmarks themselves to America.

Every factory has a story. Individually, each employed real people, individual stories in themselves. Important stories, probably most passed down

*Exton Cracker Factory.* Created by Adam Exton in his bakery, which stood on this site, the oyster cracker is a Trenton invention, and the Victorian-era factory still stands on Centre Street, now converted to lofts. In the Ferry Historic District in South Trenton on Centre Street, the building dates to 1847. It remains remarkable, perhaps, to consider the proximity of factory and housing and reflect upon the one-time integration of industry and residence, in light of the post–World War II zoning revolution that segregated city areas of use. Leading "new urban" critics call for a return to the integration of use in the contemporary city.

*Sherman Avenue.* This residential street in East Trenton was named for former Trenton mayor William P. Sherman. Part of the East Trenton neighborhood, these rowhouses were typical of housing in the late 19th century for local factory workers.

*East Trenton.* The intersection of St. Joe's Avenue and North Olden Avenue in East Trenton reveals a desolate scene. Factories and industrial buildings were predominant in the area, and are still visible from Route 1 traveling into the city. Off the highway, the area is primarily residential. Graffiti adorn the water tower.

anecdotally within families. These people got up, often walked to their factories for their shifts from their nearby rowhouses, put in their physical labor, and returned home. They lived and died in Trenton. These buildings are as much memorial to them and to the history of industrial America; in the post-industrial city, they take on the shape, form and meaning of remembrance. They are private diaries of the unspoken thoughts, the hardships and injustices as well as achievements, of those who built the nation. Think about this when you look at the broken glass, or the weeds growing between the bricks. Take nothing for granted. These hulking skeletons that permeate the city keep the past in the present.

Sherman Avenue is in Trenton's East Trenton area, cut off by Route 1 and railroad tracks from the North Trenton and Top Road sections, and flows into the Coalport/North Clinton areas. According to the Trenton Historical Society, the street was named for William P. Sherman, a former mayor of the city.[103] Today it is a street of rowhouses, with abandoned and boarded-up ones sandwiched between occupied ones.[104] The area known as East Trenton was originally part of Trenton when it was incorporated as a city in 1792, but became part of Lawrence Township, then was its own township called Milham Township (which included the Top Road area) until 1888, when it rejoined Trenton. It became a factory area with numerous mills, due to the proximity of the Assunpink Creek, and then in particular, rubber and pottery. Consistent with its industrial character, the housing was built to accommodate the workers. Anyone traveling the Northeast Corridor by train can see that rowhouse construction was typical in Eastern seaboard cities. Trenton, Philadelphia, Baltimore — look out the train as you go past.

Walk Sherman Avenue. Stand in East Trenton. Look at the factories and the rowhouses. It is here that the industrial most meaningfully contrasts with the post-industrial.

# 7. The Urbanist City

A mid–November night, and I am driving down East State Street from Hamilton into Trenton to attend a function at Marsilio's in Chambersburg. As of this writing, the restaurant is no longer functioning as a restaurant; after over 50 years of operation, it now provides catering and private party services. It is not alone. The great days of Chambersburg as a restaurant venue may be over; restaurateurs blame crime in the city and the attractions and convenience of suburban restaurants.[1] I have also heard this anecdotally. This night, though, was a retirement party for the outgoing acting director of the New Jersey State Museum.

This portion of East State Street consists of red brick rowhouses on either side of the street, cutting through the heart of the East Ward of Trenton. It is dark, with few streetlights, and those not particularly illuminating. Few people are on the streets, shadows barely glimpsed. There is the occasional bar or "night club," so proclaimed. But what is striking is the pervasive darkness, the almost complete absence of lights in windows. It is as if the city has been abandoned or is under occupation.

> [Interlude]
> "At one time, Chambersburg ('The 'Burg,' in local parlance) had as many as a dozen tomato pie establishments. Everyone had neon signs that vertically spelled out T-O-M-A-T-O-P-I-E-S," says Azzaro. "Then neon got expensive, so to be more economical, they started calling it pizza." The plenitude of pies, plus numerous bars and nightclubs, made Trenton a popular stop for sports and musical celebrities travelling between New York and Philadelphia in the 1950s and '60s. Lining the walls at Papa's and the two DeLorenzo's Tomato Pies are photos of stars (some who have eaten at the restaurants)— Jimmy Durante, Louis Prima, Keely Smith, Joe DiMaggio, and Vic Damone, to name a few. ...
> Outside Trenton, the term tomato pie is little known.[2]

I noted earlier the feel of a city and the sense of place. There are some places, like nearby Princeton, whose central downtown area with its coffeeshops, microbrewery, movie theater, bookstore, record store, clothing shops, jewelry

## 7. The Urbanist City

***Chambersburg.*** Already well-known as an identifiable part of South Trenton, Chambersburg is a principal setting for novelist Janet Evanovich's bounty-hunting Stephanie Plum and her improbable adventures. Chambersburg has also been known for its restaurants; although anecdotally, the author has been told that some have closed and business has fallen off as a ramification of the gang violence that has plagued the city. Nearby, is Delorenzo's Tomato Pies, one of the city's more famous eating establishments, and not to be confused with Pete Lorenzo's restaurant near the train station, a traditional haunt for politicians and businesspeople that has now gone out of business. In addition to the tomato pie, Trenton has been known to have other particularized names for food — such as "pencil points" for penne pasta.

stores and university campus could be a component of a city section. It could serve as a neighborhood of any major city. The difference is that if one walks far enough, one enters the small town, and knows it is not an urban environment. It lacks size. It lacks the *sense* of a city. It may be *urbane*, but it is not *urbanist*. The urbanist city needs to be large enough so that one can move from neighborhood to neighborhood, and still feel part of the fabric of the city. The city, and that feeling, deteriorates gradually. As Rae puts it, a downtown shop closes, and a new one miles away in the suburbs opens; before we are aware of it, these "small changes" have destroyed the city.[3]

New York, Chicago, Boston, Philadelphia. There are large, "world-class" cities, places that are unquestionably of a certain urban character. They look like cities as we envision cities, and they act like cities as we understand urban culture. They are what Jane Jacobs has called "great cities," as I noted earlier. And yet, each city is an aggregate of neighborhoods and separate "villages"

***Corner of East State Street and Logan Avenue.*** Entering the Wilbur neighborhood from the east, at the border of the city, a ruined building ironically posts a realtor's sign near the door. The sign states the building is available. Welcome to the post-industrial small city.

***East State Street Rowhouses.*** These rowhouses, in the Wilbur area of Trenton in the East Ward, are reflective of the variety of this form of urban housing.

within the city. Within New York City, as a student at NYU Law School in Greenwich Village, I wandered the dogleg and near-hidden streets of the West Village—and was in a different world from that merely a few blocks away, on Bleeker Street and Washington Square Park. A city is more than blocks and neighborhoods. You steep yourself in it, and you stand back from it, and you never get the dispositive angle on it.

Even in the 1990s, when urban decline was at the center of political discourse, there were voices continuing to urge that cities—the small as well as the large—continued to provide essential functions in terms of "homes, work, education and entertainment."[4] At the beginning and end of the day, the essential realization must be—too often ignored by the planners, theoreticians and politicians—that "[w]hat is sad is the inability of our adversarial political system to come to grips with the idea that cities are made up of people and it is they who make—or mar—the city."[5]

One writer, Brian Robson, has offered two factors that he has observed as contributing to the deterioration of the city and its urban civilization that are directly applicable to Trenton: decline in population (which, in Trenton's case, continued past the 1990s and into the 2000s), and indicators of economic and social distress. He contends that while urban policy benefited from expenditure of funds and public-private partnerships, it has failed in terms of a coherent strategy. On the other hand, certain European cities have turned around based on factors such as public-private partnerships that also involve higher education institutions, focused sectoral development, emphasized marketing to cities in terms of their entertainment facilities and inter-city collaboration.[6]

He concludes:

> Coherent urban policy which incorporated consistency and compassion has certainly been lacking. There have been well-meant ideas and occasional effective actions, but not enough and, as with the recent axing of the Urban Programme, often curtailed when achieving some success. Yet a civilized society depends on the successful survival of its cities. It is the hallmark of people trying to live together successfully and peacefully. Until this last part of the twentieth century, the balance always seemed to be tipping to make life in the cities better. Despite years of environmental damage, economic slump and the destruction of war, there always seemed to be a will to try to improve. There was hope. The danger we now face is the loss of that will and the snuffing out of the flickering candle of hope. No city, no civilization.[7]

In discussing the persistence of memory in Trenton and its particular identity, I had occasion to quote Douglas Rae's definition of urbanism. His factors were more of a definition of the city itself, but part of his concept of urbanist existence is more subjective: again, he wrote, "urbanist city was full of citizens who were committed to it."[8] Can we say this about Trenton? We spent some time considering Trenton as a city against the various definitions and conceits of what makes the political or sociological or even physical city. From the history and the old photographs, it would appear that Trenton experienced a commitment, not just by a few political or social leaders, but by a broader base. Even if they were not committed to the same ideology, there does seem to have been a commitment to the city. Does such a Rae-defined urbanist commitment exist today? Can we identify a particular Trentonian culture? I do not attempt an answer; I merely pose the question.

Attempting to focus on the culture of the American city as it developed in the 19th century, Gunther Barth looked at several discrete factors that enabled a variety of immigrants, from vastly different backgrounds, to nonetheless develop a particularized American urban culture: the manner in which space was divided within the city, urban newspapers, department stores, ballparks, and vaudeville houses. The city's "cultural forms" and institutions were a response to the particularities of urban life and an urbanist existence. People's notions of space, both private and public, were shaped by the exigencies of the physical nature of the city. He summarizes the interplay between the institutions therefore created as part of an urbanist existence and the physical space issues of the city:

> In the apartment house they adapted private space to a spatially divided city. The received from the metropolitan press the pieces of an urban identity and a language for communicating with each other. The department stores assured women a place in city life, and they in turn made downtown the center of urban elegance. In the ball park men were exposed to the meaning of rules in the modern city and to that basic form of urban leisure, watching others do things. The vaudeville house brought a sense of common humanity to diverse people, who emerged from the experience with social skills and cultural values that helped them cope with the intricacies of metropolitan life.[9]

Trenton as a city saw development of each of these four spaces. The 19th century saw the rise and fall of several papers, with *The Times* (then known as *The Trenton Times*) emerging in the late 19th century. It entered professional baseball's arena in 1883 with a minor league team in the Interstate League.[10] The city boasted several significant department stores.[11] The Trent Theatre was built in the early years of the 20th century for vaudeville[12]; the building was razed in 1976. The Taylor Opera House was built in 1867 and hosted Mark Twain, Ethel Barrymore and George M. Cohan; in 1921 it was converted to the Capital Theatre and is now memorialized by historical marker off South Broad Street. At one time or another, some 28 movie theaters existed in Trenton, all of which were closed or demolished or both.[13]

The same basic features of the "Gilded Age" city at the end of the 19th century and beginning of the 20th century were noted by Trachtenberg in *The Incorporation of America*: the city newspaper, department store, spectator sports, land speculation and building, the emphasis on architecture — all were part of the emerging industrial American city as marketplace.[14] Americans had always been ambivalent about their cities; Trachtenberg notes the contrast between American predilections for the shining city on the hill on the one hand, and the evils of the city *qua* Sodom and Gomorrah on the other, traced through the nation's Puritan roots. What ceased to be ambivalent was the capitalistic blood of the American city. Indeed, Monti describes the American city as the product of a bourgeois people; he calls cities "palaces of leisure."[15]

The city facilitated a particular lifestyle. It was a place of strangers, and yet it was a place of particular families that dominated its social structure. We can think back to the opening chapter and Masereel's visual image of the city, and now fill in the details. We can see a pattern of activity, a particular kind of civilization — an American civilization, an urban existence — that developed as a result of broad national events and localized interactions. In the middle of this is Trenton, a microcosm for what was occurring in industrial cities up and down the East Coast, and along the rivers and in the industrial heartland. Trenton allows us to see the patterns, make the connections. Its history is that of the country; its present reflective of the expiration of a particular way of life, and the opportunity for reinvention. Our minds may wander, and let us see where they go, and to what they return. For that is the city: a parallel to our own lives, a piece of our civilization, of our being and ethos.

Which brings us to downtown, immortalized in Petula Clark's eponymous song. Downtowns were the unifying core for the city's various neighborhoods.[16] They peaked in the 1950s, as did the American city, at least as it had been understood. Johns refers to that period, of the way the city and its lifestyle was, as dramatically different from the present because the city of the 1950s reflected "an overall cultural coherence."[17] That cultural coherence is not necessarily cause for nostalgia. The American city of the 1950s — and in particular downtown — was in many ways a racist and sexist place. Women held secretarial positions and stores catered to their perceived roles as the household shoppers. As Andres Duany et al note in *Suburban Sprawl*, "America's inner cities did not wither all at once, or by chance ... [r]acism, redlining, and the concentration of subsidized housing projects destabilized and isolated the poor...."[18]

Trenton's downtown was formed from the original Trent Town's King, Queen and Second streets, today's Warren, Broad and State streets. This was the core of the city, the scene of the First Battle of Trenton. From this heart grew the retailing establishments and offices. Trenton was "the city" to the surrounding towns, perhaps even more so than New York or Philadelphia, for a brief and shining period.

Downtown America was a place of entertainment, of style, of fashion, of business. It was the stuff of *The Man in the Gray Flannel Suit* and the business culture following World War II. In 1950, Trenton's downtown in a dense and compact city had posh hotels, movie theaters, department stores, and crowded streets. A photograph from 1946 in the *Mercer Messenger*[19] of State and Broad streets shows a remarkable scene. Cars, buses and pedestrians converge and crowd each other; this could be almost any street in New York. We note Trachtenberg's characterization: "Of all city spectacles, none surpassed the giant department store, the emporium of consumption born and nurtured in these years."[20] The massive shape of Dunham's Department Store, tall bank buildings—this was a city. This was a downtown. This was Trenton. Duany, who spent time in Trenton, notes that "fifty years ago, America's cities provided a pedestrian environment that compared favorably with the world's best cities. What has happened in the intervening decades has been sheer lunacy: in an attempt to lure auto-dependent suburbanites downtown, consultants of every ilk turned our cities into freeways."[21] Like the John Fitch Way, that is, Route 29, that severed Trenton from its wonderful riverfront park area in the name of the trinity of the automobile, progress and business.

And Trenton, like other cities, lost its retailers. Lost its offices to the suburbs. Lost its crowds to the suburban malls.

[Interlude]
*An animal rights protest directed against McDonald's methods of slaughtering chickens ruffled a few feathers yesterday afternoon at the restaurant's Cass Street location.*

**Downtown.** The clear lines of downtown Trenton's buildings are reminiscent of Precisionist paintings of this subject matter. To a large extent, the density of office and residential buildings conform to our image of a city, as distinct from simply a large town or village. The downtown today bears almost no resemblance to the vibrant, dynamic commercial and office center depicted in photographs from the early 20th century.

7. *The Urbanist City* 143

***North Broad Street.*** During Trenton's "Golden Age," Broad Street was part of the downtown shopping area. At present, its retail establishments are on a much smaller scale. Gone are the large department stores, named for the doyens of the city's retailing, such as Donnelly and Dunham, who also served on the boards of the city's leading banks and financial institutions.

> *Members of People for the Ethical Treatment of Animals (PETA) organized a small protest on the sidewalk outside the fast food restaurant, holding up signs reading, "McCruelty, I'm hatin' it," as part of a demonstration calling on McDonald's to change its slaughtering procedures."*[22]

Lest we glamorize a past that exists only in Frank Capra–style movies, we should remember that even Bedford Falls was probably not Bedford Falls. It may be a wonderful life in Capra-land, but reality is stubborn. We speak of Trenton's "Golden Age," but the urbanist city of the time was not always captured in the warm sepia-toned photographs of the time. As Rae notes of New Haven, the urbanist city at its peak nonetheless "was redolent of garbage, its streets littered with manure," marked by substandard housing for its workers, rivers fouled with human waste, cacophonous street noise from trolleys and equipment, shocking mortality rates, disease and deformity; "bigotry was routine.... Ethnic slurs ... were for many urbanites the ordinary barking noises of social distance."[23]

These specific features were not unique to New Haven. Jacob Riis told us "how the other half lives" toward the conclusion of the 19th century. New Jersey's cities were comparable: "The post–Civil War city in the United States was generally ill-built and ugly. New Jersey was no exception."[24] Particularly in Essex and Hudson Counties, people died from asthma, diarrhea and tuberculosis caused by the polluted rivers. Industrial accidents killed and injured. And the "saloon" became a fixture of the state's cities for relief.[25]

What was a physical manifestation in the 1950s was also a reflection of cultural and societal attitudes that could not abide, and did not survive. It is foolish to think they can be separated. We need to think of the new city, the new downtown, the new urban center, the new anchor for neighborhoods, in the context of the now, not the then. And we also have to recognize the realities of the digital, technological age and the presence of gangs.

North Broad Street was part of Trenton's downtown, with the core of that downtown along Warren Street, West State Street and Broad Street. The old photographs seem a work of fiction, a scene from another planet. Tall buildings, crowds, hotels, cars, stores—a place. An urban place. In the late 20th century, Trenton's great experiment with the Trenton Commons failed; no anchor stores returned to the pedestrianized East State Street. Today, a few sparks of life show up on Warren Street, but Nassau Street in Princeton, 20 minutes away, attracts more throngs to its small-town atmosphere than urban Trenton.

To be sure, the fate of Trenton's downtown is not solely due to safety concerns; small-town America has lost considerable ground to the shopping malls, for a myriad of reasons. Trenton is not alone, and is prototypical of the story of the post-industrial American city. Regardless, today North Broad Street seems a sad place, with a few retailers and a few shoppers. The downtown appears desultory, dispirited. It will take more than a few urban homesteading shopkeepers and "downtown associations" to turn it around. There needs to be a vision, but there also needs to be the perception and, fundamentally, the reality of the safe streets of Jane Jacobs. Of course there needs to be money, but money cannot reinvent a place by itself. There needs to be political will and commitment. Maybe it can come back. Some places do. Some places don't.

For now, Trenton's downtown is not merely a shadow of its former self. It is virtually non-existent. While kudos goes to the few businesses that attempt to revive it, we need to be realistic and call it what it is. People are not driving into Trenton on a Friday or Saturday night to windowshop, eat dinner, and catch the theater. They may go to the ballpark or the arena, but they generally do not wander State and Broad streets at night for their coffeeshops. Self-delusion and are knee-jerk reactions to "gentrification" are not viable pieces of urban planning, any more than is ignorance of the needs and desires of current neighborhoods and those who live in them. And a city strapped for cash, as so many cities, can only count on its government for so much, particularly if the tax base continues to decline. Cities that have brought themselves back have done so with a consensus on revival. A city that remains divided against itself as to what it wants to be, cannot be. The fears of disappearance of the city's central business district, its downtown core, have not been completely realized. To an extent, cities have revitalized their central business district, often in a "gentrified" way, so that more "meat and potatoes" stores have been replaced by boutiques; older, landmark buildings have been readapted and protected.[26] Examples of this might be Greenville, South Carolina, and Baltimore's Inner Harbor area.

As we walk Broad Street, the main shopping venue of this downsized, post-industrial city, we are walking down contemporary America. We are experiencing the most recent set of paragraphs in a long chapter.

Robert M. Fogelson calls downtown "a uniquely American phenomenon," but it now is neither what it was in the first quarter of the 20th century, either as word or place: "By the late nineteenth century it evoked a sense of bustle, noise, and avarice, just as uptown, the fashionable residential district, evoked elegance, gentility, and sophistication. As they years passed, however, many Americans began to regard downtown as déclassé, even disreputable."[27] Its change has been not only in denotation, but also as *place*, as skyscrapers and office parks spread to the peripheries and suburbs. "Downtown" as such is now no longer seen as a necessary predicate to the American city.[28] And while some may harbor the sentiment that downtowns are returning, Fogelson disputes that: downtown *qua* downtown, or at least the American downtown of film and literature, and the 1920s, is gone.[29] Technology made possible the experience of the elements of culture without the need for concentration, as found in such places as the Route 1 corridor just outside Trenton.[30]

Downtown was geographic; in New York, it was the southern tip of Manhattan in the 1830s and 1840s. It was a place of business, and assumed that role in small as well as larger cities. By 1900 it had taken on the connotation of the city's business district.[31] It was a place of railroads and skyscrapers, of professional offices and courts, of hotels and entertainment, of shops — all generally a relatively finite, and therefore congested, area. As the noise and congestion increased, so the residential population decreased. And it was this schism between business and residential uses that marked the transformation of the larger cities by the end of the 19th century and the smaller cities by the beginning of the 20th century.[32] The congregation of competitive and non-competitive businesses in the same area served the utilitarian function of convenience for meetings and concourse, and also proximity to transportation facilities. And while some were concerned about the political consequences of class disparity as wealthier residents moved from downtown, Fogelson notes "most Americans" considered this "residential dispersal as an extremely auspicious development."[33] Good city planning, in the influential view of some, accommodated separation of home and workplace. And it was this "belief in spatial harmony" that justified this separation and also prevented suburbs from viewing cities as threats, and vice versa.[34] The downtown became the city, and the city, its downtown. By the 1920s — the peak of Trenton's "Golden Years" — downtown was a thriving place. Pictures from the period show vibrancy.

Within twenty minutes of Trenton area two full-sized shopping malls — Oxford Valley, in Pennsylvania, and Quaker Bridge, a few miles north on Route 1. A little farther afield in Pennsylvania is Neshaminy Mall, and in New Jersey, the Menlo Park and Woodbridge Malls to the north, and so forth. Beyond these larger-scale malls are the smaller boutique malls, such as Market Fair in nearby

West Windsor, and the "box store" sites (words do not yet exist to adequately describe these parking lot fiestas) of Nassau Park, where Wal-Mart and others stake their claim.

It is remarkable to visit these places on a weekend. They assume the atmosphere of a family outing. Husbands, wives, couples, and children arrive and infiltrate. Where families once walked downtown in a city, they now walk across vast stretches of lined pavement to move from giant box to giant box. The boxes are externally fungible, and wear the brand insignia of their national birthright. You can be in New Jersey or Illinois or California or South Carolina; the boxes and logos are the same. They have replaced the urban downtown in the "edge city."

But on a Saturday morning in Trenton, sparse knots of people traverse the intersection of Broad and Market, and beyond that, the few lone walkers. A few cars up and down State Street. No traditional department stores. Not even a movie theater. The last movie I saw in Trenton was the original *Exorcist*.

In the urbanist city, streets provide a sense of place. In virtually every city there is one street, or one intersection, that is synonymous with the city. Hollywood and Vine for Hollywood, or Los Angeles. Fifth Avenue or Times Square

*Corner of Market and Broad.* With a hint of a Western town, the intersection of Broad and Market streets in Mill Hill is a far cry from the open-air market that once graced its namesake street. Sometimes we are left only with street names to remind us of historical significance.

for New York. Piccadilly Circus in London. In Newark, it is Broad Street, or more particularly, the Four Corners Historic District at Broad and Market. Trenton has State Street. Atlantic City is a Monopoly board. In New Brunswick, George Street is perhaps its defining artery. Elizabeth has South Broad. Camden has Broadway, but perhaps Market and Federal streets are the more well-known. In Jersey City, it is less a question of streets than squares: Journal Square, Pavonia, Exchange Place, Newport.

What do these cities look like from ground level? It varies, of course. It is always intriguing to see the jumble of architecture, the clash of styles. Old and new. The up and down silhouette of uneven buildings, some even crooked, old brick, next to glass and steel. A city resembling an ill-fitting jigsaw. But in such combinations we find character.

In his study of urban elements, *The City Assembled*, Spiro Kostof writes:

> The history of the street has yet to be written, either as urban form or as institution. It should, of course, be both. For on the one hand, the street clearly belongs to the history of architecture and urban design in the strict sense of physical fact. The street is an entity made up of a roadway, usually a pedestrian way, and flanking buildings. How each one of these is articulated, how they interact, in what ways the design of the street walls is controlled and guided — these are questions of form pure and simple. There is the matter of sidewalks; of street furniture; of paving; of trees and greenery — each with its own, as yet very incompletely known, story....
> 
> But the street as an institution is an equally critical subject. Beyond its architectural identity, every street has an economic function and social significance. The purposes of the street traditionally have been traffic, the exchange of goods, and social exchange and communication.[35]

Kostof puts the first "conscious street" in Khirokitia, in the sixth millennium BC.[36]

There are different types of traditional, intentionally designed streets: canal streets, bridge streets, boulevards (wide streets, covered streets). All streets, though, embodied a battle between public and private interests. While private streets as such were the exception rather than the rule, the war was played out in such battlefields as signage. For example, what rights are there to hang out a shingle on the public street advertising one's shop? This was the subject of legislation in 18th century England. Today, we speak of air rights and rights of views.

This politics of signage is interesting. In their work, *Learning from Las Vegas*, architects Robert Venturi, Denise Scott Brown and Steven Izenour refer to the "architecture of persuasion" on the street, or the strip, and note that "in the narrow streets of the medieval town, although signs occur, persuasion is mainly through the sight and smell of the real cakes through the doors and windows of the bakery. On Main Street, shop-window displays for pedestrians along the sidewalks and exterior signs, perpendicular to the street for motorists, dominate the scene almost equally."[37]

**Grant Avenue.** Trenton's planning maps put this street within the East Trenton "neighborhood," but the North Ward Historic Resource Survey locates it squarely within the Coalport/North Clinton area. Regardless, the street has distinctive rowhouses marked by these eyebrow windows.

Today in Trenton, as opposed to the old photograph, the signage is minimal and purely functional. There is no persuasion, no advertising as such. The audience for persuasion is dwindling.

Among my trove of photographs of Trenton is a scene from the Trenton Commons in 1999, before it was reopened to vehicular traffic; it shows three men sitting on the brick window ledge of the old City Hall at the corner of Broad and State, at the time a fast food place. A woman is about to walk past them. Through the prism of Trenton, let us make a connection to literature and the City itself. In one of his "Cities and Memories" chapters, Calvino writes of the now-rough city of Isidora, once known for its telescopes and violins: "In the square there is the wall where the old men sit and watch the young go by; he is seated in a row with them. Desires are already memories."[38] Trenton's memories are visible in the streets. They are in the minds of the people who are at home here, who remember a city of violins and telescopes. They still sit on this ledge in Trenton.

Consider the "street." The street remains important because the street is where we live. The street is where we connect, both physically and emotionally, with our city. This has importance to the photographer; as Helen Liggett has observed in her chapter devoted to "the street' in *Urban Encounters*, "Instances of connectiveness with existence make street photography part of the art of existence."[39]

One of the essential American "street photographers" of the 20th century, Bruce Davidson, understood the magic of the street. Among his projects was photographing one street in particular — East 100th Street in New York City. What compelled him? What distinguishes one street from another? The street became intertwined with lives of the people who lived on it. He wrote that "sometimes I had to force myself to go to the block because I was afraid to break the painful barrier of their poverty. But once I was there and made contact with someone and felt connected, I never wanted to leave."[40] I will emphasize one picture of his in particular — an apartment house fills over 95 percent of the frame, with a small strip across the top to show the sky and other buildings, and a small triangle of space in the bottom left, where a dozen or so people are standing around. Some are conversing with each other. One is looking into a doorway, another out into the street. The overwhelming composition of the image, though, is geometric — rectangular windows and diagonal fire escapes, all dark against a dark building.

We can find this beauty and essentiality in Trenton, if we look.

The street has also become, in some places, a barrier, if not a border both physical and psychological. As noted, Route 29 in Trenton scythed Mahlon Stacy Park from the rest of the city, eliminating an essential recreational area of the city for many. Jersey City is criss-crossed by highways. In other places, like Newark, a street such as Broad Street forms a kind of electronic fence that separates ethnic groups; Newark's history, revealed both through research and anecdotally, is of a separation of ethnic group by bounded streets.

An interesting phenomenon has developed of late in American cities: the self-proclaiming poster on their lampposts and other stands. In Trenton, there are posters identifying Chambersburg as the restaurant district. Other places identify the city, like a name badge worn by a conventioneer.

The street is also a place of entrepreneurship. The majority of businesses in this country remain small businesses, the traditional "Mom and Pop" businesses. True, the failure rate of such small businesses is high, but they remain prevalent. They are the signature of the city's commercial activity. While most of New Jersey's cities may have begun with factories and industrialization (Atlantic City being the exception), it appears more that the retailers and office workers are the mainstay of their economies. We glimpse such through the windows of the stores.

Neighborhood matters. Different streets and areas, barely blocks apart, can be so diverse in a city. Trenton's residential housing is a mix reflective of the various types of architecture and periods in the United States; some streets have rowhouses, others, Victorian-era single family homes, and each within a stone's throw of each other. What is the effect on a community's mindset when children are born into, and grow up in, houses that are literally next door to abandoned and boarded-up houses.

Ferry Street is a world unto itself, and is one of my favorite streets and areas of Trenton. Comprising, with the Delaware River, the western boundary of the proposed Trenton Ferry Historic District, it has a series of 19th century rowhouses. It is one of the city's oldest streets, and led to one of the city's two 18th century ferries. At its foot was Lower Ferry, also known as Colvin's Ferry.[41] At the corner of Broad and Ferry Street still stands the Eagle Tavern, discussed above.

So we find these reminders of the past, and sometimes they seem to put an exclamation point to Trenton as a desolate place, a shadow of its former self. But it lives, it sputters, and sometimes gains traction. Against the drumbeat of crime statistics and abandoned houses, its defenders sally forth. Real estate projects take abandoned factories or old landmarks and turn them into residential units. The success of the Broad Street Bank Building's rebirth as housing

*Ferry Street.* Ferry Street marks the avenue to the Colonial ferry terminal. On his way to his inauguration in New York, Washington was ferried across the Delaware from Morrisville to Ferry Street, and made his way to the Mill Hill area. He ate at the City Tavern, then located at the corner of Warren and State streets. Ferry Street (above) provides examples of the industrial rowhouses that marked the area; they mainly date from the latter half of the 19th century. It constitutes the western border of the 70-acre area, from South Warren to South Broad Street, of the proposed Trenton Ferry Historic District. The Trenton Historical Society in its draft application on its website notes, "The alignment of Ferry Street is one of the earliest roads in the city of Trenton and has remained a constant for over three centuries. The earliest known map representing Ferry Street dates to 1714 and shows the roadway following its present course." http://trentonhistory.org/Documents/FerryHistDistNomination.html (accessed 9 August 2009).

was much-publicized. Still, all the letters to the editor cannot take away from the present reality.

Where do we go from here in the post-industrial city? In *City*, William Whyte makes the case *for* gentrification. He writes, "The 'gentrification' charge implies that the chief threat to housing for the poor is the upgrading of neighborhoods. The problem is the opposite. The chief threat is disinvestment. And the worst culprit is the federal government."[42] He further argues for a return of the agora, the central place of ancient Greek cities. There is something about a physical concentration that offers what is now on the shelf in suburban areas through technology, but physically, there is a different kind of social interaction that cannot be replicated. Whyte explains, "It is the genius of the center city that it is *not* high-tech. What is remarkable, indeed, is how little technology it does use.... Socially, the city is a very complex place. Physically, it is comparatively simple. For the business of the center, it must have streets, buildings, and places to meet and talk. As far as essentials are concerned, it has little more than the agora of ancient Greece."[43]

He adds: "The agora at its height would be a good guide to what is right. Its characteristics were centrality, concentration, and mixture, and these are the characteristics of the centers that work best today. Physically, there are vast differences, but in the gutty, everyday life of the street they would probably be remarkably similar."[44]

The more things change, the more they stay the same. Across the century, we retain our need for human connection and contact, which the city — our creation — fosters.

Compare and contrast Trenton with another post-industrial small city, Greenville, South Carolina. Like Trenton, it has pre–Revolutionary roots as a small town, and in the years leading up the Civil War, began to become an industrial center, fueled in part by the railroads. It featured the largest wagon manufacturer in the South.[45] Following the war, its African American population grew, as did its status as a textile manufacturing center. By the opening decades of the 20th century, as Trenton was peaking in its Golden Age as well, Greenville became known as the Textile Capital of the South. And as with Trenton, industrial strikes and the post–World War II years saw a decreased population and flight to the suburbs. In the 1970s, visionary leadership over the past quarter century moved a city with abandoned buildings downtown to a thriving place of some 60,000 people today. The main thoroughfare is filled with shops and restaurants. A rejuvenated park on both sides of the river is popular and utilized. The city boasts a fine art museum. It ceased being lost.

But maybe this is a false analogy. Trenton's problems may be part of a more regional phenomenon. Whyte tells us:

> The cities of the northeastern and north-central states seem to have been hit particularly hard. A succession of demographic studies have argued that they have

had it, that they are 'aging' and functionally obsolete, being geared to a declining manufacturing economy and with an overpriced labor force — and that, in any event, they are in the wrong latitude. The message is clear. Go to the South and the Southwest. The cities in those regions, runs the argument, are expanding vigorously, offer lower rates, lower-cost housing, a more tractable labor force, and a quality of life unmatched by the cold North.[46]

To be sure, there is the War Memorial Building, with its occasional concerts. There is the Mill Hill Playhouse with its occasional productions. But just ten miles away, in Princeton, Nassau Street and Witherspoon Street throb on Friday and Saturdays nights, and most weeknights as well. People are out and about, living in, taking part in, relating and reacting to *place*.

We often speak of political will. It is an amorphous context, perhaps more understood intuitively than formally defined. Nonetheless, rhetoric is not enough. The city of Greenville, South Carolina, proclaimed vision and moved toward it. Baltimore, Maryland, did the same; I remember the enthusiasm of a cabdriver in the early days of the city's renaissance. There was something tangible, a tactile presence in the city. Pride was almost something you could touch. You feel it in Greenville.

Whether Trenton will gain comparable traction remains to be seen.

# 8. The Engineered City

Drifting through Trenton, one is struck by its contribution to engineering and the infrastructure of America. In its graveyards are John Augustus Roebling, the leading engineer behind the implementation of the suspension bridge in America, and William Borrow, a (if not the) major contributor to the development of the versatile I-beam. (More about him in Chapter 9.) The city's steel and iron works played a part in bridge construction far beyond Trenton; most emblematic, perhaps, is the Brooklyn Bridge, brought into this world by the senior Roebling and his son, Washington Augustus Roebling. Beyond bridges, Trenton also has a credible sampling of a variety of types of skyscrapers. It also features a covered roadway, euphemistically called a "tunnel," built over the remains of its historic Colonial port of Lamberton, and the Delaware and Raritan Canal, one of several of those great engineering feats of canal construction in the mid–Atlantic states during the first third of the 19th century. While not boasting the largest or most historically significant, the city provides a window on various architectural styles and a modest museum to American engineering.

So we can reflect on what the city has to teach, and look beyond its few square miles and see what there is to be seen in this small but respectable outdoor museum of American engineering.

## Skyscrapers

Trenton, like other American cities, took to the skyscraper during the late 19th and early 20th centuries as a symbol of economic growth and strength. To think about Trenton's skyscrapers, we need a bit of context.

The skyscraper was a potent symbol of the new capitalism. While the architects may have sought aesthetic resonance, the skyscraper itself was among the more prominent symbols of the emergent American economic power, coincident with the global flag-showing in the Spanish-American War of 1898 and as precursor to the American prominence in World War I and the new century.

Skyscrapers fascinate. Grounded in earth, they seem to defy gravity. If the modern city is seen as the ultimate expression of civilization and human achievement, then the skyscraper is the 20th-century threat that runs through it. It is not that a city must have tall buildings to be defined as a city: Rome, Paris and Vienna are but three examples without American-styled skyscrapers in their cores. And it is certainly true that skyscrapers may mark suburban or exurban areas. Nonetheless, the skyscraper often connotes, and at times helps define, the city. It connects us to the earth and sky at the same time.

The skyline of a city becomes its identification. Like the silhouette of a well-known person, whose nose, brow and ears lend distinctive shape, so the skyline of the city. It was not until 1876, though, that the word "skyline" came to mean the city's buildings, rather than the point where earth and sky meet.[1] One distinguishing feature of the contemporary city skyline is its private, rather

*The City.* A bird soars over the downtown and statehouse area, and we have an example of the importance of skyline to a city's identity. Although Trenton does not have the skyscrapers of Jersey City or Newark, the two largest cities in the state, it nonetheless retains the look of a city and has its own skyline. The "small city" in post-industrial America retains the infrastructure and potential to reinvent itself as an economic and cultural hub. One of the most identifiable features of the city is the Statehouse building (left center). The golden dome is a symbol not only of the state, but also of Trenton. As one approaches from the bordering state of Pennsylvania, it is not merely the city, but the state itself that beckons. Whatever else makes a city a city, we cannot ignore its "look."

than public, nature.² In fact, "by the early twentieth century skyscrapers were the most striking feature of the business district."³

The modern skyscraper is an American invention,⁴ with the Reliance Building in Chicago generally considered the first *modern* skyscraper. Following the invention of the Otis elevator in the latter part of the 19th century and steel framing, taller buildings became economic and feasible. Virtually every major school and style is represented in New Jersey's cities, and a good variety in Trenton.

Skyscrapers, and the notion of the city skyline, are not free from controversy. Even today, in Washington, D.C., there are no towering private office buildings, so as not to offset or diminish the monumental nature of the public buildings. The city as a collective entity has an identity; there has been a view that private domination of the city's image should be discouraged. Architect Spiro Kostof has written of this debate as often revolving around the shape of the skyline and its importance and relevance to the city's denizens. That skyline is familiar, an icon for the city; it is something tangible to them and at the same time "a vision to cherish and come home to; it is also their urban advertisement to the world, the front they present to visitors, and a disseminative shorthand for a broader audience still. Royal seals with city views have had currency since at least the 13th century. Cities appeared on Renaissance coins and medals, on prints and paintings, and on their cheaper modern counterparts, postcards, T-shirts, refrigerator magnets."⁵

The *Oxford Dictionary of Architecture* defines "skyscraper" as a "high multi-storey building based on a steel or concrete-framed or skeleton structure, evolved in the U.S.A. in the late 1880s after the limitations of traditional load-bearing construction had been reached with ten or twelve-storey buildings."⁶ There is no real definition as to height or number of stories. What is generally agreed is that the skyscraper is considered an American "form born and developed best on this continent."⁷ Nor is there agreement as to the absolutely "first" skyscraper, or even a consistent history of the development of the skyscraper.⁸ Writing in 1959, J. Carson Webster attempted a definition of the skyscraper based not solely on height or structure, or form or function, but a variety of considerations. These included (1) "essential characteristics" of great height, arrangement in stories with the utmost space and light in each story; (2) "necessary means" of a structural system that could accommodate these characteristics, with appropriate materials (mainly steel), and elevators, and (3) "favoring conditions" that are economic, social, technological, psychological and aesthetic.⁹ These factors remain relevant today. A very tall, multi-story building may be a "skyscraper" in its most minimal and purest sense, but these other considerations transform it into something else and establish its character and personality. At least one writer has noted the American penchant for skyscraper form as a cultural phenomenon, and which is a function of four elements—a convergence of cultural values, technological convergence, economic organizations and governmental policies.¹⁰

In this regard, Rykwert writes, "Many people were indeed dissatisfied with the modern city and its buildings and their environments, but this had little to do with "style" or "ornament" — as their self-appointed spokesmen maintained — but a great deal to do with the frustration that the alienation of merely rent-producing and characterless buildings induced. Questions of style and ornament, which may seem harmless, become dangerously misleading when they stop at the surface and consequently mask problems of social structure and of context."[11] So appearance does matter. After all, while a building can certainly be razed, enormous resources are poured into the creation of a skyscraper, and the thinking must be that this is a permanent alteration of the city's geography. Who wants an ugly building as part of the daily existence of a city?

One of the early architectural theorists to discuss urban planning was Marc-Antoine Laugier (1713–1769), who noted the importance of the entrance to a city; he recommended legible street patterns after one enters through a triumphal arch to an open plaza. As Hearn explains in *Ideas that Shaped Buildings*, "Laugier's conception is an ideal, but it is also one, as he recognized, whose realization could be imposed upon an existing city piece by piece."[12] One would be hard pressed to find a city in New Jersey or even within the United States to meet those criteria. St. Louis has its own version of a triumphal arch, and certain cities, seen from the interstate highways, present an impressive "window" view, but more often than not, we are entering a city with a keen awareness of being in its outskirts. In New York City, or more particularly the island of Manhattan, the only impressive entranceway is through Grand Central Station — a kind of triumphal arch. The rat-like maze that is now Penn Station does not count. If we enter by train as part of the Northeast Corridor, then we enter Trenton mainly by its current train station, which is an improvement over the prior one but lacks monumentality. To enter by road, even across the bridges from Pennsylvania, is to confront not an impressive or welcoming sign or vision, but the ordinary green directional signs of the interstate highway culture.

The tallest building in New Jersey as of this writing is the Goldman Sachs Tower at 30 Hudson Street in Jersey City, built in 2004 and with 42 stories. Measurements of its height vary from approximately 781 feet to 791 feet, or approximately 238 meters. As an example of Postmodern architecture, it reflects a reaction to the minimalist Modernist buildings such as the glass and steel rectangles of Ludwig Mies van der Rohe. In style, it attempts to reintegrate past styles with contemporary visions and materials.

Not all view the modern skyscraper favorably. Frank Lloyd Wright condemned its omnipresence in close quarters in the modern city:

> The skyscraper if considered as independent achievement in itself may be justifiable: a prideful thing! A tall building may be very beautiful, economical, and desirable in itself — provided that it is in no way interference with what lives

below, but looking further ahead than the end of the landlord's ruse — by inhabiting a small green park. That park is humane now. The skyscraper is no longer sane unless in free green space. In the country it may stand beautiful for its own sake.
   Exaggerated perpendicularity has no such bill of health. It is now the terrible stricture of our big city.[13]

Technologically, the invention of the elevator, together with steel frame construction, facilitated vertical growth.[14] American corporate wealth was not a function of fragmented family organizations, as in Europe, and government policies were not restricted by cultural taboos, such as in China, where taller buildings were deemed disrespectful to the emperor.[15] While New York became the preeminent location for skyscrapers, they were not as quickly embraced in smaller cities that lacked the demand for office space or the capital necessary to construct them.[16] When they were constructed, they became a focal point for the city's business district; "the skyscraper served to anchor the business core around a functional and visual landmark."[17]

The upward thrust of urban building at the end of the 19th and first quarter of the 20th century helped define the American city, and was not limited just to the major cities such as New York and Chicago.

And so Trenton, in the height of its own Golden Age *fin-de-siecle*, participated. Trenton's first skyscraper was the Broad Street Bank Building, a twelve-story Beaux Arts building at the corner of State Street and Montgomery Street. Its architect was Trentonian William A. Poland (1852–1935), who designed, among other Trenton buildings, the Second Masonic Hall. Built in 1900, it was not only the city's first skyscraper (no building in Trenton had reached higher than four stories previously), but also contained the city's first elevator and first revolving door; it was also the first to utilize the steel superstructure. Its lobby and mezzanine also served as community activity facilities, and retail establishments (including Thomas Cadwalader's cigar shop) were accommodated.[18] The original building was eight stories in 1900; a twelve story addition was added in 1913 and an eight story addition in 1923. Originally modeled after famed architect Louis Sullivan's school, it developed into an example of Beaux Arts architecture, and more particularly, French Renaissance.[19] It has been renovated into combined residential and office space in an effort toward Trenton's renewal.

We can use the prism of Trenton to think more broadly about architecture and this particular style. The Beaux Arts style derives from the Ecole des Beaux-Arts in Paris, and is notable for paired columns, patterns within patterns, high parapets, domes, projecting facades, balustrades, pilasters and pavilions. Ornaments on the building include flowers, garlands and shields. The style was prevalent from approximately 1885 to 1920. It was criticized by Frank Lloyd Wright in *In the Course of Architecture* as "Frenchite pastry."[20] The *Oxford Dic-*

***Broad Street Bank Building.*** **The first skyscraper in the city, it now stands as a symbol of the post-industrial small city's adaptive reuse. It has been renovated and currently serves as a prime residential location in center city Trenton. The Broad Street National Bank was organized in 1887, and began in a small store on South Broad Street.**

*tionary of Architecture* writes, "Scholarly, self-confident, grand, and lush, the style was perfectly attuned to the mood of Europe and America in the two decades before 1914." [21] We can stand on the streets of Trenton and look at this building, and connect to a broader movement in Western architecture.

The Broad Street Bank Building was built at a time of changing perceptions of the skyscraper, when the aesthetic value of the skyscraper itself was recognized at the birth of the 20th century.[22] The skyscraper, while embraced by some, was criticized by others as commercial and impersonal. In the early years of the 20th century, the schism between business and art seemed to lessen as some, such as Alfred Stieglitz, compared the skyscraper as an American symbol to that of the Parthenon to Greece.[23] In *New York: A Historical Atlas of Architecture*, the authors note that "by the turn of the 20th century, the architectural model for [banks] had been established as a solid limestone volume in the Beaux Arts style, with lavishly decorated interiors."[24]

The Broad Street Bank Building was important to Trenton's identity as a city, as the vision of what physically constituted a city, or at least an American city, changed with the advent of the 20th century. In particular, the influence of Beaux Arts architecture was a product of this.

The 19th-century skyscraper was initially the introduction of functionality to the metropolis; with the 20th, skyscrapers embodied symbolism as well as functionality. As one architectural critic explains:

> So at the turn of the century there was still a fairly traditional sense of what a city was supposed to be. The vaunted ambition of a nation moving to fill a continent and eager to play a major role in the international balance of power was the force that most influenced architecture in terms of style; it helped create the surge of interest in classicism — the imperialist leanings of the Beaux-Arts being a perfect reflection of the nation's new self-image — and thus came a generation of railroad stations, museums, and other structures that bespoke a commitment to civil grandeur. But the notion of how cities and buildings should look was affected only slightly. Business buildings had grown with the advent of the steel frame and the elevator, the two technological innovations that made great skyscrapers on the one hand possible and on the other hand practical, but they tended to be little more than 12 or 15 stories in height.[25]

An example of this attention to Neo-Classicism is the Trenton Trust Building at 28 West State Street, a 14-story skyscraper built in 1924. It embodies the essence of what skyscrapers were all about. It also embodies, for me, a core element of the urban aesthetic of Trenton.

The skyscraper must be "lofty," wrote the (or at least a) progenitor of the American skyscraper, Louis Sullivan, in his 1896 essay, "The Tall Office Building Artistically Considered." It was in this famous piece that he also penned the phrase "form ever follows function." In 1896, in the nascent years of modern skyscraper construction, Sullivan took it upon himself to comment on the important considerations for such buildings, not least of which concerned aesthetics. As we consider the two premier early skyscrapers in Trenton, and even the more recent ones, it is helpful to bear in mind his precepts that held such sway over skyscraper construction in 20th-century America. Among Sullivan's main concerns was coherence; he protested against the seeming mix of styles in an attempt to break up the vertical lines. He wrote that the skyscraper "must be every inch a proud and soaring thing, rising in sheer exultation that from bottom to top it is a unit without a single dissenting line that it is the new, the unexpected, the eloquent peroration of most bald, most sinister, most forbidding conditions."[26] This coherence was noted by Alain de Botton in *The Architecture of Happiness* as one of the virtues of a building, together with order, balance, elegance and self-knowledge.[27]

Consider in particular the Trenton Trust Company Building at 28 West State Street. Only 14 stories — barely a "tall building" by today's standards, but a skyscraper nonetheless. It soars. It is lofty. It is a beautiful building, with coherence, a building that speaks. O'Gorman's states in *ABC of Architecture*, "Architecture is a form of language, of communication. It speaks. It can convey through its design its place in society, its content."[28] It tells us that architecture

***Trenton Trust Company Building.*** Also known as the 28 West State Street building, this 1924 example of Neo-Classical architecture is one of the city's first and most aesthetic skyscrapers. The bank was organized in 1888. It is a striking example of the power of architecture to convey meaning. In the words of architect Louis Sullivan, written in 1896 on the skyscraper: "[W]hat is the chief characteristic of the tall office building? And at once we answer, it is lofty."

matters, that aesthetics matter, and that when we walk the streets of our cities, we want them to reflect an atmosphere of (to borrow from de Botton as to why architecture makes us happy) order, balance, elegance, coherence and self-knowledge. Of all the buildings in Trenton, this remains my favorite.

On either side of the Trenton Trust Company Building door are two portrait medallions encircled in wreaths. Four fluted pilasters grace the front, the two wider ones nearest to the arched doorway. Three carved inserts symbolize the city's or state's economy. Above them, a row of small lions' heads. Separating the 12th from 13th floor, beneath the cornice, are dentils, another Greek classical feature that resemble teeth. At the top are modillions that appear to have a leaf design. It has a steel rigid frame with a brick façade.

On the State Street entrance façade are two bas-relief profiles surrounded by bay laurel garlands. They resemble paintings of Renaissance merchants. The bay laurel leaf as used in architecture hearkens back to Greek and Roman usage as awards for athletics, poetry or military victory. This banking company was formed in 1888; 36 years later, its message to the world was one of success. The three bas relief panels above carry the Latin inscription "e pluribus unum," or "out of many, one," the inscription on the seal of the United States and, until 1956 when it was replaced by "In God We Trust," the American motto. On the side, these three panels are repeated, some with the word "thrift" engraved over them. Among the other panels on the Chancery Lane side of the building is one of the Brooklyn Bridge. Completed in 1883, the Brooklyn Bridge was engineered by John Roebling and his son Washington, two of Trenton's more renowned citizens. This bas relief is emblematic not only of the preeminence of the bridge itself, but also of the city's role in that historic structure. Further testament to the Classical architecture are the three cartouches at the 11th story, as well as the vertical scroll ancone (bracket) at the top of the arch of the door, supporting the cornice.

This one building is an education in itself, and a connection to the broader world and history of architecture. How many people have walked past this building in Trenton and barely glanced at it?

Trenton has not yet managed a skyscraper of Newark or Jersey City proportions, but the symbolism behind its skyscrapers is no less important for that. Among the tallest buildings in Trenton are the two Kingsbury Towers, examples of Brutalist architecture. These twin 21-story residential buildings were built in the early 1970s.

I find Brutalism among the more interesting of architectural styles for skyscrapers. The Brutalist name and style conjure harsh images, but the word derives from the French *beton brut*, or rough concrete.[29] Nonetheless, it is well-named. Its main period of use was from approximately 1950 through the mid–1980s. Among others, it is primarily associated with Le Corbusier (Charles-Edouard Jeanneret-Gris) in his post–1945 works. It emphasizes the imprint of the formwork, the temporary shuttering of the mold for concrete. In some cases, exposed steel is used in lieu of concrete. Some consider it a reaction to the glass and steel structures becoming prevalent at the time. The Kingsbury Towers in Trenton, New Jersey, were completed in 1972. They have the most stories of any building in the Trenton.

Kingsbury Corporation is an intriguing story. It is a non-profit corporation, and the apartments are available as affordable housing and for senior citizens. As Trenton lost population in the 1950s to the suburbs, Kingsbury was formed as a multi-racial, multi-ethnic, ecumenical effort to regain and retain that kind of diversity in the heart of Trenton.[30] Built on part of the original Stacy land, the name was selected from one of the original names for the Trent House. It has undergone various changes in ownership and management, and some believe while its original objective failed for a while, its population is now close to what that original conception was.

But from an architectural standpoint, the Kingsbury Towers are also significant. The former Pan Am Building (now the MetLife Building) in New York City is an example of Brutalist architecture, shared with Trenton. Another notable example is the Barbicon Estate towers in London.

Trenton defies its stereotypes. We can look at these buildings and draw connections, and locate Trenton as a city of the world. Think about that when you look at these twin buildings, which, I suspect, many travelers through the city, as well as natives, barely look at or otherwise take for granted.

The Department of Labor and Workforce Development Building, a 13-story, 203-foot building built in 1962, is an example of Modern architecture in the city. Modernism reflects simplicity of design and utilitarianism.[31] Early Modernism in skyscrapers may be dated from 1932,[32] and was reflected in, among other things, the "International Style," and exemplified by the large steel and glass towers of Mies, such as New York's Seagram Building. Modernist skyscrapers began to come into vogue in the 1940s and in the 1960s began moving beyond rectangular shapes, embracing cylindrical and other forms.[33] The concept of Modernism was to reject the past, and seek an aesthetic that was based upon functionalism and contemporary materials and technology. That said, it must be acknowledged that there is no unity of agreement on "one" Modernist approach. In addition to looking to the present and dismissing historical influences, Modernist architecture stresses the simple. In art, an example of this approach is found in Piet Mondrian's work of *Des Stijl* paintings with his black lines and squares of color.

Late Modernism expanded upon Modernist principles and utilized curves and colors that might otherwise not have been found within the starker lines of modernist buildings. Late Modern may refer to such buildings built between approximately 1960 and 1980. Different writers have different views as to a definition of Late Modernism; the *Oxford Dictionary of Architecture* states it is

## 8. The Engineered City 163

"architecture in which the images, ideas and motifs of the Modern Movement were taken to extremes, structures, technology, and services being grossly overstated at a time when Modernism was being questioned."[34]

Have we homogenized our cities? Are cities *qua* cities dead? Passé? Should we tear them down and start all over? Can we still find *character* in a city? In discussing modern and postmodern architecture, Jürgen Habermas writes:

> After a century's criticism of the large city, after innumerable, repeated, and disillusioned attempts to keep a balance in the cities, to save the inner cities, to divide urban space into residential areas and commercial quarters, industrial facilities and garden suburbs; private and public zones; to build habitable satellite towns; to rehabilitate slum areas; to regulate traffic more sensibly, etc., the question that is brought to mind is whether the actual notion of the city has not itself been superseded.[35]

Kingwell cites Habermas and this quotation and goes further. He wonders whether the identify of the city has been lost due to the lack of central cohesiveness, the loss of traditional (manufacturing) function and the postmodern "deadening sameness, the banal luxury" of our cities and buildings.[36]

A full discussion of Modernism and its incarnations is well beyond the scope of this book; these few comments are merely meant to flavor the discussion and provide a prelude to further reading. Trenton's few examples provide an entrée. When we look at them, do we see reflections of Mies? Do we see banality? Whatever we conclude, we have examples of the movement in Trenton and can judge in context the influence of Modernism on the architecture of this city.

Other examples of Modernist skyscrapers in Trenton include Trent Center East, a 14-story, residential apartment building built in 1965; Lafayette House, another apartment building, 12 stories high and built in 1963; the 16-story Carteret Arms Apartments; the 15-story Rowan Towers; the 13-story Luther Arms apartments; the Mary G. Roebling office building built in 1988 at 12 stories; and Two Capitol Plaza, a 16-story office building on West State Street, built in 1967.

We are using Trenton as a point of entry to the broader issues as we walk its streets. We may consider elements of the debate as we look at a building such as the Labor Building. Not all are fans. One of the leading "New Urbanists" has expressed his disdain for Modernism. James Kunstler finds that Modernism "did its immense damage" by separating contemporary construction from historical and traditional means, without sensitivity to ingrained social and urban relationships "and by creating a physical setting for man that failed to respect the limits of scale, growth, and the consumption of natural resources, or to respect the lives of other living things. The result of Modernism, especially in America, is a crisis of the human habitat: cities ruined by corporate gigantism and abstract renewal schemes, public buildings and public spaces unworthy of human affection, vast sprawling suburbs that lack any sense of community, housing that the un-rich cannot afford to live in, a slavish obeisance to the needs of automobiles and their dependent industries at the expense of human needs, and a gathering ecological calamity that we have only begun to measure."[37] Kunstler thus explains Modernism as a reaction to the industrialization and its ugliness, as an "architecture that eschewed all ornamental references to history, a purist architecture of the dawning of the twentieth century!"[38]

Do we agree?

We remain *flâneurs*. We can wander this compact city and have connection to the great architectural movements of the centuries. We are in the great open-air museum of Trenton. We can decide for ourselves. While Trenton's examples may not be the prototypical examples, they nonetheless allow us to sample, and participate in, the great architectural movements as evidenced in these high-rise buildings.

I mentioned the Goldman Sachs building in Jersey City as an example of Postmodernism. Postmodern buildings, dating from approximately 1970, seek to restore some of the more decorative aspects of pre–Modernist structures, particularly with the available of newer materials. It is less one particular style or movement, as an attempt to categorize what *The Oxford Dictionary of Architecture* indicates is "connected with a loss of faith in what were once regarded as certainties (e.g., progress, rationality, science) and with a growing acceptance of a bewilderingly large palette of images, signs, and products promoted on a scale never experienced before in the history of the world, which some ... have welcomed as offering 'complexity' and 'contradiction' in design."[39]

As Nan Ellin explains in *Postmodern Urbanism*, "Postmodern architecture has been described as multivalent, or containing many meanings. It also draws from a variety of styles, celebrating difference and pluralism. It features ornamentation, often suggestive of the human body. And it reflects a desire for communal space along with an admission that there is nothing quite adequate to fill it."[40] Postmodern urbanism, therefore, embodies (1) a return to history and monuments, contrary to modernism's rejection of same; (2) the importance of character and place, as opposed to, among others, the International Style; (3) less emphasis on function, and more on human scale; (4) less ideological bent.[41]

Trenton's principal contribution to the Postmodern dialog is the 1989, 15-story One State Street Square building. Another Postmodern tall building is the 12 story 33 West State Street building, a red brick structure that is reminiscent of the CNA Plaza Building in Chicago—another red skyscraper, more of the International School. The Emporis.com site for skyscrapers notes that 33 West State Street is mainly Modern, but has the Postmodern element to it because of "historicizing" on the State Street façade. Historically as well, it stands of the site on the Hildebrecht Hotel.[42]

We do not crane our necks too much in taking in Trenton's skyscrapers. It is a small city, and its skyscrapers are relatively small. Perhaps it will once again reach for the skies. For now, we have had a survey of some of the major architectural schools that were embraced in skyscraper instruction. A small, but nonetheless instructive, museum, and one that is replicated across the landscape of other such post-industrial cities.

## *Bridges*

Bridges are literal and symbolic, functional and aesthetic. They are artificial insertions to the landscape and become part of it. The bridge combines architecture, engineering and art. Its whole is greater than the sum of its parts. It is visible mathematics, a sculpture of line and form. The bridges of a city complement it and comprise it, and often come to symbolize it. Many considerations go into the type of bridge to span a particular crossing.[43]

Not only was Trenton home to the internationally renowned engineering family of the Roeblings, with their mansions on State Street and factory along South Broad Street, but also the city itself remains a kind of open-air museum for these engineering structures. Trenton's bridges are diverse. As it happens, Trenton has two examples of suspension bridges—the "bouncing bridge" in Stacy Park, itself a model of the Brooklyn Bridge, and the other a suspension bridge connecting the former administration building of the Roebling factory (now the Mercer County Administration Building) with another building. Various girder and beam bridges are found in the city. Its stone arch bridges are historic.

Consider them as we come across them in our perambulations.

Stone arch bridges are among the oldest type of bridge, and certainly marked many crossings in Colonial New Jersey. Trenton has several 19th-century stone arch bridges that are of historical and engineering significance. Stone symbolizes the land, and even in the 20th century, more contemporaneous stone bridges continue to have appeal. Stone as a material is conducive to the physical forces that act on the arch, so in addition to aesthetic considerations, it remains useful from an engineering context as well.

The stone arch bridge at South Broad Street crossing the Assunpink Creek, at the location of the Second Battle of Trenton, is the third stone arch bridge at the site. The first, built in 1774, featured in the First and Second Battles of Trenton. It was replaced in 1822, but this later bridge was lost and replaced by the current one. It has been identified as the oldest bridge in Trenton in the New Jersey Historic Bridge Survey.[44] Another notable stone arch bridge carries Montgomery Street across the Assunpink Creek in the Mill Hill area. This bridge, built in 1873, still has its original cast-iron balustrade. The bridge is considered significant as well for its architect, Trentonian Henry E. Finch. Finch was the architect of various Trenton churches, as well as the now-gone Taylor Opera House. He also designed the 1869 stone arch bridge carrying South Clinton Street across the Assunpink. This latter bridge is part of the abutment to the 1892 Pratt Truss Bridge across the creek and the tracks that lead to the train station; the Historic Bridge Survey cites this pair as providing a rare tandem example of 19th-century solutions to engineering and transportation considerations. The crossing is one of the most historic in Trenton."[45] Finch's third stone arch bridge, built in 1856 and carrying East State Street and Fairview Street over the Assunpink, has been so changed that it is no longer considered historically significant. It also has the 1843 historic stone arch bridge that stands at or near the site of the original 1774-built one that featured in the Second Battle of Trenton.

Trenton also features two beautiful tributes of the great age of the railroad. The massive stone railroad bridges were expensive to build. With the advent of cheaper iron, stone bridge construction for railroad bridges was less frequent, but picked up again in the 1880s for various reasons, including dissatisfaction of railroad engineers with the performance of the iron railroad bridges, and a better economic condition of the railroads to afford the investment in stone arch construction of this magnitude. Strong arch bridges were designed to carry the heavy freight trains laden with anthracite from Pennsylvania through New Jersey. As trains increased in power and weight, the older wooden bridges simply could not handle them. Exemplifying this late–19th-century construction was the 18-span, 1080-foot-long stone arch bridge built by the Pennsylvania Railroad at Trenton from 1901 to 1903, made of Clearfield sandstone.[46]

According to the application for its listing in the inventory of the National Register of Historic Places, this bridge was among those built by the Pennsylvania Railroad as part of "the most ambitious stone masonry bridge building program in the United States." Significantly, it linked by rail New York and Philadelphia, and is reported to be one of the last stone arch railroad bridges built in New Jersey.[47] Quoting a contemporary (1903) *New York Times* article, the applicant also noted the cost ($3.5 million, including the bridge and approaches), and that this stone arch bridge was "said to be the only one in the world, with the exception of the one at New Brunswick, where four tracks run parallel," streamlining the travel time. The use of stone rather than steel was consistent with the Pennsylvania Railroad engineering staff's predilection for masonry arch bridges.[48]

The Pennsylvania Railroad Bridge, now part of the Amtrak Northeast Corridor system, represents one of the last stone arch railroad bridges built in New Jersey. The Pennsylvania Railroad had ignored the city for some time. However, with the Reading's construction of its crossing, Pennsylvania bought land in South Trenton for the purpose of constructing the bridge across the Delaware, and the first train crossed on August 23, 1903.[49]

Bridges like this strong, impressive arch bridge built of stone hearken back to Roman construction and give a permanency to the environment, and a sense of the ghosts of massive freight trains whistling through the night.

## 8. The Engineered City

Similarly, to the south is the 1875 Reading Railroad Bridge near Lower Ferry Road. This structure was part of the Reading Railroad network between Pennsylvania and New Jersey, and now part of the Conrail line running from the Reading Terminal in Philadelphia to West Trenton. The Reading's assets ultimately went into Conrail (the Consolidated Rail Corporation) in 1976, now known as CSX. Today, that once-proud railroad operates movie theaters in Australia and New Zealand.[50]

While the arch bridge relies on its geometric shape to spread the load and accommodate the forces playing on it, truss bridges disseminate the loads through different types of grid patterns, and provided an efficient way to manage certain types and lengths of crossings. Trenton has two historic truss bridges, the Calhoun Street Bridge and the "Trenton Makes" bridge, which distinguish the city. However, most emblematic is the "Trenton Makes" Bridge.[51]

The Trenton Makes Bridge is more formally known as The Lower Trenton Bridge. It is a Warren Truss bridge, marked by equilateral triangles. This bridge's history and its predecessors on this site are important in the history of American bridge-building. The original bridge at this site was heralded as "one of the finest specimens of bridge architecture in the world" by John Barber and Henry Howe in their 1844 work, *Historical Collections of New Jersey*. Its builder, Theodore Burr, was one of the preeminent and sought-after bridge builders of the day. Burr improved timber bridge truss construction by adding an arc for support. Thomas Pope, who authored the first American book devoted to bridge construction, in his 1811 *A Treatise on Bridge Architecture* discussed the original bridge and placed it in a pantheon of bridges such as Caesar's Timber Bridge, and various bridges in Tibet, China, Italy, Switzerland, Africa, Norway, France and England; among the American bridges discussed, the one at Trenton was one of less than a dozen.[52]

Due to its construction and height, it survived the 1841 flood that destroyed other, newer bridges along the Delaware. In 1842, it was the first American bridge to carry an interstate railroad, but within 35 years, it was considered obsolete and replaced by other railroad and general traffic bridges. Once the Pennsylvania Railroad Company built the stone arch railroad bridge in 1908, the two steel railroad bridges were destroyed. By the 1920s, though, the general traffic bridge also could no longer function to serve local needs, so the Trenton Makes Bridge was constructed in 1928. Unlike many of the other truss bridges crossing the Delaware, this bridge has a camelback configuration. The image indicates a polygonal top chord with five slopes.[53]

The slogan "Trenton Makes, the World Takes" reflects the city's industrial prominence, the place of steel, rubber and pottery. In 1935, the sign "Trenton Makes, the World Takes" was placed on the bridge. Now principally referred to as the Trenton Makes Bridge, a logo of the bridge served as the symbol of the Trenton Titans minor league hockey team.[54]

Trenton's second principal truss bridge is the Calhoun Street Bridge.[55]

Once part of the Lincoln Highway transcontinental road route, it features a plaque that points to San Francisco and New York, reflecting its former glory along the route from New York to Pennsylvania and onward to California.

The original bridge on this site, which, like the Trenton Makes Bridge, replaced one of the Trenton ferries, was completed in 1861, after almost two years of construction and some 20 years after it was authorized. Destroyed by fire in 1884, it was replaced that year by the present wrought-iron bridge that was built on the original piers and abutments. Originally called the Trenton City Bridge, or City Bridge it was featured by its builder, the Phoenix Bridge Company, as one of the most advanced bridges in the country.[56]

It has seven spans (each nearly 180 feet long) and is a Pratt through truss, connecting Trenton, New Jersey, to Morrisville, Pennsylvania. The Pratt Truss was invented in 1844 by Thomas and Caleb Pratt. In this configuration, the diagonals are in tension and the verticals in compression, with the diagonals slanting downward and toward the center. Calhoun Street was originally known as Beatty's Ferry Road, one of the original streets of Trenton. As with other bridges along the Delaware, it replaced a ferry — in this case, Beatty's Ferry, one of two that operated in Trenton.[57]

Of lesser significance, but interesting because of its location on part of the battlefield during the battles of Trenton, is the red-painted Mill Hill Bridge, another Pratt truss bridge built in 1888 across the Assunpink Creek. The Trenton Mill Hill Organization states that at the time, this crossing for Jackson Street was part of a transportation improvement in the Mill Hill District that included work on another bridge and sidewalks.[58] A similar (though green) bridge carries South Clinton Avenue across the railroad tracks.

More familiar as part of the bridge construction of the first half of the 20h century, from approximately 1915 through 1955, are the steel girder bridges. This bridge is marked by a deck slab supported by certain types of beams or girders— either the I-beam, consisting of two flanges (top and bottom plates) welded to the web (side plate), or the box girder, utilizing four plates welded into a box shape, with flanges on top and bottom, and the webs forming the sides. Other, less-used girders, take the shape of the Greek letter pi or the capital "T."[59] The Scudder Falls Bridge skirts the interstate highway around Trenton, and reminds us of the early settlement "by the falls." [60] Another girder bridge, The Trenton-Morrisville Bridge, carries Route 1 across the Delaware.

Among the most aesthetically pleasing of the city's bridges is the 1909 aqueduct that carries the Delaware and Raritan Canal across Parkside Avenue adjacent to Cadwalader Park. The New Jersey Historic Bridge Survey describes it as follows:

> The handsome, concrete aqueduct with Neo-Classical-style balustrades and octagonal columns is the most significant "City Beautiful" bridge in the area, and it may well be the earliest. It was designed and built by the Pennsylvania Railroad to carry the canal and railroad over the entrance to Cadwalader Park

*Cadwalader Park Bridge.* This aqueduct, which carries the Delaware and Raritan Canal through Cadwalader Park and across Parkside Avenue, is a stellar example of the application of the "City Beautiful" movement in Trenton. The New Jersey Historic Bridge Survey puts its construction date at 1909 by the Pennsylvania Railroad. Cadwalader Park itself was designed personally by Frederick Law Olmsted in 1891.

which was developed after 1888 on the grounds of the McCall Mansion. The house and surrounding 100 acres are listed, but the aqueduct is not rated. It is a contributing resource to both the McCall Mansion House and the Delaware & Raritan Canal Historic District. It is also individually significant based on its type, completeness, and history.[61]

It's a bit sad to find this beautiful bridge defaced by graffiti. Someone has claimed it, but none can own it. It is there for us.

## Canals

Among the major engineering achievements of the first half of the 19th century, and a significant component of the Industrial Revolution, was the canal. The "Canal Era" was a "major phase" in 19th-century American history that contributed to the growth and creation of American cities.[62] Canals contributed to nationalism and the "binding" together of the country.[63] Although canals date back to the dawn of Western civilization, the American Canal Era leaned heavily on the transfer of European technology.[64] The Erie Canal in New York "was the first to demonstrate on a grand scale that canals would work in America."[65] New Jersey and Pennsylvania sought to compete with the Erie Canal and build their own; the mid–Atlantic canals became the most concentrated regional canal network in the nation."[66] The Delaware and Raritan Canal demonstrated the ability to link canals and rails as well; "New Jersey's canal history was more directly tied to both banking and railroad development than that of any other canal state."[67] As its name states, it linked two of the state's great rivers and established a waterway between the anthracite mines of Pennsylvania and the factories of New York.

The Delaware and Raritan Canal was in reality two canals—the main canal that reached from Bordentown to New Brunswick, going through Trenton, and the feeder canal, from around Raven Rock (near Lumberton) to Trenton, where it connected with the main canal. Nearly all of the original canal (both main and feeder) still exists.[68] Begun in 1830 and worked on by mainly Irish immigrants, and reportedly dug by hand using picks and shovels, and animal-drawn scrapers, the canal opened in 1834 and was built primarily to convey coal from Pennsylvania to New York. The canal's usage peaked post–Civil War through the 1870s, ultimately losing out to the railroads as more efficient means of transport. Trenton was the highest point of the canal, which consisted of seven locks used to raise and lower boats on their way through. In its day, the canal saw steam-powered vessels on it, as well as the mule-drawn barges. A subculture of those connected with the canal grew up. The canal and the Camden and Amboy Railroad abutted the Roebling factory in Trenton. Steamboats plied the canal.

Since the canal was a significant transportation route for coal from Pennsylvania to New York, the feeder was designed to help control the water levels, as the main canal served Bordentown to New Brunswick, facilitating New York Philadelphia traffic. The feeder, though, connected Pennsylvania's Delaware Canal at Lambertville, and also became a transitway itself for coal. From its construction in 1831 through the 1860s and 1870s, the canal was an essential artery in the circulatory system of 19th-century industrial America. An engineering feat, it was rendered obsolete with the onslaught of the railroads. *Trenton Makes, the World Takes.* The heart of the industrial northeast. Coal, iron, rubber, pottery. The cries of the mule tenders walking along the towpath, great piles of coal moving through the city. Those tending the bridges and locks were given homes; three remain—the ones at Calhoun Street and Hanover Street need restoration, while the one at Prospect Street is utilized.

At around Old Rose Road, the feeder canal joined the main canal. As we curve around on Route 1 near Old Rose Road, we can just glimpse the chain link fence from the road that separates the canal from the highway. Back in the city "aboveground," we can walk along the towpath from the area of Old Rose Road, and peer through the chain link fence and dense vegetation to where the canal goes underground, the steady sound of traffic on Route 1 on top of it drowning out the birdcalls; the highway abuts the still-extant waters above ground of the canal, the sluggish water of the canal as it goes past Old Rose Street towards Southard Street. We turn around, look back and see the glinting gold dome of the Statehouse. It was in this area, at Old Rose Road and Southard Road, that the main canal joined the feeder canal, and from which the main canal continued south to Bordentown.

The canal also tells a story. In Trenton it was an integral part of the city since it was integral to the city's industrial development. John Roebling's wire rope cable factory was located alongside the canal and the Camden & Amboy Railroad, for both transportation purposes as well as the hydraulic power. Today, the remnants of the Roebling factory along South Broad Street house Mercer County's administrative offices, including those of the County Executive and Freeholders. Part of the premises has been converted into the Roebling Market, and a light rail station is located here. Route 129, built over the canal, allows us to imagine the water flowing past, and brings the old sepia-toned pictures to life. Other factories were located along the canal and often had their own turning basins. Like much of the canal that ran along the stretch that now consists of Route 1, those turning basins were also filled in.

*Canal Tender's House.* There are three remaining canal tender's houses in Trenton. The Delaware and Raritan Canal was built in the 1830s to carry Pennsylvania coal to New York; the 30-mile feeder canal began near Raven's Rock and ended in Trenton, where the 34-mile main canal picked up and continued on to New Brunswick. The Trenton to Kingston portion opened in 1833. The canal itself was a significant catalyst in Trenton's industrial development. Peaking in 1866, it ultimately lost out to the railroads as the prime source of transportation.

Still within Trenton are walkable portions of the canal, which transverses Cadwalader Park through the aqueduct. The Calhoun Street Canal House along the Delaware and Raritan Canal feeder that runs along part of West State Street, through and out of Trenton, is boarded up, peeling, graffiti-scrawled. Despite rehabilitation efforts, it remains peeling, decrepit, lost, dead. Another ruin.[69]

So think of Trenton as a kind of museum of technology, an outdoor landscape of engineering achievement. One of its bridges spans the site of a predecessor bridge that was truly world-class and renowned. Its skyscrapers, if not of comparable renown or size, nonetheless form part of the mosaic of architectural practice. And the Delaware and Raritan Canal remains largely intact, one of the important canals of a great, lost era, and one of the midwives to the Industrial Revolution.

# 9. The Landscaped City

We tend to think of cities in terms of concrete, steel and glass, but the green of a city is as much a part of its identity, culture and look as the concrete and steel. Trenton boasts, in its way, a world-class urban park designed by the preeminent landscape architect of his time. Together with parks, cities often have remarkable cemeteries that reflect the city and are a type of park in their own fashion. They contain the stories of the city, not just its bodies. Let us stroll about and see where the paths of Trenton lead. A bit of context is appropriate, and that context is provided to some extent by an introduction to the City Beautiful movement.

The City Beautiful movement arose in the 1890s and carried into the 1920s in part as a reaction to the squalor, ugliness, corruption and incompetent government marking the American urban scene following the Civil War. Peripatetic soldiers, released from war, moved from city to city. The needs of the factories brought people into the cities. Sanitation, roads and infrastructure were overwhelmed. Municipal police forces were undertrained and inefficient. Political bosses held sway. During the last decades of the 19th century, the reformers battled for improvement. "Conferences for Good City Government" ensued in various cities, and journals sprang up to espouse the ideas that were coming forward. As an adjunct to the civic movement, architects and civic groups sought to better plan their cities and their growth. With the Columbian Exhibition of 1893 in Chicago, and the leadership of Daniel H. Burnham, city planning in America, the notion of the "beautiful city" began to take hold.[1]

William H. Wilson, in a "revisionist" examination of the City Beautiful movement, has argued for its real achievements and rejects limitations of its effectiveness based on utilitarian or functional arguments. He further opposes the proposition that the City Beautiful movement was restricted to planning, or that it was just another example of "Progressive Era reform," or that its planning component was subordinate to local politics.[2] With roots in the 19th century, it had tangible ramifications in the 20th; he argues that "the movement's concerns for converting ugliness to beauty and for controlling and enhancing economic and physical growth were compelling. Equally powerful were its desires for comprehensiveness, utility, and functionalism."[3] President Woodrow Wilson urged a "heightened sense of civic loyalty," and one way to achieve that was to install appropriate monuments, landmarks and architecture in cities to help shape that.[4]

This attempt to remove ugliness and emptiness from American cities was another fostering component of the City Beautiful movement: "The conviction that an intimate link existed between a city's physical appearance and its moral state — and that America's cities were sadly deficient on this score — was central to the 'city beautiful' movement, a surge of interest in civil betterment and beautification that began in the mid–1890s and crested in the first two or three years of the twentieth century."[5] Another component was the self-interest of the "booster" class, the capitalist civil leaders seeking expanded profits; "for some capitalists, the appeal of the city beautiful lay no deeper than their pocketbooks: ugliness, dirt, and disorder were bad for business."[6]

Ultimately, though, the core of this otherwise diffuse movement was that "it sprang from the conviction that a more livable and attractive urban environment would call forth an answering surge of civil loyalty from the urban populace, and that this in turn would retard or even reverse the decay of social and moral cohesiveness which seemed so inevitable a concomitant of the rise of cities."[7]

No one wants to live in squalor. We decorate our offices and workspaces to provide a sympathetic environment. Why should not the same instincts compel us to treat our cities in the same way?

One sees the ramifications of the City Beautiful movement in Trenton. Cadwalader Park, discussed in more detail below, was designed with these principles in mind. Among the favored architectural styles of the City Beautiful movement was Neo-Classicism, which is well-represented in Trenton's buildings such as the Mercer County Courthouse and the aqueduct carrying the Delaware and Raritan Canal from Cadwalader Park across Parkside Avenue. One of the city's early skyscrapers, at 28 West State Street, also exemplifies that return to Classical design.

## Parks

So cities are often known for their parks. New York is unimaginable without Central Park; London without the Serpentine. Urban parks are not simply oases for escape. They are an integral part of the city's fabric. They are more than just a place for the city dweller to obtain a bit of "country." They are showcases for the best of the city itself. Figures like William Cullen Bryant in New York heavily influenced urban planning to accommodate nature.[8]

The leading landscape architect of the 19th century was Frederick Law

Olmsted (1822–1903). Olmsted held the uncommon view at the time that parks were essential in an industrialized country.[9] His philosophy was to foster "the democratic use of open space."[10] In Olmsted's own words, in an 1870 essay titled "Public Parks and the Enlargement of Towns":

> We want a ground to which people may easily go after their day's work is done, and where they may stroll for an hour, seeing, hearing, and feeling nothing of the bustle and jar of the streets, where they shall, in effect, find the city put far away from them. We want the greatest possible contrast with the streets and the shops and the rooms of the town which will be consistent with convenience and the preservation of good order and neatness. We want, especially, the greatest possible contrast with the restraining and confining conditions of the town, those conditions which compel us to walk circumspectly, watchfully, jealously, which compel us to look closely upon others without sympathy. Practically, what we most want is a simple, broad, open space for clean greensward, with sufficient play of surface and a sufficient number of trees about it to supply a variety of light and shade. This we want as a central feature. We want depth of wood enough about it not only for comfort in hot weather, but to completely shut out the city from our landscapes.[11]

This philosophy is manifested in Cadwalader Park. Speaking a century after Olmsted's vision was implemented, Trenton's Division of Natural Resources landscape architect, Randy Baum, more recently was quoted as saying: "You can get lost in the park and not think you're in the city of Trenton."[12] For Olmsted, the park was a work of art, meant to resonate and restore one's equilibrium: "What we want to gain is tranquility and rest to the mind."[13] Olmsted was part of the great reformist movements that sought to eliminate the mystery and contradiction of the post–Civil War American city: "Olmsted undertook a mission to teach the metropolis about itself, to clarify its parts, its outcroppings as well as its dense centers: to teach it especially to recognize its spaces as sites of meaning."[14]

Olmsted's New York parks are world-famous: Central Park, Riverside Park, Prospect Park. Cadwalader Park, while on a lesser scale, nonetheless attests to the importance of Trenton at the time. To have the services of such as Olmsted, this man of genius and foresight, was not a trivial matter.

Cadwalader Park also permits us to meditate a bit about the more global meaning implicit in the city park. Look at this place, and consider a broader context, and how Trenton fits in with that. In the mid–19th century, "British and European parks were generally estates that had been donated to the city, or private aristocrats' gardens to which the public was allowed access."[15] The public park in Birkenhead, near Liverpool, was different: it had been designed specifically as a public park, and was the subject of an article that Olmsted wrote for a horticultural magazine in 1851. In reading his description, one sees the nascence of his philosophy as reflected in the parks in New Jersey that he laid out, even today. Birkenhead Park was classless, or conversely, frequented by all economic groups, and this pleased Olmsted. Rybczynski notes Olmsted's ironic comment "that in democratic America there was nothing comparable to what he called the 'People's Park.'"[16] A more cynical view was that "embodied in the concept of the park, then, lay a motive to eradicate the communal culture of working-class and immigrant streets, to erase that culture's offensive and disturbing foreignness, and replace it with middle-class norms of hearth and tea table."[17]

Urban parks should be democratic open spaces. They should function as the great equalizer. Unfortunately, various urban parks have gone through a transition to fearful places, where even in daylight, one may not feel completely safe. They are not refuges from the city; to the contrary, they have become part of the contemporary city's malaise. For many people, they have become places to avoid, places of fear. Who wishes to walk under a graffiti-ridden, urine-stenched arch of a grand old stone arch bridge?

This more general, pro-democracy forum is reflected in the parks in New Jersey's cities designed by Olmsted or the landscaping firm he founded. Each of Olmsted's parks embody "signature combinations of rolling landscapes, curving drives, great lawns, dedicated recreation areas, and a variety of water features, like lakes and streams. But there is another, less tangible, thread that connects them."[18]

Cadwalader Park in Trenton, developed in the early 1890s, is reportedly the only of New Jersey's urban parks that Olmsted designed personally[19] and in the last years of his career.[20] A plaque in the park indicates it was finally completed in 1901.[21] He had submitted plans for a "Central Park" in Newark with his partner, Calvert Vaux, (1824–1895), in 1868, but the project was ultimately done as Newark's Branch Brook Park by Olmsted's landscaping firm. Similarly, plans were drawn up by Olmsted or his firm for Warinanco Park in Elizabeth, New Jersey. He also designed the campus for the Lawrenceville School, not far from Trenton and along the historic old "King's Highway" that is now part of Route 206.

The preliminary plan for Cadwalader Park shows a rough oval surrounded by trees, with open spaces within, and an area toward Stuyvesant Avenue labeled "Boys Playground," reflecting then-contemporary thinking. Playgrounds were viewed from a moral perspective, not a charitable one, helped by the prevailing view that play was an essential part of development.[22]

A website featuring Olmsted's work refers to the "Seven S's" of Olmsted's design: scenery, suitability, style, subordination, separation, sanitation and service.[23] In more expansive terms, Olmsted's vision contemplated the appearance of indefinite boundaries and ever-changing vistas as one looked upon the scenery in a park and moved about, but nonetheless respecting the natural ecology of the place, and making sure that the elements harmonized (subordination) while at the same time separating areas of the park. Branch Brook Park in Newark, designed by Olmsted's firm, is a good example of this philosophy, with the southern part of the park more scenic and pastoral, and the northern part more recreational. Similarly, Cadwalader Park in Trenton separates the purely recreational area, from the circular roadways that loop around the scenic areas of the park. There are streams and ponds, and an attractive footbridge. The park features the 1909 aqueduct that carries the Delaware and Raritan Canal Feeder over Parkside Avenue near the park's main entrance. Olmsted designed the park in 1891; this bridge, in Neo-Classical style, was meant to complement the park. It was originally known as the Cadwalader Park Tunnel. Built by the Pennsylvania Railroad, it is representative of the City Beautiful movement.

Branch Brook Park in Newark itself features three bridges of architectonic significance, and water also features extensively. Interestingly, although Branch Brook Park is now renowned for its cherry blossoms, they were not part of the original Olmsted design. Branch Brook is dominated by the spires of Newark's Sacred Heart Cathedral and its arch bridges.[24]

At present, Cadwalader Park retains monuments and statuary, and Ellarslie Museum.

Among these monuments is the Mercer County Soldiers' and Sailors' Monument. The monument was cast in 1907 and dedicated in 1909 to the county's fallen soldiers and sailors during the American Civil War. On one side is a sailor; on the other side is a soldier, and atop the memorial, a member of a Civil War Color Guard, all sculpted by Charles P. Owen. Nearby is the Swamp Angel, a three-hundred pound Civil War–era cannon used by Union forces in South Carolina to bombard Charleston, South Carolina; it was installed in Trenton in 1876[25]. According to Eleanore Nolan Shuman, the percussion shell launched into Charleston in August 1863 "was also the first poison-gas shell ever fired into a city."[26] It is sobering to look at this weapon of mass destruction in the Olmsted-designed urban park in Trenton. The Camp Olden Civil War site notes that it was moved from its city location to the park in 1961 on the 100th anniversary of the Civil War.[27]

As this book was being written, it was of interest to see the park fully utilized for an Easter Egg hunt. Children rushed past the statue of John Roebling on more urgent business of finding the eggs. While it may be that the competition from adjacent green areas and the facility of the automobile has drawn people away from the urban park as such, Cadwalader Park remains essential and far from redundant.

Trenton's other principal and historic park, Mahlon Stacy Park, runs along the Delaware River. It has been sliced from the main part of the city by the construction of Route 29, also known as the John Fitch Way, and is now undergoing reconstruction to reunite the park with the central city. Located behind the state capitol complex, the area is generally reclaimed swampland.[28] The park opened in 1916. At one time, during the 1920s, the Douglass House was placed here.

There are a variety of other, smaller parks in the city. One other worth noting is the Mill Hill Park, where the lopsided truss bridge crosses the Assunpink and the Second Battle of Trenton took place, as well as part of the First Battle of Trenton. The Delaware and Raritan Canal has become a state park, with portions of the towpath and canal still accessible and winding their way through the city.

Of note, and standing near Mill Hill Park off South Montgomery Street, is the statue of George Washington. Originally centered at the Philadelphia Centennial Exposition in 1876, then bought by private citizens and installed in Cadwalader Park in 1892, the 7-ton, Carerra marble sculpture was moved to Mill Hill Park in 1976. Interestingly, it is not an equestrian statute, but rather, features Washington as he was (supposedly) crossing the Delaware. In his left hand appears a spyglass; in the statue atop the Battle Monument he also holds a spyglass, though in his left hand. It is the same posture as reflected in the Emanuel Gottlieb Leutze painting that hangs in the Metropolitan Museum of Art in New York, and of which a copy hangs at the Washington's Crossing visitor's center in Pennsylvania.

A city's principal park is like its heart. It provides balance to the physical and intellectual activity surrounding it. In a place like Manhattan, Central Park provides a true place of repose — it is large enough to contain diverse and wild areas together with more "formal" recreational areas. One can wander a fair ways in Central Park, and find spots where the civilized is blocked, and the wild remains. Cadwalader Park, designed by the same man, is not as large, of course, but neither is Trenton as large as New York. Nonetheless, at a time when Trenton's citizens mainly lived and worked in the city, and did not get in cars to drive the few miles to the suburbs, Cadwalader Park provided the same kind of comfort and balance to the urban environment as Central Park. In that sense, even though it appears to be less used than historically, it continues to provide an essential function in Trenton life.

## *Cemeteries*

New Jersey has more than 800 cemeteries, ranging from family plots to large urban cemeteries.[29] Trenton's cemeteries, like many other urban cemeteries, are contemplative places that speak to the present. Burial places are sacred ground; we feel the need to have something physical to be near, to address, even if we know intellectually that the person is "not there." In her book *The American Resting Place*, Marilyn Yalom notes the importance of this as exemplified by the treatment of many of those who perished in the September 11, 2001, World Trade Center attack, with the interment of ashes on the Ground Zero site making it sacred.[30]

## 9. The Landscaped City

The philosophy behind the American cemetery, of which Trenton's are no exception, has evolved over time; today they are as much a place of general reflection as they are final "resting places" for the deceased. Yalom notes that "from the early seventeenth century though the late eighteenth century, Euro-American cemeteries were somber places intended not only for the disposal of bodies but also for the edification of the living. They were meant to be visual reminders that death awaited everyone."[31] With the 19th century, though, attitudes began to change as cemeteries deteriorated due to a belief they were somehow infectious. Beginning with the New Burying Ground in New Haven, Connecticut, as a reaction to the disorderliness of the old New Haven Green's utilization for this purpose, the cemetery came to be seen "as a transcendent oasis that could propel the spirit above life's quotidian cares."[32] Fed by the naturalist writings of such as the poet William Cullen Bryant, "early-nineteenth century civil leaders set out to create idyllic settings that would indeed be conducive to untroubled rest."[33] This "rural cemetery movement" was reflected in New Jersey; "the enormous marble and granite memorials that fill these cemeteries provided a medium for status-conscious Victorians to display a permanent record of their achievement."[34] And in the 20th century, we have been treated to the "memorial park," which lacks the individualized tombstones of the rural or garden cemetery, and generally features more uniform markers, with more meticulous attention to landscape.[35]

Sentiments similar to those identified by Yalom are reflected in a quaint booklet about Riverview Cemetery.[36] The place to be buried in Trenton if one wants the most attractive views is Riverview Cemetery. One wanders on this hill among the famous and not-so-famous, and looks out across the Delaware River and toward the Trenton-Hamilton Marsh. The view is that experienced by the late–17th-century European settlers in the area.

Riverview Cemetery was incorporated in 1858 by act of the New Jersey state legislature, but traces its European roots back to 1685 as a Quaker burial ground where, according to the plaque facing it, in South River Walk Park, "John Lambert, with his brother Thomas, arrived from Burlington, New Jersey by boat in 1678 and took over some 2000 acres on the bluffs overlooking the Delaware. Lambert conveyed two acres to the Chesterfield Friends Monthly Meeting for use as a burial ground."[37] If not on its precise site, certainly nearby, along the Route 29 corridor, late–20th-century excavations revealed Native American burial grounds.[38] It was enlarged twice in the 19th century, including by acquisition of land owned by Joseph Bonaparte, Napoleon's brother. Landscape architect Calvert Vaux , who worked with Frederick Law Olmsted, designed part of the expansion. It now has approximately 70,000 graves on its 50 acres. The first plot was sold to Captain William E. Hunt, a Trentonian living at Lalor and Third streets.[39] The national trend described by Yalom is also referred to in *Quakers, Warriors and Capitalists*, noting that Riverview was part of the "rural cemetery movement," and before the large city park became an urban fixture, these cemeteries were meant for the city's living population as well.[40]

John Taylor, a Trenton politician and businessman who also served in the state Senate, is buried here. Taylor also developed "pork roll," also known (more locally in New Jersey) as Taylor Ham. William Dayton (1807–1864), whose grave overlooks the Delaware River, was the newly formed Republican Party's first vice-presidential candidate in 1856, obtaining the nomination over Abraham Lincoln. (Lincoln stopped in Trenton on February 21, 1861, on the way to his inauguration, and addressed the Legislature at the Statehouse, then dined at the Trenton House, and continued by train to Philadelphia and Washington.) Lincoln later appointed Dayton as Minister to France, where Dayton was instrumental in keeping France from recognizing the Confederacy.

Civil War connections in the cemetery include Brigadier General Randolph Macy, the father-in-law of General George B. McClellan, who became governor of the state and is also buried in Riverview. Other Civil War figures buried here include William Archinal (1840–1919), Civil War Medal of Honor Recipient; William Halstead (1794–1878), United States Congressman from New Jersey and Civil War Army officer (founder and first Colonel of the 1st New Jersey Volunteer Cavalry regiment); George Peter Ihrie (1827–1903), Civil War Union Brevet Brigadier General; Gershom Mott (1822–1884), Civil War Union Army Major General; Samuel D. Oliphant (1824–1904), Civil War Union Army Brevet Brigadier General; D. Lane Powers (1896–1968), United States Congressman from New Jersey; John Augustus Roebling (1800–1869), German-American Industrialist and Civil Engineer, designer of the Brooklyn Bridge; James F. Rusling (1834–1918), Civil War Union Army Brevet Brigadier General; William S. Truex (1819–1889), Civil War Union Army Brevet Brigadier General; and Evan M. Woodward (1838–1904), Civil War Medal of Honor Recipient.[41]

There is actually a web entry for a listing of persons born before 1820 who are buried in Riverview, collected by Mabel W. Howell and Elizabeth Warren in 1929.[42] This is a very different kind of place. McClellan and Roebling are among the more famous men in American history. They are here. It helps give this place a perspective.

Equally historic but in a somewhat degraded state of repair is Mercer Cemetery, situated in the heart of Trenton and what is considered the Coalport/North Clinton area. Most of the times I have been there, the gate has been locked. Inside, many of the identifying markers of notable tombstones are shattered or broken. According to the New Jersey Department of State Archives, the land for the site was aggregated in 1841; burials began in 1842 prior to the cemetery's official incorporation in 1843 by the state legislature.[43] The last burial was in 1973; for most of the latter half of the 19th century, this cemetery was supposedly the place to be.[44] However, in typical Trenton, if not New Jersey, fashion, part of the cemetery was sold in 1892 to relieve financial pressures, and the cemetery's prestige, prominence, desirability and, ultimately, use fell off. It was restored in 1992, which raises the question of what it must have looked like in 1991.

The plaque at the cemetery tells us: "Within these walls rest statesmen, politicians, soldiers and plain citizens of 19th century Trenton. Mercer Cemetery itself is a monument to their contributions to the life of this city." Seventeen historic grave sites are noted, for Sgt. John P. Beech, James Taylor, John O. Raum, William Potts Sherman, Charles Hewitt, William Borrow, Dr. John Manners, Charles Chauncey Haven, William R. McKean, Dr. John McKelway, Hamilton Family, John Briest, Capt. James Olden Paxson, Ira Wells Wood, William Young, Daniel Budd Bodine and Capt. Joseph A. Yard. White was an English-born potter who "was the first to produce white earthenware of only American materials," according to the informational marker. Apart from the soldiers, politicians and industrialists, the most notable grave here, and the most poignant to me, is that of William Borrow.

William Borrow was the shop foreman at the new Trenton Iron Company in the 1850s, owned by Peter Cooper, his son Edward, and his future son-in-law Abram Hewitt, and which was the largest of its kind, and engaged in a frantic effort to "manufacture a 7-inch (18 cm) heavy bulb-tee rail beam."[45] This was critical to the effort to provide adequate support for the kinds of buildings then being constructed in American cities as the Industrial Revolution took off. In 1853 Borrow produced long U-shaped channel beams, a kind of I-beam. By early 1854, Trenton Iron Company produced wrought-iron bulb-tee in a single piece, another step in the evolution of the I-beam. The goal was still to produce an actual I-beam, and the effort killed Borrow — he died from exhaustion at age 34 on October 1, 1854. On his grave, though, he is noted for his singular contribution to the development and production of the I-beam, a critical component of the construction industry.

In a near-contemporaneous book published in 1855 by Jacob Abbott of Harper Brothers, describing the construction of the new Harper Building, which was one of the first to use this kind of flange, Borrow's heroic efforts are detailed, in somewhat inflated prose:

> The desideratum was therefore to make a solid rolled flanged beam of the right shape and proportions, and of the weight required for the spans ordinarily adopted in the buildings of large cities. The method of rolling such flanged beams was finally brought into successful operation at the iron-works of the Trenton Iron Company, situated in Trenton, N. J. The difficulties to be overcome in contriving and constructing the necessary machinery were very great. The mass of iron required for each beam, and which has, of course, to be pressed through the rollers at almost a white heat, is enormously heavy. Then the difficulty of constructing the rollers so that the iron, in passing through between them, shall have formed upon it flauges [sic] so wide as are necessary for beams, was very serious. We can not here describe the means by which at length the end

***William Borrow Grave.*** Located in the Mercer Cemetery, this grave commemorates Borrow and his contribution to the development of the I-beam, critical to the Industrial Revolution and construction of tall buildings.

was attained.* The arrangement was invented by a young Englishman named William Borrow. He was a relative of the author of Lavengro and of the Bible in Spain. Mr. Peter Cooper, under whose general charge the operation was conducted, was specially interested in the work, from the desire to employ such beams for the purpose of making fire-proof the large edifice which he was then erecting in New York for the Scientific Institution. He calculated that he should be able to put up the machinery in four months, and at an expense of about thirty thousand dollars.

The difficulties were, however, found to be far greater than had been foreseen. Instead of four months, it was two years before the machinery was brought into successful operation, and the cost of it, instead of thirty, was a hundred and fifty thousand dollars. And when at length the machinery was made to work successfully, the designer, Mr. Borrow, suddenly became ill, and died within a week, from the prostration of all his energies, mental and physical — a martyr to the difficulties which beset the practical workers of the world, whose story is seldom told, and who die without odes or funeral orations to celebrate their triumph or to honor their memory.[46] [*The process of rolling out these immense bars of glowing iron forms a very magnificent sight. It can be witnessed at any time at the works at Trenton, which are always readily shown to visitors.]

So here in the middle of Trenton, in a worn-down cemetery that sees few visitors, a young Englishman, who adopted this city as his own, literally worked himself to death, a virtually unsung hero in American construction and industrialization. The place he worked is now a bar-restaurant near a minor league baseball field. There was a time, truly, when Trenton made and the world took, and it was the result of the lives, efforts, and deaths of people like William Borrow. People whose graves are unvisited, unremarked.

St. Michael's Church on North Warren Street traces its congregation to 1703. The current building stands where a predecessor building stood at the Battle of Trenton where Washington's troops opened fire on the Hessians. The cemetery was once larger, and now has about 100 tombstones intact. It includes some of the city's earliest families, such as the Coxes and the Williamses. In addition, Pauline Joseph Ann Holten, daughter of Joseph Bonaparte, king of Spain, and his Quaker mistress, Ann Savage are buried there.[47]

Friends Meeting Ground Cemetery, adjacent to the Friends Meeting House (described earlier), contains the grave of Thomas Cadwalader, first burger of the Free Borough of Trenton, as well as George Clymer, signer of the Declaration of Independence. Also noted earlier, the First Presbyterian Church has a cemetery that includes the grave of Abraham Hunt, a city merchant who was entertaining Hessian commander Rall the night before the First Battle of Trenton but who was also purportedly helping Washington.[48] Hunt remains a controversial figure, if not exactly at everyone's fingertips; Fischer notes he swore allegiance to both causes.[49] Fischer writes: "For Abraham Hunt and Stacy Potts and others in Trenton, the Revolution was good for business. They made the most of their opportunities, and both sides were happy to deal with them."[50]

***St. Michael's Church.*** Founded in 1703, built between then and 1748, and one of New Jersey's oldest Episcopal parishes, the church featured in the First Battle of Trenton. Over the years the building underwent various renovations. The Gothic façade reportedly was added in the 19th century.

Similarly, Lida Newberry writes in *New Jersey: A Guide to Its Past and Present* that "Hunt gave indirect assistance to Washington's victory at Trenton by pressing the Hessian commander to partake of his hospitality on the Christmas Night before the battle."[51]

Whatever he did or did not do, his remains have turned to dust in this plot of ground here in Trenton.

The green spaces of the city paradoxically reflect life and death. The traditional park has developed as a place of life and of renewal, as a place to seek and obtain balance. The traditional cemetery began as a place of death and honor, and yet has become parklike. Strolling through Riverview, with its vistas over the Delaware River, is a strangely calming experience. Trenton's parks and cemeteries, like those of other cities large and small, are integral to its character, culture and urbanity.

# PART THREE
# PEOPLE REACTING TO THE CITY

## 10. *The City of Thought*

If a city, as some suggest, is the ultimate achievement of humanity, then we can consider the city also as not only an intellectual exercise, but also a place of ideological exchange. Certainly in the pre-digital, pre-virtual age, when artists actually congregated in physical proximity in the café or tavern, ideas were exchanged, bounced around, considered, offered, rejected, in a physical place. The city was a place of excitement, a tactile place where human beings communicated with each other in the flesh. The city has also been a place of education, where people aggregate to learn skills.[1] One wonders at the impact of the Age of the Blog, where intangible expression has to a large extent replaced that physical expression.

Nonetheless, we continue to associate cities with artistic endeavor and, more broadly, intellectualism. Some refer to their graduate degrees from the "school of hard knocks," and so forth. The city is a place of cafés where writers and artists congregate; a place of galleries and museums where the cognoscenti preen. The stereotypes remain.

But there is, as with all stereotypes, a kernel of truth. The city, by virtue of its concentrated population, diversity of both people and occupations, enables a certain amount of resources to be devoted to cultural activities, which, in turn, enrich the city and help sustain it. However, the positive side of urban intellectual life, or even intellectualism itself, is one side of the coin. There is a history of anti-intellectualism as part of the American narrative that goes hand-in-glove with a distrust, if not hostility, to the city.

In the film *Mr. Holland's Opus*, Mr. Holland, a high school music teacher, is retired because the school board has decided that music is a luxury that cannot be afforded. He is told that the basics are more important. He comments to his colleague, the gym teacher and football coach, that the latter need have no worries; the football team will never be cut. The meaning was clear: pursuits such as art and music were deemed non-essential to American life. Richard Hofstadter identified the phenomenon in his classic 1963 work, *Anti-Intellectualism in American Life*, and traced its roots to the democratization of the

United States. Among other things, he also identified the impact of the loss of village life to the cities. More recently, we have the phenomenon of anti-rationalism, a smugness in not knowing certain things.[2]

There is an artistic community in Trenton. The Trenton Artists Workshop Association is a non-profit group formed in 1979 that boasts 350 members, ranging from artists to students.[3] Trenton resident and renowned artist/photographer Jon Naar organized the Trenton Artist Salon, in conjunction with Café Ole on Warren Street.[4] Gallery 125, at the corner of Warren and Lafayette streets, was opened by the Trenton Downtown Association for varied art exhibits but at least as of this writing, closed in June 2010, a victim of budget cuts[5] Various other events, such as poetry readings and slams, or other art exhibits, occur or have occurred in the recent past at different venues.[6] The city boasts the Greater Trenton Symphony Orchestra,[7] which performs a popular set of concerts on New Years' Eve each year at the War Memorial Building. The New Jersey Symphony Orchestra also avails itself of that venue. There is a Trenton Film Society that hosts the annual Trenton Film Festival,[8] and the Mill Hill Playhouse, run by the Passage Theatre Company, which provides live theater in the city.[9] The State Museum Auditorium, within the museum and capitol complex, is another venue for performances. Higher educational institutions are represented by a campus Mercer County Community College, and the site of the unique Thomas Edison University, which gives credits for one's life experience in awarding degrees, modeled after the inventor.

So if it no longer has the Taylor Opera House, or even a traditional movie theater, Trenton as a city remains a place where the kinds of cultural activity we generally think of as part of the urban experience not only exists, but also thrives. It is perhaps one of the city's secrets, and certainly one of its charms. If not Greenwich Village or Montmartre, Trenton's Lafayette/Warren/Front Street area is nonetheless a piece of the global artistic, urban mosaic.

Let us move from Trenton to a broader context, and then back again.

## *The City and Anti-Intellectualism*

Hofstadter's *Anti-Intellectualism in American Life* is an appropriate starting point. To the extent that the 19th-century American city was the city of business, Trenton was no exception. Business ultimately was good for the intellectual life of the city, and vice versa. In short, the communities needed each other. In the early 20th century, there were caricatures of the businessman, such as Sinclair Lewis's Babbitt, but the businessman himself, creating impersonal corporate structures that overshadow individuality, bears certain responsibility for the stereotype.[10] Hofstadter finds that this "tension between intellect and business has about it ... a kind of ungainly intimacy, symbolized in the fact that so many intellectuals are rebelling against the business families in which they were reared."[11] So the notion of "business" as anti-intellectual was a kind of political phenomenon, but was also successful due to its roots in conventional wisdom.[12] This hostility was a change in attitude from the early 19th century, when the "mercantile ideal" was that of a kind of business aristocracy — well-to-do, cultured, civic-responsive.[13] But as the 19th century concluded and the Industrial Revolution peaked, "the more thoroughly business dominated American society, the less it felt the need to justify its existence by reference to values outside its own domain."[14] The image of this "mercantile ideal" gave way to the image of the "self-made man," those who made it with street smarts as opposed to book learning; "there went a persistent hostility to formal education and a countervailing cult of experience."[15]

Ultimately, the 19th century fostered the history of anti-intellectualism and to a large extent, intellectuals themselves fed the tension: "partly by their own fiat, intellect had become associated with losing causes and exemplified by social types that were declining in vigor and influence, encapsulated by an impermeable world."[16]

We speak of being urbane, from the Latin *urbanus*, meaning of a city, itself with the root *urbs*, or city. There is a long history in this country of anti-urbanism. One can almost draw a circle from Thomas Jefferson's original condemnations of the city (before his later, if partial, recantations) to Frank Lloyd Wright's harangues against the concentrated city. In *The Intellectual Versus the City*, Lucia and Morton White note the contemporary concern over the plight of the nation's cities, yet write that "enthusiasm for the American city has not been typical or predominant in our intellectual history."[17] Although many refer to Jefferson's agrarian bias, particularly reflected in his *Notes on Virginia* the Whites refer to Jefferson's reaction to the yellow fever epidemic of 1800 as being a causal factor in his changed, or at least softened, attitude. They write: "For once he came to view yellow fever as avoidable, at least in newly planned cities, a powerful anti-urban argument had been met in his mind. He still disliked the European city's spirit, manners, and principles, and he would have done without those if he could, but he would not abandon the American city to disease in the name of Providence of ideological commitment."[18] In 1816, he also reflected a realization that industry was as necessary for the preservation of independence as agriculture.

Interestingly enough, as Hofstadter points out, Jefferson himself was pilloried by certain Federalists as a "philosopher" and therefore lacking the character to be president.[19]

It is perhaps no accident that anti–urbanism and anti-intellectualism are linked. It is commonplace to hear about the "city slicker" confronted by the practical, down-to-earth, common-sensical farmer or villager who doesn't "put much stock" in "book-learning." The city, by conventional wisdom, is a place of great universities, of late-night conversations in bohemian quarters over alcohol, cigarettes or drugs, of new ideas and exotic, and erotic, entertainment. But if they are linked, they are also not necessarily the same. It was possible for rural populations to resent the city for other reasons—the influx of foreigners (as if the country has not been founded by immigrants), as well as the residue of the Industrial Revolution and its concomitant poverty, crime and pollution in the 19th century.

New York features prominently, as the preeminent and largest of the American cities, in any discussion of anti-urbanism. Still, New York was not the only industrial city during the Industrial Revolution of 19th century America; certainly places like Trenton, among the hundred largest American cities at the time, had urban cultures. The city *qua* city was not limited to New York. The attitudes toward the city may have been inspired in large part by various writers' and commentators' experiences with particular cities, especially New York, but that does not mean attitudes toward cities did not affect, and continue to affect, places like Trenton. Indeed, the features of urban life that so repulsed some anti-urbanists in the 19th century—the crime, chaos and grime of the city— are among the same denominators that have caused many to write off places like Trenton that have not succeeded in reinventing themselves or otherwise adapting to the post-industrial, post–World War II world.

The literature of the new nation, particularly through the Transcendentalists Ralph Waldo Emerson and Henry David Thoreau, showed a "distrust of the America city."[20] In particular, Emerson stated in his 1844 lecture, "The Young Americans," that "the cities drain the country of the best part of its population," although Andrew Lees suggests as well that there is also a pro-urban strain in some of his writings.[21] This dislike was across the board by the 1850s, shared by "empiricist and transcendentalist, individualist and utopian socialist," and was potent.[22] Jefferson's views reflected his affinity for the land, for farming and a suspicion of the mob, which he associated with the Industrial Revolution. The 19th century's important American writers—Herman Melville, Nathaniel Hawthorne and Edgar Allan Poe—linked "commerce, crime, crowds, and conventionalism ... with the city in a horrible alliterative dream."[23] Melville in particular, in his 1852 novel *Pierre,* presented the city (New York) as a bitter place.[24] Jefferson's views on the antithetical results of cities on democracy, in the words of another commentator on urbanism and American democracy, "set the style for the treatment the city was to receive in subsequent political thought," and puts into question the White's conclusion that Jefferson truly recanted his anti-urban views.[25] Indeed, it has been observed that hostility toward "the city" has Biblical roots, reflecting the alienation of humanity from God.[26] Religious overtones remained part of the basis of hostility toward the American city well into the 19th century; Lees points to a book by John Todd called *The Moral Influence, Dangers and Duties Connected with Great Cities,* appearing in 1841, as one such example.[27]

This anti-urban feeling, as the 19th century closed, was less based in an abstract love of country versus city, but rather, was a result of more intellectual criticism itself, as exemplified in the writings of Henry Adams.[28] That hostility seemed to derive as much from prejudice as from rigorous or rational discourse. For Adams, particular components of society — ranging from the "crowd" to "bankers" to "Jews" — were the epitome of what he hated about cities.[29] To Henry James, another *fin-de-siecle* commentator, it was the chaos, ugliness and excess of the cities he observed and that formed the focus of his novels.[30] William Dean Howells was the "ambivalent urbanite," whose novels, the Whites suggest, reflect a fear of the city and a nostalgia for village life. Novelists Frank Norris and Theodore Dreiser similarly depict a hatred of New York, based in part on the suffering of the poor and the seeming indifference to it. The work of Jacob Riis in the 1890s also forced awareness of the social conditions of the city, something that urban advocates, and not simply urban critics, had to focus on.[31]

William James and Jane Addams brought a degree of pragmatism and focus on social work in the city. For James, "the operative word" was "possibility."[32] He offered *pragmatism* as a philosophy that suited the city: "a livable city on earth, one is therefore tempted to say, is the social manifestation of James' pragmatism, and that is why he is one of the first great American philosophers to associate himself with the life of the American city."[33] His disciple, Jane Addams, sought, as other reformers, "not to destroy the city but to recreate within it something lie the spirit of life as it was lived in an earlier time."[34] The city was no longer antithetical; it was something with opportunity and possibility, with the weapons for reform, including education and communication.[35]

Others influenced by James — notably Robert Park and John Dewey — sought to study and quantify the city, to understand it, to apply sociological methodology to it. However, even they, note the Whites, were distrustful, if interested: "One might hesitate to apply the term 'anti-urbanist' to them because of its suggestion of thorough disapproval of city life, but both Dewey and Park had deep reservations and feelings of uneasiness about the city of the twentieth century, reservations and feelings that arose in part from their favorable estimate of a mode of life they associated with the pre-industrial past."[36] Lees, in his book on the city and European and American thought, called Park's work "evenhanded" and helpful in creating awareness and understanding of the city, even as Lewis Mumford was "excoriating 'megalopolis.'"[37] The Whites contend that Lewis Mumford, one of the preeminent writers on the city, arguably falls within the pantheon of anti-urbanists, believing "that cities and their walls originated in and encouraged war," and that "like Emerson he thinks that the city has destroyed the whole human being."[38]

During the Depression, an anti-urbanist sentiment gained further traction, with a group of Southern poets — the Fugitives — at the forefront. Expressing an "agrarian versus industrial" mindset, poets John Crowe Ransom, Robert Penn Warren, Alan Tate and John Davidson targeted the city, including Southern cities, as hostile to Southern values of gentility.[39]

Frank Lloyd Wright was an advocate of dismantling the city as it had become, whose "inclination to demolish the city was stoner than his desire to rebuild it in anything like its present form."[40] The Whites suggest that, like Adams, he shared, at least in part, an anti–Semitic basis for disliking the contemporary city.[41] In *The Living City*, Wright identifies three "artificialities" of modern production that establish the evil of the city: rent for land, rent for money (i.e., interest) and the "unearned increment of the machine itself," that is, the profits of leverage over labor.[42] But regarding the second one, interest, he writes: "By way of the ancient Mosaic invention of 'interest,' money is now a commodity for sale, so made as to come alive as something in itself—to go on continuously working in order to make all work useless."[43]

Bigness, or at least those cities that were big enough that they lost interconnectedness and sense of community, was not preferred, and led to parochialism.[44] Bigness, industrialization, a sense of loss of control — perhaps all of these were factors that preyed on populist sentiments. Ultimately, the Whites refer to "the legacy of fear," and the fact that respected American intellectuals, and particularly its writers, have attacked American city life.[45] They write:

> An anti-urban ideology may arise from the same feelings that underlie popular attitudes, but the ideology can logically refine these feelings and give them a more respectable and authoritative form. The fact that so many intellectual figures who occupy our national pantheon said more in opposition to city life than they said in praise of it is responsible for the fact that today's city planner in America finds no powerful intellectual tradition of love for the city to which he can appeal.[46]

Following the American Civil War, when the population shift from a rural to an urban country began, "hostility toward the city has also found repeated expression in the various movements of political protest which have agitated rural America, from the Grangers tin the 1870s to the Farmers' Holiday Association in more recent times."[47] Among other reinforcing factors of this hostility were the nativist (anti-immigrant) movement and the Prohibitionists.[48]

Why the persistent hostility? We can, like the Whites, note the paradox that the city is generally considered the place where intellectuals are to be found in concourse with each other, that urbanization is increasing, and that this kind of anti-urbanism has not been found, at least to the extent expressed in America, in Europe. We can, like them, reject the simple answer of "romanticism," because the reasons of anti-urbanism reflected in their various writings have been too diverse. No theory could be built upon such divergent "views" that range from anti–Semitism to a longing for nature and a view that the city, deviating from nature, is wicked. However, "the tradition of anti-urbanism in American writing is at its best when it convey esthetic, psychological, and moral ideas, and impressions of the city's defects," and therefore current urban and city planners ignore such a tradition of criticism at their peril.[49] With the city here to stay, urban planners must move forward but with "a respect for the fundamental values of education, individuality, and easy communications among men. But unlike his predecessors, he cannot deceive himself about the *place* in which those values must be realized today"—that is, the city.[50]

I have not attempted an independent survey of the theme here, as being beyond the scope of this chapter and this book. What I have sought to do is explore, albeit briefly, the thinking of the Whites, Lees and Hofstadter as they considered America's intellectual history, its writers, thinkers and influence peddlers over the past three centuries, in the context of the city. What one concludes is that there is a discernible thread (and threat) of anti-urbanism, even by those who might be considered sympathetic to "the city." The particular reasons may be era-sensitive, but the pattern seems to have persisted. In the current American socio-political environment, race and xenophobia may also be seen to play a part, as demographics have shifted, and suburban communities become resentful of subsidizing failed cities within their counties and states.[51]

Trenton as a city may be used to reflect upon the broader phenomenon of anti-intellectualism in American history, not limited just to anti-urban suspicions. The issue of business and intellectual development is as old as cities themselves. In his *Medieval Cities,* Henri Pirenne argued, essentially, that cities arose as a result of trade, which produced a new class, the commercial middle class. Previously there had been the clergy, nobles and serfs, but with the advent of commerce, the new "bourgeoisie" arose. However, the link between cultural development and business was essential; he writes, "In no civilization has city live evolved independently of commerce and industry."[52] Cities were needed to support their needs for centralized manufacture and trade. Trenton itself reflected the development of that new bourgeoisie. We need only think of the Roeblings, the Maddocks and the Lenoxes, among others, as the leading industrial families in the city. Indeed, in Trenton we find that the founder of the city's opera house was the manufacturer of pork roll. The Roeblings and the Maddocks were among the preeminent civic leaders in the city's Golden Age. Pride in the city would seem to reflect on their corporate being as well. If there were meaning to *Trenton Makes, the World Takes,* there was also meaning to a transcendent positive image from the city to its businesses and back again.

## The City as Art

Given New Jersey's Colonial status, and its cities being among the nation's oldest, it is good to reflect on the city as a place of learning by noting the reminders in the city's geography. For example, Trenton has an Academy Street, named for the school founded in 1781 as the Trenton School Company; the building was completed and opened in 1782 as an elementary school with 40 students.[53] It was renamed Trenton Academy in 1785 with a basic curriculum,

***Academy Street.*** **This image provides a perspective on the Hanover/Academy Historic District. Abandoned houses and inhabited houses exist in proximity. This street was originally named Fourth Street in colonial Trenton, and was renamed Academy Street after the Trenton Academy that stood where the city's current public library stands.**

which expanded as its reputation grew. Among its more notable alumni was John Roebling's son, Washington Augustus Roebling. It closed in 1884; in 1900 it was sold to the Trenton Public Library, whose main branch is on Academy Street. The first reported record of a library in Trenton was 1750.[54] The "Apprentices Library" was established in 1821, and 30 years later, in 1852, the main progenitor of the current library was opened to the public in rented space in the Temperance Hall, then moved to its own building on Greene Street.[55] In 1897 Trenton's mayor, Welling G. Sickel, formed a committee to consider a free public library for Trenton, which was approved and in 1902, the current building on Academy Street was completed and the library launched.[56]

When we look at this building — the original building, and not the new addition — we see the kind of Classical architecture we associate with monumental, civil buildings. There is the portico with columns, its cornice with modillions, and all part of the American Renaissance that drew on classical construction.[57] More to the point, though, this building — and what it stands for — was part of the broader movement in American cities during the so-called American Renaissance to put an American flavor on these public buildings at the turn of the century. As McKelvey writes, "the pervasive atmosphere of the Renaissance swept over America. New state capitols in Providence, Madison,

## 10. The City of Thought

*The Cultural Complex.* The New Jersey State Museum and the New Jersey State Library are fine examples of Modernist architecture from the 1960s. Their compelling façades frame the dome of the planetarium, recently renovated to state-of-the-art standards. The New Jersey State Museum was established by Legislative enactment in 1895. The planetarium was renovated and reopened with state-of-the-art facilities in 2009. The State Library dates itself to 1796 as the official date when the Legislature entrusted the Clerk of the House with the responsibility of maintaining the state's collection of books.

Harrisburg, and St. Paul revealed the Beaux-Arts background of their architects. New libraries and art galleries in a dozen cities from Boston to San Francisco borrowed facades from French or Italian Renaissance palaces or from Greek or Roman temples."[58] We can compare it to the city hall, discussed elsewhere, and built around the same time.

So it is not just the architectural expression, but also the focus on the cultural and intellectual growth of the city — embodied by the public library — that is also represented by this building. We can stand on Academy Street and take in this building, contemplate its history, and let our mind wander to the bigger questions of American life.

Another connection to the urban world through art is triggered by a visit to the New Jersey State Museum.[59] One of the ways to do this is to focus on a particular artist who himself paid attention to capturing the city *qua* city and is represented in the museum: George Ault.

In 1989, the New Jersey State Museum in Trenton was one of several museums, including the Whitney Museum of Art in New York, which featured an exhibition of the artist George Ault's work.[60] Ault (1891–1948) lived in New Jersey for part of his life, and often painted Precisionist/Cubist style urban landscapes. The New Jersey State Museum holds one of his paintings, and it is an appropriate connection to this book that it does, since his artwork provides another kind of prism for getting at the nature of the city. While the "Ashcan School" of painters, exemplified by, among others, John Sloan, may capture the realism and squalor and humanity of city life, Ault's near-crayon-like work goes to the essence of the city's architecture and lifeblood. Not quite as abstract as Fernand Leger, not as realistic as John Sloan, not always "Precisionist," he is, for me, among the quintessential urban painters. If he lacks Edward Hopper's sense of mystery and foreboding, he nonetheless captures the power, potency and potential of the city and more of Giorgio de Chirico's isolation and estrangement. Ault is also represented in the Newark Museum by his painting, "From Brooklyn Heights."

As we look at the geometric, simplified planes of Ault's painting in the State Museum, and reflect upon his aesthetic vision of the industrial city, we can step outside the State Museum onto State Street, into the real world of an industrial city, and allow life imitating art to flow through us.

It is not so far-fetched to consider the city as a work of art in itself. In *The City as a Work of Art: London, Paris, Vienna*, Donald J. Olsen notes the apparent contradiction in terms. Those who defend the city often do so on grounds of economic necessity and efficiency, an infrastructure: "To both attackers and defenders, the city is the product of vast, anonymous forces, not an individual creation. Any beauty it might possess would be incidental to its real nature, any visible structure one imposed by historical necessity rather than artistic intent."[61] But, Olsen suggests, in at least three cases—London, Paris and Vienna—the city shape was determined not because of industrialization, but almost in spite of it. During the 19th century, like Vienna, "imperial Paris and London, too, were deliberate artistic creations not merely intended to give pleasure but to contain ideas, inculcate values, and serve as tangible expressions of systems of thought and morality."[62] He discusses this in his opening chapter of the city as luxury in terms of urban virtue and urban beauty, and the efforts made during the 19th century to develop the city itself as an aesthetic creation.

Olsen's analytical components are to view the city as monument, as home, as playground, and as document. The city as monument is meant to establish parts of the city as more than its monuments, to create great public spaces and buildings that make the city itself a testament to something greater than its mundane and workaday life. The city as home attested to the contrast of private life from public life in the city; in its outside architecture, interior space and social geography. The city as playground focuses on its hidden pleasures, gardens, cafés. The city as document involved architecture as historical evidence: Olsen notes one of his underlying assumptions that "a work of art is also a historical source, that the city, as the largest and most characteristic art form of the nineteenth century, has something to tell us about the inner nature of that century."[63] Architecture was an avenue through which the creators of the city sought to establish beauty: "A city in its public buildings necessarily reflects the aesthetic values of the regime, in its private structures the taste of those economically strong enough to participate in 'the market.'"[64] Even if the architecture in each city did not necessarily reflect a unifying theme in European civilization, it nonetheless reflected the "assumptions and convictions shared by the makers" of London, Paris and Vienna that "architecture was a language, capable of expressing complex and important ideas. Another was that such ideas ought to be directed to the service of public good and private morality."[65]

Rykwert as well comments on the importance of the "private realm" and the importance of middle-class and working-class housing to architects during the Industrial Revolution and thereafter.[66] That housing became intertwined with the other preeminent feature of the Industrial Revolution — the factory. As such, both housing and the factory — hitherto relatively unregarded by architects — became a principal focus, and a principal part of the tangible face of the urban environment.[67]

Perhaps most importantly, and most relevant to consideration of a place such as Trenton, is the notion Olsen puts forth that the city is an "embodiment of history," which provided an organizing principle: the buildings, the architecture, the entire *language* of the city "were employed and perceived by a culture that thought *historically*."[68]

In analyzing the impact of the Obama administration on the cities, this theme of anti-urban sentiment — notwithstanding that 80 percent of the United States population lives in metropolitan areas — continues, in the view of some.[69] The authors of a piece appearing in both *The New Statesman* and *The Nation*, speaking from "the left," identify this hostility as a function of racism, the "indifference of the mainstream left" such as labor unions that have not focused on the cities as such, a "political and cultural conservatism" that counterbalances the liberalism generally found in and associated with cities, and factionalism among local governments.[70]

We have moved from art to the city as art to the antithesis of aesthetic. The relevance of this to Trenton finds itself in the persistence of the centuries-old issue: the city as a place of poverty. It is not enough to rail against the city. We are not turning back. We cannot de-urbanize. If anything, writers like Kunstler and planners like Duany argue for increased urbanization and density. From an efficiency standpoint, James Lovelock notes that "a well-run city uses less food and energy than a civilization of villages and isolated farms; certainly less than the distributed exurban communities that surround most of the developed world's towns today."[71] In short, the city remains essential. It is not the enemy. If Lovelock is to be believed, it is the last best hope for the planet.

## Cultural Institutions

We have been meandering about Trenton and thinking about the city as an intellectual place. We have used Trenton to touch on broader issues of anti-urbanism and anti-intellectualism. We find that Trenton has enclaves of artistic society. We also find that Trenton has three museums of significance: the New Jersey State Museum, the Ellarslie Museum, and the Grounds for Sculpture.[72]

Museums matter.

Museums form and shape the city's intellectual life. Cities become centers for art and creativity, which in turn shape the city's image. A city is perceived to be a cultural center, a place to which artists go to vindicate themselves.

I have a vague recollection of an episode of *Star Trek: The Next Generation*, in which the captain of the *Enterprise*, Jean-Luc Picard, explains to someone (his immediate subordinate, Riker) why he reads philosophy. He says, in essence, that while mastery of science and technology is important, it is philosophy that gives it purpose and meaning. Something like that. Like when Mr. Holland in the movie says that if you eliminate music to focus on reading, eventually people won't have anything to read about. The same thought.

I once attended a reception in Trenton on behalf of the New Jersey State Museum and the Friends organization that supports the museum, as a trustee of the Friends and a board member of the Museum. A then-member of the New Jersey State Assembly, and former museum board member, said a few words, and called museums in general "food for the soul." She made that remark in the context of the pressures facing legislatures in times of deep financial crisis. What do you say when fellow legislators are arguing for money for such things as food stamps, child care and the like? Her comment addressed Picard's observation.

The Grounds for Sculpture is on the site of the old New Jersey State Fairgrounds, along East State Street Extension and just beyond the physical border of Trenton, in Hamilton Township. Fairs date back to medieval times, and in 1745 King George II granted a royal charter for the conduct of a fair in "Trenton Township." Such fairs involved sales of livestock and other commercial activity. It was the first fair in the colonies and lasted for five years; later, in 1797, the New Jersey Legislature banned fairs.[73] The notion of an agricultural fair was revived in the 19th century, and by the 1880s the "state fair" was established; in 1888, such luminaries as Annie Oakley made an appearance. By the 1970s the state fair was in decline; in 1988 the Grounds for Sculpture, led by sculptor J. Seward Johnson, purchased the grounds (which included 1920s buildings such as the Domestic Arts Building) and created a somewhat magical, if surreal, place in the middle of an industrial area spilling over from Trenton into "suburban" Hamilton.

The Grounds for Sculpture is a unique open air museum, but its influence on the surrounding industrial area is great. A variety of sculptures grace the landscape, intermixed among the factories and distribution centers. The Hamilton Train Station nearby also has some sculpture. It is an intriguing use of art in public places. A small sampling of sculptures is near the Trenton train station, in a plaza in front of office buildings, but lacks the scope and impact of the Hamilton example.

Trenton also boasts Ellarslie, the city's museum, part of the aesthetics of Cadwalader Park. It focuses on rotating exhibits but has a permanent collection highlighting the city's pottery and ceramic industries.[74] Other aspects of the collection include fine and decorative arts, and cultural history. It has been the city museum since 1978, but the Italianate villa began as a residence when constructed in 1848. This museum is another small treasure of the city's artistic reservoir. Its annual "open," which invites contributions from area artists, is in the best tradition of museums and salons that seek to support and cultivate their city's talent.

Among the premier institutions in the city is The New Jersey State Museum. It was established in 1895 with a focus on "natural history, archeology and industrial history."[75] It expanded with ethnography and fine arts collections, as well as a significant New Jersey collection and a planetarium. At present, it divides itself into, as it puts it, "four museums in one"—archeology and ethnology, cultural history, fine art and natural history. I wrote earlier of George Ault, represented in the museum's collection. Countless schoolchildren in the state made the class trip to the museum.

I had a personal hand in certain other acquisitions, most notably that of a Julian Scott[76] (1846–1901) painting, "General Washington Discussing Plans, Morristown, New Jersey." Painted in 1876–1877, this painting was known at one point as "Horse Drawn Sleigh." It depicts Washington in a colorful sleigh in conversation; a soldier walks behind, and another, on horseback, rides nearby. I was chair of the exhibition and acquisitions committee at the time, and was intrigued to be participating in building the American art collection of this significant museum. It is but one small piece of a collection, and one smaller piece of the cultural history of Trenton, but it was a privilege to have been a part of it.

This museum, once the stuff of near-mandatory school trips for so many of the state's children, as of this writing soldiers on with a determined if reduced staff and limited funding, to regain its former prominence. It is another casualty of the battle between money and will, between the statements espoused by the fictional starship captain Jean-Luc Picard and the fictional music teacher Mr. Holland on the one hand, and the "pragmatists" on the other. At the end of the day, failure to consider the intellectual life of a city as important will lead to a city's downfall. A city cannot function without its soul.

## Newspapers

A final word about the city and its intellectual life must make note of the media. Trenton remains one of the few surviving two-newspaper cities.[77] It went through a somewhat tumultuous period. Its Colonial and post–Revolution history indicated a vibrant media center, with a variety of newspapers. Isaac Collins' *New Jersey Gazette* was Trenton's (and New Jersey's) first newspaper.[78] It began in 1777 in Burlington, and relocated to Trenton in early 1778. After several Colonial-era efforts came and went, and various failed efforts through the 1830s, two newspapers gained credibility in the mid–19th century — *The State Gazette* and *The True American*.[79] *The True American* lost out in the early 20th century to the *Trenton Times*, which by the late 19th century had absorbed *The State Gazette*. In the 1980s, the *Trenton Times* dropped the city from its name in an effort by its owner, the *Washington Post*, to establish the paper as the leading newspaper in the state of New Jersey, and drive out the *Trentonian*. It failed on both counts, losing readership.[80] Today *The Times* as the *Trenton Times* is now known, remains in competition with *The Trentonian*. The latter is in tabloid form, and began in 1946 by ex–*Trenton Times* members of the International Typographic Union.

Are cities losing their daily newspapers?[81] The two-newspaper city has become less common, a victim of rising costs and competition with other sources, such as in the internet. What happens to the sense of community? The growth of the newspaper was both cause and effect of the growth of the industrial city in the 19th century, and "satisfied people's need for information about the bewildering place they found themselves in, the other inhabitants, and themselves."[82] There was a need for information an a regular basis, regarding all aspects of the city's life — economic, social, athletic, to name a few. Particularly with regard to immigrants, newspapers became the great leveler, enabling them to know and find out what was necessary.[83] Barth, in his exploration of key elements of the urban persona in the 19th century, identified the rise of the metropolitan press as one that facilitated uniformity within city life, and concluded:

> In its symbiotic relationship with the American modern city, the metropolitan press recognized people as individuals, apart from their existence as part of the masses. Beyond that, it identified them as persons who formed special groups. In beginning to address women directly, large newspapers singled out a potentially powerful segment of the urban population.[84]

So Trenton remains an anomaly, a city of two newspapers, even as its population shrinks.

The city is a city of thought. Its museums, schools and media outlets are all a part of that. Moreover, the city is a place of concentration of both people and minds. The city has always been a place of inspiration; most notably, perhaps, are the roles of Paris and New York in painting, photography, film and fiction. Trenton has featured sporadically in the written arts. Examples include drama (Thornton Wilder's 1931 play *The Happy Journey to Trenton and Camden*, poetry (Grace Cavalieri's 1990 collection, *Trenton*) and fiction (Theodore

Dreiser's *The Financier* and *The Bulwark*). Indeed, Trenton was known to Dreiser; he allegedly engaged in sexual liaisons with one of his typists, Louise Campbell, in Trenton.[85] This occurred at the Sterling Hotel; according to the New Jersey Historical Society, this hotel stood at the corner of State Street and Chancery Lane.[86] If you're wandering Trenton and pass this spot, think a moment about Theodore Dreiser.

One of the images in this book is a photograph from the capitol complex that shows the state library, museum and planetarium. They symbolize the city as a place of intellectual endeavor. I have summarized, and oversimplified, some of the points made by certain writers on the city as magnet for both artists and critics of intellectualism in American life. Trenton's role is not that of Paris or New York. Most cities' roles are not, either. But as a city, Trenton encompasses the same kinds of sentiments, and in its cultural presence, contributes nonetheless to fulfilling the role of the city as a place of contemplation, creation and composition.

# 11. The Territorial City

In this chapter I want to consider certain concepts of territoriality, and suggest two perspectives that may, at first blush, not seem to warrant juxtaposition at all. The first is that of the city as battleground, in which territory, neighborhood and street are seen as almost sovereign states between competing factions. The second perspective is that of territory as the physical appearance of the city, its legibility. To some extent, perhaps, one relates to the other; I juxtapose the discussion because the interrelationship appeared to suggest itself to me. The territorial nature of gangs is accommodated by the contours of the city. We consider the territorial nature of the city, reflecting on the ensuing violence as well as the more passive consideration of territory in terms of the legibility of the city. What I am not doing in this chapter is engaging in an exhaustive scholarly or journalistic exploration into gang warfare or causal factors of criminality, nor am I running to ground the scholarship and extensive work in the areas of urban sociology and planning. Rather, consistent with the theme of this book—that we can view post-industrial Trenton as a jumping-off point for further inquiry—I offer various preliminary thoughts and reactions as to what comes to mind in a discussion of territoriality and legibility—how people mark out their city and how people read their city.

In his provocative *The Territorial Imperative*, anthropologist Robert Ardrey undertook what he called a "close shot" of territoriality, and wrote that it is "a single aspect of human behavior which I believe to be characteristic of our species as a whole, to be shaped but not determined by environment and experience, and to be a consequence not of human choice but of evolutionary inheritance."[1] He concludes that humans act territorially from "instinct" or, more precisely, biological and evolutionary conditioning, that is, "nature," rather than from environment or learning, that is, "nurture." He identifies two particular territorial imperatives—area behavior, in which a species protects an area for the purpose of mating, and the pair territory, in which the territory is defended for purposes of brooding. Ardrey extrapolates his analysis to human behavior and the implications for nationhood — in other words, there are biological bases for what we do politically and socially.

Others have noted, though, that "both from statements by Ardrey and by projections from his thesis of the territorial imperative, gigantic theoretical leaps can too readily be made to gang delinquency and international conflict. The 'turf' of delinquent gangs, the opposition to slum clearance by slum-dwellers, the skid-row resident who fights removal, the white protest against Negro property invasions, the burglarizing intrusion on the territory of others, the frequency of intragroup crimes of violence, etc., are facile translations of Ardrey's propositions."[2]

My purpose here is not to debate Ardrey's theses or look to the variety of sources, pro and con, regarding his points. I find them challenging and thoughtful, as I do the critical view of his theories. What I want to do is simply set the stage for a look at territoriality in two facets — that of gangs and that of legibility — using Trenton as our window.

> "You don't understand. You can't control who's coming in through that door," LeGore said. "I want to be out of the city of Trenton. We have lost enough money."[3]

So spoke Jennifer LeGore, owner of Maxine's nightclub on South Warren Street in the main downtown business district of Trenton, in December 2009. An article in the Trenton press about the Trenton City Council meeting noted that she addressed the council regarding operations of the club until the end of the year. She was closing after over four years of operation, citing violence that included three stabbings within or just outside the establishment.[4]

Trenton's violence runs the gamut from individuals to gangs. Certainly violence is not unique to Trenton, nor are gangs unique to Trenton or even the city as city; suburban gang activity is not uncommon in New Jersey. Yet the city, like a living body, provides a host in which parasites function and often thrive. Abandoned houses facilitate squatting and secrecy. Concentrations of people and material things provide opportunities and targets.

Trenton needs more than just physical force to combat the problem. Post-industrial cities infested with gangs are cycling downward. In the words of Mike Davis, discussing gangs in Los Angeles:

> In a post-liberal society, with the gangplanks pulled up and compassion strictly rationed by the Federal deficit and the Jarvis Amendment, where a lynch-mob demagogue like William Bennett reigns as "drug czar" — is it any wonder that poor youths are hallucinating on their own desperado "power trips?" In Los Angeles there are too many signs of approaching helter-skelter: everywhere in the inner city, even in the forgotten poor-white boondocks with their zombie populations of speed-freaks, gangs are multiplying at a terrifying rate, cops are becoming more arrogant and trigger-happy, and a whole generation is being shunted toward some impossible Armageddon.[5]

Is Trenton a piece of Los Angeles?

New Jersey's criminal code defines "gang" as "three or more people who are associated in fact, people who have a common group name, identifying sign, tattoos or other indicia of association and who have committed criminal offenses while engaged in gang related activity."[6]

[Interlude]
> A city teen who carried out a 2006 gang shooting from the back of a bicycle when he was 15, and committed an armed bank robbery months later, has been sentenced to 10 years in prison for both crimes.[7]

We look at images from Afghanistan and reflect on the violence there. It is often presented as a desolate, hostile place. One looks at the dramatic scenery in news photos and videos of that place, and simultaneously understands that the beauty conceals an almost pathological deadliness. The terrain hides breeding grounds for terrorists, kids trained as suicide bombers who regularly slaughter people on order. It doesn't matter if their targets are innocent or guilty, civilians or soldiers. Death and martyrdom form their purpose.

Trenton is not, and yet in a certain way is, Afghanistan. A 13-year-old girl is killed by random bullets, from automatic weapons no less, in a drive-by shooting of a block party ordered by the Sex Money Murder gang against the Gangster Killer Bloods.[8] Seven men were charged with various acts connected with the killing; one "man" remained unnamed because of his age. The ages of the suspects range from 17 to 21, with one person being 31. According to the police, the hit was ordered as a consequence of a fight in a bar the night before when a Gangster Killer Bloods members was shot in the leg.[9] The leader of the gang, the one who ordered the killing, is 20 years old. Apparently none of the targets was hit; an innocent and uninvolved girl is dead. The killing occurred in the Wilbur area of Trenton. Only one of the guns was found. The "hit' was allegedly ordered by a 20-year-old "five star general" in the Sex Money Murder gang.[10]

Trenton's mayor at the time had this to say: "This was an outrageous act.... Who would spray an automatic weapon into a crowd of people trying to enjoy a Sunday afternoon? ... The community can help in two ways.... First, be the parent you need to be. Reach out to your children before they are victims or perpetrators of violence. ... Whoever did this has no regard for the lives of people and should not be able to get away. Step forward with information and help put them behind bars where they belong."[11]

Who, indeed?

Some facts.

The New Jersey Department of Law and Public Safety, and the Intelligence Division of the New Jersey State Police, issued the most recent municipal law enforcement response to the 2007 gang survey. While the report identifies at least 65 "other" gangs, the five prevalent gangs reported in New Jersey municipalities are the Bloods, Latin Kings, Crips, MS-13, Pagans Motorcycle Club and Ñeta. The percentage of municipalities reported the presence of the Bloods in 2007 was 87 percent, up from 58 percent in the 2004 gang survey. The types of violent crimes committed are common assault and aggravated assault; the report notes that "drug crimes constitute almost half of all criminal activity attributed to gangs."[12] Trenton is one of eight New Jersey municipalities in which gangs having at least 200 members are aggregated.[13] The Bloods are Trenton's largest gang, with over 200 members; the Latin Kings and Ñeta reportedly have between 101 and 150 members, and 5 Percenters has between 51 and 100 members.[14]

The report notes that "gangs are not monolithic, centrally-directed organizations" and that "Bloods and Crips street gangs are composed of numerous factions/sub-sets," and "frequently are in competition and conflict with each other as well as other gangs in the same town."[15]

What kinds of weapons do these gangs possess? In 2005, Operation "Capital City" resulted in the seizure of "numerous weapons, including a .45-caliber Thompson submachine gun, a 9 mm Intratec TEC 9 semi-automatic pistol, two shotguns, two rifles and seven handguns."[16]

What is the reaction? In 2009 an announced candidate for Trenton City Council and for whose benefit the fatal block party was held in which 13-year-old Tamrah Leonard died, was quoted in a news article as saying, "There's nothing wrong with being in a gang.... There's nothing wrong joining the Boy Scouts or joining ROTC or a fraternity. All of those are little societies or brotherhoods. It's just that one of them is more criminalized because mainly it holds more blacks and Latino children."[17] This candidate did not ultimately win the election. The *Gangs in New Jersey* report notes that Trenton and Newark "cited thirteen or more gang homicides in the previous year."[18] Is this a view shared by others? In the various interludes in this book, one senses something else — a complete lack of understanding or explanation, a frustration, a sense that events and behaviors are beyond our control. Real people die. The dialogue needs to move beyond the rhetorical and the political. If the solutions were simple, presumably they would have been implemented.

Has Trenton become a "feral city?"[19] Gang activity has been cited and recognized throughout New Jersey, including smaller towns and suburban areas; it is not a product solely of the city. However, the city as a place is more susceptible to gang activity because of "density and opportunity," and the more "gangs gain a foothold in a city, the harder it is to police any part of the civic territory, thereby offering new criminal opportunities."[20]

Enter Trenton from its eastern border of Parkway Avenue at Prospect Street, and you pass the Reservoir on your right. Taking two years to complete, its opening in September 1899 was attended by some 5,000 people and marked by a parade.[21] Owned by the Trenton Water Works, which is responsible for the city's water supply, it originally held unfiltered water. It was not until 1914 that a water treatment plant was added and, in the post–9/11 age, security cameras and monitoring systems have been added to the longstanding fence.[22] Just over a hundred years ago, parades and speeches. Now, Prospect Street cuts through a war zone, played out amid abandoned factories, rowhouses and stark brick housing projects. Trenton's efforts to sell a portion of its water works, which services surrounding municipalities, were made subject to a referendum, courtesy of a New Jersey Supreme Court decision.[23]

A few blocks to the north, in the Pennington/Prospect neighborhood, at the corner of Coolidge and Eisenhower Avenues, another innocent victim, Tajahnique Lee, a seven-year-old girl on a bicycle, was shot through the cheek by a .45 calibre bullet during a gang fight in March 2006. Just over a year later, the *New York Times* reported that "little has changed at the intersection.... Drug dealers and prostitutes openly solicit business around the clock, as a network of sentries alerts others via cellphones to the arrival of the police or any unfamiliar visitor."[24] A few blocks more to the south of the Reservoir, at the corner of Rossell Avenue and Martin Luther King Boulevard, in the North Trenton neighborhood, on June 7, 2009 13-year-old Tamrah Leonard was killed in a gang attack with automatic weapon fire at a block party. The spot is a block or so away from the mobilization point in the Mexican War of 1847, for which Trenton was to raise five companies.

And then there was the complex saga leading up to the murder of Jeri Lynn Dotson, then 23 years old, in 2004. She was a member of the Latin Kings who witnessed a kidnapping of Alex Ruiz, a member of a competing gang, who was assaulted but not killed; she was killed a day later.[25] Jose Negrete, the leader of the Latin Kings in Trenton, was ultimately convicted in May 2009 of ordering her killing,[26] following a hung jury the preceding October.[27]

At the other end of the city, the neighborhood of Chambersburg soldiers on. Novelist Janet Evanovich in her debut Stephanie Plum novel, *One for the Money*, described this area as "a blue-collar hunk of Trenton called the burg. Houses were attached and narrow. Yards were small. Cars were American. The people were mostly of Italian descent, with enough Hungarians and Germans thrown in to offset inbreeding. It was a good place to buy calzone or play the numbers. And, if you had to live in Trenton anyway, it was an okay place to raise a family."[28]

Trenton remains a city of neighborhoods. But neighborhoods lack physical walls, and in a compact, eight-square-mile place like Trenton, what affects one block affects all blocks. Territoriality may be an imperative, but the city is an intertwined system.

What of the no-man's land, the open spaces of the city?

Lofland, in *The Public Realm*, notes that activity within the public realm has been a kind of unknown territory, based on three developed lines of argument. First, various writers suggested that there was a dearth of interaction among urban dwellers in the public space due to a reaction to the overwhelming stimuli of the city. She cites writers such as Georg Simmel, Louis Wirth and Stanley Milgram for the argument that the city's sensory overload causes a shutdown and therefore asocial activity.[29] A second reason for the lack of attention given to the public realm, she believes, has been that those interested in the city have treated that space more as a thing to be crossed rather than an end in itself.[30] Finally, she notes an expressed hostility to the importance of the public realm by scholars.[31]

Yet the public realm is part and parcel of Trenton. Is it a demilitarized zone?

The London Eye, a large cantilevered observation wheel with 32 capsules, opened in 2000, and according to its website, attracts 3.5 million visitors a year.[32] It rises 135 meters and allows views of up to about 25 miles on a clear day. What is intriguing about it is that it has become a feature and fixture of London in a decade, in a city whose history stretches back millennia and which still features buildings hundreds of years old. It is possible for such a thing to become endeared by a city's citizens, an iconic point of pride.

Trenton has one place to get a view of the city as a whole — the Battle Monument. You can look at the entire city, without the overlay of political or territorial borders.

One day, I went up the Battle Monument to the observation deck. I was at first surprised to learn that one could go up; whenever I had viewed the Monument on frequent wanderings around the city, I had never observed anyone up there. On the particular day, I entered the open door, and a man, who had been seated on one of the benches in the small park at the foot of the monument, came in. He took me up — I had individualized attention. One of the pictures I took is in this book. It is noted here in this discussion of legibility — of the image of a city. Of Trenton.

It is an amazing thing to do. Knowing the recent history of the city, its violence, poverty, vacant buildings, loss of jobs — all the ailments of the contemporary post-industrial city — it is almost a breathtaking experience to look at this city from this vantage point. You don't see lines of demarcation. You can identify, roughly, neighborhoods and areas, but what you see is a city.

Are we invoking Le Corbusier here, to the wrath of the New Urbanists? Is this preposterous? Should we not concentrate on crime, on the gang warfare and violence, on the abandoned buildings, the overgrown pavement where buildings once stood, on the bleak and desolate blocks that infest the city?

These things are not mutually exclusive. Vision and reality are not tautological. If you build it, will they come? Trenton needs to be safe. You can throw police at Trenton. You could occupy it with the National Guard. You could treat it as a war zone. Ultimately, Trenton needs a dream. Needs to dream. It

***View from the Monument.*** From the top of the Trenton Monument, the city spreads before one. This view also shows Broad Street (left) and Warren Street (right) looking toward the center of the city. The column is 150 feet high. This view must be one of the best-kept secrets in the city; when the image was made, on a weekend, I was the only visitor up there. The monument links Trenton to such other Revolutionary War battle sites and their monuments, such as Saratoga and Bennington.

needs vision. A vision. Not just a master plan. It needs a reason for people to walk it, and not just to get to their cars to leave, or to get to their offices and punch a clock.

A city can be based on a dream, on a myth. It is not always a good thing. Mike Davis writes in *City of Quartz* that "compared to other great cities, Los Angeles may be *planned* or *designed* in a very fragmentary sense (primarily at the level of its infrastructure) but it is infinitely *envisioned.*"[33]

If territoriality is the *sine qua non* of the post-industrial city in general, and of Trenton in particular, can we really see it clearly? How a city's neighborhoods and territories physically integrate with themselves? How do people perceive the pieces of the city? From the top of the Battle Monument, one sees the triangle made by Broad, Warren and State streets. But on the ground, is Trenton legible?

Trenton, at the time of the Revolution, consisted of perhaps a half dozen main streets and a hundred buildings. It was not one of the largest of Colonial cities and was not even necessarily of strategic importance in and of itself. Its beginnings as a city are less important than what it became, or what its inhabitants chose to make it and how they chose to see it. As Mayernik notes, Rome in ancient times was not the Rome of its Renaissance visionaries.[34] Trenton, as it grew in the 19th century, was seen by its inhabitants, its economic visionaries, as an industrial engine. Its architecture reflects that; much of the city is "red brick" even to this day, and much of the city's housing was rowhouse construction.

If there was no Idea of Trenton, is it just a skeleton of what it was, but in spirit? Or like every other lost city, discarded after its usefulness as a manufacturing center ended, has it become something else?

Physically, Trenton was wrecked when the "freeways" cut it in pieces. It was not a situation unique to Trenton; critics charged Robert Moses with "ghettoization" as a side effect of his highway projects in New York.[35] Whatever one's view of the benefits of such expressways, there is no denying their impact on the visualization of a city.

In *The Image of the City*, Kevin Lynch provides an abstract definition of a city that focuses on the physical nature of the city, but also its perception: "Like a piece of architecture, the city is a construction in space, but one of vast scale, a thing perceived only in the course of long spans of time." He divides a city into five elements: paths, edges, districts, nodes, and landmarks and emphasizes the physical form of the city. Ultimately, he develops this theme of "legibility" of a city "where objects are not only able to be seen, but are presented sharply and intensely to the senses."[36] Another leading contemporary writer on cities, Joel Kotkin, in *The City: A Global History*, makes a similar observation: "In the end, a great city relies on those things that engender for its citizens a peculiar and strong attachment, sentiments that separate one specific place from others."[37]

Eamonn Canniffe, in *Urban Ethic: Design in the Contemporary City*, tells us that the historical city enabled us to know where the city began and where it ended. Its identity was framed by a compactness, and "the boundary between city and country was clearly expressed, often by fortifications which put a premium on dense development, and in terms of size the centre was no great distance from the edge. The whole of the city was therefore visible and knowable, a level or recognition which was supported by the identifiability of the urban pattern within the walls."[38] Today, Trenton is partly shaped and bounded by highways that function as walls against pedestrian concourse — Route 1, Route 29, Interstate Routes 95 and 295. Although Trenton bleeds into Hamilton Township along the outer reaches of East State Street or East State Street Extension, much of Canniffe's observations of old cities remain true, and Trenton's compactness does assist resolution of its boundaries.

A city functions on two levels: it is perceived by its inhabitants, and, while stable over periods of time as a framework, it nonetheless is modified by its builders.[39] While many may believe a beautiful city is an impossibility, it is important, Lynch notes, that the environment be harmonious and people live in a place that is aesthetically pleasing. He considers the visual quality of a city in terms of the mental image its citizens have of it.[40] To form a general, and not individually specific image, Lynch speaks of legibility, and studies three cities—Boston, Jersey City and Los Angeles.

Legibility is a function of identity, structure and meaning. Identity focuses on the particular object as a thing separate from others. Structure is the spatial relationship of the particular object to other objects, and meaning refers to the physical or emotional meaning to the citizen. The "independent variable" is the "physical environment,"[41] so the analysis is as to that physical environment and look at the city in terms of imageability as "that quality in a physical object which gives it a high probability of evoking a strong image in any given observer."[42] He then uses the word "legibility" as interchangeable with "imageability"; the essence of the inquiry is whether the city "would seem well formed, distinct, remarkable; it would invite the eye and the ear to greater attention and participation."[43]

The importance of this kind of analytical framework, which I am of course abbreviating here, is to find the city's image, or ultimately construct cities so that their imageability is discernible, and thereby provide pleasure and aesthetic reward to its citizens. This does not mean that the entire city must be realized at once; there are "hidden forms in the vast sprawl of our cities."[44] Ultimately, it is important that a city have an image, a look, and city design must pay heed to that. It may be that a city that is legible is also one better able to address the territoriality that has become synonymous with the gang warfare that plagues it.

Interestingly, Lynch took a New Jersey city—Jersey City—at a time when its population was larger, but its population density was not so far off that of Trenton. In 1950, when the study came out, Jersey City's population was 299,017, and Trenton's was 128,009, in areas of 13 and 7.2 square miles, respectively—at 23,000 to 17,800 per square mile, respectively. Many of the comments may be applied to Trenton as well. Jersey City, he concluded, lost its shopping center with the construction of Journal Square, and had four or five centers. We might say the same thing about Trenton: a significant shopping area has been put into place in the former Roebling factory in South Trenton, along South Broad Street. The erstwhile shopping district at the corner of Broad and State streets is virtually non-existent today; a small shopping and restaurant sector is along Warren Street. Lynch comments on the "confusion of an uncoordinated street system" in Jersey City[45]; the same may be said of Trenton. There is no real grid pattern; a few streets in the downtown area run in a limited grid, but the streets then dissolve into crooked, snaking and abrupt thoroughfares. He also notes, of Jersey City, that "the drabness, dirt and smell of the town are at first overpowering."[46] While there is no overpowering smell to Trenton, there are "drabness and dirt." The abandoned houses, the weed-overrun vacant lots, the pot-holed, uneven streets make for an image from a newsreel after a war.

Lynch's analysis focuses on visibility and districts. In Jersey City, he searched for character; at least as of 1960, a few distinct areas are cited — such as Journal Square — but his conclusion, based on "the individual sketches and interviews," was that "it became apparent that none of the respondents had anything like a comprehensive view of the city in which they had lived for many years."[47] Indeed, and ironically, what defined Jersey City was not an image or legibility of the city itself, but the view of another city — the New York skyline.[48]

There are confusing roads in Trenton, with Route 1 slicing the city from north to south, and Route 29 slicing it from east to west, and ramps and circles adding to the confusion. Overpasses and underpasses distract; there are no clearly visible landmarks to orient one's self from different parts of the city. And yet, from atop the monument, looking south toward the Delaware River and across the historic core of the city, and its downtown, the city seems to snap into focus. Broad Street and Warren Street form a clear linear expression. The city's skyscrapers identify its downtown area. To the left, in the distance, an industrial water tower identifies of the factories. To the far right, in the back, is the flag of the Statehouse. From up here, the boarded-over windows do not confront. The city looks like a city. And yet, one can't help but notice the emptiness of the streets. It may be legible from up here, but it also seems desolate.

But the Battle Monument serves another purpose — that of identity and focus. Every place should have at least one structure from which one can survey the entirety of the city. Rykwert notes the importance of monuments or other prominent features as an orienting feature of the city; they "are essential for any sane urban or rural living."[49] It is an interesting way to view the Monument beyond its historical relevance.

Legibility, or imageability, according to Lynch, may include other influences, such as symbolism and history, but his focus is on the five aspects of the physical image: paths, edges, districts, nodes and landmarks.[50] Paths are the physical channels taken by the city's citizens. Edges are the opposite; they are the boundaries or breaks. Districts are the city's sections, a binary concept in which one is either "in" or "out" of the district, which have some common or identifying factor. Nodes are the intersection and entrance/egress points of the city, or concentration points, like a square or plaza. Landmarks are also identifying features but not as entrance/egress; rather, they are identifiable for signaling direction or a more particularized location.[51]

Lynch proceeds through a factor-by-factor discussion of each of these for the three cities in his study. It is an attempt to get at the essence of what makes a city legible, by breaking down the physical factors and assessing them both objectively and based on the survey data. To what purpose? To emphasize the need for attention on the micro level to afford a macro-level solution that increases aesthetic worth, and therefore ultimately, functionality of the city. He writes: "We are continuously engaged in the attempt to organize our surroundings, to structure and identify them. Various environments are more or less amenable to such treatment. When reshaping cities it should be possible to give them a form which facilitates these organizing efforts rather than frustrates them.[52]

But it is not just the responsibility of the city planner. The city's citizens also play an important part in the re-imagining of their city: "We have the opportunity of forming our new city world into an imageable landscape: visible, coherent, and clear. It will require a new attitude on the part of the city dweller, and a physical reshaping of his domain into forms which entrance the eye, which organize themselves from level to level in time and space, which can stand as symbols for urban life."[53] While most cities, at least in the United States, may no longer possess an overriding unitary imageability, those who live there are a part of the city — they provide the emotional response — and to a large extent, I read Lynch to say, it is their perception of the city that interacts with its image and perception by outsiders.[54] So while ultimately the city is reshaped, or reimaged, with attention to the prime physical factors — paths, edges, districts, nodes and landmarks — those planning and designing a city can do so based upon the interaction and perception of the citizen. Lynch concludes by emphasizing the importance of education in developing and reshaping the image, which is a "circular" or "spiral" process: "visual education impelling the citizen to act upon his visual world, and this action causing him to see even more acutely. A highly developed art of urban design is linked to the creation of a critical and attentive audience. If art and audience grow together, then our cities will be a source of daily enjoyment to millions of their inhabitants."[55]

If we were to take this approach and apply it to Trenton, what might we conclude? Trenton does not appear to be a "legible" city. Its roads do not conform to a logical grid pattern, and its parks are not placed in any particular pattern. It forms a squashed "T," with the top along the Delaware River and the stem sticking out to the northeast. Like Jersey City, it has been trisected by Route 1 and Route 29, and then again by the Northeast railroad corridor. There are significant gaps in vacant and abandoned property. Beyond the physical, though, is there an identity of the city? Say Trenton (*Trent-un*, not *Tren-ton*) and you still conjure up a particular sense of place. To those from the city, there are fond memories of neighborhoods and a particular way of life. To those in the business and legal community, there was and, to some extent still is, a sense of community and identity. For those who still live in the city, beset by the drumbeat of gang warfare and other violent crime, with a decimated housing stock and limited resources, can the city survive as a city in a meaningful sense?

We can recall our earlier discussion of place. The city is part of us, and we are part of the city. The city is intangible as well as tangible, more than a physical thing, but transcendent. We interact with it, are transformed by it, and in turn transform it for the future. As such, public space in the city, like the mind, is

*Fisher/Richey/Perdicaris.* This historic district of the city consists of a few blocks heading west from downtown, between Berkeley Square, West End, Central West and the Delaware River and Route 29. The district was part of the residential growth of the West End, during the period of 1875 to 1930 or so. The Perdicaris family were involved with the Trenton Gas Company; Gregory Perdicaris was one of the original officers of the Trenton Public Library when it opened in 1852. Ion Perdicaris, his wife and his son were kidnapped while living in Tangiers; President Theodore Roosevelt was instrumental in helping free him. Perdicaris ultimately returned to Trenton.

important. As Mark Kingwell observes, "Contrary to common belief, cities exist in time rather than space: This is part of what makes them places. Or rather, we ought to say that cities *make space timely*, and so change our own relation to time ... the politics of public space raises questions of knowledge and reality that politics along cannot address but without which politics remain stunted and incomplete.... The task is to turn around and reenter the heart of places— to be somewhere in particular, as an embodied consciousness."[56]

The American city in a way is a relatively new city, at least in terms of Western European concepts of the city. Native American cities existed by the Mayans and the Aztecs in Latin America; no comparable cities appear to have been identified, or at least survived, in North America along the lines of, say, Chichen Itza in Mexico. The American city lacks the medieval flavor and physicality of the European city. These were not walled cities, or cities that generally grew from narrow cobblestoned streets. In many respects, these were often planned in whole or in part; Philadelphia, New York and Washington, D.C., evidence clear grid patterns, for example. Even Trenton's original streets at the time of the resolution have some geometric lines to them: Warren and Broad Street from two sides of an isosceles triangle, running from the War Memorial building to State Street. Consider the geography of Trenton in trying to read it.

One of the themes, identified in city development by Mumford, among others, is the interplay between etherialization and materialization. Etherialization is the simplification of the physical and becomes symbolic; it is part of the values and culture and memory of the city. Materialization is the "concrete" structure. The growth of the city is a function of their interrelationship.[57] Mumford later notes: "Ours is an age in which the increasingly automatic processes of production and urban expansion have displaced the human goals they are supposed to serve."[58] Regardless of the resolution of this, though, there is a more disturbing pattern Mumford identifies of the subjugation of the general welfare of a city to the arrogance and power of the few. We stand on a threshold, and the choice is ours. As Mumford noted: "If these demoralizing tendencies continue [of the resurrection of evil institutions], the forces that are now at work will prove uncontrollable and deadly; for the powers man now commands must, unless they are detached from their ancient ties to the citadel, and devoted to human ends, lead from their present state of paranoid suspicion and hatred to a final frenzy of destruction."[59]

We need to think past territoriality and approach the city as a whole. In this regard, Patsy Healey posited the city as a "shared collective resource," with a focus that "could encompass an everyday-life perspective on urban conditions and experiences, along with an economic and environmental one."[60] She argues that the current challenge "is to mould multidimensional conceptions of 'city' which both reflect and interrelate the rich diversity and complexity of contemporary urban life, while generating a discursive public realm within which people can argue about what their city is and should be."[61] She faces the same questions as the rest in trying to define the city. The city to the geographer and planner was a "physical artifact," but "the economic and social relations of the city keep escaping these definitions."[62] She notes that "the social space of what we take to be the city is thus a complex layering of the time-space rhythms of multiple time-space relations, some of which are narrowly confined to a particular part of the city, others of which spread across many places near and far from the city.... It is the density and mixity of these relational layers and multiple identities which, for some commentators, create the key qualities of a 'city-type' ambience, of 'citiness.'"[63] Cities are also, of course, economic entities; "in this conception of the city as a container of economically exploitable assets, the ambition of some policy-makers is to position 'their city' in a wider landscape of competing cities."[64]

She concludes by emphasizing that we need to think of cities not just in terms of their "physical artifacts" or static people and technology. The essence of a city "lies beyond these specific existences and materialities, although as conceived, cities are full of people, technologies and power relations. But yet

## 11. The Territorial City

cities do exist and have material effects. Their existence and their power to act lie in the way they are imagined and brought to life, and in how these imaginings then become mobilized to shape politics, public policy and projects."[65]

Can we think of Trenton as a whole that is greater than the sum of its parts?

[Interlude]
*A blacksmith shop still stands on North Olden Avenue in North Trenton. On September 2, 1887, the New York Times reported the suicide on September 1 of William H. Meyers, "a well-known blacksmith" in Trenton. Meyers reportedly took laudanum and killed himself due to "being distressed over financial matters," and left "a family of seven in almost destitute circumstances."*[66]

Specific existences and materialities. The city is its ghosts, its tangible and intangible, its unique aggregation of existences, past, present and future.

Legibility defines the image, but people who live in the city deal with reality. A century ago Jacob Riis photographed and wrote *How the Other Half Lives*, depicting the lives and living conditions of people in New York's Lower East Side. Trenton is chronically, if not terminally, ill with the same social disease that afflicted Riis's Manhattan — apathy, indifference, if not studied and deliberate woefulness. Riis' title itself set forth the dichotomy of the haves and have nots, the separation of his own class and those he was photographing. This was *the* other half. It was a separate group of people. It was not titled *How Others of Us Live*, or the equivalent. He took his title from a quotation that "one half of the world does not know how the other half lives."[67] More to the point Riis, personally affronted by the mass of suffering, corruption and squalor he witnessed as a police reporter in turn-of-the-century New York, quoted testimony presented to a New York legislative committee in the 1880s:

> By far the largest part — eighty per cent, at least — of crimes against property and against the person are perpetrated by individuals who have either lost connection with home life, or never had any, or whose *homes had ceased to be sufficiently separate, decent, and desirable to affords what are regarded as ordinary wholesome influences of home and family....* The younger criminals seem to come almost exclusively from the worst tenement house districts, that is, when traced back to the very places where they had their homes in the city here.[68]

A century later, in dissecting the riots of the 1960s, the Kerner Commission found, with eerie parallelism in its Part II, addressing the "basic causes" as to why the riots occurred:

> *Black in-migration and white exodus*, which have produced the massive and growing concentrations of impoverished Negroes in our major cities, creating a growing crisis of deteriorating facilities and services and unmet human needs.
> *The black ghettos* where segregation and poverty converge on the young to destroy opportunity and enforce failure. Crime, drug addiction, dependency on welfare, and bitterness and resentment against society in general and white society in particular are the result.[69]

And as these meditations are being written, the CQ Press, in reliance on national uniform crime statistics, published its 2008 report that placed Trenton 30th in a listing of the nation's cities with populations over 75,000 in terms of crime.[70] Newark and Camden share the top 30 spot with Trenton, making New Jersey the leader among states in the top 30, with three cities present. Out of 137 cities in the group of population 75,000 to 99,999, Trenton placed seventh.[71]

Gangs and legibility. Violence and territoriality. A piece of real estate called a city. A place of extreme violence, where five-star generals in their 20s issue orders to kill. And yet, from the vantage point of the top of the Battle Monument, the city as a whole, is a beautiful place if you can see it. Like any other city.

## 12. The City and Its Footprint

I have offered some thoughts in various thematic areas that have discussed Trenton in terms of the post-industrial city in the new millennium, set against the background of the development of the city. We have touched on a variety of facets and made connections to the broader national issues. Trenton is but one tile in the mosaic, although with its own unique characteristics. This chapter looks more particularly for the patterns of the city, and the way in which a city's footprint is planted and changed. In short, it is an effort at putting Trenton in context to its future. We will discuss the comments of two prominent "new urbanists." I want to focus more on Trenton, its neighborhoods, and planning visions in the post-industrial city, and do so by exploring certain key writers on the subject.

Joseph Rykwert has argued that cities are not accidents, and we are not helpless in our effort to shape them; "the city did not grow, as the economics taught, by quasi-natural laws, but was a willed artifact, a human construct in which many conscious and unconscious factors played their part."[1] We react to our physical city, and the physicality of the city, appealing to all our senses, "is a tangible representation of that intangible thing, the society that lives in it — and of its aspirations."[2] The city is "malleable," and we have the opportunity, and responsibility, "to do *something* to make our preferences clear.... Though the powers ranged against them seem crushingly vast and wholly impersonal, ordinary citizens are sometimes able to intervene — and some have already engaged in such action."[3] Indeed, Rykwert objects to the rationalization that the city is simply a "producer of space" or as "organic," or as corrupt places[4] or as places that have grown in linear fashion as if in predetermined fashion and now face their end in the morass of the "global village."[5] The "disordered, even chaotic city" is not the problem — the problem is the current perception of "the city as an image of social inequity."[6] It is up to us to develop strategies for shaping our city environment, period.

In developing that theme, he recounts in *The Seduction of Place* the two great urbanizing movements of the late 18th century and early 19th century, and again in the post–World War II era. Recognition of the underlying impact

***The Ice House.*** Another example of the attempt to convert factories to residences, this time in the residential Chambersburg area. Built in 1896 for the Saxony Ice Manufacturing Company, it is an example of one of the "brownfield" projects in Trenton that was part of some $250,000,000 of privately funded development.

of the Industrial Revolution, and related laws such as England's enclosure laws, that funneled people into the cities, does not go far enough. The problems of crowding and poverty in the cities may be categorized, but the real problem of "how we got here," was that "a cultural transaction with the machine never mediated the impact of machine work on the body politic. That shock was never entirely absorbed."[7]

As part of the reaction to this, 19th-century Utopian models developed as paradigms for the city. Work was seen as something that could be pleasurable; "that notion seems as remote and irrelevant in the post-industrial city as it had been in the days of the conveyor belt. Yet such a hope, however modified, is the only possible source for any urbanist's energy and application."[8] Trenton, therefore, remains a work in progress. We are not bound by what it is, or may have been. Trenton can be remade, reinvented. It can build on what it has and what it has been.

Without mentioning Lovelock or Gaia, Jeb Brugmann, taking the entire planet of cities as his menu, writes in *Welcome to the Urban Revolution: How Cities Are Changing the World*, that with a majority of people living in the world's cities, cites "are changing *everything*" and as such "we are organizing the planet itself into a City: into a single, complex, connected, and still very unstable urban system."[9] It is a sobering thought and profound responsibility.

But regarding the *Gaia Hypothesis*, or however it is framed, I am not trying to engraft a complex, subtle and 30-year-old theory that remains under development and scrutiny directly onto the city in general, or Trenton in particular. What I am suggesting is (to borrow from John Berger) a *way of seeing*, or even *another way of telling*.[10] It is another way of looking at Trenton as Everycity, or at any city. When I say a city has a soul, it is another way of saying that the city is more than the sum of its parts. It is more than simply its physical look, its emotional feel, its intellectual contribution. It is a place that transcends time. It is the product of itself, its history. The person waiting for a bus, head in hands, at an otherwise deserted street corner, is the product of experience, environment, heredity. That person is a life. Add another 80,000 or 85,000 persons, and you have Trenton. Add in the other components we have addressed, beyond population, and you have a city. The complexity and interaction of those residents forms part of the mix.

What Brugmann argues is that the city itself has certain advantages that have been turning to political efficacy, and serving as the catalyst for political, economic and environmental change. While I am not sure I agree with one of his starting assumptions—that "city builders, leaders, and managers have held a diminutive status in the world's political order"[11]—his points about the increasing influence of cities are applicable even to the smaller cities, particularly in the United States. Indeed, he begins his discussion with Machala, a small, decades-old city in Ecuador of 200,000 people that reclaimed land, built a port, and now has a significant influence on Ecuadorian politics. Why? Because "the impacts of these cities reveals a fundamentally new characteristic of our world today: that local affairs are no longer just local."[12] He provides another, negative example of the effect of mismanagement of a city or part of a city, in detailing how the Pico-Union district of Los Angeles became a breeding ground for an efficiently trained set of MS-13 gang members who, upon repatriation to El Salvador, brought their Los Angeles–gained skills with them to increase transnational criminal enterprise.[13] Each city is composed of its urban "patches," and through immigration, each city neighborhood starts to take on the characteristics of urban areas around the world, Brugmann suggests. And "density, scale, association, and extension drive development in every urban patch.... The distinct ways in which cities and their different urban patches succeed or fail in creating shared advantages determines their contributions, for better or worse, to the world City system."[14]

With these thoughts in mind, we can consider the current thinking for reshaping the footprint and the soul of Trenton. Trenton is no less a part of the world community of cities. Some suggestions have been made; let us see what is on the table. We think about these things while we are well aware of the fiscal restraints and realities of post-industrial cities like Trenton in the 21st century. Still....

The Downtown Capital District Master Plan was released in May 2008 by the City of Trenton.[15] Claiming to be implemented by 2020, it proclaims, "Its successful implementation will be driven by intergovernmental cooperation, public sector investment in Trenton's infrastructure, and private sector investment in new businesses and residences located downtown."[16] This plan addresses several neighborhoods and districts surrounding the capital area, including Mill Hill, Hanover/Academy, Riverfront, downtown, the train station area and the central business district. Three "guiding themes" were set forth as the "rules" for redevelopment: first, to "establish downtown Trenton as a 'residential community of choice'"; second, to "balance tax exempt and income producing properties in downtown"; and third, to "enhance the character of streets and open spaces to anchor investment."

Cities are comprised of neighborhoods, yet there is no consensus on what a neighborhood is; they are "notoriously difficult to define."[17] Duany and Plater-Zyberk have defined a neighborhood as having a physical center — a public space or intersection, with key buildings, such as a post office and shops— and an edge, but this is less precise and can vary; the distance is about a quarter mile or five-minute walk. It has mixed and diverse uses, interconnecting streets, and balances civic buildings.[18] This definition seems more in line with a city block than a broader neighborhood. Is SoHo in New York a neighborhood? Or are we talking about a series of small villages, almost tribal, within the city?

What makes a neighborhood? We have used this word in prior discussions without necessarily focusing on what it actually means, and without defining it. The Trenton Division of Planning issued a map dated 2003 that shows 38 separately named neighborhoods in the city.[19] The map shows black line borders, as if a neighborhood rigidly ends on one street or side of a street, or part of the way down a street. Still, if the borders are fuzzy or permeable, the core of the neighborhood does, or should, have a particular identity. Some of Trenton's identified and identifiable neighborhoods are a matter of a few streets and blocks; others seem to stretch over vast areas. There is certainly a different look between Hiltonia and Coalport, between Hanover/Academy and Berkeley Square, but the differences between Coalport, Ewing/Carroll and Miller/Wall may be less immediately discernible.

It seems a truism that a city is its neighborhoods, from the largest to the smallest. No one would contest New York's preeminent status as a megacity, an international, "world-class" city, and yet, having lived there for three years, I know it is truly a city of neighborhoods. I lived in Greenwich Village, off Washington Square West, and knew when I was leaving the "neighborhood" and entering Soho, or the East Village, or somewhere else. There is a familiarity to it. And even though we may well be in a city populated by strangers, one does see the "familiar stranger" on the street, the known face if not the known name. The familiarity of the shopkeepers, even in this homogenized age of megastores, is still something to be observed.

## 12. The City and Its Footprint

*Coalport.* This desolate building on Perry Street leads into the core of the Coalport/North Clinton neighborhood. Coalport was just that — anthracite arrived by rail and was loaded onto canal boats of the Delaware and Raritan Canal in this area, where the feeder joined the main canal. Coalport was the subject of significant focus in the 1950s and 1960s for redevelopment, an effort that failed. "Urban renewal" was seen as an alternative to consolidation of the city with surrounding municipalities, according to Judith Kovisar's essay on efforts to develop Coalport; the thinking was to raze the slums, relocate people, and apparently implant a magical new business center that would attract back the amorphous middle class and reinvigorate the city's tax base. Coalport's redevelopment in the late 1950s and early 1960s coincided with construction of the John Fitchway, the highway that split the city from Stacy Park.

When people are from Brooklyn, as I am originally, they often identify their neighborhood — Flatbush, Bensonhurst. Within Trenton, perhaps the most readily identifiable connection to neighborhood is Chambersburg. Anecdotally, people will tell you how it remains tight-knit, and how the residents watch out for each other. It is a place that was known for its restaurants and, fictionally portrayed in the Stephanie Plum novels, remains true to its image. Whether the reality comports to that idealization is a topic for another book. The main point is that neighborhoods, in their importance, serve the purpose of self-identification, community, connection and anchoring.

One of the themes of this book has been the need and ability to draw connections between the present and the past, between the tangible and the intangible, the factual and theoretical, the local and the global. I have also written of the importance of connection in the context of place. We return to that now.

*East Hanover Street.* Hanover Street, at the time of the Battles of Trenton and the Revolution, was Third Street and one of the original streets of the city. The Hanover/Academy is one of the oldest residential areas in Trenton. The city's Department of Housing and Economic Development reported in 2008 that approximately 13 percent of Trenton's 33,908 housing units were unoccupied.

Connection is important. We need to feel part of something. We need to have an identity of place. We long for home. No matter how peripatetic, everyone can call someplace *home.* We need to belong. In his wonderful and misnamed "trilogy" of five books, the late Douglas Adams has a character in the last, *Mostly Harmless,* named Random. Random was born aboard a spaceship, and though ten years old chronologically, has spent a lot of time in different times due to her mother's journalistic time-jumping. She was conceived when her mother visited a sperm bank and retrieved the sperm of the only remaining human being in the galaxy, Arthur Dent. When finally meeting her biological father, Random explains her frustration of not fitting in anywhere, of having no place to call home. I think of that when I think of the comments on various urban writers as to the need for connection, not merely with place, but for city dwellers to connect with each other as part of their common identify. This is particularly so in the high mobile society we have become. Are we fully cognizant of the long-term ramifications to us as a nation? As a people? As human beings?

Kunstler notes the importance of connection in discussing the city of Portland, Oregon, in *The Geography of Nowhere*; as a result of attention to detail and how the pieces of the city fit together, Portland's residents "understood that the city was only as good as its connections, that urban ingredients treated in isolation had no meaning."[20] Things like zoning requirements of street-level

***Berkeley Square.*** A Late Victorian community that is listed on the National Register of Historic Places, Berkeley Square features a variety of housing that includes Queen Anne, Stick style, Italian Villa, Colonial Revival, Neo-Classical, Tudor, Romanesque, and Bungaloid. Critical of the Late Victorian style as losing some of the genuineness of the Early and High Periods, Alan Gowans, writing in *Architecture in New Jersey*, notes that this period was characterized by ***bigness*** and ***richness***, comporting with the industrialization of America and its growing size and wealthy merchant classes. As part of the expanding western residential area of Trenton, which was reaching the zenith of its Golden Age between 1875 and 1925, Berkeley Square exemplifies this housing.

windows, mixed multi-family and single-family zoning, and "light rail" systems were utilized to connect the city.

As we consider what has been proposed in the current Trenton Master Plan, we should bear in mind the argument made by Jane Jacobs that the health of a city depends upon integration of uses, of residence, work and entertainment spread throughout the city. This represents a return of the city to something else, for the growth of the modern, Western city has been in terms of districts: the factory district, offices, residences, theater, and so forth. The proposed Trenton Master Plan functions along similar lines as articulated by Jacobs in emphasizing the importance of the small, the streets and neighborhoods, and the need for diversity of use and population as a way of connecting the city within itself.

It is persistently upbeat; in the analysis of community potential the Plan states, unabashedly, that

> a primary attraction for new households to move to Downtown Trenton is the access its location provides to jobs. Additionally, the lifestyle choice to live in a

city center as opposed to the suburbs, especially in new construction or renovated housing, is a strong motivator. Downtown Trenton could become an exciting alternative to life in the suburbs, or to established urban neighborhoods in Trenton like Mill Hill, which may already be overpriced for some segments of the Downtown target market. Housing products that are currently missing from the Downtown mix are primarily new, for-sale units in varying price points.[21]

In the abstract, this remains persuasive and appealing. In the reality, there is no lifestyle to be gained. The predominant meaningful employment in downtown Trenton to walk to at present is government — state, county and city. One could, of course, walk to the train and commute to New York; some do that. But to talk about a lifestyle when the amenities normally found in a city are missing — no downtown shopping to speak of, no evening entertainment, and a serious crime problem — remains merely an abstraction, although abstraction and vision have their place Addressing this, the report notes "The City has also developed one of the most effective efforts in the U.S. for reducing gang activity and chronic gun violence, and has been highly successful in reducing both property and violent crime. The number of reported crimes in Trenton declined 27 percent in 2006 from 2005, falling to the lowest level since reporting began in 1967. In response, Mayor Douglas H. Palmer stated, "Trenton is a very safe city for law abiding residents and the thousands of people who work downtown or attend sporting and cultural events."[22]

In this world, perception is reality. And while that reality must recognize the positive (the Broad Street Bank building renovation, the train station improvement — which are both also recognized in the report), in Trenton, reality remains reality. Is it "safe"?

Improvements to the capital district embody removal of the ugly and vast parking lots, which were earlier identified in the report as part of the reason for the destructiveness of the area in the first place, and replacing them with garage structures to take less space, and reinstall park areas. Part of the plan is to undo the damage to the city's cohesiveness by virtue of the John Fitch Way (Route 29) built in the 1950s that separated much of the city from the Delaware River and Mahlon Stacy Park. Similar destruction of a city's coherence occurred in Detroit with limited-access freeways imposed on a previously utile grid system.[23] Mixed use development for Willow Street is proposed; this is consistent with Jane Jacobs's admonitions for not separating a city into discrete units. It is also an attempt to undo decades of post–World War II planning that caused such grief to the post-industrial city — not merely in destroying its legibility, but in further sequestering its neighborhoods and serving as a deterrent to pedestrian traffic. An artist's conception of the capital district might remind one of Boston's Back Bay. This was, after all, a Colonial city, paved over with vast parking areas for state employees. Concomitant with that re-use are proposals for greenways and trails to eliminate the tattered areas now along the Delaware and Raritan Canal, which presently runs through the city in a depressing way.[24]

Improvements to the Mill Hill Historic Area include adaptive reuse of the classical former Sun National Bank Building, mixed-use infill construction, replacement of parking lot areas with artworks or theater, restoration of the Assunpink Creek area and the historic bridge, and improved signage.

Stating that "Trenton's commuter infrastructure is the key to unlock Downtown's economic development potential," the report notes certain historic features of the area, including Mercer Cemetery.[25] The area is sought to be developed as a "transit village," which is a multi-agency initiative within the state to build an integrated residential and commercial sector around a significant mass-transit hub. Residential development and improvements are called for in the neighboring areas, including demolition of two vacant Miller Homes high-rise apartment towers and development of an Assunpink Greenway Park.

Development of the Riverfront District will, according to the plan's authors, permit Trenton to "reclaim its connection with the Delaware River to enhance the experience of living, working and visiting Downtown. Route 29 will be rebuilt as an Urban Boulevard and surface parking lots will be replaced by pedestrian-oriented, mixed-use development."[26] Mixed-use residential and commercial is proposed, together with transforming a 2.45-acre site into a public square.

Focusing primarily on State, Broad and Warren streets (the heart of the original Revolutionary War–era city), this part of the plan focuses on adaptive reuse of several historic and prominent buildings in the city. The authors recognize the primacy of place: "Authenticity of place is one of Trenton's greatest assets. It is an important colonial city that has experienced subsequent phases of high quality growth and development. The most recent phase that has impacted the scale, character and function of downtown has been the demolition of entire blocks for the development of large-scale office complexes. This has been beneficial for Trenton in that it has a major employment base coming into downtown each weekday. Care must be given to balance the need for change with the need for preservations."[27]

Improvement of the Hanover/Academy area contains a comparable blend of renovation and mixed-use proposals, but also emphasizes expansion of the use of the Mercer County Community College facilities within the city. That would be important toward restoring the city at least to some extent as a center of education, reclaiming some of its former position when The College of New Jersey (formerly, Trenton State College) and Rider University (formerly, Rider College) were both within the city.

And the final warning by the plan's proponents: "Plans are typically judged not only by their quality but by the extent to which they are implemented. The City of Trenton undertook this plan with the intention that it would be used by staff and elected or appointed officials on a regular basis to guide decisions regarding the redevelopment of Downtown. Some plans are approved but are rarely referenced, or gradually lose relevance because they are not updated. To

***Rider College Building.*** Founded in 1865 as the Trenton Business College, as part of a chain of business colleges, the school was later incorporated as Rider College, and moved to this building at 428 East State Street in 1921. With ground-breaking in 1957 in neighboring Lawrence Township, the school did not completely locate to Lawrence until 1964. Part of the Coalport/North Clinton area, the building remains a reminder of educational institutions (including The College of New Jersey) that trace their roots to the city.

keep this Downtown Master Plan relevant, its role in City decision-making needs to be affirmed."

Interestingly enough, there are a variety of websites and blogs devoted not merely to Trenton, but to its redevelopment. One is "Reinventing Trenton,"[28] in which the blogger, among other things, appropriately refers to "cool Trenton" spots, centering in the Warren Street area and its environs. That piece, written in 2005, remains largely valid. It *is* cool to wander the Colonial-era streets, and see snippets of a real urban presence. However, efforts to gauge the effectiveness of the Master Plan and its implementation, a year down the road, have been less than successful.

That is the vision for Trenton. How does it jibe with the more global picture?

Brugmann identifies four "dominant" approaches to building a city: ad hoc city building, city systems, city models and the master-planned city.[29] The ad hoc city focuses on individual interests or needs at particular points in time. The city system involves creation of the city as a community, growing organically. City modeling is designed around a particular set of products or units that are pieced together. The master planned city, combining ad hoc and city modeling, focuses on the vision of the city's leaders as opposed to coming from the "ground up," that is, its residents.[30] He distinguishes these city-building approaches from urbanism; "urbanism is a way of developing, using, and living in the city in compatible ways to make its economics, politics, social life, and ecology coherent with consensus aspirations and values."[31] There must be a clear and agreed-on urban strategy. What he calls "cities in crisis" exist because different factions undermine the building or urbanist philosophy of the others, and in "great opportunities cities," there is no consensus or philosophy, so ad hoc building becomes the norm.

The visionary plan now on the table in Trenton represents a cogent attempt to visualize, a necessity before implementation. It is an attempt to develop an urban strategy. It is an important step in the life of this city. It is city-building.

In 1927 the architect Le Corbusier wrote that a city "is the grip of man upon nature. It is a human operation directed against nature, a human organism both for protection and for work. It is a creation," which Le Corbusier puts on a plain with poetry.[32] Troubled by what he encountered in Paris, an "old" and "crumbling" place, he observed that "when an architecture was genuinely appropriate to its environment it gave a pleasing sensation of harmony and was profoundly moving."[33] Focused on the need for planning, he compares the chaotically arranged European city to one framed by the meanderings of a pack donkey, rather than the straight-line approach of a person who has an end and proceeds toward it. He preferred the "rectilinear" cities of the United States, built on straight lines. (While New York and Washington, D.C., may be prototypical examples, a place like Trenton is not.)

But beyond the physicality of the city is something more that is relevant to Le Corbusier: the *soul of the city*: "The soul of the city is that part of it which is of no value from the practical side of existence: it is, quite simply, its poetry, a feeling which in itself is absolute, though it is so definitely a part of ourselves.[34] However, the architecture, the physical adaptation of the city, nonetheless informs our happiness and sense of well-being: "A city can overwhelm us with its broken lines; the sky is torn by its ragged outline. Where shall we find repose? In old cities famous for their beauty we walk among shapes which are co-ordinated, designed around a centre or along an axis."[35] We cannot be limited by the original skeleton of a city, which "paralyzes its growth."[36] Underscoring the importance of this, and the need to heed the city, Le Corbusier does not mince words: "The great city determines everything: war, peace and toil. Great cities are the spiritual workshops in which the work of the world is done."[37] In the current urban age, with the majority of Americans living in urban areas, these words have increased vitality.

Le Corbusier's conception was of a simplified symmetry, a concentration of skyscrapers at the heart of an efficient transportation system. James Howard Kunstler, in commenting on developmental visions for Atlanta, criticized this kind of approach as "that old bullshit from Le Corbusier, the Franco-Swiss avant-garde guru-fraud from the 1920s" and his "Radiant City, the proposal to demolish a big hunk of Paris and replace it with *Towers in a Park* connected by freeways."[38] In her *The Death and Life of Great American Cities,* Jane Jacobs speaks of integrated neighborhoods of mixed use, but finds Le Corbusier's ideas often shallow and unable to withstand reality. Kevin Lynch wrote of legibility; all of these concepts are important to understanding the sense of well-being and identity of a city.

Jacobs and Kunstler seek an approach to urban existence that focuses on walkability and mixed use. It is a reaction to the post–World War II specialization and separation of city areas. The Congress for the New Urbanism declares itself to be "the leading organization promoting walkable, neighborhood-based development as an alternative to sprawl."[39] Jacobs and Kunstler have criticized Le Corbusier for his alleged wastefulness and unreality (though I think both of them would nonetheless agree that a city can have a *soul*, and that their urgings are meant to help maintain the city's core sense of identity).

Even admirers, such as architects James Stirling and Colin Rowe, apparently began to be less than convinced by the myth that Le Corbusier appeared to have created around himself. Kunstler depicts Le Corbusier as the embodiment of the Modernism philosophy that enveloped architectural thinking after World War II, with its rejection of the horrific recent past; "his Radiant City scheme became the only model for urban development in postwar America," and which "also appealed to Americans because our existing cities were aging badly."[40] It also appealed to the "back to nature" strand of American culture, the notion of "creating a city out of buildings in a park."[41] And Modernist skyscrapers, embraced by architects such as Mies van der Rohe, moved from symbols of democracy to symbols of corporate power.[42] Kunstler's point is that Modernists eliminated more than a bad past — they (in his expression) became servants of a destructive economy that has done remarkable damage to American civilization and, as well, to its cities. Henry Hope Reed, writing in *The Golden City*, complained about Modernism and its desecration of the Classical tradition on the grounds that "where once the street was crowded with sculptured detail we are now being offered a wasteland. Where once towers graced the skyline, slabs now obstruct it. Nothing seems to escape the giant vacuum cleaner of fashion as it passes over our communities, robbing them of all embellishment."[43]

Where does Trenton fit into the debate? As we consider the city's footprint and its future, it is not enough just to look at plans. It informs the discussion to understand what Jacobs and Kunstler are saying.

Jane Jacobs's assault on then-current city planning and rebuilding, *The*

*Death and Life of Great American Cities*, was published in 1961. Is what she said still relevant? It is open to debate. Nonetheless, in seeking to understand Trenton and the role of a smaller city it may still be useful to see what she had to say, and what it may tell us about the future of a place like Trenton.

Blasting the housing projects that deteriorated cities and the expressways that gutted them, she focused on the cities themselves as the proper laboratory, and not "the behavior and appearance of towns, suburbs, tuberculosis sanatoria, fairs, and imaginary dream cities."[44] Seeing is believing; she describes the reality of the Boston's North End's vibrancy, notwithstanding the failure of its geography to satisfy "traditional" planning principles.[45] Her overriding principle that emerged from her observations "is the need of cities for the most intricate and close-grained diversity of uses that give each other constant mutual support, both economically and socially."[46]

But it is not just the "look" of things. An imposition from the outside of "order" that meets some abstract aesthetic consideration will fail, Jacobs argues, calling such pretended order "dishonest."[47] Although she cautions against application of her principles and observations to towns and what she calls (but does not define) "little cities,"[48] the principles may still apply to Trenton. While its population may have dropped it into "little city" category, it nonetheless would probably satisfy her penchant for density. Given its relatively compact geographic area, its population density of 11,153 using an area of 7.7 square miles makes it virtually as dense as the obviously much more populated Philadelphia (population 1,517,550 but density of 11,233 per square mile) and over three times as densely populated as Houston (population 1,953,631 and 3,372 people per square mile).[49]

Jacobs saw the inherent value of the city *qua* city. First tracing the genesis of destructive city planning masquerading as urban reform, she excoriates the "garden city" of Ebenezer Howard that sought to "improve" the city by thinning it out and turning it inward on itself. Howard's view of housing facing inner courts rather than the street is but one example of this. This "Decentrist" approach found sympathy with early 20th-century American urban planners; for Jacobs, "this is the most amazing event in the whole sorry tale: that finally people who sincerely wanted to strengthen great cities should adopt recipes frankly devised for undermining their economies and killing them."[50]

And then along came Le Corbusier's vertical, automobile-centric utopian "Radiant City." Jacobs notes that while opposed by the Decentrists, it was actually an outgrowth of their thinking, and dramatically influenced the balance of 20th-century urban planning through the mid- to later 20th century. However, comparing his city to "a mechanical toy," Jacobs calls the egomaniacal Radiant City a lie.[51] The last great movement, the City Beautiful movement, heralded by such as Daniel Burnham of Chicago, was also a lie to her. While its monuments were impressive and had the ostensibly admirable purpose of inspiration, the centers eventually deteriorated. When all is said and done, this "concoction" from Howard to Burnham was "irrelevant to the workings of cities. Unstudied, unrespected, cities have served as sacrificial victims."[52]

So what does Jacobs find of value in a city? What should be the focus? How do we "fix" the city? She discusses the peculiar features of a city, attacking the dogmatic assertions that she believes have underlain the premises behind city planning during the 20th century. Her predominant theme is the need for diversity of neighborhood. Next she discusses the conditions for city diversity. Her third section revolves around the forces of decline and degeneration. Finally, she focuses on the particular tactics to be used to achieve the aims addressed.

First, the peculiarities and the assets of the city. Jacobs identifies a variety of physical things, seemingly mundane, but of critical importance, and how they have been used or misused.

We look to its streets and the buildings abutting them: "if a city's streets look interesting, the city looks interesting; if they look dull, the city looks dull."[53] Key to the success of a city is safety, and ensuring safety is a street-by-street matter. And the police themselves cannot keep the peace; that comes from the people of the neighborhoods, ultimately and fundamentally. The solution is not to spread people out, but to concentrate them. Pointing to the North End of Boston, she notes the diversity of its streets but, more critically, their *use*; "a well-used city street is apt to be a safe street. A deserted city street is apt to be unsafe."[54] This is a function as well of (1) clearly delineated areas of public and private space, (2) watchfulness, and (3) continuous use.[55] Once the street is so equipped to handle strangers, the strangers become an asset on the street. The institutions of restaurants, bars and shops create traffic, and traffic begets the use and watchfulness essential to safety. She decries the "turf" solution, with its genesis in a truce-like solution to gang warfare, as an outgrowth of the Radiant City developments within a city.

Consider the South Bronx and Charlotte Street. Visited by Presidents Carter and Reagan, but transformed by community organizations and local and federal money, but with a bottom-up, as opposed to top-down, approach.[56]

In addition to safety, the city depends upon the street for contact. The public nature of the sidewalk facilitates the city's social life, causing strangers to interact intimately who might otherwise not wish such intimate or private contact.[57] The ideal neighborhood balances privacy and contact.[58] She discusses neighborhood in terms of different levels of familiarity — there are various levels of connection, often through a common denominator (i.e., the shopkeeper) but while people may see and recognize each other, they are not intrusive of each other. The bounds of privacy and contact are respected. I read her to be describing the functionality of a city as a whole based on the functioning of its parts, its neighborhoods. However, that functionality is a result of utilized streets and sidewalks. Those sidewalks do not get use in unplanned cities where residential and work neighborhoods are segregated. The more contact there is, the more sharing of experience and the more stable the unit, and therefore the city. She summarizes in this way: "Although monopoly [of a commercial or residential district for that purpose] insures the financial success planned for it, it fails the city socially."[59] Sidewalk safety and contact are also essential for integration and combating discrimination.[60] In short, "Lowly, unpurposeful and random as they may appear, sidewalk contacts are the small change from which a city's wealth of public life may grow."[61]

Sidewalks also assimilate children; Jacobs urges abandonment of the fantasy solution based on sequestered playgrounds off the street, in idyllic parks, since often those are the very gang battlefields attributed to the streets. In point of fact, it is the street that provides more watchful adult eyes, in Jacobs's assessment, or more to the point, should be under such surveillance with appropriate city planning.[62] She attributes the hostility to the street — a more decentralized approach — to the centralized playground areas to the acolytes of the "Garden City" and "Radiant City" concepts, who favor isolated and enclosed parks or playgrounds.[63] Sidewalks also provide areas of "unspecialized" play as opposed to the more regimented play forced by playgrounds with fixed equipment,[64] or in a "matriarchy" where men design playgrounds for mothers' supervision.[65]

Her next point of discussion in her description of the peculiar nature of cities is the city park and its uses. She discards the assumption that parks have a defined use or that they should; they have been misused and misperceived as provided environmental or aesthetic balance. Pointing to the four parks laid out in the original William Penn geometric design for Philadelphia, she notes that only Rittenhouse Square was successful, and that was due to its surrounding mixed residential and commercial uses. The other squares (including the "square" at Logan Circle) were all established with the same intended purpose, but have fared far differently. It success is the result of "the same basic reasons that a lively sidewalk is used continuously: because of functional physical diversity among adjacent uses, and hence diversity among users and their schedules."[66] The forced designation of a park's purpose leads the park on a downward spiral. While she notes (rather tartly) that there may a use for the "Skid Row" park, such is not the panacea for the remainder of a city's parks.[67] A city park may add attraction to a city but can be successful components of a neighborhood only if fed by diversity and continuity of use.[68]

Which leads to her final component of discussion in this part — the use of the city neighborhood. First and foremost, she contends that we need to reject the idealized vision of "supposedly cozy, inward-turned city neighborhoods" that are at the center of "orthodox planning theory."[69] The nature of the city is that it is not a small town; a small town of 5,000 people may find many of them knowing each other, and seeing each other on Main Street; the same 5,000 population within a city does not have the same degree of interconnection. The concept of a self-contained neighborhood in a city may therefore be seen to work at cross purposes with the notion of a mobile and fluid city, whose geographic areas and their uses are meant to transcend artificial and confined boundaries.

On the other hand, a neighborhood as a city unit has its particular functions, such as localized government. Ultimately, she finds three useful types of neighborhoods: "(1) the city as a whole; (2) street neighborhoods; (and 3) districts of large, subcity size, composed of 100,000 people or more in the case of the largest cities."[70] The third should function as a mediator between the small street neighborhoods and the city as a whole, and this, Jacobs says, is mainly where cities have failed.[71] Given these as the city's neighborhoods, effective city planning should seek to have "lively and interesting streets ... [and] make the fabric of these streets as continuous a network as possible *throughout* a district of potential subcity size and power ... [and] use parks and squares and public buildings as part of this street fabric ... [and] emphasize the functional identity of areas large enough to work as districts."[72]

As I have noted, there exists ambiguity as to just what a neighborhood is and, therefore, what its proper uses and functions are. Gans points out in *The Urban Villagers* that in the West End of Boston, those who lived there thought less of themselves as West Enders and more in terms of sub-neighborhoods.[73] A neighborhood's qualities can only be quantified so far by sociological methodology; the essence of it may be reduced more to "feel." Neighborhoods are not to be romanticized; Gans notes that "the West End was not a charming neighborhood of 'noble peasants' living in an axotic fashion, resisting the mass-produced homogeneity of American culture and overflowing with a cohesive sense of community. It was a run-down area of people struggling with the problems of low income, poor education, and related difficulties. Even so, it was by and large a good place to live."[74]

Having identified the physical components of a city's strengths and weaknesses, Jacobs addresses the economic workings of the city, and the conditions for city diversity: "To understand cities, we have to deal outright what combinations or mixtures of uses, not separate uses, as the essential phenomena."[75] First, she discusses the generators of diversity. Initially, population is a core component; a city can sustain a greater variety of commercial facilities that cater to discrete populations that in themselves have sufficient critical mass moreso that the small town population. In this regard, the city also generates cultural as well as economic diversity, but this is not automatic; "they generate it because of the various efficient economic pools of use that they form."[76] She cites the Bronx and Detroit as high population areas with surprisingly weak diversity and choice, setting forth four necessary ingredients for an efficacious diversity: (1) each district and as many of its components as possible should have at least two primary functions, (2) blocks and streets should be short, (3) intermixed buildings within districts should be varied in age and condition so that economic yield is varied, and (4) there should be a "sufficiently dense concentration of people."[77]

The first condition requires diversity of primary uses, that is, the anchorage function of the place, as well as secondary diversity, that of the kinds of activities present as a result of the primary uses.[78] It is particularly critical that diversity exists in the downtown area, which in effect spreads throughout the city, and it is also important to have what Jacobs calls a "vital chessman," such as in New York, Carnegie Hall, surrounded by other, lesser chessmen that can respond to it; she decries as poor planning the segregated "planning island" of Lincoln Center.[79] Such civil centers that isolate uses have a negative impact on the city. Of particular relevance to Trenton and places like it is her discussion of the effect on the city of isolating government buildings and courthouses, which should not be separated from the rest of the city.

The second, the "short block" condition, is based on the assumption that long blocks, with less opportunity for turning, fosters her point that "isolated, discrete street neighborhoods are apt to be helpless socially."[80]

The third condition seems at first counterintuitive: while one can understand the mix of old and new buildings for purposes of interest and aesthetic, why also require a mix of economic yield? Should not all buildings be as profitable as possible? Not necessarily; Jacobs argues that cities need "a good lot of plain, ordinary, low-value old buildings, including some rundown old buildings" to encourage enterprises and businesses that cannot otherwise afford the more upscale ones.[81] It is not age that makes an old building useless; it is the failure of the city to support usage of such buildings for those who can afford them that renders them useless. The phenomenon of readaptive use adds to the interest of the street. The mix of old and new buildings fosters "new primary diversity" and increases economic yield.[82]

Finally, regarding her fourth condition, she distinguishes between overcrowding and density. There is no set formula; it is a matter of expediency and what ultimately works. Density must work in tandem with diversity. And, Jacobs says in a section seeking to dispel the "myths" of diversity, diversity is good.

Having set out her main contention that responsible city planning should encourage diversity, and economically and socially integrated city districts, Jacobs notes the destructive forces contributing to city decline: self-destructive diversity, single elements in a city to dominate and destroy, and the erratic effects of public and private money to "glut or starve development and change."[83] Self-destructive diversity is a function of being a victim of its own success; the successfully diverse district drives down other districts, and ultimately loses some of the purposes to the primary purpose of its success.

Border vacuums, created by, among other things, railroad lines, can also negatively impact a city not merely by keeping people from crossing them, but also by creating impressions of single-use districts within the borders. Recognizing that edges may nonetheless have use (as also explained by Lynch in *The Image of the City*) in giving a city legibility, the edge must be a seam, though, and not a barrier.[84]

The city, after all, is the extended home of its citizen. If one walks out the door and into a bleak street walled by abandoned, boarded-up buildings, with weeds growing through broken concrete and barbed-wire fences guarding parking lots, a very different sense derives, of course, than that in which one looks out upon gardens and sweeping, occupied buildings.

Nor does it do to "unslum" a city by razing current deteriorated housing and simply replacing it with putatively higher-tax-yielding facilities.[85] The way to "unslum" the slum is to seek to maintain its population and attachment to the district, and that is accomplished, she argues, through diversity, active city public life and sidewalk safety, and, of course, financial commitment; it does not happen spontaneously.[86] If the population remains by choice, and the other factors begin to take root, the "slum" may "unslum." She speaks of self-diversification as a natural phenomenon, and growing a middle class, rather than reimplanting it.[87] And one must be patient; it does not unslum overnight. Money may shape "cataclysmic change,"[88] and while it is important, it cannot cause the kind of gradual change that sustains and stabilizes a city and its districts.

In the end, Jacobs proposes different tactics. We need to rethink subsidized dwellings, because the way we have approached it has not produced the kind of diversity of population necessary for effective city building. We need to rethink the conventional view that the automobile is the enemy of the city, since comparable if not worse congestion existed in the era of horse and buggy travel; indeed, certain city districts may not warrant mass transportation, and the automobile may be essential. Rather than look upon the automobile as the causal element of a city's attrition, appropriate planning should seek to render attrition of automobile use by accommodating more sidewalk use, increase diversity, selectively limit types of vehicles in different parts of the city with coordinated use of mass transportation. We need to pay attention to "visual order," and be realistic: "There is a basic esthetic limitation on what can be done with cities: *A city cannot be a work of art.*"[89] While art is appropriate, we should not approach the city as an artistic problem: "Istead of attempting to substitute art for life, city designers should return to a strategy ennobling both to art and to life: a strategy of illuminating and clarifying life and helping to explain to us its meanings and order-in this case, helping to illuminate, clarify and explain the order of cities."[90] In short, cities are unique creations and need to be focused on their particular districts and their specific needs and issues, rather than some abstract paradigm, and to make use of the streets and the city's particular landmarks. We need to stop thinking of salvaging efforts as "projects" that are "abstracted out of the ordinary city and set apart."[91]

She sets specific goals for appropriate city planning: diversity, "continuous networks of local street neighborhoods," elimination of border vacuums, unslumming the slums, using money in longer-term (and non-cataclysmic) ways, and clarifying the "visual order of cities" by "promoting and illuminating functional order, rather than by obstructing or denying it."[92] The "Garden City" of Ebenezer Howard and the "Radiant City" of Le Corbusier are not appropriate models for city planning because they are based on an approach in the history of scientific analysis that focuses on two variables—quantity of housing or population, and jobs—rather than accepting that the kind of complexity that is a city does not lend itself to that type of reasoning and solution.[93] Ultimately, the specific must lead to the general; an inductive approach to the city will produce realistic solutions, whereas a deductive, top-down approach, moving from general to specific, leads to absurdities.[94]

All things considered, there remains a question not only of practicality, but also of letting a place be what it is. One may have an image of an ideal city, based on a particular city one likes, or a neighborhood in which one lives, but that does not mean such will translate to all cities, regardless of size. In his essay "A City Is Not a Tree," architect Christopher Alexander praises Jacobs for her criticisms of prevalent urban deadness, but notes that every city cannot be a cross between Greenwich Village and an Italian hill town. He agrees that the kind of artificial boundaries between city "districts," in which units are meant to function as a whole vis-à-vis other units, is the foundation of the artificial city and not the optimum way for a city to operate. A tree has component units that interact with each other as a whole; the semi-lattice, where fixed and variable units are continuously interacting, is the way natural cities have grown.[95]

I have taken some time to summarize Jacobs' thoughts because, though penned half a century ago, they do appear to retain relevance when considering an industrial city, like Trenton in a post-industrial world—even if not one of her "great" cities—and as a backdrop toward evaluating the current and proposed master plan on the table. Not all will agree. Nonetheless, this way of looking at things provides a useful set of parameters to bear in mind when walking about Trenton. It helps focus attention and enables one to see, perhaps, something behind the curtains. Such thoughts enable leaders and planners to say "what if." It is only upon the articulation on the "what if" that we can get to the "maybe" and then, hopefully, the "how."

Another commentator worth being acquainted with in this regard is James Howard Kunstler. Again, in trying to understand what makes a city, it helps to see how others have written of other cities, and where Trenton does, or does not, fit. Kunstler wrote *The Geography of Nowhere*, in which he argues that the destruction of the American city, towns and countryside essentially became the American economy. It is a provocative book that attempts to explain post–World War II America and what happened to where we live, and how we feel about it. The American mindset is one of individual property ownership, a feverish obsession that Kunstler calls "extreme individualism of property ownership with all that is sacred in American life."[96] Economics, not aesthetics, drove the establishment and building of American cities: "American cities flourished almost solely as centers for business, and they showed it. Americans omitted to build the ceremonial spaces and public structures that these other functions might have called for. What business required was offices, factories, housing for workers, and little else."[97]

The city of the first half of the 19th century was an integrated place; the wealthy lived on fashionable streets near the downtown and business areas, and the "poor" were, in Kunstler's words, not yet a "permanent class of subsidized indigents" but simply people with less money.[98] Following the Civil War, that changed; the entire nature of housing became more pragmatic and simply a function of housing the largest numbers of workers possible, as American cities, fueled by industrial growth, took off. It took decades before health and safety regulations caught up with the situation, and overcame American predilections for individual rights. Ultimately, "the spread of slums, the hypergrowth and congestion of manufacturing cities, the noise and stench of the industrial process, debased urban life all over the Western world and led to a great yearning for escape."[99]

Enter the suburb.

What Kunstler calls the "crisis of place" is exemplified by the country's cities, by their "squalor and impoverishment" (he was writing in 1993), but the city remains necessary.[100] The problem is that planning is divorced from reality. It is conducted in the abstract. Kunstler quotes planner Elizabeth Plater-Zyberk: "'In the past, town planning involved *design*. If you look at the plans from the 1920s you can see very clearly the concern for public space, where the civic monuments were, the focus on neighborhoods. Today it has become totally a matter of words and numbers, like an abstract painting.'"[101] She and her husband (and co-planner in their business) send forth the message about the need to change zoning laws. Trenton remains a relevant example of this potential approach; as Kunstler notes, writing in 1993, Trenton was a "customer" of Duany and Plater-Zyberk.[102] In an article on the web titled "Three Cheers for Gentrification," Duany makes the case for gentrification as opposed to pumping low-cost housing into cities, and mentions Trenton — along with Syracuse, Philadelphia, Detroit, Milwaukee and Houston — as cities "that need all the gentrification they can get."[103] It is interesting that Trenton — a small, post-industrial city — is nonetheless seen and discussed in the same terms as much larger cities. It may well be that in evaluating their recovery and importance to the national economy, the distinction Jacobs drew in the 1960s between "great" cities and other cities no longer has the same absolute meaning.

However, it is important to distinguish between the city proper and the notion of the metropolitan area. Throughout this book I have been concerned with the city *qua* city, a particularized entity, and not the urban region. As Richard Ingersoll observed in *Sprawltown*, "Almost without notice the city has disappeared.... During the past fifty years, the exponential increase in urbanization has pushed the form of cities beyond the scale of the metropolis to that of the megalopolis: an urbanized territory."[104] However, Robert Bruegmann has argued in his closely titled *Sprawl* that there really is no good definition of "sprawl"; one could just as easily call Brooklyn "sprawl" from Manhattan even if it has all the characteristics of a city as opposed to the look and feel of Central New Jersey.[105]

Interestingly enough, one could argue that New Jersey was born in sprawl. In Hall's *History of the Presbyterian Church*, which includes a fair amount of information, tangentially, about Trenton, he quotes extensively from an observation dated October 28, 1748, by the Swedish Professor of Economy, Peter Kalm, who wrote, "On the road from Trenton to New Brunswick I never saw any place in America, the towns excepted, so well peopled. An old man, who lived in the neighborhood, and accompanied us for some part of the road, however, assured me that he could well remember the time when between Trenton and New Brunswick there were not above three farms, and he reckoned it was fifty and some odd years ago."[106] Almost three hundred years ago, one would have heard the same complaint or comment that one could, and often does, hear today.

*The more things change...*

Kunstler's recommendations for what he calls "the art of making good places"[107] basically involve "new urban" concepts that others have developed that focus on cohesiveness as opposed to the destructive discontinuity of space and place that he associates with Modernism, as well as "pedestrian pockets" that stress public space, walkability and an intelligible grid structure. With sensible urban planning that focuses on these concepts, including integrated commercial and residential uses, the countryside could also be favorably impacted.

He continues his themes in *The City in Mind: Notes on the Urban Condition*, an examination of eight North American and European cities. He stresses that city-making is an art, not a science, citing Paris; that the "Edge City" as exemplified by Atlanta is not a preferred model; that a people's history continues to impact on its present day city life and construction, as evidenced by Mexico City ("a prototype of hypertrophic 'third world' urbanism, plagued by a failed social contract, lawlessness, economic disorder, and a wrecked ecology"); that freedom and openness can overcome the historic destructive forces that collapsed a city such as Berlin; that city leaders failing to understand that there is no such thing as a free lunch will inevitably become Las Vegas; that understanding history is essential, and that Classicism may be a necessary way of thinking to save a city, a la Rome; that abandoning the notion of making a city automobile-friendly may be essential to the survival of urban identity, with Boston "demonstrat[ing] the value of city life to a culture that all but gave up on the idea," and London as the source of the unfortunate notion that country life is the salvation of an industrialized city.[108]

My synopses based on Kunstler's introductory summaries of course do not explicate all of his ideas. In *The City in Mind*, he has opted for a historic approach to showcase and contrast by example what has happened in each of these cities. It is not so much a Burkean recitation that "those who don't know history are destined to repeat it." Rather, his is an approach that insists on an understanding of history but a rejection of artificial, cultish and abstract approaches to the city, which is of relevance here.

Macro-economics, Jane Jacobs tells us in 1982 in *Cities and the Wealth of Nations*, is a shambles.[109] Focus on national economies, the example of macro-economics, is misguided; "cities are unique in their abilities to shape and reshape the economies of other settlements, including those far removed from them geographically."[110] Cities grow through import-replacing, which results in markets for its exports, increased jobs in the city, improved technology, transplanted city work, and new capital. These forces help the city grow.[111] And it is the city that supports its region; while that region may persist after a city begins to stagnate, it needs the economic engine of the city.[112]

First steps are obvious. The words of William H. Whyte, Jr., in his chapter "Are Cities Unamerican?" are particularly relevant to Trenton:

> But the rebuilding of downtown is not enough; a city deserted at night by its leading citizens is only half a city. If it is to continue as the dominant cultural force in American life, the city must have a core of people to support its theatres and museums, its shops and its restaurants—even a Bohemia of sorts ban be of help. For it is the people who like living in the city who make it an attraction to the visitors who don't. It is the city dwellers who support its style; without them there is nothing to come downtown to."[113]

This discussion of neighborhoods and planning, of old ideas and new, provides some context for understanding, or at least approaching, the current Master Plan for Trenton. While it is a truism that everything takes money, it is also true, as the Beatles sang, that money can't buy love. And so, all the money in the world cannot buy political will or sense of community. There are communities with little money that nonetheless maintain a cohesive neighborhood or district. Trenton has a footprint. It has the potential to reinvent and reshape itself, and restore legibility and a self-image of the city.

Of course, we cannot be naïve. As this book was being written, Trenton was engaged in a mayoral campaign that will bring a non-incumbent to the position.[114] Some ten candidates were running. Debate points run from experience (private sector versus public sector) to development (large-scale versus small-scale), education, and the city's financial situation. That election has been resolved. Trenton, for the first time in a long time, has a new mayor.[115] We shall see.

Problems that wrack cities like Trenton cannot be solved by vision alone. A new governor, proclaiming the state on the brink of bankruptcy, proposed a budget with significant cuts in state revenue to cities, triggering the inevitable and obvious reaction.[116] However, without vision—and without an understanding, or at least perspective—practical decisions that are made in a conceptual vacuum cannot succeed over the long term.

## 12. The City and Its Footprint

What I have tried to do in this chapter is introduce the notion of the flexibility of the Trentonian footprint. We have the vision of the current Downtown Master Plan. We have the admonitions and frameworks of the "new" urbanists. We have quite a good deal of philosophical discussion against which to evaluate that footprint and the current vision. In the midst of dealing with the very real problems of funding for social services, crime, education and the other issues of Trenton, it is nonetheless vital to bear in mind the vision. It is good to understand Jeb Brugmann's analysis and frameworks. It is good to look at what Jacobs and Kunstler have said. Whether we accept or reject their conclusions and observations, they are helpful so that Trenton's implementation of its own vision does not become rudderless, and may be evaluated in the broader context of the post-industrial world.

# 13. The City and the Photographer

Once, in Providence, Rhode Island, on some obscure street, having had a cup of coffee in a forgettable diner, I took out my camera and made ready to shoot the scene outside. The woman behind the counter asked what I was photographing. She found absolutely nothing of interest on that obscure, forlorn street in her city. I did.

The photographer goes to a "tourist" destination and no one questions him or her. Walk around Trenton, and you are stared at. You are a stranger. The more charitable think you are a journalist. What can you find? How do you capture the essence of a city? How do you document space and time? How do you "see" the city as a city, as Everycity and as its own unique place?

Photographers and the city have had a particular relationship from the inception of photography. From documentary to artistic, and the blurring of those distinctions, those behind the camera have been intrigued, fascinated, disgusted, and outraged by the urban environment. In his comprehensive study of urban photography, Peter Hales observed: "Offering not simply facts but information, they were cultural messengers, and their messages both reflected and defined how Americans saw their cities. More important, they assisted in the process by which American culture adjusted to its urbanization."[1] The urban photographer, "trained to see the city in culturally conservative ways ... made photographs that placed the city within older models of perception and thereby transformed that new and unsettling world into acceptable and comprehensible patterns."[2] The Farm Services Administration photographers of the 1930s proceeded with a similar sense of mission and urgency. As explained by Roy Stryker and Nancy Wood in *In This Proud Land: America, 1935–1943, as Seen in the FSA Photographs*, the purpose of photographers such as Walker Evans and Dorothea Lange, out in the Dust Bowl, was to "introduce America to Americans."[3]

The photographer finds subjects everywhere. The key is to look at the familiar as if it were unfamiliar. Books have been written on how to see, the art of seeing, and so forth; I mentioned earlier John Berger's classic eponymous work. Others discuss composition. If you want to photograph a city, get out and walk it. Understand it. Get a sense of place in it. It is important. Jane Jacobs demonstrates in her writings that we need to get into the streets and see the common things of a city to understand it. As Helen Liggett argues for photographic engagement in *Urban Encounters*, "To form linkages among images made of encounters among the camera, the city, and experience can reengage the city for the viewer while enacting an ethics of participation. From this perspective, a constitutive overlap exists between how we present cities and how we present ourselves."[4]

The city, Joseph Rykwert writes in *The Seduction of Place*, is "a precious, essential and inalienable part of the human achievement."[5] Think beyond the ruined staircase of the old White City. Pause to consider, and then mourn a 23-year-old man being gunned down on Bellevue Avenue between Calhoun and Fowler streets on a Wednesday night in October in the new millennium. Think beyond boarded-up rowhouses and weed-strewn vacant lots. Think a city, a place. And its relevance.

Why photograph Trenton? Because it is quintessential. As we have discussed, it is also prototypical, part of the nation's past and an essential component of its present.

***Bus Stop.*** Like most small cities, Trenton lacks a subway system, although it has a light rail as well as bus service. We tend to think of cities as walkable places or at least places where convenient mass transit alleviates the need for automobiles to get around. This image is meant to convey a sense of the city, as opposed to a small town. The stop is in front of the Corner Historic Building at Warren and State streets, now a bank but at one time home of the First Mechanics National Bank and site of other Revolutionary-era buildings.

Photography is visual poetry. A snapshot captures. The photograph frees. The photographic eye takes its subject, frames it, locates it, and expands upon it. The made image permits suggestion, extrapolation, metaphor. Free association permits connections to be made. We can see the *studium* and *punctum* of Roland Barthes in his book *Camera Lucida*, that is, the general essence of the image in its cultural and normally understood context (studium) and the pricking punctum, the jarring note, the wounding detail that shocks, that pushes the interpretation beyond the four corners of the frame. And there we move into poetry, the implicit meanings, the forced involvement of the reader/viewer to see what the photographer/poet sees, or not, or more. We may view such photographs in the spirit of Japanese haiku, where the one general image is juxtaposed with the countering detail, and we are left to make our own connections.

I have been influenced by a tradition of attempts to capture the city in American history. In *Urban Encounters,* Helen Liggett sought to provide a sense of the city by proceeding on the parallel tracks of theoretical scholarship and through "street" photography. Liggett states her purpose of presenting her text and images in order to "present an argument for approaching urban experience as a situation of indebtedness rather than as a site for enacting prior narratives."[6] My purpose has not been to present an argument, but rather to create sense of place. I have sought to portray not a situation of indebtedness but one of realization and awareness. If, as I understand Liggett, we should discard preconceptions of the contemporary urban experience (her "prior narratives") and view the city as place to which we owe our cultural present, then I agree, and I further agree that the conflation of imagery and personal reaction has a place. I have not generally purported, though, as she does, to attempt to relate Trenton in broad or specific philosophical terms to such iconic writers as Walter Benjamin. It has been enough to try to place the city in philosophical, theoretical and historic context. Aesthetically, I have photographed what resonated with me and where I found connections.

Connections are also the focus of Liggett's effort to get at the urban experience through juxtaposition of complex textual analysis of such writers as Foucault, Benjamin and Lefebvre with her own photographs of the city. Regarding "street photographers," she suggests that "their images reach beyond conventional views to present gifts of recognition."[7] She seeks to provide a sense of the city by proceeding on the parallel tracks of theoretical scholarship and through "street" photography. She searches for connecting and connections. She writes:

> I come to terms with the city by presenting "urban encounters." These encounters are based in urban experience without pretending to tell the truth or even to construct a narrative about the city. Rather than assessing the city as a site of economic production or as an object of governance, this work seeks out cities as places of life.[8]

13. The City and the Photographer 241

*Rooftops.* Ominous clouds convey a sense of drama to the city's rooftops. The top level of parking garages within a city often provide unique vantage points from which to capture unique images and make urban encounters.

I have used different authors in many cases to present the city, in both practical and abstract ways. They have helped provide a context for what I sought to photograph, and why. But just as Liggett sought her own urban experience, so did I through Trenton. It is a place of life. We should retain that thought as paramount.

Another photographer, among the masters of photography, who saw his city as a place of life that warranted photographic capture was Eugene Atget (1857–1927). Recognition of the ephemeral nature of his city drove Atget into the streets of Paris. As photographer Berenice Abbott (1898–1991) observed, to photograph the city, Atget "was inescapably drawn into ever increasing awareness of its vast history."[9] Notwithstanding the appearance of solidity, the Paris Atget knew would soon change. Some street corners might vanish. Some buildings would disappear.

Abbott, who made documentary images of New York, wrote in *Changing New York*: "To make the portrait of a city is a life work and no one portrait suffices, because the city is always changing. Everything in the city is properly part of its story — its physical body of brick, stone, steel, glass, wood, its lifeblood of living, breathing men and women."[10] Atget, that hulking and seemingly melancholy former actor, hauled his camera around Paris originally to photograph scenes that could be used by artists. Eventually, he became a chronicler of a changing city, working with an apparent sense of mission to document what was about to vanish. As we look at his images today, particularly those haunting images of empty streets. He has created a sense of timelessness; we look at those images and see history. Most importantly, we see a sense of place.

Atget's elegant and often haunting images of Paris were masterworks of composition and observation, of detail, and further conveyed a paradoxical sense of timelessness and mortality. It was as if he was aware of the ephemeral nature, even of streets and buildings, and sought to capture his city in time. This mindset and approach in turn found resonance in Abbott in her significant photographs of New York City in the 20th century. The photographer's role in understanding the city needs no explanation; all one need do is look at an Abbott image. Or, of course, one by Edward Steichen or Alfred Steiglitz, two other important photographers who captured essential elements of New York City. These are not mere curiosities of another time and place. They are efforts to capture cities as places of life. The skyline itself became a popular subject that "helped glamorize this urban image."[11]

I photographed Trenton to try to find it, set it in time and place. To contextualize it, without adornment or judgment. It was an act of preservation as well. A compelling need to preserve what so many have abandoned.

I wanted to photograph Trenton to understand it in its present incarnation in terms of where it has been and where it might go.

In his collection of New Jersey images titled *Urban Landscapes*, photogra-

13. *The City and the Photographer* 243

***West End.*** The western part of Trenton, surrounding Cadwalader Park, has several residential neighborhoods — in addition to West End, there is Cadwalader Place, Cadwalader Heights, Parkside, Berkeley Square, Glen Afton, Island, Hiltonia, and Hillcrest. Some are marked by large single-family homes on spacious lots. West End Avenue, at the eastern fringe of this general area, picks up at the end of West State Street. The steeply gabled roofs and patterned shingles on some are reminiscent of Dutch buildings. Compare this architecture and street with the photographs of Sherman Avenue on page 134 and East State Street on page 138 for contrasting views of connected dwellings in the city. The city has a diversity of single-family homes on grounds that are more reminiscent of suburban developments, and clustered, street-long rowhouses like those one sees in Baltimore or Philadelphia or Washington, D.C., along the northeast corridor rail lines.

pher George Tice agrees that some of the state's older cities provide fertile ground for the photographer, singling out Paterson (the subject of independent books), Rahway, Atlantic City and Hoboken. He found Camden "too depressing."[12] He included one image of Trenton: a men's clothing store on Broad Street, reminiscent of Atget's storefronts. His urban landscapes include small-town scenes and some rural scenes, but convey the breadth, beauty and interest of architecture in this dense and urban state. Notably, though few of his images have people in them, the human hand is evident by what has been built.

Photography matters. Despite complaints, from its inception, of manipulation, and the wealth of debate on the topic, for our purposes here we can accept the factual representation of the photograph.[13] The boarded up building is the boarded up building. Regardless of one's spin, that building exists and what captured. The reality of the graffiti-scrawled wall is the reality of the graffiti-scrawled wall. Jacob Riis used photography in much the same way as Vietnam-era photographers used imagery — to bring the war home, into the living room. Riis showed how the other half lived in unflinching, unadorned manner. And it mattered.

To photograph something compels one to learn about it. While it may be preferable to have first-hand, "life experience" of the subject, that is not always possible. Critic John Berger, in *About Looking*, discussed painter Ralph Fasenella and wrote: "Only somebody who has lived in the streets of a city, suffering some kind of misery, can be aware of what the paving stones, the doorways, the bricks, the windows, signify. At street level — outside a vehicle — all modern cities are violent and tragic."[14] I do not agree with the first sentence, but I embrace the second in part; I would add that all modern cities are also a place of undiscovered beauty.

The role of the photographer is not just to document. It is to capture the culture and mirror it, and in a way, help shape it by allowing people to see what they have created. The photographer, the maker with light, does not make the reality; the photographer frames it and enables the viewer to see it through the photographer's eyes. As Peter Bacon Hales writes in *Silver Cities: Photographing American Urbanization, 1830–1939*:

*Corner of Stockton and Hanover.* A liquor store is the only open building on this corner in the Hanover/Academy district. The boarded-up windows and graffiti and empty street make for a desolation that is a not uncommon image of the post-industrial city.

*Perry Street.* Perry Street connects or runs through three of Trenton's older and more historic areas — Hanover/Adademy, Ewing/Carrol and Coalport. It is also the home of the city's two newspapers, *The Trentonian* and *The Times.* Shown here is an example of the three-story rowhouse, one of which houses a soul food caterer. The fire department is also located on this street. During the 1968 riot, apparently one of the scenes, as reported by Paul Mickle in *The Trentonian,* was of "men driving golf balls up Perry Street into the ranks of cops wearing Little League helmets and welding masks." Perry Street is in the heart of Coalport. If there is one street that epitomizes the look and feel of the "gritty" post-industrial city, it is Perry Street.

> Between 1839 and 1939, many photographers took the city as their subject. At first silent about their craft, operating in a time when photographers seemed to most Americans more like barbers than artists, these men and women — directly or indirectly — defined and ordered their contemporaries' understanding of the urban environment, its perils and potentials. Their vision of the city became the heritage of modern America.... Offering not simply facts but information, they were cultural messengers, and their messages both reflected and defined how Americans saw their cities. More important, [sic] they assisted in the process by which American culture adjusted to its urbanization.[15]

The photographer of the city has a broader social commitment — to make sure that memory persists. To enable us to see what the lens captured, and not what faded memories have let slip, or have otherwise embellished.

Over thirty years ago a book came out called *Gritty Cities: A Second Look at Allentown, Bethlehem, Bridgeport, Hoboken, Lancaster, Norwich, Paterson, Reading, Trenton, Troy, Waterbury, Wilmington.* I mentioned this book earlier. The authors had limited text and limited photographs, with their intention to put forward a "book of photographs and introductory essays that try to convey that special [visual] character" of the cities mentioned, to capture "the strong and consistent visual impressions they conveyed."[16] More recently, South American photographer and writer Camilo Jose Vergara has embarked upon a photographic journey documenting America's "ghettos," as he calls them, in "America's least fortunate cities," including Chicago, South Bronx, Newark, and Camden, and explained that he photographed these locations

> because I find these places moving. Because their streets, panoramas of ruined buildings, their rubble, their crumbling water towers and smokestacks, have the power and beauty of desolation. Because these landscapes are visceral, they make their observers stop and reflect. Because they are isolated from the mainstream, ghettos persist and grow. If more people were to experience these places, the more quickly they may be transformed.[17]

A century earlier, Jacob Riis was active. Riis's importance cannot be underestimated, nor can the importance of photography and the ability of the photographer (or, more broadly, artist) to shape one's view of the city. Hales writes of that significance:

> Just at the moment when the grand-style photography of men like [Charles Dudley] Arnold had come perfectly to synchronize with the celebration of a laissez-faire city in which order and civility were the rewards of successful battle in the economic sphere, Riis forced his isolated audience into disturbingly close contact with that which the grand style had so convincingly excised from the photographic record and, by proxy, the book of evidence. Riis succeeded in suggesting a new photographic style that could account for the pressing realities of immigration, poverty, social threat, and uncontrolled growth. He broke down the traditional cordon sanitaire of urban photographer and thereby added significantly to the existing taxonomy of the urban genre.[18]

Most of the photographs in *How the Other Half Lives* are of people as opposed to people-less buildings and ruins. It is perhaps ironic that such images are also considered, on a certain level, to be fine art. Not that the ugly and desolate cannot simultaneously have a kind of beauty, but rather because the efforts of Riis have, after a hundred years, still not proved efficacious. The photographer of the city, though, like the cop on the beat, continues to seek to protect one block at a time.

I have found certain painters to provide inspiration for photography, whether by way of subject or composition or empathy. The French painter Jean-Francois Millet (1814–1875) depicted peasants at labor. He is celebrated for the manner in which he captured their dignity while at the same time evoking compassion Part of the new realism, his subjects achieved heroic proportions. In the present era, in the West, we do not speak in terms of "peasants." We euphemize. Nonetheless, they are living, in Thoreau's words, lives of quiet desperation.

One might assume that given the nature of photography, by definition it embodies realism. Such an assumption would be incorrect. Photography encompasses abstract as well as representational elements. Although it is also a mistake to assume that manipulated images began with digital photography, the facility and diversity of such imagery arguably has increased. Indeed, there is often so much emphasis on technique and process that subject matter — the actual content of the image — often seems secondary in the works of some.

Millet, therefore, has much to teach the photographer looking to capture the lost city. While it may not be practical to duplicate his effort photographically, one can operate by analogy and metaphor. The subject matter — street people versus peasants in the field — might be somewhat different, I suggest there is a common denominator that benefits from close study of Millet. He was an artist of the lost and the betrayed, sensitive to a broad spectrum of humanity that was "under the radar" of those who needed to comprehend.

One might argue that Millet's subjects were at least working, albeit for minimal subsistence. Does that distinguish them from the people captured here? No. They are all consumed with survival. It is not a question of choice, though presumably some would argue that as well. Who could choose a life of begging? Who imagines at five or six years old, that what they want most of life is to beg on a city street? Their expressions belie that.

Millet was not necessarily concerned with expression. The women in *The Gleaners* are unrevealed; the most visible face is only partially seen. We are presented with forms, suggestions of the people beneath. That was perhaps part of Millet's genius, as opposed to other contemporary realist painters. One could sense something of the ache in these people.

And yet, the ordinariness of lives becomes particularly special; the routine of this place is unique to this place. Lives go on. People wait for buses. They go into the liquor store, open early, at the corner of Stockton and Hanover. Laughter echoes past abandoned buildings.

Though not an urban painter, Millet would have liked painting in Trenton. He would have appreciated the working-class ethos to the city, its dignity and history of tangible accomplishment.

The city as photographic subject may also be reminiscent of the Impressionist painters and their focus on obtaining the essence of the various cities they encountered. The ethos of the city was as, if not more, important than straightforward representation. The urban photographers similarly did not simply document. They strove to convey something greater than the sum of the parts

So I approached this with the photographer's aesthetic concerns and the lawyer's obsession with facts and the citizen's outrage. I walked the city, explored its neighborhoods, and got to know it visually. Sometimes, of course, having objectivity enables one to observe a place with insights often taken for granted and therefore unnoted by those in a place. I approached Trenton as I might

***Mount Carmel Guild.*** The Mount Carmel Guild, situated within the Coalport/North Clinton area, is one of the city's architectural gems. The Guild was founded in 1920 by a Trenton bishop, the Most Reverend Thomas J. Walsh, with a mission to help the poor and needy. Its Italianate Villa style reflects its roots in inspiration by rural Italian architecture. The style is marked by the square massing and elaborate detail. Gowan, in *Architecture in New Jersey*, notes the Italianate style was one of the major Victorian period architectural contributions, derived from Classical architecture but more popular in America to the extent it shows Gothic influence. Featured in England in the 1830s, the style spread to the United States, in the mid–19th century. Another example in Trenton of Italianate Villa architecture is the Ellarslie Museum in Cadwalader Park.

approach a foreign city I was visiting for the first time, with my camera. I wanted to understand Trenton, though, as an *American* city, and as I have commented above, as emblematic of the American psyche. I did not want to conduct interviews; any quotes are from news or other sources and are meant as background for these meditations.

There are as many ways to photograph a city as there are photographers and cities. One basic approach is straightforward documentary photography: this is the object, and this is a photograph of the object. Two photographers will attempt the same thing; one will produce an image that has depth and the other, perhaps not. Both may have the same technical skill, but one will arrange the image a certain way, or achieve a resonance through contrast, lighting, or through one of the myriad of factors that go into the image. Other approaches

13. The City and the Photographer          249

***Adam and Sickle Building.*** Located at 1 West End Avenue in the West End neighborhood, this building, built around 1900 and on the National Register of Historic Places, is an outstanding example of Queen Anne architecture in the city. Distinguishing features include the use of tiles and the corner curved turret and cupola.

are to photograph details, or moments, that carry suggestions and identifiers of the city, but through the story—or Barthes's inherent contradictions and tension—convey something else of the city in particular and the universality of urban life in general.

Writer Iain Sinclair and photographer Marc Atkins produced *Liquid City*, a textual and photographic exploration of eastern and southeastern London; the Thames is the liquid flowing throughout. Among the images in the book is a slightly out-of-focus black-and-white image of "the warehouse on Durward Street," which they call in the text "a survivor."[19] The building stands as a survivor on a nondescript street, though the text informs us that it oversees the doorway where Jack the Ripper's first victim was found. One building, with a history, part of the mosaic of a city. Other stories and connections are drawn in their text. This is in London, and its stories from London, but it could just as easily be one of the old factories in Trenton.

In *Some Cities*, Victor Burgin writes:

> We cannot know a "city," only those of its places we come to frequent. Aspects of a city may be revealed to us only as we leave it forever, just a people who have

250      Part Three: People Reacting to the City

> been intimates for many years may glimpse certain aspects of each other only in the moment they part. Remembering the cities we have left, we recall only certain times spent in certain places. Places we almost never think of when we are awake may repeatedly return in our dreams....
>
> Cities new to us are full of promise. Unlike promises we make to each other, the promise of the city can never be broken. But like the promise we hold for each other, neither can it be fulfilled.[20]

Burgin writes of and photographs a variety of cities—Sheffield, London, Berlin, Paris, among others. He intersperses his photographs with textual reference. Of Sheffield, he writes, "The community of steelworkers is gone. Making nothing of steel, Sheffield makes no sense."[21] The photograph, a small black-and-white image across from this, is of some children playing on a deserted platform near equally deserted railroad tracks. They are framed by the near-black, featureless silhouettes of apparent factory buildings and a smokestack. Dark gray smoke wafts out horizontally into the gray sky. The next image is an interior, with nondescript walls of what seems to be an old apartment building, with a woman in a long coat walking toward the end. This woman appears in a variety of images, at different stages of her journey, and not necessarily in order, always with her back to us. The images connote isolation, estrangement, an almost-alien planet that once, long ago, was inhabited.

He likes to photograph people in the street. He proclaims the search for a thing and the search for a person are "inseparable."[22] The images seem to break into three types: the empty city street, the people of the street, or the posters and advertisements that mock or comment, silently, on the scene. While the pieces of each city do not match exactly, Burgin finds equivalents—a section of road here, another there—both on a street in a different city. The image of the young blonde woman tending bar, facing a pair of hands, and, off to the side, anonymous, disconnected men and woman drinking, smoking—we might be in Manet's bar, with his woman from a hundred years ago. This is the city: the equivalents, the same pieces. A bar in Paris painted by Manet; a bar in Berlin, photographed by Burgin.

Trenton has its bars. And its liquor stores. Are bars merely places of escape from the city? From life? Edward Hopper's *Nighthawks* captures the estrangement and distance of the city's inhabitants from the city itself. Night emphasizes the distance. To read, and view, Burgin is to sense the city *qua* city, and understand the commonality of the (at least Western) city.[23]

There are of course many paintings of many cities. Cities like Trenton may have a few lithographs or prints to their name, and the usual collection of photographs, but they have not generally inspired an artistic oeuvre. In the sole hotel in Trenton, the Marriott, a grouping of contemporary paintings of Trenton scenes adorns the lobby, but that is as far as it goes. A painting, no matter how realistic, remains an interpretation. Even the photographer frames a subject, isolates a portion of the city, and does so because that particular scene and set of subjects resonated. How a city is painted reveals its character. Or, more accurately stated, how the artist paints the city expresses what is seen as the city's essence.

A particular group of photographers and artists, known as the Precisionists, sought to capture the strict lines and shapes of the city. This group of painters and photographers, notably Charles Sheeler (1883–1965), took the machine and the factory as things of beauty. Precisionism may be defined in various ways, but one useful and working definition is that as a style, its works "transformed motifs into generalized, poetic accounts of lines and planes, often giving them a timeless and monumental character and avoiding any signs of individual artistic expression."[24]

Other ways to approach capturing the city border on the abstract and imagistic. If Millet provided inspiration for his realism, Fernand Leger (1881–1955) provided a counterpoint, if not natural progression, in interpreting the city by its components and in exaggerated ways. His 1919 *The City*, viewable in the permanent collection of the Philadelphia Museum of Art, bears study. Leger painted, in his own cubist (or "tubist") fashion, various "cityscapes" or urban scenes, but this one is considered iconic and the only one titled simply "The City." Leger reportedly was inspired by Paris in its creation. His fascination with things mechanical and the components of the urban experience grew out of his experience in World War I. We see pieces of things, composites of the whole—a dotted line running down the center of a road, the cables of a suspension bridge, a faceless, de Chirico–styled man descending stairs, perhaps another man operating a machine, the shapes of industry—a disc and pole, signs and advertisements, something that looks like a ship's funnel—an amalgam of shapes and portions of objects representing the industrial city. It is 1919, between the wars, and a time before the post-industrial revolution—a time when Trenton was still in its Golden Age, though nearing the beginning of the end. Trenton as a manufacturing center could have been the model for this painting (perhaps excluding the inference of a major port), replete with the sense of industrial power implicit in this work. Leger, in his own words, "sought means of succeeding in conveying a feeling of strength and power.... It is necessary to retain what is useful in the subject and to extract from it the best part possible. I try to create *a beautiful object* with mechanical elements."[25]

Sheeler, Leger and Millet are but points along a spectrum, and not necessarily linear points. Centuries ago, Domenikos Theotokopoulos, better known as El Greco, painted one of the most arresting skylines in the history of art: *View of Toledo* hangs in the Metropolitan Museum of Art in New York. We look at a dramatic, bluish scene, with an electric sky. A massive stone arch bridge is in the foreground. The city rises on a hill, its skyline dominated by the cathedral. In the curator's notes on the wall, though, we learn that this is not necessarily an accurate depicture of the city from that viewpoint. Apparently, El Greco

*Kelsey Building and Statehouse.* The Kelsey Building was built as a monument by industrialist Henry Cooper Kelsey to his wife, Prudence Townsend Kelsey; he had it designed after one of her favorite pieces of architecture — Florence's Palazzo Strozzi. It now houses Thomas Edison State College, which, like its eponymous inventor, recognizes life achievement as a basis for awarding degrees.

made some adjustments to better fit his aesthetic sense; this was justified, according to the explanation, because the painter had captured the "essence" of the city. If El Greco had had a camera and used an image-processing program to achieve the same effect, one wonders at the reaction.

We may argue that a human being's physical aspect is informed by personality, but when we look, what we see initially is the outer shell. So with the city. Before we can experience its rhythms and mysteries, we must see it physically first.

In *Invisible Cities,* Marco Polo explains to Kublai Khan: "With cities, it is as with dreams: everything imaginable can be dreamed, but even the most unexpected dream is a rebus that conceals a desire or, its reverse, a fear. Cities, like dreams, are made of desires and fears, even if the thread of their discourse is secret, their rules are absurd, their perspectives deceitful, and everything conceals something else."[26]

In Trenton there are beautiful objects. The bridge in Cadwalader Park. The columns on the City Hall. The solid bricks of the Trent House. If Marco Polo were describing Trenton to Kublai Khan, what would he say? What features would he discern that affords the place its character? What would Leger paint if he were painting Trenton? How would Marco Polo describe it? What would Millet see, applying his eye for realism and humanity from the rural to the urban?

What do we see when we take the time to look?

# *Epilogue*

I have referred several times to Trenton as a prism. It is the post-industrial, apocalyptic landscape that nonetheless contains the remnants of Eden. It is a place of villainy and generosity, of violence and culture. It is, in short, a contemporary city. As far as North American cities go, it is among the oldest that still functions as a city. Its citizens walk the same streets as their Revolutionary forebears.

Perhaps "prism" is not quite the word. Perhaps kaleidoscope better serves. I have tried to view Trenton through the kaleidoscope of history, sociology, architecture, and art. I have tried to place it in an American context, both literally and figuratively. I think that, to understand America, one needs to understand Trenton. We move, inductively, from the particular to the general. And, conversely and deductively, we move from America to Trenton.

I have not have exhausted, nor could I even try to exhaust, the depth of scholarship on the post-industrial city. There are those who may well find fault with the summaries presented, or complain about some absent train of thought. There are those who may tell me I have it completely wrong. Others may nod and say, "Yes, yes, I hadn't thought of it in that way," or, "Interesting, perhaps I will go back and read what that person had to say."

What I have tried to do is to provide a sampling, in a cross-disciplinary manner, to provide the beginnings of a conversation with Trenton, since Trenton is at the same time familiar and unfamiliar, and a prototypical example of the post-industrial city. The theme of this book is that Trenton, like other such cities, is simultaneously unique and not unique. It has its own history, style, and presence, and yet it fits into the pattern and mosaic of American cities in particular, and Western cities more generally. I have sought to bring to bear many different sources and sets of eyes with which to consider, and reconsider, Trenton. It has been an exercise that finds relevance in the familiar that is often overlooked. Trenton has its problems, but it also retains its promise. It is not alone. Throughout the country we have such places at hand. They warrant our attention, for their both intrinsic as well as extrinsic value.

# Chapter Notes

## Preface

1. Procter 193.
2. Excerpted from *Aperture*, vol. 1, no. 2, pp. 41–45, 1952 in Nathan Lyons ed., *Photographers on Photography* (Englewood Cliffs, NJ: Prentice-Hall, 1966) at 68–72.
3. Langston Hughes, "Harlem," in Arnold Ramperseo, ed., *The Collected Works of Langston Hughes*, vol. 3, *The Poems 1951–1967* (Columbia: University of Missouri Press, 2001), 74.

## Introduction

1. Jeffry M. Diefendorf, "I Love That City, but Which City? Urban Change and Urban Identity in Basel, Boston, and Cologne" [for presentation at the Warren Center, Harvard University, conference on Reconceptualizing the History of the Built Environment in North America, April 30, 2005]. http://warrencenter.fas.harvard.edu/builtenv/Paper%20pdfs/Diefendorf.pdf (accessed 22 November 2010).
2. Ibid.
3. New Jersey: Place and County Subdivision, U.S. Census, http://factfinder.census.gov/servlet/GCTTable?_bm=n&_lang=en&mt_name=DEC_2000_PL_U_GCTPL_ST7&format=ST-7&_box_head_nbr=GCT-PL&ds_name=DEC_2000_PL_U&geo_id=04000US34 (accessed 22 February 2010).
4. "We did not build great cities in the European sense, [James W.] Hughes said of New Jersey's cities. 'What happened was manufacturing firms agglomerated into tight complexes in the 19th century, and we woke up and had six overgrown factory towns.'" Laura Mansnerus, "New Jersey's Cities: Sad Urban Presence Encircled by Wealth," *New York Times*, 26 September 1999.
5. Walter Benjamin, "Baudelaire, or the Streets of Paris," in Michael W. Jennings, Brigid Doherty and Thomas Y. Levin, *Walter Benjamin: The Work of Art in the Age of its Technological Reproduction and Other Writings on Media* (Cambridge, MA: Belknap Press of Harvard University Press, 2008).

## Chapter 1

1. Cathleen Crown and Carol Rogers, *Images of America: Trenton* (Charleston, SC: Arcadia Press, 2000), 92.
2. Tom Glover's Hamilton Scrapbook, http://glover320.blogspot.com/search/label/TRENTON%20DOWNTOWN (accessed 19 December 2009).
3. Kingwell 44.
4. Tuttle 11.
5. Gillette 61.
6. Cumbler 164–65.
7. Bebout 79.
8. Tuttle 125.
9. http://www.census.gov/population/www/documentation/twps0027/twps0027.html (accessed 22 February 2010).
10. Kunstler (1993) 33.
11. http://factfinder.census.gov/servlet/SAFFPopulation?_event=ChangeGeoContext&geo_id=16000US3451000&_geoContext=01000US|04000US34|05000US34037|06000US3403737440&_street=&_county=newark&_city Town=newark&_state=04000US34&_zip=&_lang=en&_sse=on&ActiveGeoDiv=geoSelect&_useEV=&pctxt=fph&pgsl=010&_submenuId=population_0&ds_name=null&_ci_nbr=null&qr_name=null&reg=null:null&_keyword=&_industry=Census (accessed 27 February 2010).
12. Tuttle 33.
13. Bebout 42.
14. Cumbler 159.

15. Cumbler 191.
16. Walt Whitman, *Leaves of Grass* (New York: Modern Library Publishers, 1921), 67.
17. Lisa Coryell, "Trenton Man Indicted In Girlfriend's Death," *The Times of Trenton*, 28 October 2009.
18. Linda Stein, "Trenton Resident Admits Fatally Stabbing Woman," *The Times of Trenton*, 31 October 2008.
19. http://translate.google.com/translate?hl=en&sl=de&u=http://lyrik.antikoerperchen.de/georg-heym-die-stadt,textbearbeitung,25.html&ei=NSXJSrmCCcGulAe4jZmSAw&sa=X&oi=translate&resnum=1&ct=result&prev=/search%3Fq%3D%2522georg%2Bheym%2522%2B%2522die%2Bstadt%2522%26hl%3Den (accessed 4 October 2009).
20. McKelvey (1963) viii.
21. Kostof (1991) 37–40.
22. Louis Wirth, "Urbanism as a Way of Life," *The American Journal of Sociology*, vol. 44, no. 1 (July 1938): 1–24.
23. Georg Simmel, "The Metropolis and Mental Life," adapted by D. Weinstein from Kurt Wolff, trans., *The Sociology of Georg Simmel* (New York: Free Press, 1950), 409–24. http://www.altruists.org/f792 (accessed 26 July 2009).
24. Ibid.
25. Ibid.
26. Gans (1993) 52.
27. Ibid., 53
28. Ibid., 54–56
29. Ibid., 61.
30. Ibid., 65.
31. http://quickfacts.census.gov/qfd/states/34/3474000.html (accessed 9 January 2010).
32. http://en.wikipedia.org/wiki/Trenton,_New_Jersey (accessed 9January 2010).
33. C. Fischer (1975) 1319.
34. Ibid., 1320.
35. Ibid., 1321.
36. Ibid., 1232n5.
37. Ibid., 1323.
38. Ibid., 568: "How plausible is the subcultural theory of urbanism? Where there is evidence, it usually supports the theory and only occasionally contradicts it. But most of the critical tests have not been done. Urbanism probably promotes the emergence of numerous and diverse subcultures within a community. Whether urbanism promotes more intense subcultures is still uncertain."
39. A useful and introductory synopsis of the views of the three writers just discussed, and others that place these thoughts in context, is found in a course resource by Quincy Edwards of the University of Hawaii. See http://www2.hawaii.edu/~qedwards/courses/uh/301/fa08/pptx/s301.c07.fa08.pdf (accessed 10 January 2010).
40. L. Mumford (1961) 573.
41. Susan Jo Keller, "New Jersey Daily Briefing: Condom Plant to Close," *New York Times*, 19 May 1995.
42. Lovelock 2.
43. Ibid., 13.
44. Kingwell 12.
45. Calvino 137.
46. "City of Many Bridges," *New York Times*, 16 February 1896, p. 25. More recently, the city of Venice, with a population of approximately 60,000, underwent a mock funeral to symbolize its reported death as population desert it for the mainland. Rachel Donadio, "Mock Funeral for Venice Dramatizes Flight of Residents from City's Heart," *New York Times*, 16 November 2009.

## Chapter 2

1. Leick xiv.
2. Albert Fein, "The American City: The Ideal and the Real," in *The Rise of an American Architecture*, 51.
3. Ibid., 52. This was not limited to the United States; English critic John Ruskin wrote of the English city as "a wilderness of spinning wheels instead of palaces; yet the people have not clothes."
4. Fein 55–57.
5. Rykwert 132.
6. Healey 1781.
7. Jessica Bruder, "Ardent Residents of Tumbledown Trenton Say It Reflects the Soul of the State Capital," *New York Times*, 2 May 2004, p. 14NJ6 ("Jerseyana; Trenton's Fighting Words").
8. Girouard v.
9. Reader 7.
10. "Between 2007 and 2050, the world population is expected to increase by 2.5 billion, passing from 6.7 billion to 9.2 billion (United Nations, 2008). At the same time, the population living in urban areas is projected to gain 3.1 billion, passing from 3.3 billion in 2007 to 6.4 billion 2050. Thus, the urban areas of the world are expected to absorb all the population growth expected over the next four decades while at the same time drawing in some of the rural population." "World Urbanization Prospects: The 2007 Revision Highlights." United Nations Department of Economic and Social Affairs, 2008. http://www.un.org/esa/population/publications/wup2007/2007WUP_Highlights_web.pdf (accessed 20 September 2009).
11. U.S. Census Bureau, "Metropolitan and Metropolitan Statistical Areas," http://www.census.gov/population/www/metroareas/aboutmetro.html (accessed 20 September 2009).

## Notes — Chapter 2

12. "The general concept of a metropolitan or micropolitan statistical area is that of a core area containing a substantial population nucleus, together with adjacent communities having a high degree of economic and social integration with that core." U.S. Census Bureau, "Metropolitan and Micropolitan Statistical Areas," http://www.census.gov/population/www/metroareas/aboutmetro.html (accessed 27 November 2009).

13. Witold Rybczynski, "Downsizing Cities," *The Atlantic Monthly*, October 1995, http://www.theatlantic.com/past/docs/issues/95oct/rybczyns.htm (accessed 28 February 2010).

14. "Venice, as a lived-in city, is dying. A population which peaked at 164,000 in 1931 is now hovering at around 60,000." Tom Kington, "Who Now Can Stop the Slow Death of Venice?" *The Observer*, 1 March 2009, http://www.guardian.co.uk/world/2009/mar/01/venice-population-exodus-tourism (accessed 25 July 2009). Trenton's population at present is approximately 83,000.

15. *Politics*, Book 7, Chapter IV, and *Laws*, Book IX.

16. H.D.F. Kitto, "The Polis," excerpted from *The Greeks*, and found in LeGates and Stout 45.

17. *The American Heritage Dictionary of the English Language* (4th ed.) 2009.

18. Weber 66.
19. Ibid., 66–67.
20. Ibid., 68–70.
21. Ibid., 72.
22. Ibid., 76.
23. Ibid., 78.
24. Ibid., 80–81.
25. Sjoberg (1965) 83.
26. Ibid., 86.
27. Lofland (1998) 7.
28. Lofland (1973) 3.
29. Ibid.
30. Lofland (1998) xi.
31. Ibid., xv.
32. Canniffe 16.
33. Lofland (1973) 8.
34. Childe (1950) 39–42.
35. Robert E. Park, "The City: Suggestions for the Investigation of Human Behavior in the Urban Environment," in Park, Burgess, and McKenzie.

36. Edward L. Glaeser, "Are Cities Dying?" *The Journal of Economic Perspectives*, vol. 12, no. 2 (Spring 1998): 139–60

37. Rae 18–19.
38. Rybcynski (1996) 39
39. Monti 17–18.
40. Matherly 351.
41. Kingwell 149.
42. William H. Frey and Zachary Zimmer, "Defining the City," in Paddison 14–34. *See also* Edward W. Soja, "Six Discourses on the Postmetropolis," in Bridge, 188.

43. Rykwert 74 (emphasis added).
44. Reader 9.
45. L. Mumford (1961) 79.
46. Kotkin xvi.
47. L. Mumford (1961) 79.
48. Kotkin 157.
49. Kingwell 14.
50. Hiss xii.
51. Ibid., xv.
52. Ibid., 20.
53. Ibid., 24.
54. Lippard 4.
55. Ibid., 6.
56. Ibid., 9.
57. Ibid., 10.
58. Ibid., 197.
59. Rodenbach 141.
60. Ingersoll 7: "In the end, sprawl is already a mature form of urbanism, one that by now is in desperate need of restoration."

61. As considered by Joel Garreau in his book "Edge Cities," such are the new urban centers and have become "cities, because they contain all the functions a city ever has, albeit in a spread-out form that few have come to recognize for what it is. Edge, because they are a vigorous world of pioneers and immigrants, rising far from the old downtowns, where little saves villages or farmland lay only thirty years before." Garreau 4.

62. Canniffe 17.
63. Ibid., 19.
64. Bell 117.
65. Hale 8.
66. Douglas V. Shaw, "The Post-Industrial City," in Paddison at 285.
67. Ibid., 287.
68. Clark 110–12.
69. Ibid., 114.
70. Ibid., 120.
71. Kostof (1972) 250.
72. Reader 74.
73. Ibid., 48.
74. L. Mumford (1961) 571.
75. Ibid., 458.
76. Rae 11.
77. Ibid., 12.
78. *See generally* Bebout, 52–77.
79. This point has been made in various places, but for one example see Bruegman 36.
80. de Tocqueville (Book 1) 325.
81. Ibid., 325n1.
82. Ibid.
83. Rybczynski (1996) 108–9.
84. http://historymatters.gmu.edu/d/6545/ (accessed 13 March 2010).
85. See Engels in LeGates 59–66.

86. Leick 30–60 (the chapter on Uruk, in which these themes are developed).
87. Healey 1778
88. Ibid., 1779.
89. Ibid., 1779
90. Ibid., 1780.
91. Ibid., 1780.
92. Ibid., 1781.
93. Ibid., 1783.
94. L. Mumford (1961) 446–50.
95. Monti 101.

## Chapter 3

1. *Holcombe v. Trenton White City Co.*, 80 N.J. Eq. 122, 127 (Ch. 1912).
2. Koolhaas 21.
3. Ibid., 34.
4. Ibid., 64.
5. The title of Procter and Matuszeski's book is *Gritty Cities: A Second Look at Allentown, Bethlehem, Bridgeport, Hoboken, Lancaster, Norwich, Paterson, Reading, Trenton, Troy, Waterbury, Wilmington.*
6. http://www.trentonnj.org/Documents/3-4-08Most%20Walkable%20City%20in%20NJ.pdf.
7. http://www.infoplease.com/us/statistics/safest-dangerous-cities-2006.html. Trenton ranked 14th most dangerous city in 2006 out of cities with populations in excess of 75,000. In 2007, it was no longer in the top 25, but homicides for 2007 were higher than 2006. In 2008 it was ranked 30th. Ryan Tracy, "Trenton Ranks 30th in Nation in Crime Rate," *The Times*, 25 November 2008.
8. In December 2008, the New Jersey Attorney General reported 1,844 arrests as a result of a year-long coordinated local, state and federal effort, across the state. Young, "Anti-Gang Initiative Leads to 1,844 Arrests, 162 Guns," northjersey.com, 9 December 2008.
9. Cunningham 330. Tuttle notes that the actual quotation was made by one of Gibson's aides, Donald Malafronte, and was "Wherever our cities are going, I'll bet Newark gets there first." Tuttle 8–9, citing *The New York Times*, 18 March 1969.
10. Rae 360.
11. http://www.trentonnj.org/Cit-e-Access/webpage.cfm?TID=55&TPID=9125.
12. Kevin Shea, "Gang Warfare Blamed in City Deaths," *The Times*, 26 June 2007: "They grew up together on the West Ward's main drag, Stuyvesant Avenue, and its side streets. They went to school together, and if they played ball, they may have worn the same uniform. Now, they are killing each other, police say, under the banner of gang rivalry."
13. Michael Ratcliffe, "Trenton Man, 23, Identified as Victim of Drive-By Shooting," *The Times*, 8 October 2008.
14. The Obama-Biden campaign did maintain a relatively comprehensive plan for cities on their website. See http://www.barackobama.com/pdf/issues/UrbanFactSheet.pdf (accessed 29 November 2008). The McCain-Palin campaign did not mention urban policy as a separate consideration on its issues page. See http://www.johnmccain.com/Informing/issues/ (accessed 29 November 2008).
15. "1931: Temple for Trenton's Art." http://www.capitalcentury.com/1931.html (accessed 19 September 2010).
16. Millman, Jennifer. "Face to Face with Barack Obama: He Talks Education, Healthcare, Unions." http://www.diversityinc.com/content/1757/article/1880/?Face_to_Face_With_Barack_Obama_He_Talks_Education_Healthcare_Unions (accessed 19 September 2010).
17. Rae 73.
18. Ibid., 19.
19. Ibid., 113–14.
20. Lee 281.
21. Ibid., 280.
22. McKelvey (1963) 17.
23. Ibid., 18.
24. Bebout 33.
25. McKelvey (1963) 18.
26. Ibid., 19.
27. Ibid., 71–72.
28. L. Mumford (1961) 446.
29. McKelvey (1963) viii.
30. Rae 11.
31. William Carlos Williams. (1946) Paterson. (rev'd ed. prepared by Christopher MacGowan (1992, 1995 ppbck) (New York: New Directions) at xiv.
32. Mayernik 220.
33. Ibid., 221.
34. Handlin 36–38.
35. Bolton 77–100.
36. Though many may have described "the city," I happen to like the succinct way James Howard Kunstler sums this up: "Cities contain the essence of civilization. They are the marketplaces for ideas and cultural values as well as material goods. They are the repositories of cultural memory. The city, above, all, is the public realm monumentalized." Kunstler (1993) 189.
37. Jacobs (1961) 13.
38. Johns 1.
39. Alex Zdan, "3 Armed Men Sought by Authorities Following Home Invasion: 2 People Beaten, 1 Stabbed Near Trenton Bar." *The Times*, 3 November 2008.
40. Jacobs (1961) 16.
41. Ibid., 30.

42. Bebout 63.
43. Rachelle Garbarine, "Commercial Property/New Jersey; For First Time Since 80's, Trenton Is to Get a Hotel," *New York Times*, 25 June 2000.
44. Lee 281.
45. Jon Norman, "Small Cities' Fates: Population, Income and Employment Change in Smaller Metro Areas in the United States, 1970 to 2000," paper presented at the annual meeting of the American Sociological Association, New York City, 11 August 2007, http://www.allacademic.com/meta/p182656_index.html
46. Calvino 7.

## Chapter 4

1. Shuman 10.
2. For the legal bases, see *Johnson v. McIntosh*, 221 U.S. 543 (1823); see also *Cherokee Nation v. Georgia*, 30 U.S. 1 (1831); *Worcester v. Georgia*, 31 U.S. 515 (1832); *Tee-Hit-Ton Indians v. United States*, 348 U.S. 272 (1955); *Passamaquoddy Tribe v. Morton*, 528 F.2nd 370 (1975); *County of Oneida v. Oneida Indian Nation*, 430 U.S. 226 (1985).
3. Podmore 48. The New Jersey Churchscape states the origin of the congregation to 1712. http://www.njchurchscape.com/TrentonFirstPres.html (accessed 26 July 2009).
4. http://www.njchurchscape.com/Trenton-FirstPres.html (accessed 26 July 2009). See also the church's website at http://www.old1712.org/timeline.html.
5. D. Fischer 425–28. McCullough also presents a more even-handed treatment. McCullough 278–84. See also Dwyer 276–79 for mainly critical commentary on Rall from contemporary sources. See also Michael Stephenson. *Patriot Battles: How the War of Independence Was Fought* (New York: HarperCollins, 2007) 254–59.
6. Podmore 53.
7. See generally William S. Stryker, *The Old Barracks at Trenton, New Jersey* (Trenton: Naar, Day and Naar, 1885).
8. Ibid., 13–14.
9. Podmore 10.
10. Ibid., 11.
11. D. Fischer 313.
12. Podmore 60.
13. James J. Backes, "Landmarks, Taverns, Markets and Fairs," *A History of Trenton 1679–1929*, http://www.trentonhistory.org/His/landmarks.html. (accessed 27 February 2010).
14. Ibid.
15. Podmore 60–61.
16. Ibid., 62.
17. Ibid., 63.
18. Backes, "Landmarks, Taverns, Markets and Fairs."
19. Rebecca White, Nadene Sergejeff, William Liebeknecht, and Richard Hunter. 2005. "A Historical Account and Archaeological Analysis of the Eagle Tavern," http://trentonhistory.org/Documents/EagleTavern.html (accessed 6 December 2009).
20. Ibid.
21. Ibid.
22. Ibid.
23. Backes, "Landmarks, Taverns, Markets and Fairs." Backes reports its ownership based on *New Jersey Archives*, 2nd Ser., vol. v, p. 370.
24. *American Heritage Magazine*, December 1987, vol. 38, no. 8.
25. In his collection *New Jersey in Travelers' Accounts 1524–1971: A Descriptive Bibliography*, Oral S. Coad aggregates summaries and some verbatim quotes from an astounding plethora of sources. Trenton is generally described as attractive; Coad's paraphrase of Lord Adam Gordon in the 1760s had Trenton described as "a pretty country place," as having "nothing remarkable" by William Owen in 1767, as a pretty village by John Adams in 1774 (Coad's paraphrase), and as "a pretty little town" by Robert Honyman in 1775. John Adams described Trenton as "a pretty village." On the other hand, Cromot du Bourg felt it was "not so pretty" as Princeton, albeit larger. The jurist James Kent termed Trenton the largest in the state as of 1793. In 1802, the French botanist Francois Andre Michaux described Trenton as "a most delightful place of abode." Sometime between 1815 and 1817 the French aristocrat and naval officer Baron de Montlezun said of Trenton, New Brunswick and Princeton that they were notable "for regularity, cleanness, and a certain air of comfort." By 1824, Englishman Simeon De Witt Bloodgood called Trenton "a large old-fashioned town." The German Prince of Wied-Neuwied, around 1832–1834, felt, as Coad summarized, Trenton to be a "straggling town; its famous wooden bridge a useless mass of timber."
26. See generally "1784: Trenton: The Nation's Capital," http://www.trenton1784.org/index.php (accessed 30 January 2010).
27. Raum 52–53.
28. Edwin Robert Walker, "The Colonial Period," in Walker et al., http://www.trentonhistory.org/His/colonial.html (accessed 22 January 2010).
29. Marc P. Dowdell, "Churches and Religious Institutions: The Society of Friends," in Walker et al., http://www.trentonhistory.org/His/churches.html (accessed 22 January 2010).
30. Podmore 48.

31. Coad 13.
32. Hall 49.
33. Weymer Jay Mills, *Historic Houses of New Jersey* (Philadelphia: J.B. Lippincott, 1903), 273–75.
34. Podmore 81. The Statehouse History on the New Jersey Legislature's website indicates it was built in 1792 by John Doane. http://www.njleg.state.nj.us/legislativepub/statehousehistory.asp [accessed 10 July 2010].
35. http://www.njstatehouse.org/ [accessed 10 July 2010].
36. L. Mumford (1961) 79.
37. D. Fischer 303. Major James Wilkinson wrote, "If there was ever a crisis in the affairs of the Revolution, this was the moment; thirty minutes would have sufficed to bring the two armies into contact, and thirty more would have decided the combat; and, covered with woe, Columbia might have wept the loss of her beloved chief and most valorous sons."
38. Kotkin xvi.
39. http://www.hmdb.org/Marker.asp?Marker=4383 (accessed 22 December 2009).
40. Richard Hunter, "Fish and Ships: Lamberton, the Port of Trenton," in *History Traced by Route 29 Booklet Series*, http://www.nj.gov/counties/mercer/commissions/pdfs/ch_lambertonportoftrenton.pdf (accessed 22 December 2009).
41. Ibid.
42. Ibid.
43. Ibid.
44. William J. Backes, "Transportation," in Walker et al., http://www.trentonhistory.org/His/transportation.html. (accessed 14 February 2010).
45. A booklet detailing his life, Thompson Westcott, *The Life of John Fitch: The Inventor of the Steamboat*, was published in 1857 by J.B. Lippincott & Co., and can be found at http://www.history.rochester.edu/steam/westcott/ (accessed 21 December 2009).
46. Souvenir 1.

## Chapter 5

1. Kaufman vi.
2. Lofland (1998) 8.
3. Kostof (1992) 123.
4. Ibid.
5. Ibid., 124.
6. Lofland (1998) 243.
7. Whyte 9.
8. Ibid., 105.
9. "Trenton's 'Triangle' Corridor," *Mercer Business*, 1 August 1999, http://findarticles.com/p/articles/mi_qa3697/is_199908/ai_n8876963/?tag=content;col1 (accessed 24 January 2010).
10. http://www.trentonnj.org/documents/planning_downtownmasterplan/ch_2_Vision.pdf (accessed 24 January 2010).
11. Whyte 145–50.
12. Jack Burgers, "Urban Landscapes: On Public Space in the Post-Industrial City," *Journal of Housing and the Built Environment*, vol. 15 (2000): 145–64 at 147.
13. Ibid., 146–61.
14. http://www.trentonnj.org/documents/planning_downtownmasterplan/ch_5_Mill_Hill.pdf (accessed 13 February 2010).
15. O'Gorman 89.
16. Pevsner 53.
17. Ibid.53.
18. Rykwert 228.
19. McNamara 2–3.
20. Richard A. Falk, "The Relations of Law to Culture, Power, and Justice," *Ethics*, vol. 72, no. 1 (October 1961): 12–27. See also Dennis E. Curtis and Judith Resnick, "Images of Justice," *Yale Law Journal* (1727 [1987]), 96.
21. Anne Maass et al., "Intimidating Buildings: Can Courthouse Architecture Affect Perceived Likelihood of Conviction?" *Environment and Behavior*, vol. 32, no. 5 (September 2000): 674–83. © Sage Publications, 2000.
22. Kingwell 85.
23. Ibid., 89 (emphasis in original).
24. Gnichtel, "The Courts, Judges and Lawyers; Medicine and Doctors," in *A History of Trenton*. http://www.trentonhistory.org/His/Courts.html (accessed 21 September 2010).
25. Raum was Trenton's city clerk from 1857 to 1859 and its treasurer from 1867 to 1871 and wrote the first comprehensive history of the city.
26. Raum 67.
27. See Podmore 73–74.
28. For an overall history of the federal court in New Jersey, see Mark Edward Lender, *"This Honorable Court": The United States District Court of New Jersey, 1789–2000* (New Brunswick: Rutgers University Press, 2006).
29. "Court Corner Laid," *Trenton Times*, 14 May 1902, p. 1.
30. "County Executive Hughes to Seek Historical Designation for Century-Old Courthouse," press release, http://www.state.nj.us/counties/mercer/news/releases/approved/070305.html (accessed 24 November 2008).
31. Shuman, notes its completion in 1904. Shuman 89.
32. http://www.clarkecatonhintz.com/project_43/ (accessed 27 November 2008).
33. Daniel Brook. "A Blueprint for the Future," *Legal Affairs* (November/December 2005), http://www.legalaffairs.org/issues/November-December-2005/feature_brook_novdec05.msp (accessed 25 November 2008).
34. Guide at 3–1, http://www.gsa.gov/

graphics/pbs/Courts_Design_Guide_07.pdf (accessed 21 September 2010).
35. "Courthouse Highlight Architectural Innovations," June 1996, http://www.uscourts.gov/ttb/jun96ttb/design.htm (accessed 28 November 2009).
36. http://www.justiceenvironments.edu.au/cof-newsletters (accessed 28 November 2009).
37. Michael Farewell, FAIA; Michael J. Mills, FAIA; and Meredith Arms Bzdak, "From the Parthenon to the Prius: Tradition, Modernity, and the New Paradigm in Courthouse Design," March 2008, http://www.justiceenvironments.edu.au (accessed 24 April 2010).
38. Ibid.
39. Mary P. Ryan, "A Laudable Pride in the Whole of Us: City Halls and Civic Materialism," *The American Historical Review*, vol. 105, no. 4 (October 2000): 1131–70, http://www.jstor.org/stable/2651406 (accessed: 23 November 2008).
40. Handlin 38.
41. Lebovich 14.
42. Ibid., 14; Pevsner 27
43. Lebovich 14.
44. Pevsner 27.
45. Ibid., 28, 34.
46. Ibid., 53
47. Ibid., 94.
48. Ibid., 97.
49. Ibid., 97–98.
50. Kostof (1992) 95.
51. Lebovich 119
52. Bailey Van Hook, *The Virgin & the Dynamo: Public Murals in American Architecture, 1893–1917* (Athens: Center for American Places, Ohio University Press, 2003), 61.
53. Podmore 111.
54. Lebovich 206.
55. Thomas C. Folk, "Everett Shinn's Trenton Mural Revisited," in Einreinhofer 68.
56. Ibid., 70.
57. Lebovich 24.
58. Ibid.
59. Public Art in New Jersey 5. See generally Handlin 132–66.
60. "Trenton's Firemen's Monument," *New York Times*, 29 July 1892, p. 5.
61. Alex Zdan, "Firefighter Succumbs to Injuries," *The Times*, 2 April 2009.
62. "A Short History of Trenton State Prison," http://www.windsorpress.net/io_hotp.html (accessed 19 August 2009).
63. Gowans 67.
64. Gresham Sykes, *The Society of Captives: A Study of a Maximum Security Prison* (Princeton, NJ: Princeton University Press, 2007 [1958]), 5.
65. Ibid., 8.

66. "Trenton's Battle Monument; The Shaft Unveiled with Bursts of Patriotic Ardor," *New York Times*, 20 October 1893, p. 8.
67. Ibid.
68. Souvenir Trenton Battle Monument Association (Philadelphia: Oplinger & Browne).
69. According to the San Jacinto Museum website, http://www.sanjacinto-museum.org/Monument_and_Museum/Monument_and_Museum_Overview/ (accessed 24 January 2010). Comparison may also be made to the Washington Monument in Baltimore, on Mt. Vernon Place. See http://terpconnect.umd.edu/~jlehnert/welcome.html (accessed 24 January 2010).
70. Pevsner 21.
71. John Blackwell, "1931: Temple for Trenton's Arts," *The Trentonian*, http://www.capitalcentury.com/1931.html (accessed 26 November 2008).
72. Kingwell 78.
73. Ibid., 82.
74. Rybczynski (1996) 133–39.

## Chapter 6

1. Shuman 171. See also John H. Sines, "Industries and Trades," http://www.trentonhistory.org/His/industries.html (accessed 28 February 2010); Raum 234.
2. Raum 234.
3. Sines, supra, n. 1.
4. Raum 234.
5. Pevsner 273.
6. Ibid.
7. Handlin 79.
8. Ibid., 80.
9. Ibid.
10. Ibid., 84.
11. Coolidge 7.
12. Briggs 17.
13. The reader is referred generally to Cumbler 51.
14. Bebout 23.
15. Ibid., 25.
16. Ibid., 26–27.
17. Trachtenberg ix.
18. Ibid., xi.
19. Ibid., 7.
20. Ibid., 52–56.
21. Ibid., 57.
22. Cumbler 110.
23. Bebout 29.
24. Trachtenberg 139.
25. Bebout 29.
26. Trachtenberg 104–6.
27. Bebout 36–39. "New Jersey faced a real crisis in the 1880's. Her cities were being pillaged. Corporate irresponsibility was breeding

chaos. Labor violence was spreading as workingmen fought blindly against the corporate order which was reducing their pay. Ethnic and religious conflicts were engendering bitterness." Bebout 39.
28. Trachtenberg 107.
29. Cumbler 109–10.
30. Bebout 35.
31. Cumbler 181.
32. Ibid., 182.
33. Mowrey 11.
34. Ibid., 18–19. Mowrey quotes an anonymous movie producer, who had tried to market a film based on its own merit rather than profit considerations, as saying "from now on art is out." Ibid., 18.
35. Steffens, *Introduction*, http://historymatters.gmu.edu/d/5732/ (accessed 6 December 2009).
36. Kotkin 85.
37. Ibid., 95.
38. Kotkin 95.
39. Rykwert 75.
40. Whyte 299.
41. http://www.city-dat.com/forum/new-jersey/42199_trenton_3.html.
42. The information in this discussion of the Horsman dolls and factory was found generally at http://trentonhistory.org/Documents/TopTen.htm (accessed 13 February 2010); Connie Limon, "Horsman Dolls—'America's Best Known and Best Loved Dolls,'" http://ezinearticles.com/?Horsman-Dolls—Americas-Best-Known-and-Best-Loved-Dolls&id=783914 (accessed 13 February 2010); http://dollreference.com/horsman_dolls1910-1940s.html (accessed 13 February 2010).
43. http://www.preservationnj.org/site/ExpEng/index.php?/10most/archive_by_year_detail/2003/Horsman_Doll_Factory (accessed 25 April 2010).
44. Limon, supra note 42.
45. Information on this company may be generally found at http://www.vintageplumbing.com/thejlmottironworks.html (accessed 13 February 2010); http://en.wikipedia.org/wiki/J._L._Mott_Iron_Works (accessed 13 February 2010); "Mott Iron Works to Move," *New York Times*, 7 July 1902, http://query.nytimes.com/mem/archive-free/pdf?res=9502E0D81330E733A25754C0A9619C946397D6CF (accessed 13 February 2010).
46. Bureau of Industrial Statistics, Department of Labor, *The Industrial Directory of New Jersey* (Paterson: News Printing, 1918), 598.
47. Lurie 431.
48. Cumbler 108.
49. Margo Nash, "Recalling the Heyday of Trenton's Cigar Industry," *New York Times*, 14 September 2003.

50. Robert P. Porter, *Industrial Cuba: Being a Study of Present Commercial and Industrial Conditions, with Suggestions as to the Opportunities Presented in the Island for American Capital, Enterprise, and Labour* (New York: G.P. Putnam's Sons, 1899), 306.
51. Patricia Ann Cooper, *Once a Cigar Maker: Men, Women and Work Culture in American Cigar Factories, 1900–1919* (Champaign: University of Illinois Press, 1987), 163.
52. http://www.state.nj.us/transportation/works/environment/pdf/Historic_BR_Mercer.pdf (accessed 13 September 2009).
53. Ibid., An additional source of general information is http://www.vintagecityclothing.com/pages/lee-history (accessed 13 February 2010).
54. See generally http://www.oldandsold.com/articles01/article828.shtml (accessed 13 February 2010); http://auto.howstuffworks.com/1911-1915-mercer-raceabout-model-35-r.htm (accessed 13 February 2010).
55. Tom Glover's historical site aggregates several articles of the time of interest and utilized herein. See http://photos1.blogger.com/blogger/2790/1877/1600/mercerinc.jpg (accessed 13 February 2010).
56. http://4.bp.blogspot.com/_N_-W1PmSNqg/SnRqazbCokI/AAAAAAAALOk/8dwxvfrI3Sc/s1600-h/1909+THE+FIRST+MERCER+AUTOS+FROM+THE+HOWARD+PLANT.jpg (accessed 13 February 2010).
57. http://search.tacomapubliclibrary.org/images/dt6n.asp?un=1&pg=1&drequest=30958&stemming=&phonic=&fuzzy=&maxfiles= (accessed 13 February 2010).
58. http://www.trentonlofts.com/default.php?building=26&name=Cracker%20Factory. (accessed 12 October 2009). For a period piece, see the 1893 article posted on Tom Glover's historical website from the *Daily True American* reporting on Adam Exton's explanation of the history of the factor and its process, found at http://1.bp.blogspot.com/_N_-W1PmSNqg/S0dHriFBSHI/AAAAAAAAMa0/cM34ipnnT8E/s1600-h/1917+OTC+EXTON+CRACKER+HISTORY.jpg (accessed 13 February 2010).
59. Mel Fabrikant, "Cracker Factory's Near Sell-Out Shows Success of Federal Stimulus Extension," *Paramus Post*, 29 January 2010. See also "From Transition to Revival in Trenton," *New York Times*, 20 April 2008.
60. "Adam Exton," findagrave.com, http://www.findagrave.com/cgi-bin/fg.cgi?page=gr&GSvcid=34492&GRid=9372571& (accessed 28 February 2010).
61. http://findarticles.com/p/articles/mi_qa3697/is_200507/ai_n14905690/ (accessed 13 February 2010).

62. John H. Sines, "Industries and Trades," *A History of Trenton 1679–1929* http://trentonhistory.org/His/industries.html (accessed 13 February 2010).
63. See Shuman 173–83.
64. Sines, supra note 62
65. Shuman 175.
66. http://www.hmdb.org/marker.asp?marker=3922 (accessed 25 January 2010).
67. Shuman 155.
68. The friendship disintegrated "as the century wore on ... into a bitter personal and business feud." Cumbler 19.
69. McCullough 39.
70. Ibid., 46.
71. Schuyler 73.
72. Ibid., 74–75.
73. See generally http://www.inventionfactory.com/history/RHAgen/rstory/rsevol.html (accessed 14 November 2009).
74. http://www.inventionfactory.com/history/RHAgen/rstory/rsgrowth.html. (accessed 14 November 2009)
75. Anthony Coleman, "Developers Express Interest in Roebling Site," *Trenton Times*, 25 May 2009. The article mentions an entertainment company that owned the site but lost its interest in the property after a court battle. Manex Entertainment was the special effects company for the original *Matrix* film; its subsidiary, Trenton Studios, Inc., had signed a redevelopment agreement with Mercer County to turn part of the site into an "East Coast" Hollywood. I was counsel for Trenton Studios, substituting in toward the end of the litigation, and we were unable to obtain judicial relief on appeal.
76. Shuman 181.
77. Robert P. Rogers, *An Economic History of the American Steel Industry* (New York: Routledge, 2009), 126.
78. Rogers 133.
79. Ibid., 135.
80. Crown 35.
81. Shuman 184.
82. Sines, supra note 62.
83. Ibid.
84. See Trenton City Museum for a concise history of the Trenton pottery industry, http://www.ellarslie.org/about_pottery.htm (accessed 26 January 2010). This notes some of the other major potteries, including Ott and Brewer, and Willets Manufacturing Co.
85. http://www.ellarslie.org/about_pottery.htm (accessed 26 January 2010).
86. Shuman 187.
87. Ibid., 188.
88. Ibid., 188–89.
89. Ibid., 189.
90. Ibid., 190.
91. Sines, supra note 62.
92. Ibid. See also Shuman 196.
93. Shuman 195.
94. Ibid., 199.
95. Cumbler 70.
96. Ibid., 70–75.
97. Ibid., 72.
98. Ibid., 145.
99. Ibid., 146.
100. See generally Cumbler 147–57.
101. Rae 17.
102. http://lawlibrary.rutgers.edu/courts/appellate/a2475-06.opn.html. See also note 73, supra.
103. http://trentonhistory.org/streets.html (accessed 27 April 2010).
104. For an account of the failed efforts in the 1950s and 1960s to develop this area, see Judith F. Kovisar, "Trenton Up Against It: The Prescription for Urban Renewal in the 1950s and 1960s," in Schwartz at pp. 161 et seq.

## Chapter 7

1. Jim Goodman, "Clinging to Tradition as Things Change," *New York Times*, 28 October 2007.
2. Jill P. Capuzo, "The Original," *New Jersey Monthly*, 12 January 2010, http://njmonthly.com/articles/restaurants/the-original.html (accessed 28 February 2010).
3. Rae 7–8.
4. Brian Robson, "No City, No Civilization," Transactions of the Institute of British Geographers, New Series, vol. 19, no. 2 (1994): 131–41. Published by: Blackwell Publishing on behalf of The Royal Geographical Society (with the Institute of British Geographers), http://www.jstor.org/stable/622750 (accessed 19 February 2010).
5. Ibid., 131.
6. Ibid., 137, citing M. Parkinson 1991, *The Rise of the Entrepreneurial European City: Strategic Responses to Economic Changes in the 1980s Ekistics*, 350–51 and 299–307.
7. Ibid., 140–41.
8. Rae 113–14.
9. Barth 24–25.
10. McCarthy 7.
11. John H. Sines, "Banks and Commerce in Trenton," Walker et al., http://www.trentonhistory.org/His/banks.html (accessed 14 February 2010).
12. John J. Cleary, "Trenton's Recreations," Walker et al., http://www.trentonhistory.org/His/Recreation.html (accessed 15 February 2010).
13. http://cinematreasures.org/search/query=trenton&search=city&method=n&show=all (accessed 11 July 2010).

14. Trachtenberg 101–39.
15. Monti 25.
16. Johns 3.
17. Ibid., 5.
18. Duany 153–54.
19. http://3.bp.blogspot.com/_N_-W1PmSNqg/SXceOXxkHJI/AAAAAAAJXA/wpDrEfHejPA/s1600-h/Dunham's+final+final.jpg (accessed 2 November 2009).
20. Trachtenberg 130.
21. Duany 158.
22. Erin Duffy, "Animal Rights Group Targets McDonald's," *The Times of Trenton*, 16 July 2009.
23. Rae 19.
24. Bebout 36.
25. Ibid., 36–37.
26. Bruegmann 52–54.
27. Fogelson 2–3.
28. Ibid., 5.
29. Ibid., 6–7.
30. Whyte 335.
31. Fogelson 12.
32. Ibid., 20. Fogelson states that urban park landscaper Frederick Law Olmsted and urban demographer Adna F. Weber noted the phenomenon at the time.
33. Ibid., 29.
34. Ibid., 33–35.
35. Kostof (1992) 189.
36. Ibid., 190.
37. Venturi 9.
38. Calvino 8.
39. Liggett 142.
40. Bruce Davidson, "Life, Through My Eyes, Seen...," in *Bruce Davidson* (New York: Pantheon Photo Library, 1986), introduction.
41. Hewitt 21.
42. Whyte 328.
43. Ibid., 338–39.
44. Ibid., 340.
45. "Greenville, SC USA," http://www.greenvillesc.gov/neighborhoods/historic_greenville.asp. (accessed 6 September 2009).
46. Whyte 331–32.

## Chapter 8

1. Kostof (1991) 279.
2. Ibid.
3. Fogelson 115.
4. "Although low buildings with exuberant Victorian towers had been built since the 1870s, the true skyscraper was invented in Chicago in 1885." Larry R. Ford, "Reading the Skylines of American Cities," *Geographical Review*, vol. 82, no. 2 (April 1992): 181, http://www.jstor.org/stable/215431
5. Kostof (1991) 282–83.
6. Curl 617.
7. Goldberg ix. "Surely more than any other type of building the skyscraper is both quintessentially American and quintessentially of the twentieth century." Ibid., 3.
8. Rosemarie Hagg Bletter, "The Invention of the Skyscraper: Notes on Its Diverse Histories," *Assemblage*, no. 2 (February 1987): 110–17, http://www.jstor.org/stable/3171092 (accessed 10 August 2009).
9. J. Carson Webster, "The Skyscraper: Logical and Historical Considerations," *The Journal of the Society of Architectural Historians*, vol. 18, no. 4 (December 1959): 126–39, http://www.jstor.org/stable/987902 (accessed 10 August 2009).
10. Ford 180, supra note 4.
11. Rykwert 229–230
12. Hearn 290.
13. Wright 55–57.
14. Ford, 181–82, supra note 4.
15. Ibid., 182–84, supra note 4.
16. Ibid., 186 supra note 4.
17. Ibid., 188 supra note 4.
18. http://www.broadstreetbank.com/history/ (accessed 9 August 2009).
19. http://www.azobuild.com/news.asp?newsID=5431 (accessed 9 August 2009).
20. Frank Lloyd Wright, "In the Course of Architecture," *Archit. Rec.*, xxiii (1908): 163.
21. Curl 64.
22. Schleier 7.
23. Ibid., 15.
24. Bahamon and Losantos 200.
25. Goldberg 5.
26. There are many places to find this article. My internet source is http://academics.triton.edu/faculty/fheitzman/tallofficebuilding.html (accessed 1 March 2010).
27. de Botton 215–17.
28. O'Gorman 89.
29. Curl 104.
30. See the Kingsbury Corporation website, http://www.kingsburycorporation.com/pages/history/ (accessed 13 September 2009).
31. Curl 427.
32. Handlin 174.
33. Cunfliffe 240.
34. Curl 373.
35. Jürgen Habermas, "Modern and Postmodern Architecture," in Leach 233.
36. Kingwell 146–47.
37. Kunstler (1993) 59–60.
38. Ibid., 61.
39. Curl 516.
40. Ellin 111.
41. Ibid., 111–12.
42. http://www.emporis.com/application/?nav=building&id=124839&lng=3 (accessed 2 March 2010).

43. An extended version of these summarized comments is found in my book *The Bridges of New Jersey* (New Brunswick: Rutgers University Press, 2005). Further sources may be referenced therein.
44. See http://www.state.nj.us/transportation/works/environment/HistBrIntro.shtm for the introductory page, and bridges by county can be found on that page. The stone arch bridges discussed here, as well as the truss bridges, are found in the Mercer County section and, as noted, some have been discussed in more detail in *The Bridges of New Jersey*.
45. http://www.state.nj.us/transportation/works/environment/pdf/Historic_BR_Mercer.pdf (accessed 13 September 2009).
46. Richman 37–38.
47. Ibid., 37–39
48. Ibid., 38.
49. Shuman 233–34.
50. Richman 38.
51. See generally my discussion in *The Bridges of New Jersey* 84–87.
52. Richman 85–86
53. Ibid., 86.
54. Ibid., 84–87.
55. Ibid., 66–68.
56. Ibid.
57. Ibid.
58. http://www.trentonmillhill.org/historypages/mh_hist.htm (accessed 30 January 2010).
59. Richman 147–49.
60. Ibid., 149–51.
61. http://www.state.nj.us/transportation/works/environment/pdf/Historic_BR_Mercer.pdf (accessed 13 September 2009).
62. Shaw ix.
63. Ibid., ix–x.
64. Ibid., 1.
65. Ibid., 30.
66. Ibid., 58.
67. Ibid., 93.
68. http://www.dandrcanal.com/history.html (accessed 19 December 2009).
69. There are three canal houses in Trenton. http://trentonhistory.org/Documents/TopTen.htm (accessed 1 May 2010). The Calhoun Street one and the one located at Hanover Street are vacant. The one at Prospect Street is used and in good shape.

## Chapter 9

1. McKelvey (1963) 115–126. See also, generally, "The City Beautiful Movement," http://xroads.virginia.edu/~cap/citybeautiful/city.html (accessed 30 January 2010).
2. Wilson 3.
3. Ibid., 4.
4. Boyer 261–62.
5. Ibid., 262.
6. Ibid., 264.
7. Ibid.
8. Fein 57.
9. Rybczynski (1999) 21.
10. Elisabeth Ginsberg, "Olmsted Looks Beyond Central Park," *New York Times*, 21 September 2003.
11. Sutton 80.
12. Ginsberg, supra note 10.
13. Sutton 81.
14. Trachtenberg 108.
15. Rybczynski (1999) 93.
16. Ibid.
17. Trachtenberg 111.
18. Ginsburg, supra note 10. Ms. Ginsburg cites Kevin Moore, project director for the Weequahic Park Association, for the proposition that "all of Olmsted's parks were designed to foster a single ideal — the democratic use of open space."
19. Cadwalader Heights website, http://www.dathil.com/cadwalader/link_book.html (accessed 5 December 2009). Olmsted developed plans for the Cadwalader Heights, although the Cadwalader Heights website indicates his plans were for the Berkeley Square part of the Cadwalader estate. Cf. Trentonspace.com website, http://www.trentonspace.com/Articles-c-2007-10-30-42362.113122_Cadwalader_Heights_celebrates_first_100_years.html. (accessed 5 December 2009). It is perhaps odd that in his biography of Olmsted, *A Clearing in the Distance*, Rybczynski makes no mention of Cadwalader Park; the only indexed reference to Trenton relates to Olmsted traveling to the city for a meeting that apparently did not occur, and then going to Lawrenceville. Rybcynski (1999) 357–58. The National Association of Olmsted Parks website identifies Cadwalader Park in 1891 as the last of the "major urban parks" designed by Olmsted, the first having been Central Park in 1858. See http://www.olmsted.org/ht/d/sp/i/1162/pid/1162 (accessed 5 December 2009).
20. Ginsburg, "Olmsted Looks Beyond Central Park."
21. The plaque states: "A Bicentennial commemorative site recognizing America's 200th year of liberty. Cadwalader Park Named for General Thomas Cadwalader, Trenton's Chief Burgess in 1746. Promoted by Edmund C. Hill in 1884. Authorized by City Council in 1888 following a public poll. Designed by Frederick Law Olmsted of New York, nationally known park designer. Property acquired piecemeal, finally totaling over 100 acres. Park was com-

pleted in 1901. One of America's outstanding municipal park." http://www.hmdb.org/marker.asp?marker=4127 (accessed 5 December 2009).

22. http://nycgovparks.org/sub_about/parks_history/playgrounds.html (accessed 21 February 2010).

23. http://www.olmsted.org/ht/d/sp/i/1168/pid/1168 (accessed 2010 February 2010).

24. See generally http://www.branchbrookpark.org (accessed 21 February 2010).

25. "Swamp Angel: A Monument Made of the Old Gun Which Was Used in Bombarding Charleston in 1863—A Unique Memorial by the Citizens of Trenton, N.J.," *New York Times*, 1 December 1876.

26. Shuman 163.

27. http://www.campolden.org/ (accessed 13 February 2010).

28. The New Jersey Commission for the Panama-Pacific International Exposition. 1915. *The State of New Jersey* 22. (accessible at http://books.google.com/books?id=yKM-AAAAYAAJ&pg=PA6&dq="The+New+Jersey+Commission+for+the+Panama-Pacific+International+Exposition"&hl=en&ei=6Jw_TKK2C4K88gbXl8CDCw&sa=X&oi=book_result&ct=result&resnum=1&ved=0CDEQ6AEwAA#v=onepage&q&f=false, accessed 15 July 2010).

29. Lurie 127.

30. Yalom 11.

31. Ibid., 42.

32. Ibid., 44.

33. Ibid.

34. Lurie 127.

35. Yalom 47–48. She adds: "The memorial park is just one more step in the direction of taming death, a process that began in the eighteenth century when angelic faces with wings started replacing death's-heads." *Id.* at 48.

36. *Quakers, Warriors and Capitalists: Riverview Cemetery and Trenton's Dead*, http://www.state.nj.us/counties/mercer/commissions/pdfs/ch_riverviewcemetery.pdf

37. http://www.hmdb.org/marker.asp?marker=4332 (accessed 6 September 2009).

38. *Ancient Ways: Native Americans in South Trenton, 10,000 B.C. to 1700 A.D.*, http://www.state.nj.us/counties/mercer/commissions/pdfs/ch_nativeamericansstrenton.pdf (accessed 7 September 2009]

39. *Quakers, Warriors and Capitalists*, 7.

40. *Quakers, Warriors and Capitalists*, 11.

41. http://www.findagrave.com/php/famous.php?FScemeteryid=100189&page=cem (accessed 13 March 2010).

42. http://www.rootsweb.ancestry.com/~njmercer/Peo/Riverview1820.htm (accessed 7 September 2009).

43. http://www.state.nj.us/state/darm/links/guides/pmerc001.html (accessed 7 September 2009).

44. http://www.state.nj.us/state/darm/links/guides/pmerc001.html (accessed 7 September 2009).

45. Margot Gayle and Carol Gayle, *Cast-Iron Architecture in America: The Significance of James Bogardus* (New York: W.W. Norton, 1998), 142.

46. Jacob Abbott, *The Harper Establishment; Or, How the Story Books Are Made* (New York: Harper & Brothers, 1855), 36–37, http://www.merrycoz.org/books/harper/HARPER.HTM (accessed 8 September 2009).

47. Sarapin 114–16.

48. Ibid., 120.

49. D. Fischer 170.

50. Ibid., at 170–71.

51. Newberry 343. The 1784 Trenton: The Nation's Capital website suggests that Hunt, as a Lieutenant Colonel in the Hunterdon Militia, may have known of Washington's attack; the implication is that he kept Rall distracted, http://www.trenton1784.org/index.php (accessed 30 January 2010). For more on this intriguing historical event, and a fictionalized supposition of how a trial of Hunt might have gone, see http://christmasmiracle1776.com/ (accessed 30 January 2010).

## Chapter 10

1. Glaeser, "Are Cities Dying?" *The Journal of Economic Perspectives*, vol. 12, no. 2 (Spring 1998): 148–49.

2. Susan Jacoby, "The Dumbing Of America: Call Me a Snob, but Really, We're a Nation of Dunces," *Washington Post*, 17 February 2008.

3. http://www.tawa-nj.org/index.php?link=about (accessed 14 February 2010).

4. http://www.cafeolecoffee.com/art.php (accessed 14 February 2010).

5. http://www.gallery125.com/home/ (accessed 13 July 2010]. For an article about its closing, see http://www.mercerspace.com/article/80532-gallery+125+closing+ends+dream [accessed 13 July 2010]).

6. http://www.trenton-downtown.com/tdablog/ (accessed 14 February 2010).

7. http://www.trentonsymphony.org/ (accessed 14 February 2010).

8. http://trentonfilmfestival.org/ (accessed 14 February 2010).

9. http://passagetheatre.org/cms/ (accessed 14 February 2010).

10. Hofstadter 235–36.

11. Ibid., 236.

12. Ibid., 237.

13. Ibid., 247.
14. Ibid., 251.
15. Ibid., 253–57.
16. Ibid., 404.
17. White 1.
18. Ibid., 17.
19. Hofstadter 146–47.
20. White 31.
21. See quote and discussion in Lees 93, and Lees 96. He discusses the White's analysis of various nineteenth century writers, and also suggests that they acknowledge that in various cases, there is a certain ambiguity.
22. White 34.
23. Ibid., 53.
24. Lees 96.
25. Francis E. Rourke, "Urbanism and American Democracy," reprinted in Callow 345.
26. Lees 6.
27. Ibid., 92.
28. White 55–56.
29. Ibid., 58–59.
30. Ibid., 90–94.
31. Lees 12.
32. White 142.
33. Ibid., 145.
34. Ibid., 147.
35. Ibid., 153.
36. Ibid., 156.
37. Lees 13.
38. White 204–5.
39. Lees 289
40. White 190.
41. Ibid., 195.
42. Wright 34–36.
43. Ibid., 35.
44. White 174–78.
45. Ibid., 200.
46. Ibid., 201–2.
47. Rourke, in Callow 347.
48. Ibid., 348.
49. White 236–37.
50. Ibid., 238–39.
51. For an interesting discussion of the dynamic between these various factors, see John A. Powell, "Race, Poverty, and Urban Sprawl: Access to Opportunities Through Regional Strategies," *Forum for Social Economics*, vol. 1, no. 9 (1999): 28, http://www1.umn.edu/irp/publications/racepovertyandurbansprawl.html (accessed 1 May 2010).
52. Pirenne 130.
53. Podmore 65–66.
54. Raum 225.
55. Ibid., 225–29.
56. Shuman 289.
57. In addition to other architectural sources, and there are many, a good description of classical and Renaissance revival styles is also found at http://www.buffaloah.com/a/archsty/index.html (accessed 4 March 2010).
58. McKelvey (1963) 123.
59. http://www.state.nj.us/state/museum/index.htm (accessed 6 March 2010).
60. Vivien Raynor, "ART; Precisionism with Emotion," *New York Times*, 14 May 1989, p. 12NJ16.
61. Olsen 3.
62. Ibid., 4.
63. Ibid., 251.
64. Ibid., 254.
65. Ibid., 281.
66. Rykwert 101.
67. Ibid., 101–2.
68. Olsen 295 (emphasis in original).
69. Joel Rogers and Katrina vanden Heuvel, "Metropolis Now," *The New Statesman*, 17 September 2009 http://www.newstatesman.com/economy/2009/09/obama-cities-help-government (accessed 20 September 2009).
70. Ibid.
71. Lovelock 135.
72. Though technically located just outside the Trenton border, in Hamilton, NJ, I have included it because of its proximity and its located on the old State Fairground, which was integrally connected to Trenton.
73. Grounds for Sculpture website, http://groundsforsculpture.org/fairhist.htm (accessed 21 December 2009).
74. See generally http://www.ellarslie.org/ (accessed 30 January 2010).
75. http://www.state.nj.us/state/museum/about_history.htm (accessed 14 February 2010).
76. The main biography of Julian Scott is Robert J. Titterton, *Julian Scott: Artist of the Civil War and Native America*. (Jefferson, NC: McFarland, 1997).
77. These are the two principal dailies. Trenton also features at least three other newspapers: *El Latino Expreso*, published weekly; *The Monitor*, published bi-weekly by the Roman Catholic Diocese of Trenton; and *Downtowner*, published monthly.
78. John J. Clearly, "Journalism and Literature in Trenton," in Walker et al., http://www.trentonhistory.org/His/journalism.html (accessed 14 February 2010).
79. Ibid.
80. Victoria White, "Changing Times in Trenton," *New York Times*, 15 February 1987.
81. David Folkenflik, "Imagining a City without Its Daily Newspaper," http://www.npr.org/templates/story/story.php?storyId=100256908 (accessed 14 February 2010); see also Richard Pérez-Peña, "As Cities Go from Two Newspapers to One, Talk of Zero," *New York Times*, 11 March 2009.

82. Barth 59.
83. Ibid., 62–63.
84. Ibid., 109.
85. Jerome Loving, *The Last Titan: A Life of Theodore Dreiser* (Berkeley: University of California Press, 2005), 268.
86. William J. Backes, "Landmarks, Taverns, Markets and Fairs," http://www.trentonhistory.org/His/landmarks.html (accessed 6 March 2010).

## Chapter 11

1. Ardrey vii.
2. Wolfgant and Ferracuti 303.
3. Meir Rinde, "Trenton Keeps Clerk, Raises Taxes," *The Times*, 18 December 2009.
4. Ibid.
5. Davis 316.
6. N.J.S.A. § 2C:44–3b.
7. "Trenton Teen Sentenced to 10 Years in Prison for Fatal Shooting, Bank Robbery," *The Times*, 19 August, 2009.
8. Lisa Coryell, "Two Gang Members Confess to Killing Teen," *The Times*, 27 June 2009.
9. "Police ID 2 Shooters in Fatal Block Party Drive-by," *Asbury Park Press*, 26 June 2009, http://www.app.com/article/20090626/NEWS/90626022/3-N.J.-block-party-slay-suspects-in-court, (accessed 19 July 2009).
10. Paul Mickle, "2009 in Review: The Day Tamrah Leonard, 13, Was Murdered," *The Trentonian*, 4 January 2010, http://www.trentonian.com/articles/2010/01/04/news/doc4b41675c00f38666327679.txt (accessed 14 February 2010).
11. "Surveillance Tape Could Help Solve Murder of Teen," *Pennington Post*, 10 June 2009, http://www.buckslocalnews.com/articles/2009/06/10/pennington_post/news/doc4a2fe8703bc72923136577.prt (accessed 19 July 2009).
12. *Gangs in New Jersey* (Trenton, NJ: New Jersey State Police, Intelligence Section, 2007), 1–2. This was the third such gang survey made in New Jersey in six years. http://www.state.nj.us/njsp/info/pdf/njgangsurvey-2007.pdf (accessed 15 July 2010).
13. Ibid., 27.
14. Ibid., 29.
15. Ibid., 3.
16. "Division Of Criminal Justice Indicts Trenton 'Bloods' Gang Members Arrested in Operation 'Capital City' on Racketeering and Drug Charges," New Jersey Attorney General Press Release, 31 March 2006, http://www.newjersey.gov/lps/dcj/releases/2006/capitalcity_0331.htm (accessed 19 July 2009).
17. "Gang Members Invited to Trenton Block Party Where 13-Year-Old Girl Was Fatally Shot," *Associated Press*, http://www.nj.com/mercer/index.ssf/2009/06/gang_members_invited_to_block.html (accessed 9 August 2009).
18. *Gangs in New Jersey*, 30.
19. Kingwell 15–16.
20. Ibid.
21. "Trenton Reservoir Finished," *New York Times*, 21 September 1899.
22. "Water Supply Security Gets Post-Terror Upgrades," http://sierraactivist.org/article.php?sid=27453 (accessed 29 June 2009).
23. Erin Duffy, "Court: Referendum Required for Water Utilities Sale," http://www.nj.com/mercer/index.ssf/2010/04/court_water_utilities_sale_mus.html (accessed 2 May 2010). See generally http://www.trentonwater.com. The case is captioned in *re Petition for Referendum on City of Trenton Ordinance* 09-02 (A-70-09) (decided April 6, 2010).
24. David Kocieniewski, "A Little Girl Shot, and a Crowd That Didn't See," *New York Times*, 9 July 2007.
25. David Kocieniewski, "In Prosecution of Gang, a Chilling Adversary: The Code of the Streets," *New York Times*, 19 September 2007.
26. Artemis Coughlan, "Gang Boss Will Pay for Slay of Young Mother," *The Trentonian*, 29 May 2009.
27. Artemis Coughlan, "Jury Hung in Boom Bat Murder Trial," *The Trentonian*, 28 October 2008.
28. Janet Evanovich, *One for the Money* (New York: HarperCollins, 1994), 1.
29. Lofland (1998) xvii.
30. Ibid.
31. Ibid., xviii.
32. http://www.londoneye.com/ExploreTheLondonEye/History/Default.aspx (accessed 5 October 2009).
33. Davis 23.
34. Mayernik 15–88.
35. Robert A. Caro, *The Power Broker: Robert Moses and the Fall of New York* (New York: Vintage Books, 1975).
36. Lynch (1960) 1, 46 .
37. Kotkin 157 .
38. Canniffe 13.
39. Lynch (1960) 2.
40. Ibid., 2–3.
41. Ibid., 9.
42. Ibid.
43. Ibid., 10.
44. Ibid., 12.
45. Ibid., 25.
46. Ibid.
47. Ibid., 29.
48. Ibid.,

49. Rykwert 133.
50. Lynch (1960) 46.
51. Ibid., 47–48.
52. Ibid., 90.
53. Ibid., 91.
54. Ibid., 94–95.
55. Ibid., 120.
56. Kingwell 19.
57. L. Mumford (1961) 112–113.
58. Ibid., 570.
59. Ibid., 572.
60. Healey 1778.
61. Ibid., 1779.
62. Ibid., 1779–80.
63. Ibid., 1780.
64. Ibid., 1781.
65. Ibid., 1783.
66. "Trenton Blacksmith Commits Suicide," *New York Times*, 2 September 1887.
67. Riis 1.
68. Ibid.
69. http://historymatters.gmu.edu/d/6545/ (accessed 13 March 2010) (emphasis in original).
70. Ryan Tracy. "Trenton Ranks 30th in Nation in Crime Rate," *The Times*, 25 November 2008
71. For full results, see the CQ Press website, http://os.cqpress.com (accessed 27 November 27 2008).

## Chapter 12

1. Rykwert 5.
2. Ibid., 6.
3. Ibid., 7 (emphasis in original).
4. Ibid., 11.
5. Ibid., 17–18.
6. Ibid., 19.
7. Ibid., 42.
8. Ibid., 73.
9. Brugmann ix (emphasis in original). For a contrarian view to those who view the "country" as the ultimate green solution, see David Owen, *Green Metropolis: What the City Can Teach the Country about True Sustainability* (New York: Riverhead Books, 2009).
10. See John Berger, *Ways of Seeing* (London: Penguin Books, 1972).
11. Brugmann x.
12. Ibid., 4.
13. Ibid., 8.
14. Ibid., 32.
15. See generally http://www.trentonnj.org/Cit-e-Access/webpage.cfm?TID=55&TPID=9125 (accessed 6 March 2010). The textual summaries in this chapter that refer to the Master Plan are taken from this site; more specific quotations have direct cites to the particular sections.

16. See http://www.state.nj.us/ccrc/masterplan.html (accessed 6 September 2009).
17. Brent D. Ryan, "The Once and Future Neighborhood," http://www.architects.org/documents/publications/ab/spring2009/The_Once_and_Future_Neighborhood_spring_09.pdf (accessed 14 February 2010).
18. Andres Duany and Elizabeth Plater-Zyberk, "The Neighborhood, the District, and the Corridor," in *The New Urbanism: Toward an Architecture of Community*, ed. Peter Katz and Vincent Scully (New York: McGraw-Hill, 1994), reprinted in Legates 206–11.
19. Moving roughly from west to east, these are Hiltonia, Glen Afton, Rotary Island, Hillcrest, Cadwalader Park, Parkside, Island, Cadwalader Place, Berkeley Square, West End, Fisher/Richey/Perdicaris, Stuyvesant/Prospect, Top Road, North Trenton, Battle Monument, Humboldt Sweets, North 25, Central West, Downtown, Mill Hill, Hanover/Academy, Train Station, Ewing/Carroll, Coalport, Miller/Wall, East Trenton, Wilbur, Circle F, Greenood/Hamilton, Villa Park, Chambersburg, Arena, Chestnut Park, South Trenton, Waterfront, Duck Island and Franklin Park. Although there is a "Ferry District" noted on the Trenton Historical Society website and apparently application is being made for its qualification as an historic district, there is no identified neighborhood called Ferry District, which seems to be encompassed within Downtown and South Trenton.
20. Kunstler (1993) 202.
21. http://www.trentonnj.org/documents/planning_downtownmasterplan/ch_3_Econ_Assessment.pdf {accessed 6 March 2010).
22. "Trenton Records Lowest Crime Rate in City's History in 2006m" http://www.trentonnj.org/Cit-e-Access/webpage.cfm?TID=55&TPID=6966 (accessed 2 May 2010).
23. Kunstler (1993) 193.
24. Various development plans for the city's canal section have been proposed. See, for example, "Delaware and Raritan Canal State Park Development Plan Draft October 2002," http://www.dandrcanal.com/pdf/drcanal_develop-plan_oct02.pdf; "Delaware and Raritan Canal State Park Master Plan," 2nd ed. (1989), http://www.dandrcanal.com/pdf/DRCC_MasterPlan_2ndEd_1989.pdf; "The Delaware & Raritan Canal: The Past, The Present and the Promise: The Proceedings" (2005), http://webcache.googleusercontent.com/search?q=cache:8ymifi_8UwOJ:www.tcnj.edu/~mluc/events/documents/DRProceedings.doc+%22delaware+and+raritan+canal%22+trenton+prospect+calhoun+tender+house+2005&cd=1&hl=en&ct=clnk&gl=us (all accessed 2 May 2010).
25. It erroneously lists General George B.

McClellan as being buried here. He is not. He is buried in Riverview Cemetery.

26. http://www.trentonnj.org/documents/planning_downtownmasterplan/chap_8_Central_Business_District.pdf (accessed 28 November 2010).
27. http://www.trentonnj.org/documents/planning_downtownmasterplan/ch_7_Riverfront_District.pdf (accessed 6 March 2010).
28. http://livingonthenet.com/wordpress/ (accessed 6 September 2009).
29. Brugmann 103.
30. I have simplified in this summary. Brugmann spends a fair amount of time on these concepts; see Brugmann 92–110.
31. Ibid., 201–2.
32. Le Corbusier xxi.
33. Ibid., xxiv.
34. Ibid., 58.
35. Ibid., 60.
36. Ibid., 84.
37. Ibid., 85.
38. Kunstler (2001) 45.
39. http://www.cnu.org/who_we_are (accessed 27 September 2009).
40. Kunstler (1993) 78.
41. Ibid., 79.
42. Ibid., 80.
43. Reed 13.
44. Jacobs (1961) 6.
45. Tuttle notes that her description of the neighborhood would have been applicable to Newark's First Ward but whereas Boston's North End was revived because its residents took matters into their own hands, Newark's First Ward redevelopment efforts were unsuccessful when "urban renewal" was forced on them. Tuttle 138–139. A comparable lesson may be drawn with regard to forced development in the name of "urban renewal" of Trenton's "Coalport" area. See Judith F. Kovisars, "Trenton Up Against It: The Prescription for Urban Renewal in the 1950s and 1960s," in Schwartz 161.
46. Jacobs (1961) 14.
47. Ibid., 15.
48. Ibid., 16.
49. http://www.demographia.com/db-uscity98.htm (accessed 13 March 2010).
50. Jacobs (1961) 21.
51. Ibid., 23.
52. Ibid., 25.
53. Ibid., 29.
54. Ibid., 34.
55. Ibid., 35.
56. Grogan 23.
57. Jacobs (1961) 55.
58. Ibid., 59.
59. Ibid., 71.
60. Ibid.
61. Ibid., 72.
62. Ibid., 74–78.
63. Ibid., 79.
64. Ibid., 81.
65. Ibid., 83.
66. Ibid., 97.
67. Ibid., 99–100.
68. Ibid., 111.
69. Ibid., 114–15.
70. Ibid., 117.
71. Ibid., 121.
72. Ibid., 129.
73. Gans 11.
74. Ibid., 16.
75. Jacobs (1961) 144.
76. Ibid., 148.
77. Ibid., 150–51.
78. Ibid., 161–62.
79. Ibid., 167–68.
80. Ibid., 178.
81. Ibid., 187.
82. Ibid., 197.
83. Ibid., 242.
84. Ibid., 267.
85. Ibid., 270.
86. Ibid., 279.
87. Ibid., 282.
88. Ibid., 293.
89. Ibid., 372 (emphasis in original). Cf. pp. 194–195.
90. Ibid., 375.
91. Ibid., 392.
92. Ibid., 408–9.
93. Ibid., 428–39.
94. Ibid., 440–41.
95. Christopher Alexander, "A City Is Not a Tree," originally published in *Architectural Forum* (April–May 1965), reprinted with permission in Gabree 106.
96. Kunstler (1993) 96
97. Ibid., 33.
98. Ibid., 34.
99. Ibid., 37.
100. Ibid., 189.
101. Ibid., 259.
102. Ibid., 260.
103. http://www.docstoc.com/docs/4708982/Three-Cheers-for-Gentrification-By-Andres-Duany-These-days (accessed 3 October 2009).
104. Ingersoll 3.
105. Bruegmann 2–5.
106. Hall 57–58.
107. Kunstler (1993) 249.
108. Kunstler (2001) x–xiii.
109. Jacobs (1982) 6.
110. Ibid., 32.
111. Ibid., 47.
112. Ibid., 57–58.
113. Whyte 24.
114. Meir Rinde, "Mayoral Hopefuls Field Queries," *The Times*, 4 March 2010.

115. L.A. Parker, "Tony Mack Beats Manny Segura in Landslide to Be Trenton's First New Mayor in 20 Years," *The Trentonian*, 16 June 2010.
116. See, for example, Trentonian Staff, "Trenton Mayor Doug Palmer: Christie's Cut Tells Trentonians to 'Drop Dead'!" *The Trentonian*, 18 March 2010 http://www.trentonian.com/articles/2010/03/18/news/doc4ba19e20430c9756515825.txt (accessed 2 May 2010).

## Chapter 13

1. Hales 2.
2. Ibid., 2–3.
3. Stryker and Wood 9.
4. Liggett 15.
5. Rykwert 20.
6. Liggett vii.
7. Ibid., 144.
8. Ibid., ix.
9. Abbott Berenice, *The World of Eugene Atget* (New York: Horizon Books, 1964).
10. Quoted from http://www.encyclopedia.com/doc/1G2-3404700012.html (accessed 26 November 2009).
11. Kostof (1991) 281.
12. George A. Tice, *Urban Landscapes: A New Jersey Portrait* (New Brunswick, NJ: Rutgers University Press, 1975), "Statement."
13. Books have been written as to the "truthfulness" of the photograph. That discussion is beyond my efforts here. See, among others, Susan Sontag's *On Photography*, Roland Barthes's *Camerca Lucida*, and Jerry L. Thompson's *Truth and Photography*. And of course, John Berger's *Ways of Seeing* and the writings of Walter Benjamin.
14. John Berger, "Ralph Fasanella and the City," in *About Looking* (New York: Pantheon Books, 1980), 96.
15. Hales 1–2.
16. Procter and Matuszeski vii, 3
17. Camilo Jose Veragra, "Images as a Tool of Discovery, The Camden Website," 28 June 2005 http://www.fas.harvard.edu/~cwc/builtenv/Paper%20PDFs/Vergara.pdf (accessed 13 January 2008).
18. Hales 342–43.
19. Sinclair 182–83.
20. Burgin 7.
21. Ibid., 10.
22. Ibid., 32.
23. Reaktion Books has put out a series of such endeavors. Perhaps it is testament to the montage effect of these works that they cannot be easily summarized, but need, like a city, to be experienced.
24. Erika Langmuir and Norbert Lynton, *The Yale Dictionary of Art & Artists* (New Haven: Yale University Press, 2000).
25. Judi Freeman, "Léger, Fernand," in *Grove Art Online. Oxford Art Online*, http://www.oxfordartonline.com/subscriber/article/grove/art/T050075 (accessed November 23, 2008).
26. Calvino 44.

## Bibliography

1. U.S. Bureau of the Census, table 12: "Population of the 100 Largest Urban Places: 1890," http://www.census.gov/population/www/documentation/twps0027/tab12.txt.

# *Bibliography*

I have sought to include books I relied on, consulted or felt were of sufficient importance, either historically or contemporarily, to note. It may be possible to assemble an exhaustive bibliography on "the city," but such is beyond the scope of this work or my endeavors and intentions. First, exploration of the city encompasses several disciplines, including, without limitation, sociology, political science, economics, and even literary studies. Second, within disciplines are many discrete areas of study; urban planning books will overlap somewhat, but generally encompass works not necessarily including in the histories of cities. Some books are devoted to a particular facet of urban life, such as the rise and fall of the downtown, or race relations. Third, the number of journals devoted to urban studies, as well as the plethora of articles in cross-disciplinary journals, not to mention newspaper articles and internet sites that touch on the topic, are vast. Finally, with regard to Trenton itself, while the body of relevant and available books is finite, the number of newspaper articles is of course voluminous. Much is available on-line; archives and other fee-based databases enable the reader to pursue research in *The Times of Trenton* and the *New York Times*, among others. A line had to be drawn, and I have identified here those sources that bear on the topic, warrant further exploration, and often contain their own bibliographies. Some works or portions of works were available online as well (when available through Google books, e.g., or academic websites, or online newspaper archives, these references were cited as in the normal course, without the particular books. google.com URL, no more than I would cite the particular library from which a book was borrowed). Some were accessed through anthologies or collections; these have generally been noted. In some instances, certain authors have several more books than the one or two noted; even though they may be relevant to students of the city, I have not made an effort to include them all, such as those by Mike Davis, for example. Any blatant omissions are purely my responsibility and based on my own discretion or ignorance, and no meaning should be attached as to any lesser or greater importance of any work listed versus not listed. Historical markers are referred to; there are sites that contain them, such as Historical Markers Data Base, www.hmdb.com, and other specialized sites.

Special mention must be made of the Trenton Historical Society's website, www.trentonhistory.org, and its plethora of articles and other materials. The website was consulted frequently and, where appropriate, particular articles or books online were cited in endnotes. For information on Camden, see http://www.ci.camden.nj.us/history/history main.html and http://www.cchsnj.com/ (Camden County Historical Society. For Newark, see http://www.oldnewark.com/ (Old Newark Web Group) and http://www.thirteen.org/newark/history.html. Other Trenton-related websites of interest include http://ruinsoftrenton.wordpress.com and www.trentonian.com.

Allen, Rodney F., and Charles H. Adair, eds. *Violence and Riots in Urban America*. Belmont, CA: Wadsworth, 1969.

Ardrey, Robert. *The Territorial Imperative*. New York: Dell, 1966.

Atkins, Marc, and Iain Sinclair. *Liquid City*. London: Reaktion Books, 1999.

Bahamón, Alejandro, and Àgata Losantos. *New York: A Historical Atlas of Architecture*. New York: Black Dog and Leventhal, 2008.

Banfield, Edward C. *The Unheavenly City Revisited: A Revision of the Unheavenly City*. Boston: Little, Brown, 1974.

Barth, Linda J. *Images of America: The Delaware and Raritan Canal*. Charleston, SC: Arcadia, 2002.

Beauregard, Robert A. *When America Became Suburban*. Minneapolis: University of Minnesota Press, 2006.

Bebout, John E., and Ronald J. Grele. *Where Cities Meet: The Urbanization of New Jersey*. Princeton: D. Van Nostrand, 1964.

Bell, David, and Mark Jayne, eds. *Small Cities: Urban Experience Beyond the Metropolis*. London: Routledge, 2006.

Bergreen, Laurence. *Marco Polo: From Venice to Xanadu*. New York: Vintage Books, 2007.

Botton, Alain de. *The Architecture of Happiness*. New York: Vintage Press, 2006.

Boyer, Paul S. *Urban Masses and Moral Order in America: 1820–1920*. Cambridge: Harvard University Press, 1978.

Braudel, Fernand. *The Structures of Everyday Life: Civilization and Capitalism 15th–18th Century*, vol. 1. Translated and revised by Siân Reynolds. New York: Harper & Row, 1979.

Bridge, Gary, and Sophie Watson. *The Blackwell City Reader*. Oxford: Blackwell, 2002.

Briggs, Asa. *Victorian Cities*. Berkeley: University of California Press, 1993 [1965].

Broderick, James F. *Paging New Jersey*. New Brunswick, NJ: Rutgers University Press, 2003.

Bruegmann, Robert. *Sprawl: A Compact History*. Chicago: University of Chicago Press, 2005.

Brugmann, Jeb. *Welcome to the Urban Revolution: How Cities Are Changing the World*. New York and London: Bloomsbury Press, 2009.

Callow, Alexander B., Jr., ed. *American Urban History: An Interpretive Reader with Commentaries*, 3rd ed. New York: Oxford University Press, 1982.

Calvino, Italo. *Invisible Cities*. Translated by William Weaver. New York: Harcourt Brace Jovanovich, 1972.

Camisa, Harry, and James Franklin. *Inside Out: Fifty Years Behind the Walls of New Jersey's Trenton State Prison*. Windsor, NJ: Windsor, 2003.

Canniffe, Eamonn. *Urban Ethic: Design in the Contemporary City*. New York: Routledge, 2006.

Caro, Robert A. *The Power Broker: Robert Moses and the Fall of New York*. New York: Alfred A. Knopf, 1974.

Childe, V. Gordon. "The Urban Revolution." In *The City Reader*, 3rd ed., edited by Richard T. LeGates and Frederick Stout. New York: Routledge, 2003 [1950].

Clark, David. *Post-Industrial America*. New York: Methuen, 1985.

Coad, Oral S. *New Jersey in Travelers' Accounts*. Metuchen, NJ: The Scarecrow Press, 1972.

Collins, Richard G., Elizabeth B. Wasters, and A. Bruce Dotson. *America's Downtowns: Growth, Politics and Preservation*. Washington, DC: The Preservation Press, 1991.

Coolidge, John. *Mill and Mansion: A Study of Architecture and Society in Lowell, Massachusetts, 1820–1865*, 2nd ed. New York: Russell & Russell, 1967.

Crown, Cathleen, and Carol Rogers. *Images of America: Trenton*. Charleston, SC: Arcadia Publishing, 2000.

Cumbler, John T. *A Social History of Economic Decline: Business, Politics and Work in Trenton*. New Brunswick, NJ: Rutgers University Press, 1989.

Cunliffe, Sarah, and Jean Loussier, eds. *Architecture Styles: Spotter's Guide*. San Diego: Thunder Bay Press, 2006.

Cunningham, John T. *Newark*. Newark: New Jersey Historical Society, 1966.

_____. *This Is New Jersey*. New Brunswick: Rutgers University Press, 1994.

Curl, James Stevens. *Oxford Dictionary of Architecture*. Oxford: Oxford University Press, 1999.

Davis, Mike. *City of Quartz: Excavating the Future in Los Angeles*. New York: Vintage Books, 1992.

de Tocqueville, Alexis. *Democracy in America*. Translated by Gerald Bevan. London: Penguin, 2003 [1835].

Dear, Michael J., ed. *From Chicago to L.A.: Making Sense of Urban Theory*. Thousand Oaks, CA: Sage, 2002.

Dehaene, Michiel, and Lieven de Cauter. *Heterotopia and the City: Public Space in a Postcivil Society*. New York: Routledge, 2008.

Donald, James. *Imagining the Modern City*. Minneapolis: University of Minnesota Press, 1999.

Dorwart, Jeffery M. *Camden County, New Jersey: The Making of a Metropolitan Community, 1626–2000*. New Brunswick, NJ: Rutgers University Press, 2001.

Douglas, George H. *Skyscrapers: A Social History of the Very Tall Building in America*. Jefferson, NC: McFarland, 1996.

Duany, Andres, Elizabeth Plater-Zybert, and Jeff Speck. *Suburban Nation: The Rise of Sprawl and the Decline of the American Dream*. New York: North Point Press, 2000.

Dwyer, William M. *The Day Is Ours!* New Brunswick: Rutgers University Press, 1998 [1983].

Einreinhofer, Nancy, project director. *Public Art in New Jersey during the Period of the American Renaissance*. Wayne, NJ: The Museums Council of New Jersey, 1990.

Ellin, Nan. *Postmodern Urbanism*. Cambridge, MA: Blackwell, 1996.

Engels, Freidrich. [1845] 1958. *The Condition of the Working Class in England*. Translated by W.O. Henderson and W.H. Chaloner. Oxford: B. Blackwell, 1958 [1845]. See also the translation of "The Great Towns" chapter in LeGates and Stout at 59–66.[1]

Fainstein, Susan S., Normain I. Fainstein, Richard Child Hill, Dennis Judd, and Michael Peter Smith. *Restructuring the City: The Political Economy of Urban Redevelopment*. New York: Longman, 1983.

Fischer, Claude S. "The Effect of Urban Life on Traditional Values," *Social Forces*, vol. 53, no. 3 (March 1975): 420–32, http://www.jstor.org/stable/2576584 (accessed 17 December 2009).

_____. "On Urban Alienations and Anomie: Powerlessness and Social Isolation," *American Sociological Review*, vol. 38, no. 3 (June 1973): 311–26, http://www.jstor.org/stable/2094355 (accessed 17 December 2009).

_____. "The Public and Private Worlds of City Life," *American Sociological Review*, vol. 46, no. 3 (June 1981): 306–16, http://www.jstor.org/stable/2095062 (accessed 17 December 2009).

_____. "The Subcultural Theory of Urbanism: A Twentieth-Year Assessment," *American Journal of Sociology*, vol. 101, no. 3 (November 1995): 543–77, http://www.jstor.org/stable/2781994 (accessed 17 December 2009).

_____. "Toward a Subcultural Theory of Urbanism," *American Journal of Sociology*, vol. 80, no. 6 (May 1975): 1319–41, http://www.jstor.org/stable/2777297 (accessed 17 December 2009).

Fischer, David Hackett. *Washington's Crossing*. Oxford: Oxford University Press, 2004.

Fleming, Thomas. *New Jersey: A History*. New York: W.W. Norton, 1984 [1977].

Fogelson, Robert M. *Downtown: Its Rise and Fall, 1880–1950*. New Haven, CT: Yale University Press, 2001.

Frieden, Bernard J., and Lynne B. Sagalyn. *Downtown, Inc.: How America Rebuilds Cities*. Cambridge: MIT Press, 1989.

Gabree, John, ed. *Surviving the City: A Sourcebook of Papers on Urban Livability*. New York: Ballantine Books, 1973.

Gans, Herbert J. *People, Plans and Policies*. New York: Columbia University Press, 1993 [1991].

_____. *The Urban Villagers: Group and Class in the Life of Italian-Americans*, rev. ed. New York: The Free Press, 1982 [1962].

Garreau, Joel. *Edge City: Life on the New Frontier.* New York: Anchor Books, 1992.

Garvin, Alexander. *The American City: What Works, What Doesn't,* 2nd ed. New York: McGraw-Hill, 2002.

Gies, Joseph, and Frances Gies. *Life in a Medieval City.* New York: Harper & Row, 1981 [1969].

Gillette, Howard, Jr. *Camden After the Fall: Decline and Renewal in a Post-Industrial City.* Philadelphia: University of Pennsylvania Press, 2005.

Girouard, Mark. *Cities and People.* New Haven: Yale University Press, 1985.

Gleeson, Patrick, ed. *America, Changing....* Columbus: Charles E. Merrill, 1968.

Goldberger, Paul. *The Skyscraper.* New York: Alfred A. Knopf, 1981.

Gowans, Alan. *Architecture in New Jersey.* Princeton, NJ: D. Van Nostrand, 1964.

Gratz, Roberta Brandes. *The Living City.* New York: Simon & Schuster, 1989.

Greenagel, Frank L. *The New Jersey Churchscape.* New Brunswick, NJ: Rutgers University Press, 1989.

Grogan, Paul, and Tony Proscio. *Comeback Cities: A Blueprint for Urban Neighborhood Revival.* Boulder, CO: Westview Press, 2000.

Hales, Peter Bacon. *Silver Cities: Photographing American Urbanization, 1839–1939,* rev. ed. Albuquerque: University of New Mexico Press, 2005.

Hall, John. *History of the Presbyterian Church in Trenton, NJ,* 2nd ed. Trenton, NJ: MacCrellish & Quigley, 1912.

Hall, Peter. *Cities in Civilization.* New York: Pantheon Books, 1998.

Halprin, Lawrence. *Cities.* Cambridge, MA: MIT Press, 1963.

Handlin, David P. *American Architecture,* 2nd ed. London: Thames & Hudson, 2004 [1985].

Healey, Patsy. "On Creating the 'City' as a Collective Resource." *Urban Studies,* vol. 39, no. 10 (2002):1777–92.

Hearn, Millard Fillmore. *Ideas That Shaped Buildings.* Cambridge, MA: MIT Press, 2003.

Hewitt, Louise. *Historic Trenton.* Trenton, NJ: Smith Press, 1916.

Hiss, Tony. *The Experience of Place.* New York: Alfred A. Knopf, 1990.

Hofstadter, Richard. *Anti-Intellectualism in American Life.* New York: Vintage Books, 1963.

Ingersoll, Richard. *Sprawltown.* New York: Princeton Architectural Press, 2006.

Jacobs, Jane. *The Death and Life of Great American Cities.* New York: Vintage Books, 1992 [1961].

Johns, Michael. *Moment of Grace: The American City in the 1950s.* Berkeley: University of California Press, 2003.

Kaufman, Edgar, Jr., ed. *The Rise of an American Architecture.* New York: Praeger, 1970.

Ketchum, Richard M. *The Winter Soldiers.* Garden City, NY: Doubleday, 1973.

Kezys, Algimantas. *Cityscapes.* Chicago: Loyola University Press, 1988.

Kingwell, Mark. *Concrete Reveries: Consciousness and the City.* New York: Viking, 2008.

Konvitz, Josef W. *The Urban Millennium: The City-Building Process from the Early Middle Ages to the Present.* Carbondale: Southern Illinois University Press, 1985.

Koolhaas, Rem. *Delirious New York: A Retroactive Manifesto for Manhattan.* New York: Oxford University Press, 1978.

Kostof, Spiro. *The City Assembled: The Elements of Urban Form through History.* London: Thames & Hudson, 1992.

———. *The City Shaped: Urban Patterns and Meanings through History.* Boston: Little, Brown, 1991.

Kotkin, Joel. *The City: A Global History.* New York: Random House, 2005.

Kunstler, James Howard. *The City in Mind.* New York: Simon & Schuster, 2001.

———. *The Geography of Nowhere.* New York: Simon & Schuster, 1993.

Lambert, Camilla, and David Weir, eds. *Cities in Modern Britain.* Glasgow: Fontana/Collins, 1975.

Landau, Sarah Bradford, and Carl W. Condit. *Rise of the New York Skyscraper 1865–1913.* New Haven, CT: Yale University Press, 1996.

Landry, Charles, and Franco Bianchini.

*The Creative City*. London: Demos, 1995.
l'Anson, Richard. *Urban Travel Photography*. London: Lonely Planet, 2006.
Le Corbusier. *The City of Tomorrow and Its Planning*. New York: Dover Publications, 1987 [1929].
Leach, Neil, ed. *Rethinking Architecture: A Reader in Cultural Theory*. London: Routledge, 1997.
Lebovich, William L. *America's City Halls*. Washington, DC: The Preservation Press, 1984.
Lee, Francis Bazley. *History of Trenton, New Jersey: The Record of Its Early Settlement and Corporate Progress*. Trenton, NJ: J.L. Murphy, 1895.
Lees, Andrew. *Cities Perceived: Urban Society in European and American Thought, 1820–1940*. Manchester: Manchester University Press, 1985.
LeGates, Richard T., and Frederic Stout. *The City Reader*, 3rd ed. New York and London: Routledge, 1997.
Lepik, Andres. *Skyscrapers*. New York: Prestel, 2004.
Lewis, Michael J. *American Art and Architecture*. London: Thames & Hudson, 2006.
Liggett, Helen. *Urban Encounters*. Minneapolis: University of Minnesota Press, 2003.
Lin, Jan, and Christopher Mele, eds. *The Urban Sociology Reader*. New York: Routledge, 2005.
Lippard, Lucy R. *The Lure of the Local: Senses of Place in a Multicentered Society*. New York: The New Press, 1997.
Lofland, Lyn H. *The Public Realm: Exploring the City's Quintessential Social Territory*. New York: Walter de Gruyter, 1998.
\_\_\_\_\_. *A World of Strangers: Order and Action in Urban Public Space*. New York: Basic Books, 1973.
Logan, John R., and Harvey L. Molotch. *Urban Fortunes: The Political Economy of Place*. Berkeley: University of California Press, 1987.
Lovelock, James. *The Vanishing Face of Gaia: A Final Warning*. New York: Basic Books, 2009.
Lurie, Maxine N., and Marc Mappen, eds. *Encyclopedia of New Jersey*. New Brunswick: Rutgers University Press, 2004.
Lynch, Kevin. *Good City Form*. Cambridge, MA: MIT Press, 1981.
\_\_\_\_\_. *The Image of the City*. Cambridge, MA: MIT Press, 1960.
Masereel, Frans. *The City*. New York: Dover, 1972.
Mayernik, David. *Timeless Cities: An Architect's Reflections on Renaissance Italy*. Boulder, CO: Westview Press, 2003.
McCarthy, Tom. *Baseball in Trenton*. Charleston, SC: Arcadia, 2003.
McCullough, David. *The Great Bridge: The Epic Story of the Building of the Brooklyn Bridge*. New York: Simon & Schuster, 2001.
\_\_\_\_\_. *1776*. New York: Simon & Schuster, 2005.
McGreevy, John, ed. *Cities*. New York: Clarkson N. Potter, 1981.
McKelvey, Blake. *The Emergence of Metropolitan America 1915–1966*. New Brunswick, NJ: Rutgers University Press, 1968.
\_\_\_\_\_. *The Urbanization of America 1860–1915*. New Brunswick, NJ: Rutgers University Press, 1963.
McNamara, Martha J. *From Tavern to Courthouse: Architecture and Ritual in American Law, 1658–1860*. Baltimore, MD: The Johns Hopkins University Press, 2004.
Miles, Malcolm, and Tim Hall, with Iain Borden, eds. *The City Cultures Reader*, 2nd ed. London: Routledge, 2004.
Monti, Daniel J., Jr. *The American City: A Social & Cultural History*. Malden, MA: Blackwell, 1999.
Mowry, George E. *The Urban Nation: 1920–1960*. New York: Hill and Wang, 1965.
Mumford, Kevin. *Newark: A History of Race, Rights and Riots in America*. New York: New York University Press, 2007.
Mumford, Lewis. *The City in History*. New York: Harcourt, 1961.
\_\_\_\_\_. *Sticks & Stones: A Study of American Architecture and Civilization*. New York: Dover, 1955 [1924].
\_\_\_\_\_. "What Is a City?" In *The City*

*Reader*, 3rd ed., edited by Richard T. LeGates and Frederick Stout. New York: Routledge, 1961 [1937].

Museums Council of New Jersey. *Public Art in New Jersey during the Period of the American Renaissance*. Wayne, NJ: Museums Council of New Jersey, 1990.

Newberry, Lida, ed. *New Jersey: A Guide to Its Present and Past*, rev. ed. New York: Hastings House, 1977 [1939].

O'Gorman, James F. *ABC of Architecture*. Philadelphia: University of Pennsylvania Press, 1998.

Paddison, Ronan, ed. *Handbook of Urban Studies*. London: Sage, 2001.

Park, Robert Ezra, Ernest Watson Burgess, and Roderick Duncan McKenzie. *The City*. Chicago: University of Chicago Press, 1967.

Pevsner, Nikolaus. *A History of Building Types*. Princeton, NJ: Princeton University Press, 1976.

Pfautz, Harold W., ed. *Charles Booh on the City: Physical Pattern and Social Structure*. Chicago: University of Chicago Press, 1967.

Pile, Steve, Christopher Brook, and Gerry Mooney, eds. *Unruly Cities?* London: Routledge, 1999.

Pirenne, Henri. *Medieval Cities: Their Origins and the Revival of Trade*. Translated by Frank D. Halsey. Princeton: Princeton University Press, 1970 [1925].

Podmore, Harry J. *Trenton Old and New*. Revised and edited by Mary J. Messler. Trenton: MacCrellish & Quigley, 1964.

Polo, Marco. *The Travels of Marco Polo*. New York: New American Library, 1961.

Pongsmas, Napassakorn. *Configuration of Public Space and Social Sustainability of Urban Neighborhood: A Case Study of the City of San Diego at the Dawn of the Twenty-First Century*. Ph.D. diss., Texas Tech University, 2004, http://etd.lib.ttu.edu/theses/available/etd-07012008-31295019476752/unrestricted/31295019476752.pdf (accessed 21 November 2009).

Poppeliers, John C., and S. Allen Chambers, Jr. *What Style Is It: A Guide to American Architecture*, rev. ed. Hoboken, NJ: John Wiley & Sons, 2003.

Procter, Mary, and Bill Matuszeski. *Gritty Cities*. Philadelphia: Temple University Press, 1978.

Rae, Douglas W. *City: Urbanism and Its End*. New Haven, CT: Yale University Press, 2003.

Raum, John O. *History of the City of Trenton, New Jersey*. Trenton: W.T. Nicholson, 1871.

Reader, John. *Cities*. New York: Atlantic Monthly Press, 2004.

Réda, Jacques. *Les Ruines des Paris*. Translated by Mark Treharne. New York: Reaktion Books, 1996.

Reed, Henry Hope. *The Golden City*. New York: W.W. Norton, 1970.

Richman, Steven. *The Bridges of New Jersey*. New Brunswick, NJ: Rutgers University Press, 2005.

Riis, Jacob A. *How the Other Half Lives*. New York: Dover Publicatons, 1971.

Rodenbach, Georges. *Bruges-la-Morte*. Translated by Mike Mitchell and Will Stone. Sawtry: Dedalus, 2005 [1892].

Rybczynski, Witold. *City Life*. New York: Simon & Schuster, 1996.

———. *A Clearing in the Distance: Frederick Law Olmsted and American in the 19th Century*. New York: Scribner, 2003 [1999].

———. *The Look of Architecture*. New York: Oxford University Press, 2001.

Rykwert, Joseph. *The Seduction of Place*. New York: Vintage Books, 2002 [2000].

Salvadori, Mario. *Why Buildings Stand Up: The Strength of Architecture*. New York: W.W. Norton, 1980.

Sarapin, Janice Kohl. *Old Burial Grounds of New Jersey: A Guide*. New Brunswick, NJ: Rutgers University Press, 1994.

Schleier, Merrill. 1983, 1986. *The Skyscraper in American Art: 1890-1931*. Reprint, New York: Da Capo, 1986 [1983].

Schuyler, Hamilton. *The Roeblings: A Century of Engineers, Bridge-Builders and Industrialists*. Princeton, NJ: Princeton University Press, 1931.

Schwartz, Joel, and Daniel Prosser, eds. *Cities of the Garden State: Essays and Suburban History of New Jersey*. Dubuque, IA: Kendall/Hunt, 1977.

Scully, Vincent. *American Architecture and Urbanism*. New York: Praeger, 1971 [1969].

Shaw, Ronald E. *Canals for a Nation: The Canal Era in the United States: 1790–1860*. Lexington: University of Kentucky Press, 1990.

Shepherd, Roger. *Skyscraper: The Search for an American Style 1891–1941*. New York: McGraw-Hill, 2003.

Shuman, Eleanore Nolan. *The Trenton Story*. Trenton, NJ: MacCrellish & Quigley, 1958.

Sjoberg, Gideon. "The Origin and Evolution of Cities." In *America, Changing...*, edited by Patrick Gleeson. Columbus: Charles E. Merrill, 1968 [1965].

———. *The Pre-Industrial City: Past and Present*. New York: The Free Press, 1960.

Smailes, Arthur E. *The Geography of Towns*. Chicago: Aldine, 1966 [1953].

*Souvenir of Trenton*. 1904. http://www.archive.org/details/souveniroftrento00tren (accessed 28 December 2009).

Speck, Jeff, Elizabeth Plater Zyberk, and Andres Duany. *Suburban Nation: The Rise of Sprawl and the Decline of the American Dream*. New York: North Point Press, 2000.

Stansfield, Charles A, Jr. *A Geography of New Jersey: The City in the Garden*, 2nd ed. New Brunswick, NJ: Rutgers University Press, 1998 [1983].

Steffens, Lincoln. *The Shame of the Cities*. Mineola, NY: Dover, 2004 [1904].

Steinman, D.B. *The Builders of the Bridge: The Story of John Roebling and His Son*. New York: Harcourt, Brace, 1945.

Strauss, Anselm L. *Images of the American City*. New Brunswick, NJ: Transaction, 1961.

Stryker, William S. *The Battles of Trenton and Princeton*. Boston: Houghton, Mifflin, 1898.

———. *Trenton: One Hundred Years Ago*. Trenton, NJ: MacCrellish & Quigley, 1878. http://ia311208.us.archive.org/2/items/trentononehundre00stry/trentononehundre00stry.pdf (accessed 28 December 2009).

Sutton, S.B., ed. *Civilizing American Cities: Writings on City Landscapes*. New York: Da Capo Press, 1997.

Tester, Keith, ed. *The Flâneur*. London: Routledge, 1994.

Tietz, Jürgen. *The Story of Modern Architecture*. Cambridge: H.F. Ullman, 2008.

Trachtenberg, Alan. *The Incorporation of America: Culture and Society in the Gilded Age*. New York: Hill and Wang, 2007 [1982].

Tuttle, Brad. *How Newark Became Newark: The Rise, Fall and Rebirth of an American City*. New Brunswick, NJ: Rutgers University Press, 2009.

Veit, Richard F. *New Jersey Cemeteries and Tombstones: History in the Landscape*. New Brunswick, NJ: Rutgers University Press, 2008.

Walker, Edwin Robert, Clayton L Traver, and the Trenton Historical Society. *A History of Trenton: 1679–1929*. Princeton: Princeton University Press, 1929. Note: although a book in its own right, this is a compendium of chapters authored by different people and is available on the Trenton Historical Society's website, http://trentonhistory.org/1929history.html.

Washington, Jack. *In Search of a Community's Past: The Story of the Black Community of Trenton, New Jersey 1860–1900*. Trenton, NJ: Africa World Press, 1990.

Watkin, David. *A History of Western Architecture*, 2nd ed. London: King, 1996 [1986].

Weber, Max. *The City*. Translated and edited by Dan Martindale and Gertrude Neuwirth. New York: The Free Press, 1958.

White, Morton, and Lucia White. *The Intellectual Versus the City: From Thomas Jefferson to Frank Lloyd Wright*. Cambridge, MA: Harvard University Press, 1962.

Whyte, William H., Jr., ed. *City: Rediscovering the Center*. Philadelphia: University of Pennsylvania Press, 2009 [1988].

———. *The Exploding Metropolis*. Berkeley: University of California Press, 1993 [1957].

Williams, Oliver P., and Charles R. Adrian. *Four Cities: A Study in Comparative Policy Making*. Philadelphia: University of Pennsylvania Press, 1963.

Wilson, William H. *The City Beautiful Movement Creating the North American Landscape*. Baltimore, MD: Johns Hopkins University Press, 1994 [1989].

Wirth, Louis. "Urbanism as a Way of Life." In *America, Changing...*, edited by Patrick Gleeson. Columbus: Charles E. Merrill, 2003.

Wright, Frank Lloyd. *The Living City*. New York: Mentor Books, 1963 [1958].

# Index

Numbers in **_bold italics_** indicate pages with photographs.

Abbott, Berenice 242; *Changing New York* 242
Abbott, Jacob 181
*ABC of Architecture* 101, 159
*About Looking* 244
Academy Street 191, ***192***, 193
Adam and Sickle Building ***249***
Adams, Douglas: *Mostly Harmless* 220
Adams, Henry 189
Adams, John 88, 89
adaptive reuse 124–125, 127, 216, 223
Addams, Jane 189
African-Americans 151
Alexander, Christopher 233
American Bridge Company 128
*The American City* 43, 57
*The American Resting Place* 178–179
*America's City Halls* 108
ancient cities 33
Anderson, William A. 130
Anderson Street 75
anti-intellectualism 185–191
*Anti-Intellectualism in American Life* 185–187, 191
anti-Semitism 189, 190
anti-urbanism 33, 187–191, 195
architecture 95–115, 147, 195; American 72; "American Renaissance" 192; Beaux Arts 100, 104, 113, 158–159, 193; Brutalism 161–162; Bungaloid 221; Classical 161, 192, 235, 248; Colonial Revival 221; columns 103, 192; cornices 161; Dutch ***243***; Egyptian 112; Federal 73; Georgian 71, 106; Gothic 184; Greek Revival 79; Italianate 73, 113, 197, 221, 248; landscaping 173; Late Modernism 162; laurels 161; Modernism 162–163, 164, 193, 226, 235; modillions 161; monumental 113–114; Neo-Classical 100, 105, 106–107, 159, 160, 168, 174, 221; pilasters 161; porticos 192; Post-Modernism 164; Queen Anne 221, ***249***; Renaissance 109, 193, 207; Romanesque 221; Spanish Mission Revival 125; Tudor 221; Victorian 133, 149, ***221***

*Architecture in New Jersey* 221
*The Architecture of Happiness* 159
Ardrey, Robert: *The Territorial Imperative* 200–201
Aristotle 39–40
"Ash Can" School 109, 194
Assunpink Creek 82, 83, 90, 99, 135, 165, 166, 223
Atget, Eugene 242
Atkins, Marc: *Liquid City* 249
Atlanta, Georgia 76, 235
Atlantic City, New Jersey 243
Ault, George 194
automobile industry 125

Baltimore, Maryland 76, 135, 144, 152, 243
Barbicon Estates 162
Barrymore, Ethel 140
Barth, Gunther 140
Barthes, Roland 249; *Camera Lucida* 240
baseball 60, 66, 98, 140
Battle Monument ***37***, 82, 90, 99, 112–113, 115, 127, 178, 205–***206***, 209; designer 113
Baudelaire, Charles 10
Baum, Randy 175
Bebout, John E. 15, 120
Bell, Daniel: *The Coming of Post-Industrial Society* 49–50
Bellevue Avenue 65, 239
Benjamin, Walter 10
Berger, John 217, 239; *About Looking* 244
Berkeley, Lord 78
Berkeley Square 211, 218, ***221***, 243
Berlin, Germany 235, 250
Birkenhead Park, Liverpool 175
blacksmiths 213
*Blazing Star* 84
boat industry 117
Bonaparte, Joseph 179, 183
Bordentown, New Jersey 170, 171
Borrow, William 153, 181–182; grave ***182***

281

# Index

Boston, Massachusetts 73, 76, 91, 99, 137, 193, 208, 227, 228, 230, 235
Botton, Alain de: *The Architecture of Happiness* 159
Boyden, Seth 18
Branch Brook Park, Newark 175, 177
bridges 165–169; arch 165; beam 165; girder 165; railroad 166; suspension 165; truss 166–168
Briggs, Asa: *Victorian Cities* 118
Broad Street 13, 62, 78, 79, 82, 87, 90, 91, 100, 104, 109, 111, 141, *143*, 144, 145, *146*, 148, 150, 158, 165, 206, 208, 209, 212, 223
Broad Street Bank Building 150, 157, *158*, 222
Brook, Daniel 105
Brooklyn Bridge 128, 129, 130, 161
Brown, Denise Scott: *Learning from Las Vegas* 147
Bruegmann, Robert: *Sprawl* 234–235
*Bruges-la-Morte* 47
Brugmann, Jeb: *Welcome to the Urban Revolution: How Cities Are Changing the World* 216–217, 224
Brunswick Avenue *15*, 31, 78
Bryant, William Cullen 174, 179
*The Bulwark* 199
Burgers, Jack 98
Burgin, Victor: *Some Cities* 249–250
Burlington, New Jersey 17, 81, 179
Burnham, Daniel 173, 228

Cadwalader, Thomas 157, 183
Cadwalader Heights *4*, 243
Cadwalader Park 112, 120, 168, 172, 174–177, 197, 243, 248, 253
Cadwalader Park Bridge 168–169, *169*, 174; monuments 177
Cadwalader Place 243
Calhoun Street 48, 64, 87, 168, 239
Calhoun Street Bridge 75, 167–168
Calhoun Street Canal House *171*, 172
Calvino, Italo: *Invisible Cities* 10, 30, 44, 77, 148, 253
Camden 10, 14, 16, 17, 18, 19, 53, 60, 69, 105, 214, 243, 246
Camden and Amboy Railroad 170, 171
*Camera Lucida* 240
Campbell, Louise 199
canals 169–172; "Canal Era" 169; canal tender's house *171*; Irish labor 170
Canniffe, Eamonn: *Urban Ethic: Design in the Contemporary City* 207
Carroll Street *107*
Carter, Jimmy 65
Carteret, Lord 78
Carteret Arms Apartments 163
Cavalieri, Grace: *Trenton* 198
cemeteries 178–184; philosophy 179; "rural cemetery movement" 179; *see individual cemeteries by name*

Central Park, New York City 174, 175, 178
Centre Street 133
Ceramic Art Company 131
ceramics industry 116, 117, 127, 130–131, 135
Chambersburg 125, 127, 136, *137*, 204, 216, 219; restaurants 136, 149
Champale Brewery 92
Chancery Lane 161, 199
*Changing New York* 242
Channing, William Ellery 33
Chicago, Illinois 76, 110, 127, 137, 155, 157, 164, 173, 246
"Chicago School" 25–26
Chichen Itza, Mexico 211
Childe, V. Gordon 42
cigar industry 117, 125
Cincinnati, Ohio 76
cities: ancient 33, 51, 151; approaches to building 224–225; art of the city 20–22, 191–195, 232; assets 228; character 43, 90; class 57; "collective resource" as 212; cultural institutions 196–197; Decentrist approach 227; decline 139; defining 24, 36, 38–44; details 73–75; disease 143; estrangement 25–26, 42; failure 51–57; feel 74; footprint 215–237; history and 78–94; "idea" 70–73, 207; legibility 207–210, 213, 214; lifespan 51; look 74, 207, 227; Medieval 108–109; memory 58–62, 70, 91; mixed use 230–233; monuments 34; neighborhoods 139, 149, 204, 218–219, 222, 229–230, 232; oldest 108; purpose 91; "rectilinear" 225; Renaissance 71; riots 54–55; skylines 39; small 76; "soul" 51, 56–57, 225; symbols 34–35, 45, 210; Utopian models 216; Victorian 118
*Cities* 45
*Cities and the Wealth of Nations* 236
City 84, 150
*The City* 40–41
*The City: A Global History* 45, 91, 207
*The City as a Work of Art: London, Paris, Vienna* 194–195
*The City Assembled* 147
City Beautiful Movement 114, 168, 169, 173–174
city halls 99, 108–110
*The City in History* 45, 52, 90
*The City of Mind: Notes on the Urban Condition* 235–236
*City of Quartz* 206
Clinton Street 165–166, 168
Clymer, George 88, 183
CNA Plaza Building 164
coal 127
Coalport/North Clinton District 135, *148*, 180, 218, *219*, 224, 245, 248
Cohan, George M. 140
"Coketown" 57, 70
The College of New Jersey 223

# Index

Collins, Isaac  198
Colonial Avenue  88
Colvin's Ferry  150
*The Coming of Post-Industrial Society*  49–50
*Concrete Reveries*  46
*The Condition of the Working Class in 1844*  55, 118
Coney Island  61–62
Continental Congress  84
Coolidge, John  118
Coolidge Avenue  204
Cooper, Peter  36, 127, 128, 129
"Corner Historic"  84, **84, 239**
Cornwallis, Charles  83
corporations  120–121
courthouses  **60**, 99–108; Clarkson S. Fisher Courthouse 105; history 101; Mercer County Civil Court 107; Mercer County Courthouse **100**, 103, 104, 174; message 102–3, 106; Richard J. Hughes Justice Complex 97, 105, 107; United States Courts Design Guide 106
Coxe, Daniel W.  117
crime  20, 21, 63, 64, 65, 136, 200–204, 214, 222, 237, 239; gangs 65, 201–204, 208, 214; Operation "Capital City" 203; safety and 228
Crips  202, 203
Cumbler, John  14; *A Social History of Economic Decline*  120–121

Dalí, Salvador: *The Persistence of Memory*  61
Davidson, Bruce  149
Davidson, John  189
Davis, Mike  201; *City of Quartz*  206
Day, Horace H.  132
Dayton, William L.  82, 180
*Death and Life of Great American Cities*  9, 226, 227–233
de Chirico, Giorgio  194, 251
Delaware Canal  170
Delaware and Raritan Canal 18, 69, 168, **169**, 170–172, 178
Delaware River  150, **154**, 179, 184, 211, 222, 223
demographics  17–18, 28, 191
Department of Labor and Workforce Development Building  162
de Toqueville, Alexis  54
Dewey, John  189
Dickinson, Philemon  99
Diefendorf, Jeffrey M.  7
doll industry  117
Dotson, Jeri Lynn  204
Douglass House  83, 90, 177
downtown  140, 141–147, **142**, 208, 218, 222, 223
Downtown Capital District Master Plan *see* Trenton Master Plan
Dreiser, Theodore  189, 198–199; *The Bulwark* 199; *The Financier*  199

Duany, Andres  142, 195, 218, 234; *Suburban Sprawl*  141
Duck Island  92
Dunbar, Hiram P.  131
Duncan, John H.  113

Eagle Tavern  150
*Eagle Tavern*  **85**, 85–86
Eakins, Thomas  113
East Trenton  **134**, 135, 148
East Ward  136
*An Economic History of the American Steel Industry*  130
"edge cities"  39, 49, 77, 235
Einstein Alley  51
Eisenhower Avenue  204
elevators  156, 157
El Greco  251; *View of Toledo*  251
Elizabeth  10, 15, 16, 81, 87
Ellarslie Museum  196, 197, 248
Ellin, Nan: *Postmodern Urbanism*  164
Emerson, Ralph Waldo  33, 188
Emporis.com  164
Engels, Friedrich  68; *The Condition of the Working Class in 1844*  55, 118
engineering  153–172
Erie Canal  169–170
Essex County  143
Evanovich, Janet  137; *One for the Money*  204
Evans, Walker  238
"Everycity"  15
Ewing/Carroll District  **107**, 131, 218, 245
*The Experience of Place*  46
Exton, Adam  127
Exton, John  127
Exton Cracker Factory  127, **133**

factories  69, 116–135, **216, 250**; first American 117
"Factory Street"  117
fairs  196
Fairview Street  166
Fasenella, Ralph  244
ferries  15, 19, 85, 150, 168
Ferry Historic District  85, 128, 133, 150
Ferry Street  78, 150, **150**
*The Financier*  199
Finch, Henry E.  165
First Battle of Trenton  14, 74, 78, **79**, 81, 90, 141, 165, 183
First Mechanics Bank  84
First Presbyterian Church Cemetery  183
First Presbyterian Church of Trenton  79, **80**, 82, 87, 90, 112, 183
Fischer, Carl G.  75
Fischer, Claude  28–29
Fischer, David Hackett  90, 183; *Washington's Crossing*  79
Fisher/Ritchey/Perdicaris Historic District  **211**
Fitch, John  79, 92–93

# 284 Index

Five Points 82, 87
*flâneur* 2, 13–14, 20, 28, 29, 53, 164
Fogelson, Robert M. 145
Foucalt, Michel: *Of Other Spaces* 99
Fowler Street 64, 239
Franklin, Benjamin 69, 82
freeways 207
French Arms Tavern 84
Friends Meeting Ground Cemetery 183
Friends Meeting House 87, **88**
Front Street 73, 82, 90, 91, 186
"Fugitive" poets 189
Fulton, Robert 93
furniture industry 117

"Gaia Hypothesis" 30, 216, 217
gangs *see* crime
*Gangs in New Jersey* 203
Gangster Killer Bloods 202, 203
Gans, Herbert: *The Urban Villagers* 230; *Urbanism and Suburbanism as Ways of Life: A Reevaluation of Definitions* 26–27
"Garden City" *see* Howard, Ebenezer
gentrification 144, 150, 234
*The Geography of Nowhere* 220, 233–235
Gershwin, George 22
*ghettoization* 207
Gibbons, Edward: *The History of the Decline and Fall of the Roman Empire* 51
Gibson, Kenneth 64
"Gilded Age" 140
Gillette, Howard 14
Girouard, Mark 36
Glaeser, Edward L. 42–43
*The Gleaners* 247
Glen Afton 243
"Golden Age" of Trenton 14, 100, 132, 143, 145, 157, 191, 221
*The Golden City* 226
Golden Swan 85
Golden Swan Tavern 23
Goldman Sachs Building 156, 164
*Goodyear Patent Case* 131–132
Goodyear Rubber Company 131
Gowans, Alan: *Architecture in New Jersey* 221
Grand Street 122, 125
Grant Avenue 31, **148**
Greater Trenton Symphony Orchestra 186
Greeley, Horace 109
Green, Samuel 117
Greenville, South Carolina 77, 144, 151–152
Grele, Ronald J. 15, 120
Griffith Electric and Supply Building **128**
*Gritty Cities* 2, 63, 245–246
Grounds for Sculpture 98, 196–197

Habermas, Jürgen 163
Hales, Peter 238; *Silver Cities: Photographing American Urbanization, 1830–1939* 244–245, 246

Hall, James 127
Hall, John: *History of the Presbyterian Church in Trenton* 88, 235
Hamilton, Alexander 79
Hamilton Township 15, 98, 127, 129, 207
Hanover/Academy District 192, **192**, 218, **220**, 223, **244**, 245
Hanover Street 87, **220**, **244**
*The Happy Journey to Trenton and Camden* 198
Harper Building 181
Harrisburg, Pennsylvania 121, 193
Harrison, William Henry 90
Harrow, Isaac 116, 117
Hawthorne, Nathaniel 188
H.D. Lee Factory 125, **126**
Healey, Patsy 56, 212–213
Hearn, Millard Fillmore: *Ideas That Shaped Buildings* 156
Henry Clay and Bock Company 125
*hererotopias* 99
Hermitage 88–89, **89**
Hessians 81, 82, 90, 183
Hewitt, Abram S. 127
Heym, Georg 21
highways *see* freeways
Hillcrest 243
Hiltonia 218, 243
Hiss, Tony 47; *The Experience of Place* 46
*Historic Homes of New Jersey* 88
*Historical Atlas of Architecture* 158
*A History of Building Types* 101
*History of the City of Trenton* 103, 117
*The History of the Decline and Fall of the Roman Empire* 51
*History of the Presbyterian Church in Trenton* 88, 235
Hoboken 114, 243
Hofstadter, Richard: *Anti-Intellectualism in American Life* 185–187, 191
Hopper, Edward 22, 45, 194; *Nighthawks* 250
Horsman, Edward Imeson 123
Horsman Doll Factory 122–124, **123**
Hotchkiss, Nelson 79
Hotel Hildebrecht 2, 68
Hotels 76
Houston, Texas 76
Hoving, Thomas 95
*How the Other Half Lives* 213, 246
Howard, Ebenezer 227, 228, 233
Howell, Mabel W. 180
Howells, William Dean 189
Hudson County 143
Hudson County Courthouse 101
Hunt, Abraham 183–184
Hunt, William E. 179

I-beam 153, 168, 181
ice 127, 216
Ice House **216**

## Index

*Ideas That Shaped Buildings* 156
*The Image of the City* 207–210, 231
Impressionists 247
*In This Proud Land: America, 1935–1943, as Seen in the FSA Photographs* 238
*The Incorporation of America* 119–120, 140–141
Industrial Revolution 52, 121, 127, 133, 172, 187–188, 216
industrialization 18, 20, 30, 60, 68, 151, 170
Ingersoll, Richard: *Sprawltown* 234
*The Intellectual Versus the City* 187–191
intellectualism 185–191
*Invisible Cities* 10, 30, 44, 77, 148, 253
iron and steel industry 116, 117, 127–130
Island 243
Italian-Americans 204
Izenour, Steven: *Learning from Las Vegas* 147

Jacobs, Jane 9, 76, 221, 239; *Cities and the Wealth of Nations* 236; *Death and Life of Great American Cities* 9, 226–233; Le Corbusier, on 226, 227–228
James, Henry 189
Jeanneret-Gris, Charles-Edouard *see* Le Corbusier
Jefferson, Thomas 72, 108, 187, 188; *Notes on Virginia* 187
Jersey City 10, 15, 53, 54, 69, 101, 103, 112, 149, 154, 156, 161, 164; Lynch on 208–209, 210
J.L. Mott Iron Works 124–125, 131
John Fitch Way 177, 222; *see also* Route 29
Johns, Michael: *Moment of Grace* 74
Johnson, J. Seward 105, 196

KatManDu 66, 98, 129
Katyn Memorial 112
Kelsey, Henry Cooper 252
Kelsey, Prudence Townsend 252
Kelsey Building 73, **252**
Kennedy, John F. 65
Kerner Commission 54, 213–214
King Street *see* Warren Street
King's Highway 82, 87
Kingsbury Towers 9, 161–161
Kingwell, Mark 44, 114, 163, 211; *Concrete Reveries* 46
Koolhaas, Rem 61–62
Kostof, Spiro 24, 155; *The City Assembled* 147
Kotkin, Joel: *The City: A Global History* 45, 91, 207
Kovisar, Judith 218
Kublai Khan 10, 30, 77, 253
Kunstler, James 163–164, 195, 226; *The City of Mind: Notes on the Urban Condition* 235–236; *The Geography of Nowhere* 220, 233–235; Le Corbusier, on 226
Kuser, Anthony R. 126
Kuser, John L. 126, 127

labor 132, 134
Labor and Workforce Development Building 9, **60**
Lafayette, Marquis de 84, 90
Lafayette House 163
Lafayette Street **73**, 186
Lalor Street 179
Lambert, John 179
Lambert, Thomas 179
Lamberton 91–92
Lange, Dorothea 3, 238
Las Vegas, Nevada 147, 235
Latin Kings 202, 203, 204
Laugier, Marc-Antoione 156
Lawrence Township 135, 224
*Learning from Las Vegas* 147
Lebovich, William L. 110; *America's City Halls* 108
Le Corbusier 161, 205, 225–226, 227–228, 233
Lee, Francis Bazley 68, 69
Lee, Henry D. 126
Lee, Tajahnique 204
Lee Jeans 125
Lee Union Alls Factory *see* H.D. Lee Factory
Lees, Andrew 188, 189, 191
Leger, Fernand: *The City* 251
LeGore, Jennifer 201
*Leni Lenape* 78
Lenox, Walter Scott 131
Lenox Family 191
Leonard, Tamrah 203, 204
Liggett, Helen: *Urban Encounters* 148–149, 239–242
Lincoln, Abraham 83, 90, 180
Lincoln Highway 75, 168
Lippard, Lucy: *The Lure of the Local: Senses of Place in a Multicentered Society* 46–47
*Liquid City* 249
Liverpool, England 175
*The Living City* 190
Lofland, Lyn 96; *The Public Realm* 41, 204–205; *A World of Strangers* 41
Logan Avenue **137**
London, England 147, 162, 194, 195, 235, 249, 250
Los Angeles, California 53, 76, 127, 146, 208; gangs 201, 217
Louisville, Kentucky 76
Lovelock, James 30, 195, 216
Lowell, Massachusetts 117–118
Lower Trenton Bridge **34**, 75, 167, 168
*The Lure of the Local: Senses of Place in a Multicentered Society* 46–47
Lynch, Kevin 226; *The Image of the City* 207–210, 231

Machala, Ecuador 217
Maddock, Thomas 131
Maddock Family 132, 191

Madison, Wisconsin 193
Mahlon Stacy Park 64, 129, 149, 177, 218, 222
Marco Polo *see* Polo, Marco
Market Street 103, 104, 109, **146**
Marriott Hotel 250
Martin Luther King Boulevard 204
Mary G. Roebling Building 163
Masereel, Frans 20–21, 141
Matherly, Walter J. 44
Maxine's 201
Mayernik, David 71, 207
McCall Mansion 169
McClellan, George B. 83, 86, 180
McCullough, David 128–129
McKelvey, Blake 69–70, 192
Mechanics and Manufacturers Bank 84, 239
*Medieval Cities* 191
Melville, Herman 188
Mercer, Hugh 103
Mercer Automobile Company 125–127
Mercer Cemetery 180–181, **182**, 223
Mercer County Administration Building 165, 171
Mercer County Community College 223
*Mercer Messenger* 141
Mercer Raceabout 125–126
Mesopotamia 33
MetLife Building 162
*The Metropolis and Mental Life* 25–26
Mexico City, Mexico 235
Meyers, William H. 213
Miami 76
Miami Beach 76
Mies van der Rohe, Ludwig 162–163, 226
Milgram, Stanley 205
Mill Hill 77, 103, **104**, **146**, 165, 168, 218, 222, 223
Mill Hill Bridge 168
Mill Hill Park 178
Mill Hill Playhouse 98, 152, 186
Miller Homes 223
Miller/Wall 218
Millet, Jean-François 246–247, 251, 253; *The Gleaners* 247
Mills, Weymer Jay: *Historic Homes of New Jersey* 88
*Moment of Grace* 74
Mondrian, Piet 162
Monroe, James 74, 79
Montgomery Street **48**, 83, 87, 90, 157, 165, 178
Monti, Daniel: *The American City* 43, 57
monuments 112–113; Bennington 206; Saratoga 206
*The Moral Influence, Dangers and Duties connected with Great Cities* 188
Morris, Lewis 84
Morris Canal 18
Morrisville, Pennsylvania 168
Moses, Robert 207

*Mostly Harmless* 220
Mott, Jordan Lawrence 124
Mount Carmel Guild **248**
movie theaters 140
Ms-13 202, 217
Mumford, Lewis 45, 56, 70, 102–103, 189, 212; *The City in History* 45, 52, 90; etherialization and materialization 212
museums 98, 193–194, 196
music of the city 22

Naar, Jon 186
National Advisory Commission on Civil Disorders *see* Kerner Commission
national capitalism 120–121, 132
Native Americans 78–79, 81; Kildorpy 78; *Leni Lenape* 78; *Sanhicans* 78; trails 82
Neary, J.S. 94
Negrete, Jose 204
Ñeta 203
New Brunswick 69, 81, 122, 132, 147, 166; and canals 170
New Burying Ground, New Haven 179
New Haven 43, 53, 64, 76, 143, 179
New Jersey: Assembly 84; Department of Agriculture **60**; Department of Environmental Protection 9; early settlement 78; municipalities 38–39; state government buildings **60**; tallest building 156
New Jersey Department of State Archives 180
*New Jersey Gazette* 198
*New Jersey: A Guide to Its Past and Present* 184
New Jersey Historic Bridge Survey 165, 168–169
New Jersey Iron and Steel Company 66, 92, 128
New Jersey State Fairgrounds 196
New Jersey State Library 97, **193**
New Jersey State Museum 48, 97, 186, **193**, 193–194, 196, 197; Friends of the New Jersey State Museum 196
New Jersey State Prison 111, *111*
New Jersey Steel Company 132
"new urbanism" 133, 215, 226; and Modernism 163–164
New York, New York 15, 50, 69, 75, 76, 85, 87, 107, 108, 127, 129, 137, 139, 146–147, 149, 157, 162, 163, 166, 168, 170, 174, 193, 198, 211, 213, 218; anti-urbanism and 188–189, 222, 231, 242, 251; neighborhoods 219
Newark 10, 14, 15, 16, 17, 18, 19, 53, 54, 64, 69, 103, 114, 147, 154, 161, 175, 214, 246
Newark Museum 194
Newberry, Lida: *New Jersey: A Guide to Its Past and Present* 184
newspapers 140, 197–199; "two newspaper cities" 198
*Nighthawks* 250

## Index

Norris, Frank 189
"North Jersey" 17
North Trenton 135, 204
Northeast Corridor 50, 58, 135
*Notes on Virginia* 187

Oakland, California 76
Obama, Barack 65, 195
*Of Other Spaces* 99
O'Gorman, James: *ABC of Architecture* 101, 159
Old Barracks 81, 82, 90, 117
Old Masonic Temple 2
Old Rose Road 170–171
Old Slater Mill 117
Olden Avenue 134, 213
Olmsted, Frederick Law 17, 58, 169, 174–176, 179; parks 175; philosophy 176–177; "Public Parks and the Enlargement of Towns" 175
Olsen, Donald J.: *The City as a Work of Art: London, Paris, Vienna* 194–195
*One for the Money* 204
One State Street Square Building 164
Owen, Charles P. 177
*Oxford Dictionary of Architecture* 155, 162–163, 164
Oyster cracker 127

Pagans Motorcycle Club 202
Palazzo del Brotto 108
Pan Am Building *see* MetLife Building
pape industry 117
Paris, France 39, 154, 194, 195, 198, 225, 226, 235, 242, 250
Park, Robert 42, 189
parks 112, 173–178, 229; small parks of Trenton 178; *see individual parks by name*
Parkside 243
Parkside Avenue 168, 174
Parkway Avenue 203
Passage Theatre Company 186
Passaic Street *9*
Paterson 10, 15, 69, 243
Peace Street 73
Penn, William 87
Pennington/Prospect 204
Pennsylvania Railroad 166, 169, 177
Pennsylvania Railroad Bridge 166
Perdicaris, Gregory 211
Perdicaris, Ion 211
Perry Street 219, **244**
*The Persistence of Memory* 61
Perth Amboy 17, 75, 81
Petty's Run 116
Pevsner, Nikolaus 109; on factories 117; *A History of Building Types* 101
Philadelphia 15, 50, 69, 73, 75, 76, 85, 87, 88, 92, 108, 129, 135, 137, 166, 170, 211, 227, 243, 251
Phoenix Bridge Company 168

photography 10, 149; city and 238–253; role 244; visual poetry, as 240
Pirenne, Henri: *Medieval Cities* 191
Pitney, Mahlon 104
Pittsburgh 76
place, sense 7, 24, 34, 44–49, 65, 136, 195, 210–211, 220, 223, 242
Place Vendôme 113
Plater-Zyberk, Elizabeth 218, 234
Plato 40
Podmore, Harry J.: *Trenton Old and New* 87
Poe, Edgar Allan 188
Poland, William A. 157
Polo, Marco 10, 18, 30, 44, 77, 253
population 3, 8, 16–17, 28, 38, 39, 70, 75–76, 94, 208, 227
post-industrial city 4, 49–53, 55, 70, 151, 154
*Postmodern Urbanism* 164
pottery *see* ceramics
Potts, Stacy 117, 183
Pratt, Caleb 168
Pratt, Thomas 168
Precisionists 251
Princeton 87, 122, 144
Princeton: Battle of 79, 91, 103
Princeton University 50
prisons 110–112
Prospect Street 203, 204
Providence, Rhode Island 192, 238
public art 97, 110–111, ***111***
*The Public Realm* 41, 204–205
public space 41–42, 96–99, 114, 205, 211, 235; European 101; parks and 175–176

Quakers 87, 111, 179
*Quakers, Warriors and Capitalists* 179
Queen Street *see* Broad Street

race relations 54
"Radiant City" *see* Le Corbusier
Rae, Douglas 43, 52, 53, 67, 70, 139–140, 143
Rahway 243
railway stations 114, 127
Rall, Colonel Johann 79, 82, 88, 91, 183
Ransom, John Crowe 189
Raum, John O.: *History of the City of Trenton* 103, 117
Read, Charles 92
Read, John 51, 52; *Cities* 45
Reading Freight Station 127
Reading Railroad 167
Reading Railroad Bridge 167
Reagan, Ronald 65
Reed, Henry Hope: *The Golden City* 226
Reliance Building (Chicago) 155
Rider University 223, **224**
Riis, Jacob 2, 143, 244, 246; *How the Other Half Lives* 213, 246
riots 213–214, 245
Riverfront 218, 223

Riverview Cemetery **83**, 179–180; Civil War soldiers buried in 180
Roberts, Spencer 109
Robson, Brian 139
Rodenbach, George: *Bruges-la-Morte* 47
Roebling, Charles G. 130
Roebling, Ferdinand W. 61, 126, 127, 130
Roebling, Ferdinand W., Jr. 130
Roebling, John Augustus 18, 36, 126, 128–130, 153, 161, 171, 180
Roebling, Karl W. 130
Roebling, Washington Augustus 130
Roebling Factory **36**, 132
Roebling Family 120, 127, 130, 132, 165, 191
Roebling Market 97
Roebling Steel and Wire Company 128
Rogers, Robert P.: *An Economic History of the American Steel Industry* 130
Rome, Italy 154, 207, 235
Roosevelt, Theodore 211
Rossell Avenue 204
Route 1 170, 171, 207, 209
Route 29 149, 177, 179, 209, 222
Route 95 207
Route 129 171
Route 295 207
Rowe, Colin 226
rowhouses **134**, **135**, **138**, 149, **243**
rubber industry 117, 127, 131–132, 135; vulcanization 132
Ruiz, Alex 204
Ryan, Mary P. 107
Rybczynski, Witold 43, 114, 175–176
Rykwert, Joseph 156, 195, 209, 215; *The Seduction of Place* 44, 215, 239

St. Clair, Arthur 84
St. Louis, Missouri 76, 156
St. Joe's Avenue **134**
St. Mary's Cathedral 131
St. Michael's Church 183, **184**; cemetery 183
St. Paul, Minnesota 121, 193
Sandburg, Carl 116
San Diego, California 76
San Francisco, California 75, 76, 107, 168, 193
*Sanhicans* 78
San Jacinto, Texas 113
Saxony ice Company 127, 216
Schenck, Garret 131
Scott, Julian 197
Scudder Falls Bridge 168
Seagram Building 97, 162
Second Battle of Trenton 82–83, 90, 91, 165, 166, 178
Second Masonic Hall 157
*The Seduction of Place* 44, 215, 239
"sense of place" *see* place, sense of
Sex Money Murder Gang 202
*The Shame of the Cities* 121
Sheeler, Charles 251

Sheffield, England 250
Sherman, William P. 134, 135
Sherman Avenue **134**, 135
Shinn, Everett 109
shopping 13, 144, 145–146
Shostakovich, Dmitry 22
Shuman, Eleanore 116, 130, 131
Sickel, Willing G. 192
sidewalks 229
signage 147
*Silver Cities: Photographing American Urbanization, 1830–1939* 244–245, 246
Simmel, Georg 205; *The Metropolis and Mental Life* 25–26
Sinclair, Iain: *Liquid City* 249
Sines, Hohn 117
Sjoberg, Gideon 41
skyline 154–155; Frank Lloyd Wright and 156–157; Trenton skyline **154**
skyscrapers 9, 121, 145, 153–165; definition 155; new urbanism and 226
Sloan, John 194
*A Social History of Economic Decline* 120–121
*The Society of Captives: A Study of a Maximum Security Prison* 111
*Some Cities* 249–250
"South Jersey" 17
South River Walk Park 179
South Trenton 137, 208
Southard Street 170–171
Spanish-American War 153
Spokane 76
sprawl 77, 234–235; *see also* suburbs
*Sprawl* 234–235
*Sprawltown* 234
Springfield Rifle 128
Stacy, Mahlon 87, 116–117
Stacy Park *see* Mahlon Stacy Park
stagecoach 87
*The State Gazette* 198
State Street 13, **27**, 31, 48, 73, 79, 82, 84, 91, 97, 98, 100, 118, 125, 136, **138**, 141, 144, 146, 147, 148, 157, 159, 161, 163, 166, 172, 199, 206, 207, 208, 223, 239, 243
Statehouse 89–90, 97, **154**, 209, **252**
steamboats 92, 170
steel industry *see* iron and steel industry
Steffens, Lincoln: *The Shame of the Cities* 121
Steichen, Edward 242
Stevens, Wallace 24
Stieglitz, Alfred 158, 242
Stirling, James 226
Stockton Street 48, **244**
streets 147–149, 228; "Main Street" 147; types 147
Stryker, Roy: *In This Proud Land: America, 1935–1943, as Seen in the FSA Photographs* 238
Stuyvesant Avenue **65**
*Suburban Sprawl* 141

suburbs 53, 60, 142, 234–235; see also sprawl
Sullivan, Louis 159, 160
Sun National Bank Building 223
Swan Street 127
Sykes, Gresham M.: *The Society of Captives: A Study of a Maximum Security Prison* 111

Taft, William Howard 124, 131
Tate, Alan 189
taverns 86; *Blazing Star* 84; *City* 84, 150; Eagle Tavern **85**, 85–86; *Golden Swan* 85; *Thirteen Stars* 84
taxis **27**
Taylor, John 109, 180
Taylor and Speeler 131
"Taylor Ham" 180
Taylor Opera House 109, 140, 165, 186
*The Territorial Imperative* 200–201
territoriality 200–201, 206, 212, 214
theaters 113–114
"theories of the city" 25–29
Theotokopoulos, Domenikos see El Greco
Third Street 179
*Thirteen Stars* 84
33 West State Street Building 164
Thomas Edison State College 252
Thomas Maddock and Sons 120, 131
Thoreau, Henry David 188, 246
Tice, George: Paterson and 243; *Urban Landscapes* 242–243
*Times of Trenton* 63, 140, 198, 245
Todd, John: *The Moral Influence, Dangers and Duties Connected with Great Cities* 188
"Tom Thumb" 109
tomato pies 136
Top Road Section 135
Trachtenberg, Alan: *The Incorporation of America* 119–120, 140–141
Transcendentalists 188
Trent, William 71, 72, 73
Trent Center East 163
Trent House 71, 253
Trent Theatre 140
Trenton Academy 191–192
Trenton Artist Salon 186
Trenton City Hall **100**, 109–110, 253; "old city hall" 109
Trenton Commons 97, 144, 148
Trenton Division of Natural Resources 175
Trenton Film Festival 186
Trenton Film Society 186
Trenton Fire Department 110
Trenton-Hamilton Marsh 61, **63**, 179
Trenton Historical Society 86
Trenton Iron Works 128, 129, 132, 181
Trenton Makes Bridge see Lower Trenton Bridge
*Trenton Makes the World Takes* motto 58–60, 62, 64, 117, 167, 170, 191
Trenton Marine Terminal 92

Trenton Master Plan 64, 97, 218–224, 236–237
Trenton Morrisville Bridge 168
Trenton neighborhoods see individual name
*Trenton* 198
*Trenton Old and New* 87
Trenton Poster Advertising Company **93**
Trenton Public Library 192, 193
Trenton Reservoir 203, 204
Trenton State College see The College of New Jersey
Trenton State Prison see New Jersey State Prison
Trenton *Thunder* see baseball
*The Trenton Times* see Times of Trenton
Trenton Train Station 196–197, 218
Trenton Trust Company Building 159–161, **160**, 174
Trenton Water Works 203
Trenton websites 224
*The Trentonian* 67, 113, 198, 245
Trentonians 67
*The True American* 198
Tuttle, Brad 14, 15, 16
Twain, Mark 140
28 West State Street Building see Trenton Trust Company Building
Two Capital Plaza 163

Universal Hagar's Spiritual Church 107
"urban beauty" 194
*Urban Encounters* 148–149, 239–242
*Urban Ethic: Design in the Contemporary City* 207
*Urban Landscapes* 242–243
urban planning 145, 210, 229
urban renewal 218
*The Urban Villagers* 230
urbanism 49, 67, 68, 136–152, 187, 235; baseball 140; department stores 140, 142; newspapers 140; vaudeville 140
*Urbanism and Suburbanism as Ways of Life: A Reevaluation of Definitions* 26–27
*Urbanism as a Way of Life* 25, 26
urbanization 38, 52, 70

vaudeville 140
Vaux, Calvert 179
Venturi, Robert: *Learning from Los Vegas* 147
Vergura, Camilo Jose 246
*Victorian Cities* 118
Vienna, Austria 154, 194, 195
*View of Toledo* 251

Waln, Robert 86
Walsh, Thomas J. 248
War Memorial Building **35**, 98, 112, 113, 152, 186, 212
Warren, Elizabeth 180
Warren, Robert Penn 189
Warren Street 13, **23**, 31, 58, 79, **81**, 82, 84,

87, 90, 91, 98, 129, 131, 141, 144, 186, 201, 206, 209, 212, 223, 239
Washington, George 82–83, 84, 91, 92, 150; sculpture 178
Washington, D.C. 76, 211, 243
Washington's Crossing 91
*Washington's Crossing* 79
watch industry 117
Waterfront Park **66**
Weber, Max: *The City* 40–41
Webster, Daniel 90, 100, 103; *Goodyear Patent Case* 131–132
Webster, J. Carson 155
*Welcome to the Urban Revolution: How Cities Are Changing the World* 216–217, 224
Wells, Gideon 117
West End **243**
Wetmore, James 105
White, Lucia: *The Intellectual Versus the City* 187–191
White, Morton *see* White, Lucia
White City Amusement Park 61–62, **63**, 64, 75, 239
Whitefield, George 88
Whitman, Walt 20, 34

Whitney Museum of Art 193
Whyte, William H. 96; *City* 151–152, 236
Wilbur neighborhood **137**
Wilder, Thornton: *The Happy Journey to Trenton and Camden* 198
William Young & Co. 131
Williams, Ralph Vaughan 22
Williams, William Carlos 70
Willow Street 127
Wilson, Woodrow 174
Wirth, Louis 43, 205; *Urbanism as a Way of Life* 25, 26
Wood, Nancy: *In This Proud Land: America, 1935–1943, as Seen in the FSA Photographs* 238
Works Project Administration 105
World Columbian Exposition 110
*A World of Strangers* 41
World War II Memorial 58, **59**
Wright, Frank Lloyd 156–157, 187, 189–190; *The Living City* 190

Yalom, Marilyn: *The American Resting Place* 178–179

www.ingramcontent.com/pod-product-compliance
Lightning Source LLC
Chambersburg PA
CBHW030103170426
43198CB00009B/475